A GUIDE TO THE GODS

A GUIDE TO THE GODS

AN ESSENTIAL GUIDE TO WORLD MYTHOLOGY

COMPILED BY

RICHARD CARLYON

QUILL
William Morrow
New York

Originally published in Great Britain in 1981 by William
Heinemann Ltd.

Library of Congress Cataloging-in-Publication Data
Carlyon, Richard.
    A guide to the gods.
    Includes index.
    1. Gods. 2. Goddesses. I. Title.
[BL473.C37 1982b]   291.2'11   82-7557
ISBN 0-688-01332-5   AACR2
ISBN 0-688-01333-3 (pbk.)

ISBN 0-688-09208-X

Printed in the United States of America

First Quill Edition

1 2 3 4 5 6 7 8 9 10

For Graham Tarrant
with gratitude for his inspiration, skill and support.

Contents

Foreword

There has never been a human society without a god of some kind. There has never been a culture that did not express an awareness of the divine, and these expressions have been as varied and as colourful as the cultures themselves. Gods and goddesses have appeared in every conceivable guise, possessing every possible character, mirroring every human attitude, opinion, virtue and vice. Their stories are a history of the human psyche and are the common heritage of us all.

The object of *A Guide to the Gods* is to make these stories accessible, reflecting the humanity, reverence and humour of our fellow men at all times and in all places. At the same time, the book catalogues the many follies into which we may fall if we cease to exercise our reason and sense of humour.

It has not been possible to include every god that has been worshipped; so little is known about so many that such an exercise would be both tedious and futile. And it has only been possible to hint at the wealth of ritual, music, dance and living myth that go to make up the activity of worship. This is a guide to gods, not to religions.

The reader will find that changing tastes, diverse sources and unregulated myth-making have made many of the stories paradoxical, non-sequential, undisciplined and fantastic. That is part of their charm; the gods do not follow our rules.

The spelling of names has been regularized to an acceptable standard with alternative spellings and aliases provided where sensible. For the Chinese gods I have used the old orthography, since the new method of transcribing Chinese names is as yet generally unfamiliar.

Richard Carlyon

Editor's Note

Many of the situations and events described in this book are common to more than one god; the relationships and associations of the deities are sometimes prolific and often complex. To repeat all the information under each relevant entry would not only be monotonous but would make the book unmanageably long. Where necessary, therefore, the reader is referred to a more specific or detailed account of things; in other cases, a fuller picture will emerge through the reading of several related entries. As with the gods themselves, one thing tends to lead to another.

The gods and goddesses are recorded alphabetically in each section. Those shown in italics in the text have an entry of their own elsewhere in the book. The general index at the back will indicate where.

A GUIDE TO THE GODS

Africa

The continent excluding Egypt

Agassou
Panther fetish of the royal house of Dahomey.

The panther symbolizes strength, bravery and cunning; it represents a purely spiritual force. It is not a god, but a signpost pointing towards a god. Each tribe in Dahomey has its own fetish, just as the whole race has its own supreme god and individuals have their own *Legba* (demon) and *Fa* (destiny). (See *Mawu*.)

Akongo
Supreme god of the Ngombe of the Congo.

Akongo once lived among men, and was quite happy to do so. Men, however, were more and more disagreeable. They would argue with each other all the time, and were noisy, selfish and litigious. One day they had a really violent argument and went so far as to indulge in fisticuffs. Akongo was so disgusted by their lack of restraint that he went off by himself into the deep forest, where he hid. Since that time no one has seen him.

Another story tells how humans once lived with Akongo in heaven. One of the women was such a nuisance that Akongo put her, her daughter and son, a load of sugarcane, cassava and corn into a basket and lowered them down to earth. Earth had never been inhabited before. The humans set about cultivating the plants they had brought with them from heaven. The woman urged her children to mate with each other in order to produce offspring. Her daughter was keen on the idea but the son took a lot of convincing. Finally he gave in.

The daughter went wandering off into the forests and there she met a hirsute man-like creature. It was a case of Beauty and the Beast. The girl shaved the new creature to make him look more like a man. What else passed between them is not specified but the child that was subsequently born was an evil sorcerer. The hairy creature had bewitched the daughter in more senses than one.

To make things a little easier for those on earth Akongo set two giants to hold up the sky with tall poles. In the east was the giant Libanja, in the west the giant Songo. Sometime in the distant future they will tire of their task and let go of the poles. That will be the end of the world, for the sky will then come crashing down. There will be so little space left that men will have to become lizards and live with their bellies on the ground.

Akovodoun
Cult of the dead in Dahomey.

There are two main kinds of worship among the people of Dahomey. Akovodoun is concerned with the dead, human spirits, ancestors and such. The other form, Tovodoun, involves the worship of non-humans: spirits, gods, demons, fetishes and destiny. The word *vodoun* was transported with the slaves to Haiti, along with many of the native African gods and ceremonial skills. There it mingled with elements of insular Indian religion and Catholicism to produce the religious system *voudoun*, which we call 'voodoo'. (See *Haitian* gods in American section.)

Akuj
Supreme god of the Turkana peoples of Kenya.

Akuj is a benevolent deity and may be consulted by anyone, no matter how humble. He has devised a strange method of divination through which to communicate with mankind. The enquirer asks his question and then throws his sandal into the air. From the way in which the sandal lands, an answer is obtained.

Amma
Supreme god of the Dogon tribe of Mali.

Amma made the stars by throwing lumps of clay up into the sky. In order to procreate, he fashioned a woman out of clay: this was the earth. His first attempt to mate with her was foiled by a termite hill, which formed her clitoris. This was a sign of her potential masculinity; Amma excised it to make her truly feminine. This first mating produced a monster in the shape of a jackal. What was more monstrous was that the jackal was single, and therefore unable to reproduce. Amma's second union with the earth woman produced the *Nummo* twins; these were both bisexual with the potential of either sex. Acts of excision and circumcision were required to complete them. The Nummo twins had snake-like attributes, including forked tongues. They in-

3

vented speech, and seeing that their mother the earth was naked wove coiling plants with which to cover her.

The jackal, alone and incomplete, committed incest with the earth, and tried to grab the coils of the plants which he thought contained the power of speech. All he did was to defile the earth and this was to cause future disasters for mankind.

Amma saw that things were not going too well. Once more he mated with the earth and produced another set of twins. These two were to be the ancestors of the Dogon. They mated and produced four boys and four girls. Each of the boys was assigned one of the elements – earth, air, fire, water – and one of the points of the compass – north, south, east, west. In addition, each boy was made responsible for one of the following human activities: magic, trade, medicine and agriculture. Meanwhile the jackal, whose name was Ogo, went about his business, which was to cause as much mischief as possible.

Anansi

The spider trickster. Originally a creator god, he became the central figure of many Ashanti (Ghana) stories as a culture hero and trickster.

A typical tale relates how Anansi won the stories of the sky god *Nyankopon*. Anansi had gone to the god, who was known to have the best stories, and offered to buy them from him. He respectfully asked the price and was told jestingly by Nyankopon that it was a python, a hornet, a leopard, and a nature spirit. Anansi agreed to the price and said that he would add his old mother to it for good measure.

First Anansi went after the python. He took the advice of his wife, Aso, and cut a branch from a tree. He acquired some rope and then went walking near the python's home. As he went along he pretended to be arguing loudly with someone. The python appeared, curious to know what the matter was. Anansi told him that he was having a disagreement with his wife, who said that the branch he was carrying was longer than the python. The python suggested that Anansi measure the branch against him to find out, and stretched his body alongside it. Quick as a flash Anansi wound the rope round branch and python and fastened it securely. He then took the helpless python to Nyankopon.

4

Next Anansi went in search of a hornet, taking a gourd of water with him. On spotting a swarm of the insects, he poured some of the water over his head and shoulders and placed a big plantain leaf on top. He then sprinkled the rest of the water over the hornets, inviting them to shelter from the 'rain' in his gourd. The hornets thanked him effusively for his kindness and took him up on the offer. Anansi swiftly plugged the opening in the gourd and took the captured hornets to Nyankopon. The sky god reminded him he had more to pay.

Anansi found a track used by a leopard and dug a concealed pit in the middle of it. Then he went away. Next morning he visited the pit and sure enough there was the leopard. The animal asked to be helped out. Anansi said he would if the leopard promised never to attack him or his family. The leopard agreed. Anansi put two sticks across the pit and told the leopard to put his front paws up on them; the animal obeyed and as he waited in this vulnerable posture for further instructions, Anansi drew his panga and sliced open the leopard's skull. He took the body to Nyankopon who told him he still had to bring a nature spirit, or elemental.

Anansi went away and made a large doll out of wood. He smeared the doll with resin and attached a string to it. Then he placed the doll where the spirits would find it, putting a bowl of food alongside. Anansi hid nearby, holding the end of the string. Along came the elementals; one of them saw the food and asked if she could have some. Anansi tweaked the string and the doll nodded in reply. The nature spirit took some of the food and thanked the doll politely, but the doll failed to respond. The spirit repeated her expression of gratitude, but the doll remained mute. The spirit, now angry, asked her sisters what she should do about it. 'Hit it' was the reply. The spirit struck the doll and her hand stuck. Then she hit it with her other hand; that too was held by the resin. The spirit butted the doll with her belly, which in turn stuck fast. Anansi sauntered out of his hiding place and trussed up the trapped spirit. He took her and his mother to Nyankopon who gave him all the stories and said that in future they would be known as 'The Spider's Stories'. (See *Wulbari*.)

Ataokoloinona
Son of the supreme god of Madagascar.

His name means 'water is strange'. He was sent down to earth by his father, the great god *'Ndriananahary*, in order to inspect the earth and report back on its possibilities as a place to inhabit. Ataokoloinona found the earth so hot and dry that he burrowed down into the ground in an attempt to cool himself. He was never seen again.

Balubaale
Collective name for the Bagandan (Uganda) gods of earth, death, the rainbow, lightning and plague.

Bumba
Creator god of the Bushongo people of the Congo.

Bumba created the sun, moon and stars by vomiting them up. Then he brought up eight species of animals from which all the others are derived. He created Heaven and Earth and they lived together as man and wife. After an argument Heaven left home in a rage, and they have been separated ever since.

Cagn (I Kaggen)
'Praying mantis', creator god of the Bushmen of south Central Africa.

Men do not know where Cagn lives, though this knowledge is held by the antelope and eland. He has a wife, Coti, and two sons, Cogaz and Gewi. The source of Cagn's power is said to be located in one of his teeth; he is a sorcerer and shape-shifter and often uses the shape of an antelope. Cagn owns a pair of magic sandals which can be turned into dogs when danger threatens and he needs protection. He was once ambushed by some thorns that had previously been men. They managed to kill Cagn and then some ants arrived and feasted on his flesh. After the ants had finished their meal Cagn's dry bones connected up again and he came back to life. (See *Kwammang-a*.)

Chwezi

Hero gods of the Nyoro of North Uganda. There are nineteen of them, each assigned to elemental forces such as rain, earthquake, sun, moon, et cetera. They form the basis of a cult which believes in spirit possession and animal sacrifice.

Danh

Snake god of Dahomey, also known as Dan Ayido Hwedo. The origin of the Haitian god *Dan Petro*.

In Dahomey Danh's shrines have their outer walls decorated with wavy lines. His worshippers dance in single file with serpents about their necks. The dancers take care to select harmless snakes for this event. As Dan Ayido Hwedo, the snake god was thought to encircle the world, making it one with itself. He is described as the Rainbow Snake and frequently shown with his tail in his mouth, a universal symbol of wholeness and unity. (See the *Great Rainbow Snake* in the Oceania section.)

Dugbo

Chief god of the earth in Sierra Leone. He is worshipped by the Kono and Tembe peoples.

Dxui

Creator god of the Bushmen of south Central Africa. Known as Tsui to the Hottentots and as Thixo to the Xhosa and Ponda peoples.

Dxui assumed the shapes of many different plants and flowers on successive days, residing in a flower or plant for a whole day and becoming himself again at night. He went on in this manner until he had been involved with the whole of botanical creation.

Fa

God of destiny in Dahomey.

Fa is the personal fate of each man. The people of Dahomey acknowledge no such concept as the one we express by the words 'accident' or 'chance'. Everything that happens is either predestined or the result of human or divine actions. Man must attune himself with his own *fa* and this is done through divination, which may be performed in various ways. The behaviour of animals and birds is significant, as are the marks on animals chosen for sacrifice. Another frequent method uses palm nuts. When a good omen is obtained it means that the success of the enterprise in question is assured. In a sense the success has already occurred, even though it lies in the future relative to the time of divination. If failure is indicated it means that the person has done something wrong in the meantime, or else there has been intervention by a god, spirit or sorcerer.

Sorcerers called *bokonon* prepare strings of palm nuts for people, representing the person's *fa*. They are kept safe as a sort of insurance policy. The sorcerers perform divination in an operation which has similarities to the art of geomancy. Nuts are tossed from hand to hand and allowed to spill onto the ground. When only one or two nuts remain the sorcerer makes either a long or a short mark on a tray of sand. After repeated tossings a sequence of long and short marks is obtained. The pattern they form is studied and an answer formulated. It is interesting to compare this system to the I Ching, the Chinese 'Book of Changes', and also to traditional Western geomancy.

Famien

God of fertility of Guinea. He is also the sovereign of good health and a sterling champion against sorcerers and demons.

Famien is often represented by a cave but may also be carried around in a bag in the form of a knife. The bag contains a second knife which is used to slay goats and chickens dedicated to Famien, on a *quid pro quo* basis for his services.

The sacred bag of Famien is more than an amulet; it is a powerful weapon, for it contains the true power of the god. It may be compared to the *grigris*, commonly found in that area of Africa, from Senegal to Angola. *Grigris* are bundles of all manner of sacred and efficacious talismans such as human and animal bones, skulls, crab's claws, fur, cloth, leaves, thread, bells, coins and dried snakes; the more unusual the item the better. They are used in magic, divination and as weapons of personal psychic self-defence. Similar objects are to be found all over Africa.

Ge (Gou)
Moon god of Dahomey.

Son of the god *Mawu*, he was lord of the sand and formed a triad with his father and with *Lisa*, who when feminine was regarded as his mother. The correct sacrifice to Ge was a white cock.

Gu
God of war and smiths of the Fon in West Africa.

Gu gave men tools with which to build houses, till the fields and make boats. He also supplied them with weapons and cutting edges. It is likely that he is linked to *Ge* and possibly to *Ogun*.

Gunab
Hottentot god of evil and the adversary of the good god *Heitsi-Eibib*. Gunab lived under a pile of stones, and is credited with creating the rainbow.

Guruhi
Evil god of Gambia.

Guruhi demanded sacrifices and often poisoned and tortured his opponents. In return for worshipping him his adherents were promised power over even the greatest chiefs in the land. It was forbidden for any uninitiated man, or any woman or child, to look upon him or enter his shrine. He was represented by a stool, a symbol of power, on which was an iron ball. This ball was supposed to have fallen from the skies. The worship of meteors and aeroliths is not confined to Africa. Wherever they have fallen they have been considered as heaven-sent and worthy of reverence.

Heitsi-Eibib
Benign sorcerer god of the Hottentots.

Heitsi-Eibib was a shape-shifter and was born either to a cow or to a virgin who had consumed a magic herb. He was not a creator god but he gave men and animals their special characteristics by means of curses. These made some animals bold, some shy, some aggressive, some submissive. For example the lion originally lived in trees like some inadequate bird, but he was cursed by the god and as a result became earthbound. When Heitsi-Eibib began putting a curse on the hare, that animal took to his heels and has been running scared ever since. The running skill of the hare was to prove fatal to mankind. Hare once overtook an insect who was bearing a message from the moon to men. The message said that, like the moon, men would die, but after that they would grow strong and live again. Hare volunteered to pass on the message but he got it all wrong, telling men that they would die and stay dead. Moon heard what Hare had said and angrily hit him with a stick, splitting the animal's nose. But the damage had been done, for mankind believed the words of Hare.

Heviosso (Xevioso)
God of thunder in Dahomey, associated with *Legba*.

In ancient times Heviosso was offered human sacrifices, but after the arrival of the Europeans a bull was used instead. The animal has its throat cut very slowly, the object being to draw off as much of the living blood as possible, for living blood is the true life-force. When the god accepts the sacrifice bells are rung and the thunder chant, Ho Ho Ho, is shouted by all the priests and worshippers. The sacrifice is followed by eight days of dancing.

Adherents of Heviosso have special ways of greeting cult superiors and also those outside the cult. The former are greeted in the following manner: the worshipper crouches down with his hands clasped and places them in between the hands of his superior fellow initiate. Then he wiggles his bottom from side to side. Laymen are welcomed in a less evocative way, the initiate greeting an outsider by making a thunder-noise in his throat. The dances for Heviosso represent copulation with the earth; other dances are dramatic representations of the character of the thunder god. The dancers work themselves into a frenzy and rush about destroying plants and huts and attacking the bystanders. They sometimes go as far as to wreck the shrine of the god.

Huveane
Creator god of the Basuto people of Lesotho.

Huveane made heaven and earth, and like many African creator gods experienced a great deal of trouble from men. He hammered some pegs into the sky and climbed up them, removing them from below as he went to prevent men from following. He went higher and higher until he was lost from sight. And he has never been seen since.

Juok
Creator god of the Shilluk peoples of East Africa.

Juok found white sand in the north and from it made white men. He travelled down the Nile and used its mud to make brown men. Then he arrived south of the cataracts, discovered black earth and from it made black men.

Juok decided to give men legs so that they could walk. He then realized that men needed arms to grow food, so he gave them two, one to manage a hoe and the other to pull up weeds. Next came eyes to see what they were doing, and a mouth to eat with. With the mouth Juok included a tongue, and having made man capable of speech, gave him ears in order to hear. And believing that man was now just about perfect, he left things at that.

Kaka-Guia
Funerary god of the tribes of the Volta area. A bull-headed god who performed the duty of a psychopomp, a bringer of dead souls to the supreme god, who in this area was called Nyami (*Nyame*). He communicated with the living via the minor gods of the locality, whose numbers and names are excessive.

Kalumba
Creator god of the Luba of Zaire.

After he had made men Kalumba realized that Life and Death were coming along the road to meet them. So he ordered Goat and Dog to guard the way. They had instructions to let Life through, but to detain Death. Left alone, Goat and Dog argued about which one of them was the more clever. Dog claimed that he could stay awake long enough to stop Death, but Goat said that he couldn't. Then Goat went away for a while and Dog made a watch-fire. He stood resolutely at his post while the darkness closed in. After many hours Dog dozed off and as he was slumbering, Death came along the road. He crept past the sleeping

11

Dog and went on to find mankind. The next day it was Goat's turn to watch. He too built a fire in the evening and stayed fiercely awake. Life came along the road and Goat arrested him, with the result that Life was unable to get through and save men from Death. (See *Wuni*.)

Kho-dumo-dumo
Demon of the Basuto people of Lesotho.

The demon arrived on earth suddenly and began swallowing everything it could find, chickens, dogs, goats, cows, people. It went from village to village, gulping down every living thing. One woman who was pregnant managed to evade the common fate by rubbing herself with ashes and hiding in the corner of a cattle-pen. She lay very still and Kho-dumo-dumo overlooked her. Soon after the demon had gone the woman gave birth to a baby boy. She placed it carefully down on the floor and went to fetch some bedding. She was gone only a minute, but when she returned her baby had grown into a strapping hulk of a warrior. She told her son all about Kho-dumo-dumo. The warrior, named Ditaolane, raced after the demon and killed it with his spears. He began slicing the body open but one of the men inside cried out; Ditaolane's knife had cut his leg. The warrior operated more carefully, avoiding the great lumps inside the demon's belly. At last he managed to make a big enough hole for all to escape through. In gratitude, the men made Ditaolane their chief, giving him all the cattle he could desire.

Ditaolane ruled peacefully for a long while, but the man whose leg he had accidentally cut harboured a grudge. The man was jealous of the warrior's success and began to poison people's minds against him. He tried many ways of killing Ditaolane but the chief outwitted his attempts. At last Ditaolane lost interest in living any longer, and allowed himself to be killed. When he was dead his heart came out of his body, changed into a bird, and flew away.

Kokola
Guardian god who inhabits a cave on the shores of Lake Victoria. People from distant places who go to fish in the lake will leave

12

their possessions in his cave with perfect security, for none would dare steal anything watched over by Kokola.

Kwammang-a
God of the Bushmen of south Central Africa.

It was from Kwammang-a's discarded shoe that the god *Cagn* first made Eland. Shortly afterwards Kwammang-a killed and ate Eland, but not before Cagn had stolen the animal's gall. When he was alone he burst the gall and its contents temporarily blinded him. He wiped the gall-liquid off with a feather and threw the feather up into the sky, where it became the moon. Kwammang-a described Cagn as his grandfather, but that does not prove any relationship. The term could have been one of respect, or even of disrespect.

Kyala
Creator god of the Nyakyusa of South West Tanzania.

Kyala was promoted from being a humble local god to the chief god and then the sky god. He became so important and elevated that he was no longer worshipped, for he was too far above men to bother himself with their petty worries.

Legba
Evil genius of Dahomey.

Each man has his personal Legba near his house in the form of a mound of clay in human shape. From the clay protrudes a moulded phallus and the figure is protected by a straw thatch. In front of the *legba*, which represents the master of the house, stand small clay pots, one for each member of the family. The pots are regularly filled with offerings of food and the *legba's* phallus is anointed with oil and flour. From time to time a chicken is sacrificed and its feathers stuck to the moulded phallus with blood. Sometimes small wooden figures called *boitchyo* are found in the shrine. It is thought that these could represent human sacrifices – either in lieu of or as a token of the offering.

In Dahomey the god Legba is associated with *Heviosso*, the thunder god. When a bull is sacrificed to Heviosso his worshippers also give a smaller tribute, a kid, to Legba. Legba is considered to be a devil, a good indication that he was originally an important god. Deposed gods often become devils. Legba is the original of the complex Haitian god of the same name.

Libanza
Supreme god of the Upotos of the Congo.

Libanza once ordered that all the inhabitants of the earth and the moon should attend his court. The moon people immediately did as he asked. Libanza told them that because of their respect for his wishes the moon would only die for two days a month, and otherwise would enjoy immortality. Eventually, and with much reluctance, the earth people appeared. Libanza angrily informed them that as they had not bothered to obey him promptly they would suffer death.

Lisa
Chameleon deity of Dahomey.

Alias Leza or Lissa, this deity is closely linked with the great god *Mawu*. Sometimes Lisa is a god, sometimes a goddess. When female she is either the wife or the mother of Mawu. Lisa commonly forms a triad with Mawu and *Ge*. The first two humans to arrive on earth brought with them some sacred beads called *lisaje*, 'Lisa's beads', and instituted the worship of Mawu and Lisa. The correct sacrifice to Lisa is a white goat and a white chicken.

Lisa sent the chameleon to protect those humans who were spreading the cult of Mawu and Lisa. He knew that they would meet trouble so he made the chameleon go in front of the humans and reflect what was there, so that they would be forewarned.

With Mawu, Lisa also forms an androgynous divinity referred to as Mawu-Lisa. This concept is the starting point of various Haitian ideas of which *Marassa* (see American section) is the most obvious

Macardit
Demon spirit of the Dinka peoples of the Sudan.

Macardit is the 'outsider', a malicious force which inflicts injuries, injustice and disaster on mankind. Any such tragedies which have no obvious explanation are blamed on Macardit.

Massim-Biambe
Omnipotent creator god of the Mundang people of the Congo.

Two deities called Phebele (male principle) and Mebeli (female principle) had a child. Massim-Biambe gave this child the gifts of breath, of life and of a soul. The child was called Man. Massim-Biambe also gave souls to the animals. Every death means that a soul is released; it leaves the body and enters the earth down a long hole, and then waits for the time when it will enter a female body in order to create a new life. The souls of men create new men, the souls of animals create new animals.

Massim-Biambe is invisible and has no describable form, but he communicates with men through the intermediaries of holy objects. These are called *grigris* or, sometimes, fetishes.

Mawu
Chief god of Dahomey.

Mawu was creator of all things and although he is worshipped he is really far too elevated to be concerned with men. No sorcerer, however skilled and powerful, can manage to bring the god down to earth. Mawu has no shrines or priests. He is often shown as part of a trinity with *Lisa*, the chameleon god, and *Ge*, the moon god. After creation had been perfected the three gods toured the earth to inspect it; wherever they stopped they carved crosses on the nearby rocks.

Having no official shrines means that Mawu is prayed to privately. For when he created man he also created abstract forces to act as his intermediaries; these forces may be called gods or fetishes. The royal fetish is *Agassou* the panther, and there are more than fifty others in Dahomey, each of which looks after a clan. Apart from Agassou the major fetishes are Nesshoue, the river; *Heviosso*, the thunder; *Danh*, the snake; and *Sagbata*, the smallpox. The correct sacrifice to Mawu is a sheep.

Mawu is joined with Lisa to form a male-female god called Mawu-Lisa, who is the ancestor of all the gods of Dahomey. Mawu-Lisa is said to have been born from an ancient and shadowy androgyne named *Nanan-Bouclou*. To the Fon of Benin in West

15

Africa, Mawu is a goddess; she was the creatress of everything and is identified with the moon. She has male characteristics as well. She gave birth to a son, Lisa, identified with the sun. Sun and moon combined to make a single god, referred to as King of the Gods.

Muluku
Supreme god of the Macouas of Zambesi.

Muluku made the earth; he dug two holes and from one came a man and from the other a woman. He gave them land to cultivate and tools, seeds and crockery. He told them to dig and plant the seeds, to build a house and to cook food in the utensils. Instead of listening to his words the man and woman chewed the raw seeds, spoiled and broke the crockery, discarded the tools and then went to the forest to hide. Muluku was annoyed. He summoned a male and female monkey and gave them the same sort of things he had given to the man and woman. He also gave them the same instructions. The two monkeys dug the earth, built a house, harvested the grain and cooked it in the pots. They ate the food off the plates Muluku had provided. The god was pleased. He cut off the monkeys' tails and stuck them onto the two disobedient humans, saying that they would be monkeys from now on, and the monkeys would be humans.

Mulungu
Creator god of the Yao of Malawi.

Mulungu lived happily on earth with his animals until the arrival of men. It was a chameleon who found the first two humans; they had mysteriously appeared in his fish-weir. He told Mulungu of the newcomers but the god decided to wait and see what these humans were like before deciding what to do. The men made fire and set the bush alight; they chased out all the animals and began killing them. Then they devised all manner of traps and snares for the people of Mulungu. The god knew it was time to leave. He asked a spider to spin him a thread up to heaven, and thus escaped from the evil ways of mankind. (See *Nyambi*.)

16

Mungo (Mungu)
God of the Giryama of Kenya.

In return for the offering of a goat and a chicken Mungo will send rain. Having performed the sacrifice, the priest beats loudly on a buffalo horn and makes his request. He then ties a strip of white cloth to the roof of the house and leaves it there until the rain comes.

Nampa
Spirit of Senegal. He is present in a fetish made of roots and leaves pounded together and rolled into three balls. His worship is restricted to the initiated.

Nanan-Bouclou
Original god of the Ewe tribe of Dahomey, Nanan-Bouclou was both male and female and created *Mawu-Lisa*. He was far too remote to be worshipped and has little significance nowadays, although he is sometimes connected with the panther fetish *Agassou*. In Haiti Nanan-Bouclou is remembered, but in a reduced role. There he is god of herbs and medicine.

'Ndriananahary
Supreme god of the Malagasy peoples of Madagascar.

'Ndriananahary sent down his son *Ataokoloinona* to see if the earth was suitable for habitation, but Ataokoloinona disappeared into the ground and never emerged again. 'Ndriananahary dispatched his servants, called men, to look for his son. They wandered all over the earth, suffering greatly for the place was hot and rocky. From time to time they sent back one of their number to the god to ask for new orders; but these messengers, the dead, never returned. To help men in their search for his son 'Ndriananahary sent rain to cool the burning rocks and to make the soil fruitful. And that is how it is.

Ndura
'The jungle'. The nearest thing the pygmies of Central Africa have to a god

Ndura nee bokbu, 'the jungle is everything'. The pygmies are *bamiki ba'ndura*, 'children of the jungle'. They have no leaders, politics, laws, classes, priests, rules, or taxes. They survive through their flexibility and their intimate knowledge of the jungle and its moods. They cheerfully provide food for villagers at grossly unfair rates, for this has the effect of keeping the latter out of the jungle and therefore unacquainted with its secrets.

'Nenaunir
Storm god of the Masai of Kenya.

'Nenaunir is an evil god and linked to the rainbow, which once swallowed the earth. The Masai attacked the rainbow with their spears and arrows and forced him to give it back. This story may be interpreted as a flood myth.

'Ngai
Creator god of the Masai of Kenya.

'Ngai made the earth and then the first man, Kintu, whose mistakes introduced death into the world. Another version of the arrival of death tells how the god gave his favourite, Le-eyo, a magic formula to recite over dead children to ensure their immortality. Le-eyo did not bother to do this until one of his own sons died. 'Ngai told him it was too late, and ever since then death has had power over men. 'Ngai gives each man at birth a guardian angel who protects him from all hazards and carries away his soul after death. Evil souls are taken to a desert, good souls are placed in wide and rich pastures among vast herds of cattle; for a dairy farm is a good approximation to the Masai idea of Paradise.

Ngewo-wa
Creator god of the Mende of Sierra Leone.

Ngewo-wa made all things, including a man and a woman. The humans called him Maanda, 'grandfather', and continually pestered him with requests for things. The god always gave them what they asked for saying to them, 'Ngee' ('take it'). So they called him Ma-ngee, 'grandfather-take-it'. The god grew exhausted with the couple's unending demands, so one night while they slept he went away to find a new place to live. The man and woman woke up, looked for their god and saw him in the sky; he was spread out wide so they called him 'Ngee-wolo-nga wa-le', which means 'grandfather-take-it-is-spread-wide'. From this expression came the name Ngewo-wa.

Ngewo-wa devised a plan to preserve peace and quiet on earth. He made two fowls and gave one to each human, telling them that if either party wronged the other he would take away the wrongdoer's chicken. The plan worked well and Ngewo-wa came down to earth for the last time and said goodbye to mankind for ever.

Ngworekara
Demon king of the Fan of the Congo.

Ngworekara was predictably ugly, wicked and vengeful. He ruled over a kingdom of evil spirits, who were the souls of the dead. He was cruel and tyrannical and could even condemn the miserable spirits to a second death. His subjects were not the most beautiful of creatures, being described as having long straggly hair, dirty ears, droopy noses, and lips like the ends of elephants' trunks. These spirits made their dwellings on mountain tops, where their noxious presence would cause men to feel dizzy and afraid.

Nkosi Yama'kosi
Title of the supreme being of the Ndebele of Zimbabwe. It means King of Kings and is often applied to leading politicians and statesmen.

Number Eleven (Dubiaku)
Culture hero and ancestor of the lesser gods of the Ashanti of Ghana.

Number Eleven was the youngest of eleven children who exasperated their mother by devouring all the food she had; there was never anything for her to eat and she was starving to death. The mother came to an arrangement with a certain tree which grew over a pumpkin patch; she would send her children to pick pumpkins and the tree would drop branches onto them, killing

19

them. It was the only way the mother could think of to survive. But Number Eleven realized the plot and tricked the tree into dropping its branches too early. He and his brothers safely collected the pumpkins and, as usual, ate up every last spoonful.

Their mother went to the sky god and complained; the god promised to sort things out. He arranged several ambushes, but clever Number Eleven evaded them all. So the sky god decided to send the children to the village of Death, where they were to obtain a number of golden objects: a pipe, a snuff-box, a chewing-stick and a whetstone. Death welcomed the children and prepared sleeping mats for them; she waited eagerly for nightfall when she intended to eat them with her gleaming red teeth. One by one the boys dropped off to sleep, each boy sharing a mat with one of Death's own children. Only Number Eleven remained awake. Death became impatient and asked the child why he was not sleeping. He replied that he would like a smoke first. Death brought him her golden pipe. Still Number Eleven stayed awake. She asked him again and the child requested a pinch of snuff; Death brought her golden snuff-box. Then Number Eleven asked for a chewing-stick and finally for some food. Death lit the fire with her golden whetstone and then went out to get water for cooking. Number Eleven had secretly cut holes in her water calabash to delay her return. By the time she got back he had wakened his brothers, sent them away and placed cloth bundles in their places. Death came in and killed the sleeping children, or so she thought. She had in fact killed her own brood. Number Eleven, who had gathered all the golden objects together, now made a dash for the door. Death followed but the child evaded her and joined his brothers who were hiding up a tree. When Death came walking below, Number Eleven could not resist urinating over her head.

Furiously Death chanted a spell and one by one the children fell out of the tree. When it was Number Eleven's turn he jumped down just before the end of the spell, forestalling its effect. Death, hoping that all the children had been killed by their fall, climbed up into the tree to check that no one had escaped. While she was up there, Number Eleven leapt to his feet and called out the same spell; Death toppled out of the branches and landed with such force that she was killed.

Number Eleven set about reviving his brothers with a magic ointment, but as he applied it to the pile of twisted bodies some of it spilt on Death. The boys revived, but so too did Death. She came to and chased after them. Number Eleven, being the smallest, could not run as fast as the others. They all reached the river before him and swam across. Number Eleven was stranded and helpless for he was unable to swim, so he turned himself into a stone. His brothers, seeing his great danger, began bawling and yowling like whipped curs. Death, who had by now arrived on the opposite bank, could not stand the noise the boys were making and decided to silence them with a well-aimed missile. She looked about for something to throw at them and noticed a stone on the river bank.... Death picked up the stone and flung it vengefully across the water; as the stone landed it changed back into Number Eleven. For Death this was the last straw; she knew she was beaten. She told Number Eleven that she would not bother him again, and furthermore if he did not harbour any of her justified victims she would reciprocate by letting his friends go. Number Eleven agreed to this arrangement, and thus became a minor god and the ancestor of all the lesser divinities of the Ashanti.

Nummo (Nommo)
Spirit couple of the Dogon tribe of Mali. They were the first perfect pair to be born to the earth and the god *Amma*.

Nyambe
God of the Koko of Nigeria.

Nyambe lived among men, and there was no such thing as death in the world because the god had provided them with a magic tree. When men grew old they went and lived under the tree for nine days, and it rejuvenated them. As time went on men began to act in a blasé fashion towards Nyambe. They stopped treating him with honour. He was upset at being ignored and called them all together, then challenged them to break a bundle of sticks. The men were unable to do so. Nyambe pointed out to them that if they had bound themselves closely to him, like the bundle of sticks, they would have had great strength from the unity. But since they had decided to drift away from him, he was going to punish them. He uprooted the tree of life and walked away into the sunset. And without its magic men began to die.

Nyambi (Nyambe)
High god of the Barotse of Upper Zambesi.

Nyambi created all things and lived on earth with his wife Nasilele.

There was a man called Kamonu who followed the god everywhere and copied everything he did. He saw Nyambi forging iron and imitated him; he made spears and began killing animals. The god was angry with such destructive behaviour and drove Kamonu away. But the man returned, and Nyambi forgave him. Kamonu came pestering Nyambi again, his pot had broken and his child had died. He demanded that the god give him spells to mend the pot and revive the child. Nyambi refused and went to live on an island in the middle of a lake. But Kamonu built a raft and poled it over to the island. The god went to live on a mountain crag; Kamonu scaled the cliffs and joined him. Nyambi ordered a bird to fly over the earth and search for a place where he would not be constantly accosted by Kamonu, but men of all kinds had settled everywhere and such a spot was not to be found. Nyambi got a spider to spin a thread up to heaven. He blinded the spider so that he would never be able to repeat the effort, then he escaped up the thread.

But Kamonu was not to be defeated so easily; he got friends to help him build a tower of logs. The tower rose higher and higher towards heaven, then it faltered and collapsed. Kamonu still watches and waits. He sees the sun rise and greets it, thinking it is Nyambi; he sees the moon come up and greets it, thinking it is Nyambi's wife Nasilele. He has never given up hope of seeing the god once more. (See *Mulungu*.)

Nyame
High god of the Twi of West Africa.

Before birth, souls are taken to Nyame and washed in a golden bath. Then the god gives the soul its destiny and drops some water of life into its mouth. This water contains a living and breathing image in miniature of the high god himself. The soul is then in a fit state to be born into a human body.

Nyamia Ama
God of storms, rain and lightning of Senegal. Sometimes he is
called god of the sky, sometimes he is considered as the invisible
and remote supreme god. He controls all the atmospheric
phenomena.

Nyankopon (Nyankopon Kweku, Onyankopon)
Sky god of the Ashanti of Ghana.

Like many gods Nyankopon used to live quite happily near men;
in fact he was so close to them that a certain old woman kept
hitting him with her pestle pole as she mashed yams. One day the
god decided he had had enough of this treatment and left. The
people blamed the old woman, for now they could not meet the
god and talk to him in the way they had been used to. More to the
point, they could no longer get what they wanted from him. The
old woman came up with a solution to the problem. She told the
people to bring their mortars, the hollowed logs in which they
mashed their yams, and instructed them to set the logs up end to
end so that they would reach the sky, where Nyankopon had
gone. The people did so and their structure almost reached its
goal. Indeed all they needed was one more log; but there were
none left. Then the old woman had another idea. She suggested
that they take the bottom log and put it on the top, that way they
would be able to reach Nyankopon's hiding-place. The people
readily agreed and the man at the base of the tower took away the
first log and handed it up to the top.... When the dust had
settled and the injured had quit screaming and the dead had been
counted, the people realized they would never see the sky god
again.
　　However, Nyankopon was not a vengeful god. He wanted to
give men eternal life and sent them a message saying that those
who died would have new life with him, in the sky. He entrusted
this message to a goat. The goat set off towards mankind but then
stopped to browse at an attractive-tasting bush. Nyankopon,
who was watching, sighed with exasperation and sent down a
sheep with the same message. The sheep succeeded in finding
men but, not being the most intellectually gifted of animals, got
the message all wrong. Nyankopon had said that men would die

23

but that would not be the end; but the sheep informed his audience that they would die and that *would* be the end. And when the goat eventually arrived with the correct message, men would not listen to it. (See *Anansi* and *Wulbari*.)

Nyasaye
God of the Maragoli people of Kenya.

Nyasaye is aided in his work by spirits, symbolized by round stones surrounding a pole representing the god himself. Sacrifices to Nyasaye are performed in the following way: millet is mixed with water and the officiating elders take mouthfuls of the mash and spit it onto the feet and heads of the women and children gathered about the shrine. They then kill a chicken and daub its blood on the heads and feet of the worshippers.

Nzambi
Great goddess of the Bakongo people of the Congo. Alias Nzambi Mpungu, she is considered as male in some parts of the Congo and called Zambi.

Nzambi made the world. Several stories relate how she then appeared to men as a poor, tired and destitute old woman. She asked for help; some spurned her, others gave aid willingly. Those who helped the goddess were magnificently rewarded and those that denied her charity were punished. Nzambi used her divine power to expose all manner of faults in people's characters. In one tale she had presented Crab with a body and legs, and promised to give him a head. Crab was full of pride and self-esteem; he invited everyone to be present at the great ceremony where he would be honoured by the goddess. Arrogantly strutting among the guests, he was so full of himself that he could not even walk straight. Nzambi saw his pretentious behaviour and chided Crab for it; she announced to the waiting crowd that because of his pride she would not after all be giving Crab a head; and let that be a lesson to them all.

Crab crept away shamefully. Ever since then he has hidden from people, scuttling under rocks, and when he does have to look about he is compelled to raise his eyes straight out of his body, for he still has no head.

Nzame
High god of the Fan people of the Congo.

Nzame is a shadowy god, impossible to represent in clay, wood or stone. He lived on earth with his three sons, Whiteman, Blackman and Gorilla. Blackman and Gorilla and all their kin were disobedient and so Nzame took his considerable wealth, his wives and his son Whiteman and went away to live on the west coast. Gorilla and his kin went off into the jungle to seek food. Blackman and his folk remained where they were, but without the resources and help of Nzame they were forced to live an ignorant and perilous life, merely managing to survive. Both Blackman and Gorilla and all their people are still irresistibly attracted to the west, where Nzame lives with his rich white son.

Obassi Osaw
High god of the Hausa of the Niger.

Obassi Osaw provided everything on earth for men except fire. Men wanted fire and sent a boy to the god to ask for some. Obassi Osaw was indignant and sent the boy scurrying back empty-handed. The chief of the men then went to the god himself to ask forgiveness for their presumption. Obassi Osaw rejected him. On his return the chief was mocked by the boy; he too had returned empty-handed. The boy said he would go and steal fire from the god. He went to the heavenly house of Obassi Osaw and made himself useful by preparing the god's food and serving it to him with every mark of respect and humility. He stayed there, doing anything that was asked of him willingly and cheerfully. He never complained and made no demands. After a while Obassi Osaw got used to having the boy around. One evening he sent him to fetch a lamp, which along with the fire was kept in the house of the god's wives. The boy went to the house, waited while the lamp was lit and brought it back promptly. In the weeks that followed he was often dispatched on a similar errand.

One evening when he went for the lamp one of the wives asked him to light it, as she was too busy. The boy lit the lamp from the fire, then took an ember and wrapped it in leaves, hiding it about his person. He took the lamp back to the god. The boy then made an excuse to go out, collected some dry wood and set it alight; he covered the smouldering wood with leaves and returned to the house. That night when everyone was asleep the boy crept out, took the burning wood and hurried back to earth. There he made the first fire for men.

Next morning Obassi Osaw noticed smoke rising from the earth. He sent down his son from heaven to investigate. His son sought out the boy and asked him if he had stolen the fire. The boy admitted quite openly that he had. The son of the god said that as a punishment the boy would be made lame. But fire stayed on earth.

Ogun (Ogoun)
God of iron and warfare of the Nago and Yoruba peoples of West Africa.

When the gods first arrived on earth their way was barred by an impenetrable thicket of thorn bushes. Ogun stepped forward with his machete and cut a way through for them. As a result, Ogun is called upon by men to remove any difficulties in their way; to smooth the path to the desired end.

Apart from being a smith god, Ogun also looks after hunters, goldsmiths, barbers and truck drivers, all of whom rely on iron and steel. He is also a god of justice, and oaths are sworn on a lump of iron; such oaths being as binding as those sworn on the Bible. (See Haitian god *Ogoun* in the American section.)

Omumbo-Rombonga
The tree of life of the Herero Bushmen of South West Africa.

From this great tree men were born. It also produced cattle and other animals. The world into which they emerged was made and maintained by *Cagn*, who had decreed that all animals should have the power of speech. But now men cannot understand the language of animals.

The idea of a Tree of Life is a recurrent concept in many diverse cultures. Examples may be found from all over the world.

Rock-Sene
God of the Serer people of Gambia.

Rock-Sene is both kind and destructive; he sends rain to swell the harvest and also strikes men and crops with his thunderstorms.

Rock-Sene heard that both the Sun and the Moon had passed by a waterfall in which their respective mothers were bathing. Sun was abashed and looked away modestly from his mother, but Moon stared hard at hers. Rock-Sene thereupon made the Sun bright, so that people would not be able to look on him and would remember his modest behaviour as they turned away their heads. The Moon on the other hand was made dimmer, so that people could stare at her as much as they wanted to, as she had stared at her mother.

Ruwa
High god of the Djaga of Kilimanjaro.

Ruwa was more of an organizer than a creator; he freed men from a pot in which they had been confined by breaking it open, gave them the means of survival, and planted bananas and yams for them. In the middle of the new garden he planted a special yam called Ukaho, which was forbidden to mankind. They could eat anything but that. Ruwa visited earth each dawn and sunset to make sure that all was going well.

One day when he was away a stranger came to the garden and asked for food. He was offered bananas and yams but said that he had met Ruwa on his journey and the god had told him that the time had come for the yam Ukaho to be cooked and eaten. The people followed the stranger's instructions. The smell of the special yam was carried afar by the winds and one of Ruwa's angels arrived, attracted by the unmistakable aroma. When he saw the people eating the yam, he grabbed the cooking pot and the remaining portions and hurried away to Ruwa with the evidence. Ruwa sent the angel back with the message that because the people had believed a stranger rather than obeying their god, they would be vulnerable to accident and destruction. Ruwa would allow their bones to break, their eyes to burst, and death to claim them.

Another story about how death came to the earth because of men not obeying the commands of Ruwa is this: The god had arranged that when men grew old they could become young again by sloughing off their wrinkled skins. They were enjoined to do this in private, for if anyone saw it happen the spell would be broken. An old man decided that the time had come to shed his skin, so he sent his granddaughter out to fetch water. He had previously bored holes in the calabash so that the girl would be gone for a long time. But the girl was more alert than he thought; she noticed the holes and plugged them at once, filled the cala-bash and returned to the house sooner than expected. The old man was caught half out of his skin. He cried out that death would now come because of her intrusion. The angry folk drove the girl out into the jungle. There she suffered a fate worse than death at the hands of various simians and became the mother of all the 'Cursed Children', that is to say the baboons, apes and other monkeys that live in the jungle.

Sagbata
God of smallpox in Dahomey.

Sagbata was greatly feared on account of his lethal nature. In ancient Dahomey, before the arrival of Western medicine, he was a very powerful god for his priests were able to spread the killer disease at will, using dried and infected scabs. The priests had dis-covered for themselves a means of immunization and so were able to wield terrible power over the people. Shrines to Sagbata were painted on their outer walls with a design of small spots, a chilling reminder of the god's influence. In recent times Sagbata has been considered an earth god and it is claimed that he is the son of *Mawu.*

Sakarabru
God of medicine, justice and retribution of the Agni people of Guinea.

Sakarabru is represented by a ball of maize and other *grigris,* or talismans. He is feared, for he is swift to punish men for their mis-deeds. He is particularly active during changes of season and during the critical phases of the moon. His devotees perform a dance for him in which they become possessed by his power, as demonstrated in a shaking frenzy.

Shango
Storm god of the Yoruba of West Africa.

He is warlike, aggressive and a magician. His weapon, the thunderbolt, is represented by a double-headed axe which bears a striking resemblance to the hammer of the Nordic *Thor*.

Unkulunkulu
High god of the Amazulu; known as Nkulnkulu to the Ndebele (both Zimbabwe)

Unkulunkulu's name means 'old, old one'. The earth was already made when he appeared from a reed patch. With him came all living things, plants and animals. He was very much a god of the earth, having nothing to do with the heavens. He showed men everything about them, giving things names and describing their uses. He also instituted human reproductive powers and organized men under the leadership of chiefs.

Waka
Benign rain god of the Galla of Ethiopia.

Waka controls all the rain and rituals must be performed to propitiate him, but he is on the whole a kind god. He may be approached directly by devotees or through the intercession of a man of knowledge. Such a man will have studied history, divination and the rules which govern religious ceremonies.

We
Supreme god of the Kasena of Upper Volta.

We used to live near earth, but a certain old woman kept slicing bits off him to add to her stew-pot. As a result the god decided to move up to heaven.

Wulbari
Supreme god of the Krachi of West Africa.

In former times Wulbari lay on top of mother earth, and there was little space for men between them. The proximity of mankind soon became unbearable to the god for several reasons.

First of all there was an old woman who kept thumping him with her pole when mashing yams (the god *Nyankopon* had a similarly painful experience). Then there was the smoke from cooking fires which made the god's eyes water and turn red. Finally there were a number of people who had acquired the habit of wiping their dirty hands on Wulbari to clean them.

In time-honoured fashion Wulbari decided to leave for heaven. He settled down there and collected the animals round him in a zoological court. The spider *Anansi* was employed as an officer in the palace guard. Anansi begged a corncob from Wulbari, went down to earth and played a complex series of confidence tricks on men. The result of it all was that he acquired a hundred slaves in return for the single corncob. Glowing with pride from the success of this mission, Anansi became a braggart. One day he boasted that he was cleverer than Wulbari; the god overheard the claim and summoned Anansi to the throne. Wulbari told the spider that he would be given the chance to prove himself, all he had to do was to go away and fetch 'something'. Wulbari would not say what that 'something' was.

Anansi left the palace, called all the birds to him and took one feather from each. With the multicoloured plumage he created an extraordinary feathery costume. He put it on and went and sat in a tree opposite the palace. All the courtiers came to view the exotic and peculiarly plumaged fowl, wondering what kind of bird it was. They sent for Wulbari but he was unable to identify it. Someone suggested that if Anansi were there he would be sure to know. By the way, where was the spider? Wulbari said that he had sent Anansi to fetch 'something', and the 'something' he had in mind was the Sun, the Moon and Darkness! The courtiers roared with laughter at Wulbari's roguery.

When the crowd had dispersed, Anansi climbed down off his perch, discarded his feathers and hastened off into the forest. It was not too difficult for a confidence trickster of his calibre to purloin the Sun, Moon and Darkness. He put them in a bag and strutted back to Wulbari's palace. There he declared that he had fetched 'something'. The courtiers crowded into the throne room and Anansi opened the bag and took out Darkness. Everyone was plunged into total blackness, and there was a good deal of cursing and not a few stubbed toes. Next Anansi took the Moon out of his bag, throwing a little light on the scene. Then he hoisted out the Sun. The effect was devastating. Used to the dark, many of the courtiers were permanently blinded; others more fortunate got away with severely damaged eyesight. Only a few escaped. And that was how blindness came into the world.

Wuni
Supreme god of the Dagamba people of Ghana.

In the old times men did not die, they were slaves forever. But they wanted to be free, so they sent Dog to Wuni with a plea that they be emancipated. As Dog approached the home of the god he passed an old woman tending a cooking fire, on which there was a covered pot. Dog licked his lips in anticipation and stopped. The old woman shouted at him but Dog stared blissfully at the pot, thinking of the food it must contain. Goat had heard the men give their message to Dog and had followed him out of idle curiosity; when he saw Dog hanging about the fire he decided to go and give the message to Wuni himself.

Meanwhile the old woman had brought a child from the hut; she undressed the infant and took the lid off the cooking pot . . . and began bathing the child in the warm water. Dog growled a few rude things beneath his breath and trotted off on his errand. He soon met Goat who was striding back from the house of Wuni looking proud and happy. Goat told Dog he need not worry about the message for he, Goat, had personally delivered it to the god. Dog asked him to repeat the wording which Goat cheerfully did: men had grown tired of their unending slavery, and wished to die. Dog went hot all over; Goat had got the message wrong. All men wanted was to be delivered from slavery. He ran all the way to Wuni and stammered out the correct message. But it was too late, the god had made the arrangements with Death. (See *Kalumba*.)

31

America

NORTH AMERICAN ■ MEXICAN
SOUTH AMERICAN ■ HAITIAN

Agloolik
A good spirit of the Eskimo. One of the throng of deities who assisted or impeded the Eskimo in their harsh and unremitting struggle for survival. He lived under the ice and helped hunters and fishermen in their efforts.

Aipaloovik
A sea-living god of the Eskimo.

Aipaloovik was evil, and did his best to injure mariners by dashing up out of the depths and biting them. His profession was murder and his leisure-activities included destruction, vandalism and mayhem. Think of him as a divine hit-man.

Akna
'The mother', Eskimo goddess of childbirth.

Ataentsic
Iroquois/Huron mother goddess from heaven.

Ataentsic dwelt in heaven where her father was the first celestial inhabitant to suffer death. She used to speak to her father's dead body and it would reply, giving her advice. When she was of age the corpse told her to go to a chief and marry him. Ataentsic set off alone, and after overcoming the dangers of the journey arrived at a huge tree which sheltered the tepee of the chief. She became his wife. When she was pregnant her husband became suspicious and thought that she had been having an affair with a dragon of fire. Maliciously the Northern Lights suggested that he dispose of her. The chief rooted up the large tree, leaving a huge hole. Angrily he took hold of his wife and their new born daughter, Wind Breath, and threw them into it.

Ataentsic and her child fell through the hole in heaven; below was an unending ocean. The goddess's descent had been noticed by an otter, a muskrat and a turtle. They hastened to look for some earth for Ataentsic to land on. The muskrat found some and placed it on the turtle's back. Then the birds caught hold of Ataentsic and her child and landed them safely on the fresh earth.

Mother and daughter lived happily on earth. When she was of age Ataentsic's daughter was visited one night by the Lord of

Winds. She conceived and twins were formed inside her. The twins were jealous of each other and before they were born began fighting. They fought so furiously that their mother died. Ataentsic rescued the twins and from their mother's body created the sun and moon. The twins were named *Ioskeha* and *Tawiscara*.

Aulanerk
A friendly Eskimo deity who brought men joy. He lived in the sea, was naked, and his movements caused the waves.

Aumanil
A good spirit of the Eskimo. He controlled the movements of the whales and so was important to Eskimo economy. Despite his marine obligations he lived on dry land.

Awonawilona
Zuni Indian supreme god, the maker of all things. Awonawilona had dual sexuality, a not uncommon trait among creator gods.

Big Heads
Demonic deities of the Iroquois Indians. They were huge, bodiless heads covered in long hair from which protruded sharp-nailed claws. With open mouths and fiery eyes the Big Heads flew about in storms, the wind keeping them up by their masses of hair.

Coyote
A demon clown figure among the North American Indians.

Coyote represented the breaking free of negative power from the universal order of things. The Montana Sioux claim he invented horses, which they considered as a type of adapted dog. Coyote is a folk-hero; though not a regular god he was always sneaking about on the periphery of the divine world, causing trouble.

Ga-Oh
Iroquois god of the winds; a giant cannibal who used stones as missiles and rooted up great trees.

Gendenwitha
Iroquois goddess of the Morning Star.

The great hunter Sesondowah once saw a wonderful elk and gave chase, but it turned out that the animal was a spirit. It led him up to heaven where he was captured and bound by the goddess Dawn. He was forced to become her guard and stand at her door. One day Sesondowah looked down to earth and saw a beautiful girl, and fell in love with her. He managed to transform himself into a bird, then flew down to earth and brought the girl back to heaven. Dawn was very angry at what he had done and tied him securely to the doorpost; she transformed the girl into a star and fixed her to her forehead where she became Gendenwitha, the Morning Star. Sesondowah and Gendenwitha can see each other, but they can never come together.

Hino
Iroquois thunder spirit and god of the sky.

Hino destroyed evil things with his fire arrows. He was married to the Rainbow. Once when mankind was threatened by the Big Water Snake, Hino recruited a boy called Gunnodoyak and trained him to fight the creature. Gunnodoyak didn't do too well: the Big Water Snake swallowed him. Hino had to kill the snake himself and rescue Gunnodoyak. As a sort of consolation prize Gunnodoyak became one of Hino's immortal helpers.

Huruing Wuhti
Creator god/gods of the Hopi Indians.

Huruing Wuhti was not one but two gods. He/they made the earth and the animals and then decided to make men. He/they took clay, moulded it, sang a spell, and so man and woman were created. It is not known if he/they had any schizophrenic tendency/tendencies.

Ioskeha
Creator god of the Iroquois and Hurons.

With *Tawiscara*, Ioskeha was a twin son of the Lord of Wind and the girl Wind Breath, daughter of the fallen goddess *Ataentsic* (*q.v.*). He and his brother fought while still in the womb and thus caused their mother's death. His twin brother claimed that Ioskeha had started the fight, and so Ataentsic drove him away. Ioskeha went to his father for help. His father gave him weapons to hunt with and maize seed to plant. Ioskeha created all manner of animals and began cultivation of crops. These soon fell prey to the spells of a dwarf demon named Hadui, who caused them to sicken. Ioskeha defeated the demon and took from him the secrets of curing diseases; he also won from him the magical and ritual herb called tobacco. He set free the sun and moon from the captivity imposed upon them by his brother and let them inhabit the sky, out of reach of evil. Then he set about creating the races of mankind.

All this time he had been jealously watched by his twin Tawiscara. Everything he did the latter imitated, trying to prove that he was as powerful as his twin. But the creations of Tawiscara were failures; they were full of defects and came out monstrously disfigured. Finally Ioskeha lost his patience and sent his brother into distant exile.

Keelut
An evil Eskimo earth spirit, who looked like a hairless dog.

Kitcki Manitou
Algonquin Supreme Being.

Kitcki Manitou was the Great Spirit present in nearly every North American mythology. To the Sioux he was Wakonda, to the Oglala, Wakan, Tanka.

To the Algonquin Kitcki Manitou was the Uncreated, the Father of Life, the Master of Light, the God of the Winds. He dwelt in Heaven and was above all powers. Longfellow, who ransacked Algonquin myths wholesale for 'Hiawatha', calls him Gitchee Manitou. The idea of a Supreme Being is found in many primal religions; in no way does this indicate monotheism.

Manitou
Algonquin name for the spirit of divinity inherent in every created thing. Man must control the lower Manitous in stones, fire, wood

and such and try to acquire the help of the powerful Manitous in the wind, rain and sun. The Iroquois equivalent is 'Orenda'; the Eskimo word for the same essence is 'Innua'.

Michabo
'Great hare', Algonquin founder of the human race.

According to the Algonquin, Michabo was born on the island of Michilimakinak. He made the earth, deer, water and fish. He drove away the cannibal spirits and helped mankind by inventing the fishing net. He was a shape-shifter and could take on many different animal forms. He inhabited the House of Dawn, where he was host to the souls of good men, feeding them on succulent fruits. He created men by mating with a muskrat.

Na'pi
'Old man', creator god of the Blackfoot Indians.

Na'pi made the world and created a woman and her son out of clay. The woman immediately wanted to know if they would always be alive. Na'pi had to admit that he hadn't thought about it. He threw a buffalo chip into the river saying that if it floated then people would die, but only for four days, after which they would live again. If the dried buffalo dung sank, then people would die and stay dead. It floated. The woman, who was something of a gambler, disagreed with the god's test. She said that she would throw a stone into the river. If it floated people would live for ever, if it sank people would die and stay dead. That way living people would have more sympathy for each other.

She threw the stone into the river. Of course the wretched thing sank.

Nokomis
Algonquin goddess of the earth.

Nokomis' name means 'grandmother' and she fed all living things, plants, animals and men. According to Longfellow, she was swinging about on a grapevine in the moon when a rival 'cut the leafy swing asunder', causing the goddess to fall to earth where she bore Wenonah, who was to be the wife of Hiawatha.

Onatha
Iroquois goddess of wheat.

Daughter of the mother goddess Eithinoha, Onatha was abducted by a demon whilst looking for dew; he took her into his underworld kingdom and made her a prisoner there. The sun began to look for her; at last, after shining on the earth for many weeks, Onatha appeared out of the ground. She returned to the cultivated fields and grew strong and healthy under the sun's care.

Oshadagea
'Big eagle of the dew', the Iroquois guardian of the west.

Oshadagea fought the demons of fire who tried to destroy vegetation by draining it of moisture. He combated them by flying from the west with a great lake of water in the hollow of his back. With this water he moistened the vegetation, reviving it.

Pah
God of the moon of the Pawnee Indians.

At the orders of the great god *Tirawa*, Pah took his place in the west to give light to men during the night. He mated with *Shakuru* the sun, and they had a son. The Morning Star and the Evening Star had also mated and produced a daughter.

The son and the daughter were placed on earth, and were the ancestors of mankind.

Pukkeenegak
Eskimo goddess of clothes-making and childbirth. Pukkeenegak was a kindly spirit who procured food for her worshippers. She was always prettily dressed, wore big boots and had a tattooed face.

Sedna
Eskimo goddess of the sea and its creatures.

Sedna was greatly feared, being gigantic and one-eyed. But she was not always like that. She was once a beautiful and desirable maiden who scorned all lovers, until a handsome hunter paddled up in his kayak and wooed her with soft words and fair promises.

39

She liked the look of him and they were married; but soon came the terrible truth. Her husband was not human but a bird-spirit who had fallen in love with her and had assumed human form to court her. Sedna's father, Angusta, came to her rescue and managed to carry her off in his boat, concealed under a pile of furs. Pursued by the phantom hunter, Angusta refused to give back his daughter or even let her be seen. Torn by heartbreaking despair, the demon lover gave a tragic cry and turned back into a sea-bird. At that moment the sky darkened and the sea boiled up into a furious storm.

Horrified at his own daring in the face of the spirit and in mortal dread for his own life, Angusta cast his daughter into the sea as a propitiatory sacrifice. Sedna grasped the boat, trying to clamber to safety. Her terrified father took his ivory axe and began hacking at her hand. He cut off her finger-tops which fell into the sea and became seals, then her finger-stumps, knuckles and parts of her hand. From these bloody fragments were born other sea creatures, walruses and whales. The sea swallowed Sedna and became calm. Angusta reached his shore tent, tied up Sedna's dog and fell into an exhausted sleep. That night the sea flooded; man and dog were swept away, to join Sedna in the bitter depths.

Sorcerers wishing to visit Sedna to demand the release of seals for hunting must pass first through the realms of death then cross an abyss where a wheel of ice turns unceasingly and a gigantic cauldron of seal meat eternally seethes. Having got past her enormous guard dog the petitioner can meet the goddess. To return, he has to travel over another dreadful abyss on a bridge as narrow as a knife edge.

Shakuru
Sun god of the Pawnees.

Among the Plains Indians the most important ceremony of the calendar was the famous Sun Dance. This festival involved the discussion of inter-tribal politics, the recognition of acts of valour, ceremonial dances, and a lengthy process of self-mutilation by young men wishing to fulfil vows or prove their manhood. Young warriors would attach themselves to tall poles by hide ropes which were tied to sharp stakes, and then pushed through skin and flesh on the chest. The warrior would lean his whole weight on the ropes and circle about the pole, following the movement of the sun in the sky. This painful process lasted the whole of the day or until the small stakes were entirely ripped out of the living flesh by the warrior's weight and movement. The sun dance was more than just a dramatic public spectacle; it had a deep influence on the soul of the warrior undergoing it, and was a sincere expression of his desire to overcome the limitations of his human frailty.

Shakuru was placed in the east at the creation by the god *Tirawa* (*q.v.*).

Spider Woman
Navaho spirit who taught the *Twin War Gods* (*q.v.*) how to overcome the dangers on their journey to their father, the Sun. She gave them charms and magic formulae so that they could negotiate the crushing rocks, the cutting reeds, the tearing cacti and the boiling sand.

Stone Giants
Iroquois and Huron monster-gods.

Vociferous, violent beings who threw huge stones about the place and were not loth to chew on a tasty Indian or two for dinner.

Tawiscara
God of the Iroquois and Hurons. Twin brother of *Ioskeha* (*q.v.*).

Tekkeitsertok
Eskimo god of the earth. He was the most powerful of their gods and owned all the deer. His favour was sought at the hunting season with widespread sacrifices.

Thunder Bird
American Indian god of thunder revered by most tribes and nations. His eyes flashed lightning and the noise of his wings made the thunder. He sustained growing things by sending rain, and was attended by minor spirits in the shape of hawks and eagles.

41

Tirawa
Creator and sky god of the Pawnee Indians.

Tirawa arranged the dwelling place of man in the shape of a circle, edged all round with sky. You may verify this by climbing to the top of the nearest mountain and taking a look. This fact is represented in the Hako ceremony where the priest draws circles in the sand with his toes.

Tirawa lived in heaven with his wife Atira. He declared his intention of creating men and ordered the gods to help him, promising them each a portion of his power to enable them to do so. *Shakuru* the sun was placed to give light and heat, Pah the moon was assigned the night. The Evening Star was placed in the west and called the Mother of All Things. The Morning Star, a soldier god, was set to guard the east borders; Pole Star was sent north and Death Star south. Tirawa spaced four other stars between them as supports for the sky.

Evening Star was ordered to send a thunder storm into the middle of which Tirawa cast a stone; it made a hole through which a huge ocean could be seen. Tirawa gave the four major stars clubs and told them to beat the ocean; they did so and the waves divided to reveal the land. The god then ordered the stars to sing creation songs; the songs caused another storm which broke up the earth into hills and valleys. Again they sang, and again a fresh storm broke out. After four such songs and four storms they had created plants and trees, streams and rivers, and the germination of seeds. Tirawa ordered the sun and the moon to copulate. They produced a son. The Evening Star and the Morning Star followed suit and brought forth a daughter.

Tirawa ordered Lightning to inspect the earth; he took with him a sack of storms which contained the constellations. Lightning put down the sack and began hanging up the constellations on the sky. A wicked star called Coyote-Deceiver sent a wolf to steal the sack. The wolf opened the sack and all the storms rushed out; death was also loosed. The wolf was killed instantly and ever since then death has been at large.

By now the two children of the sky were old enough to be taught the ways of men – the skills of speech, clothing, fire-making, hunting, agriculture, body-painting and tobacco-smoking. The man was taught how to conduct religious rituals and sacrifices. In time other stars had children and sent them to earth where they formed a tribe with the first man as their chief. He passed on all his knowledge to the others. Life would have been perfect were it not for death.

Tootega
Eskimo deity who looked like a little old woman. She lived on an island in a stone house and had the enviable ability of being able to dispense with kayaks, umiaks and other craft. She simply walked across the top of the water.

Torngasoak
Major Eskimo god, the Good Being.

There seems to be some disagreement about Torngasoak's appearance. Some say he looked like a bear, some like a tall man with one arm; others say that he was no bigger than a man's finger. And of course there are those who state, with depressing but ineluctable finality, that he had no shape at all. Something that everyone is agreed upon is that he was a good sort of chap.

Twin War Gods
Navaho Indians.

The Twin War Gods set off on a journey to their father, the Sun, having first been briefed by *Spider Woman* (*q.v.*) on the hazards facing them. They passed safely through the four dangers – crushing rocks, cutting reeds, tearing cacti, and boiling sand – and came to the house of the Sun. They passed savage bears, serpents, winds and lightnings, soothing them with the magic words Spider Woman had taught them. They entered the huge square house which was built of turquoise, and saw handsome men and women who wrapped them in sky-clothes and put them on a shelf where they lay quietly. Their father came in, took off the sun from his back and hung it on a peg on the west wall, where it jangled for a while. Then he pulled the wrapped twins off the shelf, unrolled their covering and furiously threw them on to some spikes. But the twins, grasping the life feathers given to them by Spider Woman, managed to bounce back unhurt. Then their father attempted to steam them to death in a sweat-lodge. They were saved by wind given them by Spider Woman.

Pretending to acknowledge the twins as his sons, the sun god offered them a pipe to smoke. But they were warned in time by a caterpillar that the pipe was poisoned; the insect gave them something protective to put in their mouths. They smoked the pipe contentedly, saying it was good. At last the god was convinced, and was proud to declare that the twins were indeed his sons.

Chalchihuitlicue
'Precious green lady' or 'Precious jewel lady'; goddess of storms, youthful beauty, whirlpools, spring growth and love.

Reeds were collected from the lake with which to adorn Chalchihuitlicue's temple, and it was a custom that anyone coming near the priests carrying out this ritual would be set upon, beaten and robbed. Her festival was a day of visits, practical jokes, and the eating of a special porridge. Chalchihuitlicue was beautiful and desirable, but was possessed of a formidable and uncertain temper. She wore a skirt covered with jade, carried amaranth stems with streamers specked with spots of rubber, and wore a cotton head-dress similar to that worn by the witch *Tlazolteotl*. Her special colours were blue and white, and to please the goddess it was necessary to offer her flowers, mushrooms (hallucinogenic) and cotton head-dresses.

Chantico
Goddess of fire, the home and fertility.

Chantico was that principle of female uncertainty of which we are all well aware. She is reminiscent of a description of life given by Jane Austen: that human experience consists of two interwoven strands, one of pure pleasure and the other of pure pain. Her symbols include a red serpent and cactus spikes. She has a golden face, and under her authority are wealth and the precious stones found in the earth.

Cinteotl
God of maize.

Cinteotl was the deified maize plant, the supplier of earthly food. Sometimes he had female form. Always he was protected by the water gods. A Mayan carving shows him as a young man with maize growing from his head. At his festival people would cut themselves and drip their blood onto reeds in his honour. He is connected with *Yum Caax* and thought to be the inspirer of the North American spirit of the corn.

Coatlicue
'Serpent lady'; goddess of the earth.

Coatlicue was the mother from whom all things came. She was both positive and negative, both womb and grave; she produced and she devoured. As the earth, she was the gigantic mother capable of supporting all life, but she also caused famines and earthquakes. She is variously represented as a serpent, the great crocodile Cipactli, and as a giant frog. Her cult was linked with that of the jaguar.

'She of the serpent skirt' was especially reverenced by the common folk, who depended on the earth for their survival. But one could never be sure of her; sometimes she was fruitful, sometimes the dealer of disaster. All one could do was worship her and hope for the best. Coatlicue's gigantic dragon-like jaws are the symbol of the first day of the Mexican calendar, for the earth is the beginning of everything. (See *Tezcatlipoca*.)

Coyolxauhqui
'Golden bells'; moon goddess.

The Earth Mother became pregnant and her children, the stars, were horrified. They felt it was a shameful state of affairs and plotted to kill her before she could bear the new child. Coyolxauhqui got to hear of the plot and ran ahead of the assassins to warn her mother. She reached the cave where the Earth Mother was confined just ahead of her furious siblings. As she arrived outside the cave the baby was born. He was *Huitzilopochtli* (an aspect of *Tezcatlipoca*) and had emerged fully-grown and armed ready for battle. Hearing the approaching mob he stepped calmly out of the cave and started to shoot. He killed everyone he saw, including the unfortunate Coyolxauhqui. Too late he was informed of his sister's fidelity. In order to make amends he cut off her head and tossed it up into the sky, where it became the moon. Golden bells can still be seen on the cheeks of the moon – the golden bells from which she derived her name. (See *Tecciztecatl*.)

Huitzilopochtli
'Blue hummingbird on the left' (south). An Aztec tribal god and aspect of *Tezcatlipoca*.

Huitzilopochtli is associated with the sun at its zenith and is god of war and young men. He first appeared to the Aztecs in a vision when they were a small, oppressed tribe. He ordered them to move about, carrying his image with them. The Aztecs became nomadic, settling in temporary homes, urged to move on by the image and persecuted by a succession of local rulers through whose lands they had to pass. At last they reached some small islands on a lake and the image declared that this was destined to be their home, Mexico. From these islands they prospered and grew in strength, conquering their neighbours and controlling lands that eventually reached the size of an empire.

It was an empire based on military organization and run with utterly ruthless cruelty. Huitzilopochtli was rewarded for his help with the hearts and blood of tens of thousands of prisoners captured in battle. The conquered peoples provided a steady and increasing stream of victims for ritual slaughter. The god's festival was a twenty-five day orgy of blood. Apart from mass sacrifices on an obscene scale there were mock battles in which captives were employed. To give these horrid dramas a touch of reality, the unfortunate actors were killed.

Huitzilopochtli's cult inspired Aztec resistance against the Spaniards; but behind the glorious warrior there lurked death. The resistance was fierce but doomed. It could, and did, have but one result.

Ilamatecuhtli
Mother goddess.

Ilamatecuhtli's festival in winter was marked by a horrible example of misplaced devotion. A woman was sacrificed, her heart cut out and her severed head carried at the front of a dancing procession. The horror of this practice was counter-balanced by a sort of slapstick clowning. People would hide bags of wool about them and when they passed a woman in the street, they would whip out the bags and beat her with them, just for fun.

Itzcoliuhqui
'Twisted obsidian one'; god of darkness, biting cold, volcanic eruptions, disaster and destruction.

Itzpapalotl
'Obsidian butterfly'; a beautiful female demon who was definitely not to be trusted. A chilling mixture of sensuality and death, the original vamp.

Mayauel
Goddess of *pulque* (fermented drink).

Mayauel was a farmer's wife and was looking after the *agave* patch when she saw a mouse exhibiting unmistakable signs of inebriation. She tried to scare it off, but it laughed in her face with the bravado of a hen-pecked husband tumbling out of a bar at closing time. She noticed that the mouse had been drinking the juice of the *agave* plants. Mayauel and her husband collected some of the juice and put it aside when they went out to work. The juice fermented. They returned in the evening and tasted it; then they took another drink, and then another. Eventually they fell asleep, dead drunk. The grateful peasantry of Mexico were pleased with the discovery, so much so that they made Mayauel into a goddess.

Mayauel is represented enthroned on a cactus plant, carrying a looped cord to show that she helped women in childbirth. The night was her special time. The military Aztec aristocracy, who were puritanical to the point of perversion, did not approve of the goddess. They were not concerned about the health of the peasants; all they were worried about was that their young warriors might get drunk and disgrace their nation by falling about in public.

The Aztecs made cunning use of Mayauel to undermine the influence of the god *Quetzalcoatl*. They showed her tempting Quetzalcoatl with a drink which would incapacitate him. The suggestion being that he was a weak god and not one that any right-thinking Aztec priest, warrior or politician should support.

Meztli
Moon god; see *Tecciztecatl*.

Mictlantecuhtli
'Lord of the land of the dead', patron of the North. As god of the Underworld, he looked after those souls who reached his kingdom.

Mixcoatl

'Cloud serpent'; god of hunting. During his part of the calendar weapons were made for the army, especially spear-throwers and javelins; weapons which stung from afar. He was god of the Tlaxcalan tribe.

Ometecuhtli

The supreme deity of ancient Mexico; a god of duality. being both male and female.

Ometecuhtli created and sustained everything, holding the earth as a grain in a drop of water in his hand. Superior to all other gods, too elevated to be counted among their colourful ranks, he was a philosophical concept of a totally different dimension. Unknowable, he had no temple for men could not expect any experience of him; he was too remote, too far above and beyond the universe to be bothered by such paltry things as weather, food, life or death.

Quetzalcoatl

A wind god.

'Precious twin' or 'feathered serpent' – both meanings are valid, though the first is probably the original sense. Quetzalcoatl is a complex god originating from the first lord of the Toltecs, with accretions from an ancient Olmec god called Longnose. He was god of the winds, of sea-breeze and of life-breath. His rounded loin cloth is supposed to hint at a priapic aspect in his character.

A main characteristic of the god is duality and uncertainty, and this is linked to the behaviour of the planet Venus, which was his star. He is the Morning Star, the planet lifting itself out of darkness; an image replete with the idea of kingship. On the other hand the Feathered Serpent is the green earth which swallows the planet after its descent. His cult is rife with yet more uncertainty; like man's sexual nature the sea-breeze cannot be relied upon. Quetzalcoatl wore the wind jewel as an emblem of this unreliability. Another of his symbols is the rubber ball; like the unsure god and the unsure fate of the warrior in battle, the ball bounces off the wall of the 'game court' at unpredictable angles. As the ball bounces, zooms, approaches and retires it imitates the erratic movements of the planets among the stars.

The cult of Quetzalcoatl, once supreme, had been challenged and overshadowed by that of the wizard god *Tezcatlipoca*. There seems to have been an actual political struggle with the losers, the devotees of Quetzalcoatl, leaving to found a new cult centre and city at Chichen Itza. The surviving cult in Mexico was looked after by a group of nobles and many of the ceremonies were secret to the inner circle.

The Emperor Montecuzoma Xocoyotzin's devotion to Quetzalcoatl was seen in two ways. One was the planning of his military response to the Spaniards in accordance with his obser-vations of the planet Venus; anyone seeking proof of the falli-bility of the pseudo-science of astrology need look no further than this tragic example. The second, and probably more fasci-nating, aspect of the Emperor's devotion was his belief that the Spanish conqueror Cortes was the reincarnation of Quetzalcoatl. They were expecting a pale-faced man with a black beard wearing certain clothes and jewels. When Cortes arrived he happened to be wearing things which the Aztecs immediately recognized as the insignia of the god. This raises an interesting question – how much did Cortes know about the prophecies and folklore sur-rounding the supposed return of Quetzalcoatl? Have we given him full credit, for it was certainly the psychological impact of his arrival which successfully paved the way for what seemed a suicidal attempt at conquest.

In marked contrast to other Mexican gods, Quetzalcoatl was benign and good. There was only one human sacrifice to him each year. Compared to the blood-drenched worship of the other gods this record, though in our eyes imperfect, stands out as being nearly humane. It is ironic that because of the myths surrounding a relatively good god the doom of all the others, proud, fierce and bloody as they were, was finally sealed. It was certainly justice, of a sort. (See *Mayauel*.)

Tecciztecatl
God of the moon.

Tecciztecatl was a wise old man who carried a white shell on his back. Also called *Meztli*, he sometimes wore butterfly wings to symbolize his flight through the heavens. He was the moon at the height of its path. Although replaced by the goddess *Coyolxauhqui*, he was retained in the calendar and in certain rituals.

Tezcatlipoca
'Mirror that smokes'; the foremost of all the gods of Mexico.

Tezcatlipoca was The Shadow, 'He who is at the shoulder'. Evil god of magicians, he ruled the world. Originally he wrestled with the great crocodile, Cipactli (see *Coatlicue*), an aspect of Mother Earth. He lost a foot to her, but managed to drag her from the primeval waters to create the earth; in doing so he tore off the crocodile's lower jaw, thus preventing her from sinking back. Tezcatlipoca's name refers to the mystic clouding of the obsidian mirror used in divination. He was god of the warriors, controlling the reeds from which weapons were manufactured. He required to be glutted with blood, and human hearts.

One had to beware when out at night near dark woods, for if you investigated a glowing light and a sound as if of wood being chopped, you would come across Tezcatlipoca – a ghastly skeletal creature with fiery eyes and slobbering tongue. You would soon realize that the noise you mistook for wood being cut up was in fact the sound of his ribs opening and shutting like loose gates in the wind, revealing the creature's insides. If you were cursed with this apparition there was but one way of escaping with life and sanity intact. This was to approach the grisly Tezcatlipoca, thrust your hand into the bloody cavity when the ribs opened, grasp hold of the palpitating heart, and wrench it out.

Titlacauan
An aspect of the god *Tezcatlipoca*.

During the time sacred to him in the calendar the priests spread a bowl of flour on top of the temple pyramid. They watched the flour; at night a single human footprint would appear on it. This was a sign of the god Titlacauan/Tezcatlipoca; he was one-footed for when he dragged the earth monster from the primeval waters he lost a limb to its crocodile jaws. This monster, Cipactli, was an aspect of *Coatlicue*, the Earth Mother.

Tlaloc
The rain god.

The proper incense to burn for Tlaloc was rubber; he was pleased by its smell, and the black smoke it gave off symbolized the dark rainclouds. He was Lord of Waters and in his temples were kept bowls containing four kinds of rain: the kindly morning showers, the fertile midday rain, the evening rain suitable for planting, and the dark hail which ruined crops. He was an ancient fertility god and ruled over a humid southern paradise full of rainbows, butterflies and flowers. Despite this charming environment, he required unending human sacrifices on a vast scale.

Tlauixcalpantecuhtli
'Lord of the house of the dawn', that is to say the whole of the planet Venus rather than an aspect of it. A dangerously destructive deity.

Tlazolteotl
Lady of Witches.

Tlazolteotl is depicted in a pre-Columban drawing in a startlingly familiar way: she is shown riding naked on a broom, wearing a horned head-dress with crescent moon. She grasps a red snake and has a crescent-moon decoration on her nose. She is flanked by the blood-stained rope of a suicide, a serpent's head, a human heart, a sacrificial blade, and a flower.

Tlazolteotl is a sad clue to a dark aspect of the Aztec mind. The Aztecs were fanatical puritans, running a cruel priest- and soldier-dominated society in which there predominated a tragic inability to accept natural sexuality. Harsh repression and suppression drove the Aztec priesthood into horrifying extremes of aberration. Enforced guilt led to self-mutilation which led to human sacrifice. Human sacrifice grew into mass slaughter of defenceless victims, including babies and children.

The worship of the Lady of Witches was stained with fanaticism. Girls of ordinary families were taken and dedicated to Tlazolteotl by a merciless priesthood. They were trained as prostitutes; then they were thrown into the military barracks where young soldiers, who had undergone inhuman discipline to expunge every vestige of humanity in their souls, used them as sexual objects. It was a cynical action on the part of the leadership to give the youths a safety valve for their suppressed but inevitable needs. When they had fulfilled their function the wretched children were declared by the priesthood to be contaminated. They were seized and their throats cut ceremonially. Their pathetic corpses were taken and cast into the swamps, like so much rubbish. Love, affection, humanity, the healthy and joyful expression of man's sexual nature, none of these had any part in the perverted ideals of the priesthood.

There is a sad duality about the image of Tlazolteotl. She had a broom – a cleansing broom – to sweep away what the priesthood described as filth; yet at the same time she was blamed for creating that filth. Hers is a sobering and tragic story

Tonatiuh
God of the sun.

Ruler of fate, Tonatiuh took with him on his heroic journey all warriors who had met brave deaths and all women who had died in childbirth. He was constantly thirsty and required blood to drink. In order to keep him moving and to ensure his return, the Aztecs offered him a daily sacrifice of human hearts and blood

Ueuecoyotl
'Old, old coyote'; god of sex and irresponsible gaiety.

Often confused with *Xolotl* because of his beastly behaviour Ueuecoyotl was the manifestation of socially unacceptable, uncontrollable impulses. He was unexpected, irrational and, something the Aztecs could not forgive, fun. Ueuecoyotl falls into the category of 'trickster' gods in the company of *Anansi*, *Coyote*, *Maui*, *Loki* and others. (Refer main index.)

Uixtochihuatl
Goddess of salt.

She was sister of the rain gods and her cult was marred by human sacrifice. Women victims were offered to her at the pyramid of Tlaloc.

53

Xilonen
Goddess of maize. Her festival was celebrated with feasts of maize, gruel and tamales.

Xipe Totec
The Flayed God; god of agriculture and penitential self-torture.

Xipe Totec gave man food by being skinned alive, just as the maize is skinned to reveal the corn. With horrible and perverse reasoning the Aztecs celebrated his festival by skinning captives alive.

The god was represented wearing a mask of human skin, with one eye torn out as an offering of extreme pain. He is the 'red' aspect of *Tezcatlipoca*. The Aztecs believed that only through extreme suffering could the god be induced to give corn. It shows once again how far into madness the fanatical application of dogma can take mankind. And of course it wasn't the Aztec priests and leaders who suffered so horribly, but always some poor peasant or captive.

Xiuhtecuhtli
Lord of Fire; god of domestic and spiritual fire.

Xiuhtecuhtli's ceremony, 'Making of New Fire', occurred once every fifty-two years. All fires were doused and fresh flames kindled on the heart of the inevitable human sacrifice. This new fire was distributed among the temples by the priests, and thence to all the palaces, mansions and homes of the people. The priests of the god were astronomers and regulators of the calendar; their task was crucial for the whole of Mexican culture depended on the calendar. Apart from this major festival, minor ceremonies took place for Xiuhtecuhtli during which sacrificial victims were slowly roasted to death.

Xolotl
'The Animal'; lord of the Evening Star.

Xolotl was an unfortunate creature in every sense; he was deformed and his feet pointed backwards. A dispenser of bad luck, it was his task to push the sun down into the abyss of night. He was responsible for bringing both man and fire from the Underworld.

Yacatecuhtli
God of merchants.

His name means 'Lord Nose', which is not an exclamation of bewilderment but has the sense of 'he who goes before'. His image was a bundle of staves carried by merchants on their journeyings. The blessing of this image with incense and the occasional human sacrifice (with bought slaves for he was a commercial god) was carried out in secret, so as not to annoy the nobles by a display of wealth. As a result little is known of his worship and festivals, which were all held behind closed doors. His symbol is reminiscent of the *rangga* (cult objects of Oceania), also of the medicine-bundles of the American Indians and the *tjurungas* of the Australian aborigines. We might also include in this class of sacred objects the god-sticks of the Maoris (though they had a specific function), the *palladia*, the *ancilla* of Rome and the crane-skin bag of the Celtic *Mannannan*.

Mexican merchants, *pochteca*, held a lowly but special place in society, for they conveyed news as well as goods from place to place. They were forbidden to wear weapons and were recognized by their fans, which they carried to cool themselves on the road. The merchants made the only worthwhile maps of Mexico and the surrounding lands, and one of these maps was used by the Spanish conqueror Cortes to help him cross the forests of the Yucatan peninsula.

Yaotl
Lord of the Darkness.

A tribal god of a group with a migratory story curiously parallel to that of the Aztecs. This is most probably indicative of a migration legend common to many Mexican tribes. Yaotl is the equivalent of *Tezcatlipoca*; he is darkness opposed to light.

Acat
The god of life among the Maya. He was responsible for the development of children in the womb.

Apu Punchau
'Head of the day'; another name for the Inca Sun. (See *Inti*.)

Ariconte
A Tupinamba (Brazil) god who is one half of a set of famous, mythical twins.

Ariconte and his twin Tamendonare were born at the same time from the same mother, yet they had different fathers. One was the god *Maira Ata*, the other a mortal man named Sarigoys. It is not known which father was responsible for which twin. The twin brothers were mortal enemies, but that didn't stop them from having a series of exciting adventures together. Their mother had been eaten by cannibals while they were quite small. They were rescued and brought up by a kind woman, and when they were old enough the twins went out to find their mother's killers. They lured them to an island and caused a storm to flood it, covering the killers who then were changed into tigers.

The twins then set off to look for their father; they found him leading a quiet life as a village wizard. He set them tests before acknowledging them as his sons. The wizard was the god-hero Maira Ata; Sarigoys seems to have dropped out of the story at this stage. He made them shoot at targets but their arrows remained up in the air. Then they had to leap between the two parts of the clashing stone Itha-Irapi. One of them got crushed so the other put the pieces back together again and they managed the test.

Maira Ata was not entirely satisfied but, being like all fathers, gave them another chance: they had to go and steal the bait used to catch a certain fish which was the Food of the Dead. The fisher was a divinity called Agnen whose sole purpose in life seems to have been to oppose the twins. Once more one of the twins was torn into bits and put together again by his brother. After that, their father acknowledged that they were his son/sons. But which was which and who was who?

Auchimalgen
Araucanian (Chile) moon goddess.

In the depressing and spiritually dangerous world inhabited by the Araucanians, Auchimalgen was the only one who cared anything at all for mankind. She frightened away evil spirits and was some sort of comfort to the people against the sea of disasters which continually beat against them. When she turned red it was a warning that some important person would die. Not that they could do anything about it, but it was always handy to know. Auchimalgen was the wife of the sun, who was *not* worshipped by the Araucanians. Perhaps he was too happy.

Bacabs
Mayan gods of the four winds; their pillars held up the vault of heaven.

Backlum Chaam
Mayan god of male sexuality

Bochicha
The sun god of the Chibcha (Columbia); he created civilization and all the arts.

Bochicha defeated a demon called Chibchacum in an epic battle and punished him by forcing the demon to carry the world on his shoulder. From time to time Chibchacum gets restless and moves his burden from one shoulder to the other, causing earthquakes.

Bochicha was honoured by a sacrificial victim called a *quesa*. This was usually a ten-year-old boy taken from the home village of the god. The boy was cared for lavishly in the temple until fifteen years old. Then masked priests took him to a pillar representing the sun, bound him to it and shot him dead with arrows. His heart was excised as an offering and his blood collected in sacred vessels. Compared with what went on among the Aztecs one might describe this sacrifice as almost civilized.
(See *Thomagata*.)

Catequil
The Inca god of thunder and lightning; he carried a mace and a sling.

The proper offering to Catequil consisted of children, but despite this dark connection the god was supposed to be the father of all the twins that were born. The Incas ran a highly sophisticated and well-organized society. For political reasons they admitted all sorts of ancient and primitive deities to their pantheon; in, of course, a subservient role. But they were not the first men to make religious compromises for the good of their political power. Nor were they the last.

Chasca
'The long-haired star' of the Incas. A personification of the planet Venus and imagined to be a servant of the sun. Under the care of the planet came princesses, girls and flowers.

Chiquinau
God of the air of the Niquiran Indians (Nicaragua).

Chonchonyi
A revolting Araucanian (Chile) god who looked like a large human head with long, flappy ears. This inhabitant of men's nightmares used his ears as wings in his search for victims. Most of all he liked people who were weak and lying helpless on their sick-bed. When Chonchonyi had located a suitable victim he would bide his time until the miserable wretch was alone. Then he would fly in, murder the invalid and suck his blood.

Colo-Colo
Araucanian (Chile) deity.

Colo-Colo emerged from a cock's egg; in fact he was a basilisk. He drank the saliva of his victims, which would cause a fever in the unfortunate person resulting in death.

Gucumatz
Guatemalan god of agriculture and civilization.

Gucumatz was the son of the Sun and Moon and his name means 'feathered snake'. As a shape-shifter he could assume any animal form; he lived in both heaven and hell. He is associated with the god *Hurukan* (*q.v.*) as a subservient partner in a series of adventures.

Huaillepenyi
Araucanian (Chile) god of fog.

Huaillepenyi looked like a sheep (female) with a calf's head and a seal's tail. He lurked on river banks, lake and sea shores. Not surprisingly, he was blamed for any deformed children that were born.

Hunab Ku
Head of the Yucatan Maya pantheon, the 'one god'. Also called Kinebahan – 'eyes and mouth of the sun'.

Hurukan
Guatemalan god of whirlwind and thunder from whom we get the word hurricane.

Hurukan was someone to be reckoned with and even the son of the Sun and Moon, *Gucumatz*, held him in great respect. He created the first fire by rubbing his sandals together, a picturesque image which connects lightning with ordinary fire made by friction. Encouraged by his friend Gucamatz, he made the earth and all the animals. He ordered the animals to worship him but they could only manage a series of yells, grunts, squeaks, roars and whistles. Hurukan was not pleased and condemned the animals to be eaten; rough justice when you consider that it was he who created them in the first place.

Hurukan and Gucumatz then set about making men out of clay, but not a word of praise was forthcoming. They tried making men out of wood, with predictable results. Silence. Angrily they destroyed their handiwork, but some of the little creatures escaped and survive to this day as monkeys. The gods then tried making men out of maize, and women to accompany them. Success.

But things soon went wrong; because the sun had not yet

arrived the men began complaining that they couldn't see. Hurukan gave them fire and divine knowledge, but the lack of sun, the lack of universal illumination, divided mankind. They dwelt apart, and different languages were developed. At last the sun, moon and stars appeared. Grateful mankind sang praises, and cutting themselves about the arms, shed drops of blood as offerings of thanks.

This habit of blood-offering developed into the sacrifice of humans. It was a wise choice for the worshippers, but not so good for their victims.

Inti
Inca sun god.

Inti was visualized as a human with a bright face surrounded by sun rays. It was believed that he crossed the sky, dived into the sea and swam under the earth, reappearing again in the east, refreshed after his dip. His three sons were significant figures in the Inca pantheon: Choun (*Viracocha*), *Pachacamac* and *Manco Capac*. The Inca (rulers, not the people at large) claimed descent from Inti and only they were allowed to speak his name.

Cristobal de Molina, a Spanish priest, has left a report of the great annual feast of Inti Raymi to celebrate the harvest of maize in 1535. The Inca himself led the chanting which lasted from before sunrise to sunset; there were continual animal sacrifices, and llamas were thrown for the common people to catch 'and this caused great sport'. Other offerings included bales of coca leaf (used by the Indians for its pain-killing and sustaining properties when chewed). Effigies of past Incas were set up under awnings – great numbers of men were employed to fan the statues and keep off the flies. After eight days of chanting and sacrifices the Inca took a hand plough and broke the earth, this act making it possible for agriculture to continue.

Itzamna
Mayan god of healing.

A son of the Sun, Itzamna had the power of bringing the dead back to life. His sign was a red hand to which the sick prayed for healing. In return for presents, pilgrimages and squirrel sacrifices, the god made sure the fields remained fertile and that water did not fail. He was also god of drawing and letters.

Ixzaluoh
Mayan goddess, wife of *Hunab Ku*.

Ixzaluoh, whose name means 'water', is praised for the invention of weaving. Anyone who has watched the wind ripple a lake will understand the link between her name and her discovery.

Kulkulcan
Serpent god and the Mayan form of the Mexican deity *Quetzalcoatl* (*q.v.*); the city of Quirigua was devoted to his worship. Some have foolishly attempted to link his name with that of the Irish hero Cuchulain

Kurupira
Tupinamba (Brazil) deity; a gnome of the Amazonian forest.

Kurupira is a protector of animals but is not too fond of men; no doubt because of their taste for meat. He is a little fellow and if you spot him in the dark undergrowth you cannot mistake him, for his feet are turned backwards.

Maira Ata
A hero god of the Tupinamba (Brazil) who figures in the story of *Ariconte* (*q.v.*).

Maire-Monan
Tupinamba (Brazil) god; 'the transformer' and successor to *Monan*.

Maire-Monan taught the Tupinamba their laws and agriculture. If men were evil he would punish them by changing them into animals. This annoyed men so much that they arranged a celebration, the culmination of which was the lighting of three bonfires over which Maire-Monan was expected to jump. The god's reactions are not recorded, but he had no choice in the matter. The first jump was successful, but on the second jump the heat of the fire made him faint in mid-leap. He collapsed into the flames and exploded with an almighty bang, producing thunder and lightning and shooting himself up into the sky, where he became a star.

Mama Quilla
Inca goddess of the moon.

Mama Quilla was both wife and sister of the Sun; her image was a silver disc with a human face. She was the protectress of married women. Incestuous relationships among the gods were commonly mirrored in royal families all over the world. As late as 1558 Pope Julius III sanctioned the incestuous marriage of the Inca, Sayri-Tupac, at the request of the King of Spain; and to the immense political advantage of the Spanish occupiers of an uneasy and rebellious Peru.

Manco Capac
Solar god of the Incas.

Manco Capac was the youngest of four brothers who were the sons of the Sun. They had emerged from the caves of Pacari-Tambo. The eldest son selfishly claimed the whole of the earth for himself, ignoring the needs of his brothers. Manco Capac was greatly angered by this. He lured his brother into a mountain cave and trapped him there forever by sealing the entrance with huge stones. The god then took his second brother to the top of a precipice and pushed him over the edge. As the luckless sibling plunged to the ground, Manco Capac used magic to change him to stone. The third brother had witnessed these deeds, and realizing the determination and ruthlessness of Manco Capac, he took flight and was never seen again.

Manco Capac then founded the city of Cuzco and assumed the hegemony of the world, being worshipped as Son of the Sun. His father was *Inti* and two of his brothers were *Pachacamac* and *Viracocha*.

Masaya
Goddess of volcanoes among the Niquiran (Nicaragua).

After earthquakes and tremors Masaya was propitiated by human offerings. The unhappy victims were delivered to her via the crater. She looked like a ghastly old hag with black skin, sagging bosom and wispy hair. Apart from fear she instilled respect, for she was given to oracular utterances.

Meuler
Araucanian (Chile) god of whirlwinds and destructive typhoons. Meuler was in charge of the winds and is represented as a lizard fleeing for cover from the impact of the typhoon.

Mictanteot
Goddess of the Underworld of the Niquiran (Nicaragua). She received some of the souls of the dead; the others, more lucky, were received in heaven.

Misca
Niquiran (Nicaragua) god of merchants.

Monan
Tupinamba (Brazil) ancient hero god.

Monan's name means 'old one' and he created mankind. Then he had a change of heart and destroyed the world with flood and fire. This antediluvian Monan should not be confused with his successor, *Maire-Monan* (*q.v.*).

Ngurvilu
Araucanian (Chile) god of water, the sea and lakes.

If an Indian suffered a swimming or boating accident then it was the fault of Ngurvilu, for he lurked in the water in the shape of a wild cat whose tail terminated in a dreadful claw. He used this weapon to strike at people, out of sheer malice.

Nohochacyum
Mayan god of creation.

Nohochacyum was always at war with an evil god, Hapikern. Defender of mankind, his name means 'grandfather'. His parents were two flowers. He had three brothers, one neutral, one kind, and one not so kind.

63

Pachacamac
Pre-Inca god of the earth and consort of *Pachamama*

To the coastal population of Peru, Pachacamac was the supreme god, and was retained by the Inca for political reasons. He was the rival of *Viracocha* (*q.v.*) and created skill and diversity among men by adapting the humans created by that god. His inclusion in the Inca pantheon was uneasy. Atahualpa, the Great Inca, treated Pachacamac's high priest coldly, explaining to the Spanish conqueror Francisco Pizarro that the oracle of the god had given him three predictions, all of which had turned out to be disastrously wrong. Atahualpa encouraged the Spaniards to desecrate the temple complex of Pachacamac, and found them not unwilling to help.

Cieza de Leon records an Indian legend that Pachacamac was originally a tall white man who could work miracles and exhorted people to love each other; de Leon calls him Tici-Viracocha. Another myth tells how Pachacamac emerged from a sacred cave along with other gods, his brothers. Sacrifices of animals and humans were carried out every year in his honour. His father was *Inti* and his brothers were *Manco Capac* and *Viracocha*

Pachamama
Inca goddess of the earth, wife of *Pachacamac*.

Pihuechenyi
Araucanian (Chile) demon. Pihuechenyi was a winged snake with a vampire's taste for blood. He descended at night onto anyone sleeping in the forest, for a quick midnight snack.

Pillan
Araucanian (Chile) god of thunder.

Like all Araucanian gods, Pillan was malevolent and had to be appeased. He caused earthquakes and volcanic eruptions as well as thunder and lightning. He was helped in his mischief by squads of evil spirits who were constantly at work making people ill, disturbing the weather, blighting crops et cetera. Amongst this unpleasant gang were snakes with human heads who caused comets and shooting stars. It need hardly be said that such phenomena presaged coming disasters for the miserable Araucanians

Supai

Inca god of death. A morose and greedy character whom the Incas tried to placate every year by the sacrifice of a hundred children. They were not too successful, and death is still as greedy as he ever was.

Tamagostad

Chief god of the Niquiran (Nicaragua), who lived with his consort Zipaltonal in the east. Together they created everything on earth.

Thomagata

Chibcha (Columbia) god of thunder.

Of terrifying aspect, Thomagata rushed about like a fiery ball, delighting in turning men into animals. The sun god *Bochicha* (*q.v.*) fought against him and made him impotent with a swift kick where it hurts. Despite this embarrassing setback Thomagata still retained his right to appear at ceremonies; he was described as having one eye, four ears and a long tail.

Tupan

Tupinamba (Brazil) god of thunder and lightning.

Tupan was a stocky young man-god with wavy hair. Whenever he visited his mother, and he was fond of visiting her, his journey caused a storm on earth, the noise of thunder being the creaking of his boat. The Tupinambas acknowledged him but did not worship him.

Urcaguary

Inca god of underground treasures. He is represented as a snake with a deer's head and his tail is adorned with gold chains.

Viracocha

'Foam of the lake'; supreme Inca god, son of *Inti*.

The 'invisible god', synthesis of sun god and storm god, Viracocha carries a thunderbolt and is crowned with the sun. His origins are pre-Inca and, along with *Pachacamac* (*q.v.*), he was retained and included in the Inca pantheon more through politics than faith. He was son of the Sun and brother to Pachacamac and *Manco Capac*. He lived in Lake Titicaca and represented water's power of bringing forth life. He was also the god of water, and wears a beard which is the symbol of it. He had neither flesh nor bones yet could run very swiftly. His eventual disappearance into the sea is analogous to the story of the Mexican god *Quetzalcoatl* (*q.v.*); and some writers have hinted that Tici-Viracocha (confused with Pachacamac) could possibly have been an early European traveller, a missionary bringing the Christian ideals of love to the New World before the voyages of the Spanish and Portugese.

Viracocha gave out oracles and required sacrifice. From time to time he appeared on earth in the guise of a wandering beggar, ragged and scorned. In his divine aspect he weeps, and his tears fall and replenish the earth. His wife, and sister, was called Mama-Cocha. The raising of Viracocha from a mere sun god to the supreme deity seems to have coincided with the imperial expansion under Pachacute Inca Yupanquil, the ninth Inca. This monarch was an administrative genius and his pushing forward of Viracocha seems not unconnected to the fact that his predecessor, the eighth Inca, shared the same name as the god. Inca Viracocha had been something of an oracle; he predicted the coming of the Spaniards, so much so that when they arrived they were called *viracochas*; just as the Aztecs had called them *teules*, 'gods'.

Vizetot
Niquiran (Nicaragua) god of famine.

Yum Caax
Mayan god of maize.

Yum Caax signified life, riches and joy. He is shown as a young man with a curiously slanted forehead. The Mayan aristocracy used to bind their children's heads with boards to make them tall and flat, representing a cob of maize. The Mayan were deeply and emotionally attached to the soil and agriculture. Making their children look as much like maize as possible was clearly gratifying to their psychology.

Agwe

Haitian god of the waters; also of wind, thunder, cannon-fire, boats, sea-shells. He is the Voodoo equivalent of the Roman Catholic St Ulrique.

Agwe's ceremony is expensive and complex. First of all a sacrificial ram is chosen and then dyed blue. A square wooden raft is constructed to hold offerings. Round the raft are painted the symbols of Agwe: fishes, boats, shells. There is an image of a mermaid accompanied by a dove; she is La Sirene (a sea aspect of the love goddess *Erzulie*). Symbols represent other gods of the Voodoo pantheon, *Damballah, Ayida, Ogoun,* as well as the crab Agassou.

A feast is prepared – cakes, sweets, vegetables, pigeons, mutton, chickens, wine, rum and champagne. The day is filled with prayers and preparations, until in the evening special songs are sung to the accompaniment of a conch shell. A huge bed is prepared for Agwe and his consort La Sirene. They are believed to spend the night there.

Early the next morning the raft, the ram, ceremonial drums, a huge seven-tiered wedding cake, baskets of pigeons and chickens, huge amounts of food and drink are all taken down to the sea. They are loaded on to a boat, along with the *hougouns* (male priests and worshippers) and *mambos* (female worshippers). The boat goes out to sea, to the place the followers believe is above the underwater island home of Agwe, Z'ile Minfort. When they sense they have reached the right spot the raft is loaded with all the food and drink. The chickens and pigeons are slaughtered and piled on as well; the huge wedding cake takes pride of place.

With a convulsive start one or more of the worshippers becomes possessed. They all know that the god is present; water is poured over those who are entranced, for Agwe must be kept wet.

The blue-coloured ram is taken to the side of the boat and thrown into the sea as the first offering. Then the heavy raft, loaded with its burden of good things, is lifted bodily up and slid into the water. It floats for a while, then suddenly sinks. The people in the boat burst into joyful song, for the god Agwe has accepted their offering.

Ayida
Haitian rainbow goddess, female counterpart of *Damballah*.

Azacca
Haitian god of agriculture.

Azacca is thought of as a younger brother to the god *Ghede*, who treats him in a high-handed way. Unlike his stylish and sophisticated brother, Azacca is a peasant. He exhibits self-consciousness and insecurity; he will grab his food and huddle with it in a corner, gobbling it down with no attempt at good manners. He is coarse, boorish, loud and sexually crude. But to his credit he is also hard-working, shrewd, simple and affectionate, unlike his dandified and cynical brother.

Azacca is thought to be a Voodoo god of Indian rather than African origin. His name probably derives from *zara*, 'corn', or *maza*, from which we get the word 'maize'.

Badessy
Minor sky god of Haiti.

Originally from Dahomey, Badessy is associated with *Damballah*. Along with other elemental deities he is regarded as rather *passé* by the sophisticated *serviteurs* of Haiti. A *serviteur* is a person who is 'ridden' or possessed by the *loas* (gods). Males are called *hougouns*, females *mambos*.

Bossu
A malevolent Voodoo spirit.

Bossu is part of the criminal underworld and a 'soldier' of *Maît' Carrefour*. He was possibly derived from an ancient king of Dahomey called Akadja, for there is a Kadja Bossu. The spirit is a member of a large clan of Bossu and his sign is a man with three horns. He is related to *Mounanchou*, a work god and rival of the terrifying *Ogoun*.

Brigitte
Maman Brigitte is the female counterpart of the god *Ghede*, especially in his aspect of Baron Samedi. She protects the graves

in cemeteries marked with his cross.

Damballah
Serpent god of Haiti.

African in origin, Damballah is sometimes associated with the Mexican Feathered Serpent (*Quetzalcoatl*). He is a benign, paternal sky god whose blessing is reward enough. He is so wise and exalted that it is useless trying to bother him with petty human concerns and worries. He has an affinity for water, and special pools (*bassins*) are built for him to bathe in. He loves to climb trees and recline at ease in the branches. Life does not affect him; he links past with future.

Damballah is often visualized as a great arch in the sky; part of his body is coloured, like *Ayida* the rainbow, his female counterpart. With Ayida he represents sexual totality; together they are coiled about the earth. Not surprisingly, the suitable offering to Damballah is an egg, which is his special symbol. Many minor deities are linked to him for he is the proof of eternal goodness, patron of the rains, and of streams and rivers created by the rains.

Dan Petro
Haitian god of farmers; originally African god *Danh*.

Dan Petro has snake-like attributes; he is not malevolent but has many malevolent subjects. He is the father of the tribal gods who contributed to the new Caribbean pantheon.

Erzulie
Haitian goddess of love, beauty, flowers, jewels, dancing and fine clothes.

Erzulie is as totally unlike the fecund Earth Mother of other religions as it is possible to be. She is the poignant mistress, the muse of beauty, the goddess of dreams, ever going beyond reality and fact into exquisite fantasy. She is thought of as being fabulously rich, languidly luxurious to the point of neurasthenia. She is elaborately stylized and formal in movement; she dresses with painstaking emphasis on detail, with exaggerated indecision. The whole universe hangs in the air as she compares scarves, her eyes and mind flitting from one to the other, until at last she makes a selection, only to change her mind again. Her presence transforms the everyday into something magical, fraught with perfumed mystery. Before she comes it is necessary to prepare for her the best of everything, scented soap and thick towels, rich cakes, extravagant confections, and champagne, which must always be kept ready for her to sip and reject, and sip again.

In addition to being so demanding, Erzulie is the soul of generosity, lavish with her gifts, her affections and her body. She greets all men with warm embraces. She is sexually involved with all three major gods of Voodoo, *Damballah*, *Agwe*, and *Ogoun*. She wears three wedding rings. Her exuberant physical generosity comes from sincere love rather than mere promiscuity.

Yet Erzulie's gaiety is tinged with sadness. She will be happy and frolicsome, flirting, sipping champagne and laughing, and then suddenly be plunged into tears and racking sorrow. She is conscious of betrayal; she is cosmic innocence besmirched. In this aspect she is, with reason, especially worshipped by prostitutes. She is at once pure virgin and bright-eyed coquette, constantly yearning for a perfection which is forever unattainable.

Erzulie is a critical link with the sublime; through her heart men can rise to wonderful heights, and the gods can come down to meet mankind. She possesses her *serviteurs* with a mysterious strength. It is a well-attested fact that even old women, when 'ridden' by her, can flirt and dance like supple-bodied young girls for hours on end, with no subsequent ill-effects.

Ghede
Haitian god of the dead.

Ghede's colour is black and his sign a square cross on a low tomb. He is also lord of life, for the mysterious portal through which the dead pass is also that door through which the gods arrive, bringing life. In his chamber are kept grave-diggers' tools and also a sculpted phallus. His dance is the dance of copulation; he is the beginning and the end. Ghede is a protector of children and has healing powers. He is also the cosmic corpse. He is of African origin and is often linked with Baron Samedi, the keeper of cemeteries and lord of zombies.

The phallic side of the god's character is expressed in his amusement at man's attempts to deny or camouflage his inevitable erotic nature. He delights in seeking out the refined and pious and confronting them with lascivious gestures, in exposing their fraudulent attitudes. No one can elude him. *Serviteurs* who are 'ridden' by him (*i.e.* those who fall into a trance and express his character in their behaviour) are tested. They are given rum mixed with twenty-one of the hottest spices known. Only Ghede can drink the burning mixture. Only Ghede can stand the fiery fluid sprayed in his eyes without blinking.

Ghede exhibits positive behaviour, and is full of self-mockery. He poses as a beggar and will wolf down piles of food; he often gatecrashes into ceremonies of other gods, causing chaos and embarrassment by his behaviour. He goes as far as to throw fits just to upset people. And all the time he is watching out of the corner of his eye, wickedly gauging the effect of his performance.

Ghede is instantly recognizable; he wears a black coat, top hat, dark glasses (often with one lens missing), carries a cane and smokes a cigar or elegant cigarette. He is also called Baron La Croix, Baron Piquant, Baron Cimetière. He speaks in a nasal voice, and wickedly deals in opposites; he is elegant and ragged, sensual and unfeeling, forces men to dress as women, and women to dress as men. He mixes life with death, for he is also lord of sorcery. No one can indulge in magic without his permission, and through his power bodies are brought back to life from the grave; they are called zombies. As you dig up a corpse you must sing a song to the god with the refrain: 'Hold that man, don't let him go, hold that man!' Ghede is wise, shrewd and an experienced trickster, but he will give you his advice unstintingly. It is up to you if you trust it.

There is a true story which shows the nature of the god. Some years ago in Port au Prince a huge crowd was seen approaching the Presidential Palace. As it came nearer it was seen that leading the crowd was not one but several Ghedes. All the *serviteurs* were dressed in black tail-coats, top hats and dark glasses; they twirled canes and gestured elegantly with cigars and cigarettes. It was a mass manifestation of the god. They reached the palace and demanded money for a feast. Their request was promptly, not to say hurriedly, met. The delighted Ghedes strutted away to enjoy themselves.

71

Legba
God of the crossroads, the psychic crossroads where the Above meets the Below.

Legba's colour is white, dogs are sacred to him, and he is of Dahomey origin. He is guardian of the gates, the 'old man', the sun, parent and protector of all life. He manages to be both man and woman, and also phallic god of Dahomey. He is god of the intersection of the two worlds; he is the interface and is described as being 'on both sides of the mirror'. No Voodoo *bounfor* (cult building) is without its *poteau-Legba*, the wooden pillar which is the prop of the universe. Any prayers or requests must mention Legba first of all.

Legba leans on a stick, and one of his symbols is the *macoutte* (straw sack). With stick and sack he totters forward into the future. In Dahomey, he is recognized as *Fa*, 'destiny'. One of his Haitian titles, Grand Chemin, refers to the road to the other world on which he travels. Legba has no fixed abode, he is always on the move. He wears a wide hat to keep off the sun, for he is a king and kings must not be touched by it (cf. royal umbrellas in Africa), and he always carries a pipe and tobacco with him. Sacrifices to Legba are performed in a special way. A chicken is taken and its neck twisted until it is dead. Then the bird's feathers are stuck to the *poteau-Legba* with its blood.

Mait' Carrefour
'Lord of the crossroads'; god of magicians.

This Haitian god is brother to Baron Samedi (see *Ghede*) and of Kalfu Indian descent. Mait' Carrefour is a young man who has the power of disruption; he is capable of unleashing bad luck and undeserved disasters onto any man, however well prepared. He makes the best laid plans turn into chaos. He has the power to release the demons of night, and is strong enough to bind them up again. He is shown with his muscular arms raised out crosswise. Mait' Carrefour is also the moon and is at his most powerful at midnight. Understandably, he is a patron of magicians.

Marassa
Twin gods of Voodoo. (See *Lisa* in African section.)

The Marassa are symbolic of man's twinned nature, matter and spirit, human and divine, mortal and immortal. They are the first children of God and their feast is at Christmas. They represent the beginning of all things, and the beginnings of all things. They are worshipped at harvest time and on All Souls' Night (though they share between them but one soul).

Linked to them is the idea of *Marassa-trois*. It involves a different way of counting, of looking at things. In Voodoo one plus one equals three: count one for each part, one plus one equals two, and add the new totality they create; that makes three. The relationship makes both parts meaningful, one plus, and plus one.

Marinette
Earth goddess of Haiti, wife to *Ti-Jean Petro*.

Mounanchou
A minor god of Haiti.

Mounanchou is seen as an executive; he wears a business suit, carries a briefcase, is pompous and fond of keeping people waiting. He is a divine PR man, part of the official apparatus. He is worshipped because he has power; the power of the bureaucrat in modern society. Interestingly he is also assumed to be corrupt, to have criminal associates especially in the Bossu clan. (See *Bossu*.)

Nanan-Bouclou
Dahomey primal god who was both male and female. He created the twins, *Mawu-Lisa* (see Africa section), from whom all the Voodoo gods descended.

Ogoun
God of war, politics, fire, iron and thunderbolts.

Ogoun is an heroic figure, originally war god of the Nago peoples of the Hausa Empire of West Africa. From warrior and ruthless champion he came to control iron, the main ingredient of war. In Voodoo his power is seen as political. He is a functional god (*loa travail*) and as such is susceptible to flattery and praise. He consorts with *Erzulie*, the goddess of love, and because of his

73

association with fire is opposed to the sea and water. His colour, inevitably, is red. The god's presence is saluted by the fumes of rum; the liquor is poured on the floor and set alight. He is greeted by playing the national anthem and a military salute.

Ogoun is fierce with pent-up energy and anger; he seems always on the point of explosion, ready to scream and fight at a second's notice. He can perform incredible feats, which have been well-attested. One of them is to take a sharp sword or machete, place it on his diaphragm and lean his whole weight on to it. He will also press sharp points and blades against his flesh, leaving the skin unmarked. Ogoun is always swearing and exclaiming 'By thunder!' If you are near him and he shouts out 'My balls are cold!' it is an indication that he wants rum. According to his mood, he will either swallow down the drink in great gulps or else spit it out in a fine spray.

Politically Ogoun is a wheeler-dealer, a fixer, an opportunist. It has been pointed out that many of his priests are Masons. Voodoo is a synthesis of African animism, Indian cults and Roman Catholicism. The admixture of Masonry, a phenomenon which the Roman Catholic Church anathematizes and proscribes, is of more than passing interest. (See *Ogun* in African section.)

Simbi
Voodoo patron of the rains and of magicians of a benevolent nature.

Simbi shares functions and characteristics with other Haitian gods. Radiating and overlapping into other domains, he is Simbi en Deux Eaux. He is a snake in form, but a shy creature of fresh water. He originates from several of the different African cultures which have contributed to Voodoo.

Ti-Jean Petro
A serpent deity, son of *Dan Petro*.

Whenever Ti-Jean Petro appears, his first action is to shin up the nearest post, column or tree. Usually he does nothing else but stay up there, happy with his position.

Asia

CHINESE ■ JAPANESE ■ INDIAN

Ao
Gods of rain and the sea; the four dragon kings.

The dragon kings were the subjects of the Jade Emperor (*Yu-Huang-Shang-Ti*). Each was assigned a portion of the earth and an area of sea; and each owned a palace of crystal staffed and maintained by fish and crabs. Other forces under their command patrolled the sea bed, each dragon king being responsible for his own territory.

During droughts the dragon kings were much worshipped; noisy processions of music and dancing would follow a cloth effigy of a dragon through the streets of the town. Rural areas also honoured their local dragon kings, for every stream and river had its own example of this particular god. The names of the four brother kings were Ao Ch'in, Ao Kuang, Ao Jun and Ao Shun.

Ch'ang-o
Goddess of the moon and wife of *I*.

I had been given the drink of immortality by the gods, and one day when he was out his wife drank it. *I* found out and his anger was so blistering that a frightened Ch'ang-o fled to the moon for refuge. There she begged help from the Celestial Hare, who agreed to fight on her side. After a few blows had been exchanged the Celestial Hare persuaded *I* not to punish his wife. Ch'ang-o was an extremely beautiful young woman so it was not too hard for her to mollify him. *I* made peace with her. Ch'ang-o continued to live in the moon; she had a palace there and her husband was a constant visitor.

Ch'eng-Huang
God of walls and ditches.

Each town or village had its own Ch'eng-Huang, usually a prominent local sage or official promoted to godhood after his death. The identity of the Ch'eng-Huang was often revealed to people in dreams, though the actual choice was made by the gods who set the examination for the post. The Ch'eng-Huang not only protected the community from outside attack, but also took an active part in exposing wrongdoers whose behaviour constituted an internal threat. He would identify them to the local governor in dreams. The festival of the god of walls and ditches was celebrated in spring. A procession of his statue was accompanied by Mr Black (nightwatchman spirit) and Mr White (day watchman spirit), and by his personal assistants Mr Horse-face and Mr Ox-face. In addition there was an escort of demons with gongs and much noisy jollity. (See *Ma-Mien* and *Niu-Y'ou*.)

Chih-Nii

Goddess of spinners and daughter of *Yu-Huang-Shang-Ti*, the Jade Emperor (for whom she wove robes and clouds).

One day Chih-Nii and a group of friends went down to earth to bathe in a river. While they were in the water a cowherd came along and stole their clothes. The goddess went after him but he had hidden the garments – without them it was not possible for her to reascend to heaven. She made the best of the situation by marrying the cowherd, and later they had two children. After some years together Chih-Nii managed to discover the hiding-place of her stolen clothes; she put them on and returned to her celestial home.

The cowherd was unhappy without his wife and was advised by his ox (who happened to be a spirit in disguise) to go to heaven and seek an audience with the Jade Emperor. The ox volunteered to show him the way there. The cowherd saw the Emperor and asked for the return of Chih-Nii. The Emperor was touched by the love shown by the cowherd and realized that his daughter was equally in love with him. But it was impossible for them to live together, either in heaven or on earth, for the daughter was an immortal and the cowherd a mere man.

The Emperor came to a compromise; he declared that they could meet every seven days. But obviously he had not expressed himself too clearly, for the goddess and her husband thought that he meant they could meet only on the seventh day of the seventh month of each year. The Emperor had turned each of them into a star and placed them on opposite banks of the Celestial River. (She is the star Alpha in the Lyre, he is the Beta-Gamma pair in Aquila.) Once every year a group of magpies arrives and builds a bridge of sticks over the Celestial River so that they may meet each other. On earth on that day it always rains, and the rain is a sign that the happy couple are weeping with joy.

Ch'in-Shu-Pao
A guardian god.

Ch'in-Shu-Pao was a T'ang Dynasty military hero who was elevated to the divine status and given the job of guarding doors. On one occasion he successfully defended the Jade Emperor (*Yu-Huang-Shang-Ti*) from an enraged dragon who blamed his misfortune on the former and tried to enter the palace to take revenge. He was helped in this exploit by two other pairs of heroes, *Tien Wang* and *Heng-Ha-Erh-Chiang*. In recognition of their service the Emperor ordered that their portraits should be painted on the doors. (See *Men-Shen*.)

Erh-Lang
Guardian god who chased away evil spirits.

Called 'Second Lord', Erh-Lang was the nephew of the Jade Emperor (*Yu-Huang-Shang-Ti*). He was a shape-shifter and had up to seventy-two different bodily forms. He was once swallowed by the Transcendent Pig whom he then slew for his foolhardiness. Erh-Lang was a popular god in China and was widely worshipped.

Fan-K'uei
God of butchers.

A prominent figure in the turmoils which surrounded the rise to power of the Han Dynasty. Formerly Fan-K'uei had worked as a humble dog-skinner. When he achieved a position of power he was adopted as patron by the local butchers and soon rose to divine status.

Feng-Po
The Earl of Wind. He carried the winds in a large flagon made of goatskin.

Feng-Po-Po
Goddess of winds. She replaced *Feng-Po* (the Earl of Wind) and

would ride through the clouds on a swift tiger.

Feng-Tu
Chief town of the land of the dead.

The Chinese hell was not just one locality but a complete land with towns, villages and fields. Here reigned the Yama kings (see *Yeng-Wang-Yeh*). Crossing over to the entrance of hell, the Demon Gate, were three bridges: a gold one reserved for gods and deified humans, a silver one for the souls of the just, and a plain wooden one for the souls of the damned. These last unfortunates were continually falling over the edge of the wooden bridge, which had no parapet or handrail. They plunged into the river which flowed beneath and were torn to bits by the brass snakes and iron dogs waiting in the waters.

Fu-Hsing
A god of happiness. He was a deified human, and his symbol was the bat. (See *Shou-Hsing*.)

Heng-Ha-Erh-Chiang
The 'Sniffing General' and the 'Puffing General'; guardian gods of Buddhist temples.

Sniffer has his mouth closed and from his nostrils emits a stream of deadly light. Puffer has his mouth open and blows out foul smells fit to stun one senseless. The two gods were to be found painted each on a leaf of the traditional Chinese double-doors. Later they were replaced by the Heavenly Kings. (See *T'ien-Wang*.)

Hou-Chi
'Prince Millet', an ancient harvest god.

Hou-Chi was much venerated by the peasantry, for he ensured that their crops would be fruitful. He was prestigious enough to have been adopted by the Chi clan as their eponymous ancestor. Later he was to be overshadowed by Celestial Prince *Liu*. Hou-Chi is shown as a kindly old man with millet stalks growing on his head.

Hsuan-T'ien-Shang-Ti
Supreme Lord of the Dark Heaven, Regent of Water.

This god was a powerful exorcist and master of demons. He was shown as a gigantic human figure with wild hair, dressed in a black robe with a golden breastplate. He stands barefoot on a turtle around which is coiled a serpent.

Hu-Shen
God of hail.

Hu-Shen was worshipped because his powerful hail could destroy a growing crop in a few minutes. His veneration was therefore placatory. He was persuaded not to send his hail by prayers and offerings of the usual kind, wine and grain.

I
God of bowmen, often called the 'excellent archer'.

In primeval times there were ten suns, not just one. Each division of the day had its own sun which appeared alone during its allotted period. One day, however, things went badly wrong; getting their schedules mixed up, all ten suns appeared in the sky at once. Their combined heat was so fierce that it threatened to burn up all life on earth. The 'excellent archer', I, saved the earth by shooting nine of the suns out of the sky. They fell dead at his feet in the shape of ravens.

I's wife was the beautiful moon goddess *Ch'ang-o*.

I-Ti
God of wine. He was a mortal who invented the art of wine-making – and was deified for outstanding services to humanity.

Kuan-Ti
God of war and fortune-telling.

Kuan-Ti was originally a famous general of the Han Dynasty who died a martyr's death at the hands of the kingdom of Wu. His worship was active well into this century, up to the time of the Republic.

Kuan-Ti was dressed in green and had a red face; to the mass of the population he was a judge and helper. He helped predict the future by means of numbered slips placed in a bamboo container. The container was shaken until one of the slips fell out. The number on the slip was found in the prophetic books, and the appropriate verse applied to the enquirer's question. (See *Shou-Ts'ang*.)

Kuan-Yin (Kwannon)
Goddess of mercy.

Kuan-Yin was originally male and the Indian *Boddhisattva* Avalokiteshvara, 'the merciful lord of utter enlightenment'. Avalokiteshvara chose to remain on earth to bring relief to the suffering rather than enjoy for himself the ecstasies of Nirvana.

Kuan-Yin, sometimes possessing eleven heads, is surnamed Sung-Tzu-Niang-Niang, 'lady who brings children'. She is shown dressed in white, seated on a lotus and carrying a child. She was goddess of fecundity as well as of mercy. Her help was sought by those suffering from disease, and she was therefore universally popular. Her temple on Miao Feng Shan (Mount of the Wondrous Peak) attracted large numbers of pilgrims, who used rattles and fireworks to emphasize their prayers and attract her attention.

K'uei-Hsing
God of examinations.

Originally an assistant to *Wen-Ch'ang* (god of literature), K'uei-Hsing became the centre of an important cult. The sophisticated bureaucracy of the empire was controlled by men who had come top in competitive examinations. This system of choosing leading administrators was doubly advantageous from the viewpoint of the Emperor; he was served by the best brains and also avoided the risk of real power falling into the hands of aristocratic, dynastic families. Brilliant individuals with no strong family ties proved his safest agents.

K'uei-Hsing was, so it is said, a brilliant scholar who had come first in his examinations. But when the Emperor saw him he refused to give him the required imperial affirmation of his success. The reason was because K'uei-Hsing was, to put it mildly, incredibly ugly. In despair the brilliant but grotesque candidate decided to end it all. He threw himself into the sea, but a turtle swam under him and returned him to land. After this sign of divine favour the Emperor had no choice but to acknowledge the examination result.

K'uei-Hsing is shown standing on the turtle called Ao and holding a corn measure and writing brush. The brush is to mark the name of the successful candidate and the measure is used to assess the knowledge and talents of all the examinees. K'uei-Hsing was naturally popular with students and civil servants. The best way of obtaining his help was to work hard for the examinations, but the occasional prayer and offerings of incense didn't go amiss.

Lao-Tien-Yeh
'Father-Heaven', a title of the Jade Emperor (*Yu-Huang-Shang-Ti*).

Lao-Tzu
A philosopher who was a contemporary of Kung-Fu-Tzu (Confucius). He was assigned divinity by the popular mind and considered an incarnation of the Celestial Master of the First Origin, one of the main triad of Taoist gods (see *Yu-Huang-Shang-Ti*). After compiling the book Tao te Ching, Lao-Tzu mounted a green ox and ambled away into the sunset, never to be seen again by mortal eyes. The book he left, the Tao te Ching, is a collection of maxims, probably from various sources. It is organized in two parts and contains the basis of Taoist thought. It is a sublime creation by any standards.

Lei-Kung
God of thunder.

More feared than adored, Lei-Kung had few shrines. He was an ugly fellow with blue skin, wings and claws. Clad in a loincloth, he carried drums and hammer and chisel. The chisel, like a thunderbolt, was deployed against wicked humans. The hammer was used to strike the chisel and to beat the drums. As an executive of celestial justice Lei-Kung sought out undetected crimes and punished the wrongdoers. Occasionally he needed human help to detect malevolent spirits who disguised themselves as men or animals. He was the god to turn to if you wanted to maliciously inform against your neighbours or other people. Lei-Kung controlled only the thunder and was not responsible for lightning.

Liu
God of crops; a Celestial Prince, he became Superintendent of the Five Cereals – rice, barley, millet, sorghum, wheat.

Lu-Hsing
God of salaries and employees. His symbol was the deer, Lu, on which he was often shown mounted. (See *Shou-Hsing*.)

Lupan
God of carpenters. Lupan was considered to be a god of amazing skill; it was said that he once made a wooden falcon which could fly.

Ma-Mien
'Horse-face', a bailiff of the Yama kings.

With his companion 'Ox-head' (*Niu-Y'ou*), Ma-Mien's job was to conduct people to hell. Chinese bureaucracy extended past death; Ma-Mien needed an official warrant, signed and sealed, before he could act. He presented the warrant and conducted the soul back for judgement. Every guardian and door god he passed had to see his credentials. This paperwork was considered necessary for otherwise any common-or-garden demon might assume a disguise and try to arrest human souls. Ma-Mien received his orders from *Ch'eng-Huang*, the god of walls and ditches. The god kept lists of all the inhabitants of his area and so could make up the warrant accurately.

For the Yama kings, see *Yeng-Wang-Yeh*.

Meng
Lady Meng lived just outside hell and prepared the broth of oblivion (*Mi-Hung-T'ang*). All souls returning from judgement were compelled to pass her door and had to drink of the brew. Their memories were erased like wiped tapes, but they still retained

the ability to feel pain. Pain remained with them even if they were reincarnated as animals, birds or insects.

Meng-T'ien
God of the writing brush. A military man who was deified for inventing the writing brush, which is after all mightier than the sword.

Men-Shen
Gods of the door.

There were several pairs of such guardian gods, found painted on the front doors of houses and temples. One was normally white-faced and the other had a coloured face. The most prominent pair were Shen-T'u and Yu-Lu. Another noteworthy couple were Yu-Ch'ih-Ching-Te and *Ch'in-Shu-Pao*. Buddhist temples had Generals 'Sniffer' and 'Puffer' (*Heng-Ha-Erh-Chiang*) and also the Heavenly Kings (*Tien-Wang*).

Mi-Hung-T'ang
The broth of oblivion.

This wonderful drink was brewed by the Lady *Meng* who lived on the borders of hell. It caused humans to forget every detail of their former lives, to forget their time in hell, to forget even their ability to speak. Everything was erased from the mind, which was left as blank as that of a newborn babe. After drinking the broth of oblivion the soul was ready to be reborn on earth, either as an animal or a human according to its former behaviour. If the soul was to be reborn as an animal, the appropriate skin was thrown over its shoulders and it was taken to the Red River. From the parapet of Pain Bridge the soul was cast into the swift scarlet stream which hurried it to its rebirth. (See *Yeng-Wang-Yeh*.)

Niu-Y'ou
'Ox-head', a sort of spirit constable for the Yama kings (see *Yeng-Wang-Yeh*) and for the god of walls and ditches – *Ch'eng-Huang*. His constant companion was 'Horse-face' (*Ma-Mien*).

Pa-Cha

In life a famous soldier, Pa-Cha was in death worshipped as the most effective deity against locusts. He is shown in a soldier's tunic, with an eagle's beak. His fingernails are excessively long, like talons. The idea was that he could combine his soldier's training with his raptor's armoury and mobility to attack the potentially devastating swarms of locusts.

Pa-Hsien
The Eight Immortals.

These were seven famous men and one woman who had attained immortality through merit; they were permitted to eat the peaches of immortality (*P'an T'ao*) at the banquets of Queen Mother *Wang*. They were usually found in attendance on the god of long life, *Shou-Hsing*.

One of the Eight, Li of the Iron Crutch, was a beggar with a gourd and crutch. While his soul was visiting the philosopher *Lao-Tzu* his body was left in charge of a disciple who mistakenly cremated it. When Li came back there was no body for him so he was forced to use that of a beggar, recently vacated on account of starvation.

Of the other Immortals, Han Chung-Li (or Chung-Li of the Han period) was a smiling old man who radiated happiness. Chang-Kuo-Lao was an old man who owned a marvellous donkey that travelled at incredible speeds; it could then be folded up and stowed away in a pouch. Lan-Ts'ai-Ho was a travelling minstrel whose philosophical songs caused him to be snatched away to heaven by a stork, which is a nice reversal of our own popular image. Lu-Tung-Pin was a hero of early Chinese literature who was shown carrying the famous Flying Sword with which he killed the Yellow Dragon. Han-Hsiang-Tzu and T'sao-Kuo-Chiu were disciples of Lu-Tung-Pin. Ho-Hsien-Ku ('immortal maiden Ho') was the one female Immortal.

P'an-Chin-Lien
Goddess of prostitutes.

In life P'an-Chin-Lien was a widow who indulged in unbecoming habits. The frequency and variety of these habits angered her father-in-law to such an extent that he felt constrained to apply a short sharp shock. He did this lethally with a long sharp sword. P'an-Chin-Lien was honoured, if that is the right phrase, by her more professional contemporaries and became the goddess of that calling.

P'an-T'ao
The peaches of immortality.

In the orchard of heaven grew the miraculous peach trees. They bore fruit only once every three thousand years, and this fruit formed the main dish at the banquets given by the Queen Mother *Wang*, wife of the Jade Emperor (*Yu-Huang-Shang-Ti*). Only gods and immortals were invited to eat the fruit. Among humans the peach was the symbol of long life.

Pi-Hsia-Yuan-Chun
'Princess of streaked clouds', daughter of the Emperor of the Eastern Peak, *T'ai-Yueh-Ta-Ti*. Alias Sheng-Mu, this goddess was the protectress of childbirth and of women and children. She wore a headdress adorned with three birds with wide wings. She was attended by two ladies, one who brought children, the other who ensured good sight for babies. The connection of light and eyesight with childbirth is reminiscent of the Greek goddess of birth *Ilythia*, who carried a torch.

Pi-Hsia-Yuan-Chun is complemented by the compassionate *Kuan-Yin*.

Shen-T'u
Guardian god.

This ancient divinity was a companion of a god called Yu-Lu. Their job was to guard the gates of hell and prevent a mass breakout, which would certainly be a nuisance to the living. They stood by a great door under a massive peach tree on a mountain on the borders of hell. When a ghost or a fretful soul managed to make a run for it the guards would seize it and punish it. The punishment was solitary confinement – solitary that is apart from a couple of hungry tigers. (See *Yeng-Wang-Yeh*.)

Shou-Hsing
God of longevity; he formed a triad with *Fu-Hsing* (god of happiness) and *Lu-Hsing* (god of salaries).

Shou-Hsing had a prominent and somewhat bulbous bald head, his eyebrows and whiskers were white and venerable. He leaned on a staff and carried a peach of immortality (*P'an-T'ao*). He was a domestic god; he had no public shrines but was universally worshipped in a land which honours its old people. Shou-Hsing was the arbiter of the life-span of men. He had tablets on which were inscribed the date of everyone's death. But he was not a hard god and it was sometimes possible, if you treated him well, to persuade him to make certain favourable adjustments to those dates.

Shou-Ts'ang
Servant god of the great *Kuan-Ti*.

When Kuan-Ti received a justified complaint from the victim of any wrong, he would send Shou-Ts'ang to execute justice. Shou-Ts'ang played the part of squire and groom to the god of war; he accompanied him everywhere and looked after his horse and armour. Like most functionaries, he was a somewhat colourless character.

Shui-Kuan
'Agent of Water', part of a triad of Taoist gods which included the 'Agent of Heaven' and the 'Agent of Earth'

Shui-Kuan was the principle which defended men from evil of all kinds. Sins were confessed to the agents in this way: the sinner wrote down his failings in triplicate; one copy was burned (sent to heaven), one was buried (sent to earth), and the third was weighted and sunk in a nearby river or lake. Every fortnight Shui-Kuan received offerings of cakes shaped like tortoises. Also offered to him were cakes whose knot forms represented the links of a chain. (See *T'ien-Kuan* and *Ti-Kuan*.)

Sung-Chiang
God of thieves. A renowned bandit and troublemaker who was elevated to godhood.

Sun-Pin
God of cobblers.

Before Sun-Pin's time men went barefoot or wore simple sandals; this left the toes vulnerable. Sun-Pin was a soldier, a general no less, and suffered the painful misfortune of having his toes cut off in battle. After he had recovered the skills of balancing and walking, he decided that to hide his deformity he would cover the front of his feet with shaped containers of leather. Before too long he had invented shoes and had earned the undying gratitude of many generations of shoemakers.

T'ai-Yueh-Ta-Ti (Tung-Yueh-Ta-Ti)
The Great Emperor of the Eastern Peak.

This god was assigned custody of the affairs of mankind. He was subject to the Jade Emperor (*Yu-Huang-Shang-Ti*) and lived on the peak called T'ai-shan in Shantung Province. He was protector of animals as well as of men, and everything to do with the welfare and prosperity of both was under his domain. He was a powerful and respected figure, and his main temple in Peking was the head of a wide-ranging divine bureaucracy which contained over eighty separate departments.

Heaven ran its affairs through a celestial civil service, divided into ministries and agencies. It was staffed by selection from among the ranks of the dead, and if normal Chinese practice was anything to go by they probably had to sit a fiercely competitive written examination.

As representative of the Jade Emperor, the Emperor of the Eastern Peak was accorded imperial dress, status and income. He was worshipped in a rich temple and was far too important to be seen in the homes of his followers. If they wanted anything, they had to go to him.

Tien-Hou
Empress of Heaven.

Tien-Hou was a mortal woman whose brothers were sailors, each of them sailing on different ships. One day when they were all away Tien-Hou fell into a coma. She was revived with great difficulty and her first words were a protest that they had awakened her too soon. Then three of the brothers returned with the story that all their ships had been caught in a storm at sea, but their sister had appeared to them miraculously and led three of the vessels to safety. However she was revived before she had had time to locate the fourth ship; the fourth brother never returned, for his vessel had foundered in the storm. Tien-Hou died young, but she constantly returned to help sailors and others in times of danger. People named her Princess of Supernatural Favour and came to regard her as holy. As time went on she was thought of as Queen then Empress of Heaven.

T'ien-Kuan
'Agent of Heaven', one of a triad of Taoist gods.

T'ien-Kuan brought men happiness. In theatrical form, he was depicted as a masked dancer who said a prologue to the main play and distributed bits of paper on which were written wishes for happiness. These were given to the audience. (See *Shui-Kuan* and *Ti-Kuan*.)

Tien-Mu
Goddess of lightning.

Tien-Mu produced her lightning from mirrors which she held in both hands. A thunder storm in ancient China involved a number of gods who co-operated to produce the right effects. Apart from Tien-Mu, any producer wishing to put on this particular drama needed *Lei-Kung* (thunder), *Yu-Tzu* (rain), *Yun-T'ung* (clouds) and *Feng-Po* (wind). Crowd extras in the form of demons and the occasional guest appearance by a dragon or two added to the scenic effects.

Tien-Wang (Mo-Li)
The Heavenly Kings.

These were four brothers, Buddhist gods whose duty was to guard doors. They were guardians of the Four Directions. Originally from India, their names were Vaisravana, Virudharka, Virupasa and Dhrtarastra. Each carried an object which, when mortals they had used to control the elements. These objects were a sword, a guitar, an umbrella and a marten (the animal). The sword raised tempests, the guitar governed the winds, the umbrella controlled the light of the sun and the marten killed and consumed malicious spirits. Because of their potency and aggressive energy the Mo-Li were ideal sentries. (See *Chin-Shu-Pao*.)

Ti-Kuan

'Agent of Earth', one of a triad of Taoist gods. Ti-Kuan had the power to forgive the sins of men. (See *Shui-Kuan* and *T'ien-Kuan*.)

Ti-Tsang-Wang-Pu-Sa
God of mercy.

The darker regions of the Chinese hell were gloomy places, full of despairing souls. Were you to find yourself in those caverns you would most likely be visited by a holy man whose way was lit by a brilliant pearl. The tinkling sound of the metal rings on his staff would announce his approach. It would be Ti-Tsang-Wang-Pu-Sa and he would do all he could to help you. He would even try and stop you from being reincarnated as something or somebody evil. Ti-Tsang-Wang-Pu-Sa is the Chinese equivalent of the Buddhist *Boddhisattva* named Ksitigarbha. He had renounced personal experience of Nirvana in order to wander through the infernal regions helping ordinary people. He is depicted as a smiling monk, robed and with a halo about his body as well as one about his head; he carries the pearl which gives light and the staff adorned with metal rings. (See *Yeng-Wang-Yeh*.)

Ts'ai-Lun
God of stationers. He was credited with the invention of paper.

Tsai-Shen
God of wealth.

Tsai-Shen was the most resoundingly successful and popular of all the ancient Chinese gods. Even atheists worshipped him. Every year his birthday was celebrated in every household with the sacrifice of a carp and a cock. He was a magisterial figure dressed in exquisite silks, and was minister of a whole department of wealth with many fiscal and economic deities under his control.

Ts'ang Chien
God of writing.

Like many things, the art of writing depended on the combination of several talents. The intermeshing of talents is indicative of a general attitude of interdependence in the Chinese mind. Interdependence is the root of technology and its flower was seen in the many advances of Chinese culture. There are several different poetic myths as to the origins of the actual characters of Chinese calligraphy; some claim they were marks made by birds hopping across sand, some claim they were first seen in twigs, and some claim they were brought to China as marks on the coat of a divine horse.

Tsao-Wang
God of the hearth.

Every household had its hearth god who was a kind of recording angel. He would listen to everything that was said and watch all that was done, and note it down. Every year he would go to the Jade Emperor (*Yu-Huang-Shang-Ti*) with an annual report on the family. The Emperor would then consider their past behaviour and decree the family fortunes for the coming year.

The hearth god had a wife who recorded the words and actions of the women of the house. Both deities were represented by pictures painted on paper, and had a daily offering of incense. When the time came for the annual report to be submitted, the god's mouth was sweetened with confectionery (to ensure sweet words in the report) and the paper image was burned. As the flames consumed the paper, the family let off firecrackers to help Tsao-Wang on his upward journey. While the god was absent for the few days it took him to get to Heaven and back the family could do and say as it pleased, for their deeds and words were not recorded or held against them. But their freedom was not total; in the absence of their hearth god the family was vulnerable to all manner of disasters.

Tu-Ti
Gods of the locality or *genii locii*.

Despite their lowly position in the celestial hierarchy, the Tu-Ti were popular and well-liked deities. In fact every place, house, street, farm or town, had its own locality god. They were generally kindly and respectable old men, suitably clad for their part of the world. They were always accompanied by their wives. Locality gods may be regarded as invisible watchmen, seeing that their little domains ran smoothly and came to no ill.

Wang-Mu-Niang-Niang
Alias Hsi-Wang-Mu, 'Lady Wang', she was the wife of the Jade Emperor, *Yu-Huang-Shang-Ti*, and lived on Mount Khun-lun. Lady Wang was the keeper of the peaches of immortality (*P'an-T'ao*) and the ruler of the Western Paradise, the future home and reward for the virtuous.

Wen-Chang-Ta-Ti
God of literature.

Instead of a picture or graven image, Wen-Chang was represented in people's houses by a tablet on which his name and title were inscribed in fine calligraphy. He was the patron of literature and verse; his symbol was the crane, a poised and elegant bird which was regarded as a personification of literary style.

Wen-Chang achieved divinity only after seventeen busy incarnations. He was helped by *K'uei-Hsing*, god of examinations, and by a minor god, called 'Red Jacket'. This last assistant looked after students who had not done their work up to standard, occasionally exerting his influence and helping a lazy scholar to succeed.

Yeng-Wang-Yeh
'Lord Yama King', the foremost of the ten Yama kings or Lords of Death.

Lord Yama King screened the newly-arrived souls in hell and decided where they should go: either to a special court or to be punished or sent straight back to the Wheel of Transmigration (rebirth). There were ten law courts in hell, each specializing in the hearing and sentencing of specific crimes. In addition there were eighteen dungeons, each offering a different form of torture or punishment.

After passing through the first law court presided over by Lord Yama King, the soul might be sent to one of the following. Second court: dishonest agents and bungling doctors. Third court: forgers, rumour-mongers, liars and corrupt administrators. Fourth court: misers, dishonest shopkeepers and merchants, blasphemers. Fifth court: murderers, atheists and erotomaniacs. Sixth court: all sacrilegious men. Seventh court: grave-robbers, slave-traders and slave-owners, cannibals. Eighth court: those guilty of disrespect towards their parents. Ninth court: arsonists and those who have died in accidents. Tenth court: the Wheel of Transmigration.

The Yama kings were all dressed alike in royal robes and only the very experienced could tell them apart. They were helped in their difficult and exhausting task by hordes of spear-carrying, horn-headed court ushers. (See Indian god *Yama*.)

Yu-Huang-Shang-Ti
The August Supreme Emperor of Jade alias Yu-Ti, August Person of Jade alias *Lao-Tien-Yeh*, 'Father Heaven'.

The Jade Emperor lives on the highest level of heaven with his court. At the moment he is the Supreme Emperor; he was preceded by the Celestial Master of the First Origin and after him will come the Celestial Master of the Dawn of Jade of the Golden Door. His palace is similar in all respects to that used by the earthly Emperor and under him is a complete civil service, army, courtiers and family. He is always depicted wearing royal robes and seated on a throne.

The earthly Emperor was the special devotee of the Jade Emperor and made solemn offerings to him of silk, jade, wine and meat. The Jade Emperor created men. He moulded them from clay and put them out to dry. Then it clouded over and rain came down. The Emperor rushed out to bring them under shelter, but the rain had already spoiled some of them. Which is why some men are born sickly or even deformed. He is married to the Queen Mother *Wang*. (See *Chih-Nii*.)

Yu-Tzu
God of rain.

Yu-Tzu helped the other weather gods, when they got together, by sprinkling rain onto the earth. He carried the rain in a large ceramic pot and distributed it by plunging a sword into the vessel and shaking the water off the blade in droplets.

Yun-T'ung
God of the clouds.

One of several Chinese weather gods, Yun-T'ung was in fact a litte boy; he delighted in collecting and piling up heaps of clouds.

Aji-Suki-Taka-Hi-Kone
God of thunder.

One of several such gods. Aji-Suki-Taka-Hi-Kone was born noisy and grew up even noisier. He made such a din that they carried him up and down a ladder. That is to say he was heard receding and approaching. Sometimes he was placed in a boat which sailed about the islands of Japan, and that is why the thunder is heard echoing from shore to shore. He was the father of Prince Cataract, *Taki-Tsu-Hiko*, the god of rain.

Ama-No-Minakanushi-No-Kami
The Divine Lord of the Middle Heavens, the Pole Star. Stars were not normally worshipped, but later Chinese and Buddhist influence introduced the idea of sidereal divinities to the Japanese.

Ama-No-Uzume
A fertility goddess.

Ama-No-Uzume was one of the companions of *Ninigi* when he journeyed to earth. She performed an obscene and comical dance to provoke the laughter of the gods in order to entice the hidden sun to emerge. The dance had associations with the return of fertility to the earth; it was symbolic of planting the seed to await the sun after its winter recess. (See *Amaterasu*.)

Amaterasu
Goddess of the sun.

Amaterasu was born from the washing of the right eye of the god *Izanagi* and was given command of the Plain of the Heaven, the sky. She was loaded with shining gems. The Imperial Family claim both descent and divinity from her. Apart from other tasks Amaterasu was involved in sacerdotal functions, one of which was to weave the robes of the gods, a habit still kept alive by modern Shinto priestesses.

Amaterasu's brother was the maniac *Susanoo*. One day he climbed up to heaven to see her and told her that he was going to visit his mother in hell. He suggested that they should each create a few offspring as symbols of mutual trust. Amaterasu chewed up Susanoo's sword and blew the fragments in a mist from her mouth. Out of the mist came three goddesses. Susanoo took Amaterasu's gems, munched them up and blew out a mist from which five male gods appeared. Susanoo grew so excited at his success that he quite lost his head. He went yelling and whooping like a madman through the rice fields, breaking down the dykes, trampling on the crops and blocking the ditches.

Amaterasu tried to pretend that it was all boyish spirits and forgave her brother. She had other things to think about, the festival of first fruits was approaching. But the unspeakable Susanoo went and squatted in the temples, soiling them with excrement. Hard as it was, Amaterasu still forgave him. She and her women sat quietly in the weaving-shed making robes for the gods. Suddenly they heard a noise above them, the sound of a pair of feet, the heavy drag of a large object over the tiles. A hole was kicked through the roof and there appeared the raw and bloody carcass of a flayed horse. As the horrible object crashed to the floor, one of the women collapsed and died. It was another of Susanoo's little jokes.

All this was too much for the goddess; she fled to a dark cave and hid deep inside it. In the absence of Amaterasu, the sun, the world was plunged into cold darkness. At first the gods were not too bothered, but then they had the seriousness of the situation brought home to them: under the cover of darkness millions of devils had emerged to wreak joyful and unrestrained havoc on the world.

The gods held a meeting to decide what to do. The god of wisdom devised a plan. The gods collected cocks, a mirror and strings of jewels. They hung the mirror and jewels on a *sakaki* tree outside the cave in which Amaterasu was hidden. Then the goddess *Ama-No-Uzume*, an earthy lady not noted for modesty, mounted an upturned tub and began to dance. The cocks crew loudly as the dancing goddess worked herself into a frenzy. She tore off her garments and performed an impolite dance sequence. The gods roared with unrestrained laughter.

The clamour made by crowing cocks, drumming feet and guffawing gods penetrated the cavern in which Amaterasu was sulking. Her female curiosity got the better of her and she crept to the cave entrance and peeped out. Her brilliant reflection flashed back at her from the mirror, the jewels on the tree glinted and glistened. Amaterasu came out a little further to see what it was. Suddenly she was grabbed and hauled out, the cave entrance was sealed by rope and the gods rejoiced, for the sun had returned to the world once more.

Ama-Tsu-Kami

The name given to the gods of heaven to distinguish them from the gods of earth (*Kuni-Tsu-Kami*).

In former ages the gods of heaven used to visit earth fairly often, for there existed a bridge, Ama-No-Hashidate, between the two places. The gods of heaven were neither malicious nor omniscient; they had to keep in touch with worldly affairs either through messengers or through divination, second sight, and other ways of fortune-telling. The bridge has long since collapsed into the sea, and this has not made things easier for either gods or men. Heaven is very like Japan, with the same sort of landscape and plants. It is crossed by Ama-No-Gawa, the Heavenly River.

Amatsu Mikaboshi

God of evil, 'august star of heaven'. Alias Ama-No-Kagaseo, 'brilliant male'.

Ame-No-Hohi

Ame-No-Hohi was sent down from heaven to find out what was happening on earth; this was after the god *Ame-No-Oshido-Mimi* had refused to get involved. The gods waited and waited. Three years passed. They sent down his son after him. To this day there has been no news.

Ame-No-Oshido-Mimi

Son of the goddess *Amaterasu*.

The goddess sent Ame-No-Oshido-Mimi to be ruler of the earth, but as he approached it over the floating Bridge of Heaven he saw what an unruly place it was, full of noise, unrest and trouble. The god did a prompt about-turn and went back to heaven, where he declared that he didn't want anything to do with men and their affairs. Ame-No-Oshido-Mimi was one of the few sensible gods of history. (See *Ame-No-Hohi*.)

Ame-No-Wakahiko
A courageous god who was sent down to earth to be its ruler.

Ame-No-Wakahiko was armed with a bow and arrows. When he arrived on earth he met and married the daughter of *O-Kuni-Nushi*. Time passed. The gods began to fret as they heard nothing from him. They decided to send down a messenger, and chose a pheasant. The pheasant flew down, searched about and then landed in a tree opposite Ame-No-Wakahiko's house. The people noticed the pheasant and an old woman loudly declared that it was a bird of ill-omen. Before the pheasant had a chance to open its beak, Ame-No-Wakahiko had grabbed his bow and one of his celestial arrows, aimed and fired. The arrow went clean through the divine messenger and carried on upwards, piercing the screen of heaven. It fell, bloodstained, at the feet of *Amaterasu*. The gods were stunned. *Take-Mi-Musubi* recognized the arrow as one of his; he had given it to Ame-No-Wakahiko. With a curse he grabbed the arrow and flung it aside. The arrow fell out of heaven, and just as Ame-No-Wakahiko was congratulating himself on a good shot, it came whizzing back and landed in his heart. Ame-No-Wakahiko toppled over, dead. The old woman had been right; it was a bird of ill-omen. (See *Haya-Ji*.)

Benzaiten
Goddess of love.

Originally a Hindu goddess, she rides on a dragon and plays the *biwa*. She is one of the gods of happiness (see *Shichi-Fukujin*).

Bishamon
God of happiness and war.

Originally a Hindu deity, Bishamon carried a small pagoda and lance. It might seem paradoxical to us to have one god for both happiness and war, but Bishamon was a god who protected men against the assaults of disease and devils. He therefore had to be suitably armed and armoured. War often brings wealth and so Bishamon was regarded as one of the seven gods of happiness.

He is often shown with a flaming wheel as a sort of halo, the same design of wheel seen in Hindu iconography. It may be regarded either as the Wheel of Fate, *dharma*, or as simply a sun symbol.

Chimata-No-Kami
God of crossroads.

Originally a phallic deity, Chimata-No-Kami was a guardian of roads and footpaths. His phallic talisman was set up at crossroads, representing the creative force, which was positive. Although elbowed aside by Buddhism and imperial decrees, the cult still persists in unfrequented places. (See *Izanagi*.)

Gozu Tenno
The ox-headed Celestial King; god of plague.

Gozu Tenno was probably a foreign import. In later times he was identified with the god *Susanoo*. The Chinese had an ox-headed spirit (*Niu Y'ou*) who was probably the inspiration for Gozu Tenno.

Haya-Ji (Haya-Tsu-Muji-No-Kami)
God of the whirlwind.

Haya-Ji was responsible for transporting the god *Ame-No-Wakahiko* down from the Plain of Heaven to earth. He was a monstrous looking creature with a huge bag on his back. From this bag he let out the winds.

Hikohohodemi
A hero-god.

With his brother *Hosuseri*, Hikohohodemi was born to the goddess *Kono-Hana-Sakuya-Hime*. He was a clever huntsman and his brother was a skilled fisherman. One day they thought it fun to try out each other's equipment. Neither of them had much luck, Hikohohodemi with his brother's net and fish-hooks and Hosuseri with his brother's bow and arrows. In fact things went rather badly for Hikohohodemi and he lost his brother's best hook. Hosuseri was furious when he found out; he refused to accept back his fishing tackle until it was complete. Hikohohodemi decided to go down into the depths of the sea to look for the missing hook.

101

On the ocean bed the god was seen by a maiden who was very attracted by his manly figure. She was the daughter of the sea god *O-Wata-Tsumi*, and she took Hikohohodemi to her father's palace and presented him there. Hikohohodemi explained the reason for his trip. The sea god ordered a search to be made for the lost hook. Meanwhile Hikohohodemi was betrothed to the maiden and married her subaqueously. The hook was found in a fish's mouth and returned to the bridegroom. After a pleasant stay Hikohohodemi declared that he really ought to be getting home. The sea god gave him two magic stones, one to make the tide come in and the other to make it go out.

Hikohohodemi returned home and gave the hook back to his brother. Far from being grateful, Hosuseri continued his moans and complaints. Hikohohodemi threw the first stone into the sea; the tide rose and rose. It went on rising until the terrified Hosuseri promised to stop his harassment and honour his brother. Hikohohodemi threw the second stone into the sea and the tide receded.

The sea maiden arrived, as she had promised she would. She was pregnant. When her time came she warned her husband not to be near, and not to look into the delivery room. Hikohohodemi was overcome with curiosity and found a chink in the wall to peep through. After his wife had given birth she turned into a dragon and left for the sea, leaving the baby on dry land. A few days later her sister arrived to look after the infant. In time the child grew up and took his aunt as wife. One of their sons was Jimmu-Tenno, founder of the Imperial Family of Japan.

Hiruko
God of the morning sun and guardian of children's health.

Hiruko was reputed to have been the brother of the god *Ninigi* and grandson of *Amaterasu*, the sun goddess. He was probably a local god retained in a subservient role.

Hisa-Me
'Frowning-women'; female devils who live in the land of the dead. An aggressive and unattractive bunch who are also called *Shiko-Me*.

Hoderi

One of the triplets born to *Kono-Hana-Sakuya-Hime*, wife of the god *Ninigi*. This particular child seems to have disappeared, for he is not mentioned again. His brothers, *Hosuseri* and *Hikohohodemi*, are well known

Ho-Masubi (Kagu Zuchi)
God of fire.

Ho-Masubi's birth caused the death of his mother, the goddess *Izanami*. His father, *Izanagi*, was so distraught that he killed the baby. From the child's blood came eight gods, and from his dismembered body came eight mountain gods.

Despite being so energetically disjointed, Ho-Masubi made his home on a mountain called Atago in Kyoto province. His popularity is not unlinked to the fact that the wood and paper houses of the Japanese are so vulnerable to fire. His good graces were sought by sacrifices and placatory amulets. He was especially revered in the Imperial palace.

There are two kinds of fire. *Kiri-bi*, made by the friction of wood, and *uchi-bi*, made by striking sparks from steel and stone. This second fire is considered the purer and is used for rituals and for cooking.

Two aspects of Ho-Masubi strike one as of more than passing interest. The first is his association with mountains; fire and mountains often go together in mythology. The second is the use of the image of a boar as a protective charm. Like fire whipped by the wind, the boar is swift and destructive.

Hosuseri
Son of *Kono-Hana-Sakuya-Hime* and brother of the hero-god *Hikohohodemi* (*q.v.*).

Inari
God of rice.

Inari was a popular god and had many shrines. He was shown as a bearded old man sitting on a sack of rice. His attendants were foxes, and sometimes the animal was worshipped in his place. Foxes were the god's messengers. Later his domain was extended to include all kinds of prosperity, and he was honoured by shop-keepers and merchants. In the old days Inari was a smith-god with special responsibility for the forging of sword blades. He is also shown holding a sheaf of rice straw and a pot of rice wine.

Izanagi
A creator god.

After the original three self-made divinities there were seven generations of gods. The last of these, Izanagi, and his wife, *Izanami*, were assigned the task of solidifying the earth. Standing on the floating Bridge of Heaven, Izanagi churned the sea with his lance. The water began to thicken, rather like butter; a drop of ocean fell from the lance and solidified, making the island of Onokoro.

The two deities made their home on the island, and set up a sacred column. They began to perform the rites of sexual union; this was done by each of them walking around the column in opposite directions until they met. The goddess Izanami praised the beauty of Izanagi. This was a mistake, for the child they conceived after their meeting was a monster. They set him adrift on a raft of reeds. Then Izanami gave birth to . . . an island. This issue was also rejected. They tried to find out the reason for the strange births by consulting the other gods. They were told that as they met after walking round the column it was necessary for the male to speak first, to take the initiative. Izanagi and Izanami performed the ritual again, this time in the correct way. They then settled down to produce many gods. The last of these was the god of fire, *Ho-Masubi*, whose birth caused his mother such pain that she perished.

Izanagi could not be consoled after Izanami's death. He decided to go down to hell to seek her out. When at last he found her Izanami admitted that she had already eaten of the food of hell, and so was unable to return to earth. She said she would discuss the matter with the god of the Underworld and left to find him, warning her husband not to follow her. But of course Izanagi did. He entered the dark palace of the god of hell, carrying a flaming torch he had made from his comb. His startled wife tried to conceal herself but it was too late; Izanagi saw that her body was already decomposing. Furious and ashamed, Izanami sent the demon women, called *Hisa Me*, after him. Izanagi took to his heels with the female devils in hot pursuit. He had to use all his skill and magic to shake them off in the dark labyrinthine caverns. Then he found that the thunders and soldiers of hell were also after him. Izanagi reached the slope which leads from the land of the dead to earth; he raced up it and came to a peach tree. Plucking three peaches from it, he turned on his pursuers and pelted them with the missiles. The infernal army fled in disarray, for the peach is the sign of life and hope, the antithesis of all that is meant by hell. Izanagi then blocked the entrance of the Underworld with a vast boulder.

Stained by the impure soil of hell, Izanagi went to wash himself in the river. As he undressed, each article of clothing became a god; then his stick became the phallic god of the crossroads (*Chimata-No-Kami*). The water washed off the dirt of hell, and the dirt became harmful gods. Seeing this, Izanagi had to create a series of good gods to compensate. He also produced all the gods of the sea. Then Izanagi washed his face. From his left eye was born *Amaterasu*, the sun; from his right eye came *Tsuki-Yomi*, god of the moon. His nose gave forth *Susanoo*, guardian of the seas. The two eye-gods obediently went to their domains, the Plain of Heaven and the Kingdom of Night. Susanoo, however, immediately began to cause trouble and Izanagi was forced to chase him away. Thus were the gods created.

Izanami
Divine mother; sister and wife of the god *Izanagi*.

Izanami helped Izanagi in the creation of the Japanese islands and the many gods. After an initial failure, during which monsters were born, they produced the gods of the Wind, Trees, and Mountains, as well as several others. The final birth was that of the god of fire (*Ho-Masubi*), whose delivery caused the death of Izanami. She descended into the Underworld, where her consort followed her in an effort to bring her back. But he failed. (See *Izanagi*.)

Kami
A general name for certain divine beings including famous men, trees, mountains, rivers, winds or anything in nature that is special or unusual. The word *kami* signifies divinity as in *Ama-Tsu-Kami*, 'the gods of heaven', or in *Kuni-Tsu-Kami*, 'the gods of earth'. It is not, however, an exact translation of our word 'god'

Kami-Musubi
Goddess mother of *Sukuna-Bikona*. She resurrected the slain god *O-Kuni-Nushi* at his own mother's request.

Kami-Nari
God of rolling thunder.

One of several thunder gods. Kami-Nari was widely worshipped and his main shrine is at Kashima. His shrines contain holy swords, which are symbols of his power.

Kappa
A water demon.

Kappa was a skinny little character with a large head and a curious hairstyle reminiscent of that of a Western mediaeval monk. He lived in rivers and ponds and used magic to draw travellers and others into the water where they would drown. But if Kappa did approach you there was one sure way of avoiding a watery grave. What you had to do was to bow to him in the correct and polite fashion, bending at the waist with your head low. Being a punctilious and none-too-bright sort of fiend, Kappa would gravely return the compliment. As he bowed low the water he was hoarding to drown you in would pour out of a hole in the top of his head. So it paid to be polite, even to demons.

Kawa-No-Kami
God of *kawa* or rivers.

Important rivers had their own special deities, but all streams and rivers were under the control of Kawa-No-Kami. Occasionally flooding rivers were appeased by human sacrifice.

Kono-Hana-Sakuya-Hime
Daughter of the mountain god *O-Yama-Tsu-Mi*.

Kono-Hana-Sakuya-Hime married the god *Ninigi*. She became pregnant so speedily that Ninigi was convinced that she had been unfaithful to him. To prove him wrong she built a house without doors in which to give birth. She declared that at the moment of delivery she would set fire to the house. If the child was not Ninigi's then the flames would consume them both. She gave birth safely to twins (some say triplets), the brothers *Hosuseri* and *Hikohohodemi*. Her honour was vindicated.

Kuni-Tsu-Kami
The name given to the gods of earth to distinguish them from the gods of heaven (*Ama-Tsu-Kami*).

Nai-No-Kami
God of earthquakes.

Nai-No-Kami is a recent addition to the company of gods, his worship being instituted in the seventh century A.D. We can see in Nai-No-Kami how gods are introduced. The human mind reacts to a dynamic force of nature, in this case a series of severe earthquakes, and quite naturally wants to identify the force responsible in order to form a relationship. The desire to influence the force is a more potent motive than mere fear. Humans are above all reasonable creatures and are always ready to talk. If the force seems overwhelmingly powerful then a subservient attitude complete with rituals, sacrifices and propitiatory acts is assumed. The deity is given a name in order that he may be addressed personally, then a parentage and place among the company of gods. Fears and hopes are then solidified into ritual, and a priesthood with vested interests appears. A strong ruling caste, either of warriors as in Japan, bureaucrats as in China, or priests as in the Aztec empire, will encourage the development of gods, absorbing and regulating all new ones, lest they grow too powerful. If real divine revelation should chance along then it is either suppressed or emasculated. A multiplicity of gods, however they arose, is of great help to autocratic systems, for they absorb much of the raw and unformulated psychic energy of the people, energy that may otherwise find a political outlet. We must always remember that there is a world of difference between god and God.

Naka-Yama-Tsu-Mi

God of mountain slopes; one of the eight mountain gods produced from the dismembered body of the baby god of fire (see *Ho-Masubi*).

Ninigi

Divine grandson of the sun goddess *Amaterasu* (*q.v.*) who sent him to rule over the earth. The goddess gave Ninigi the sword Kusanagi, the mirror which had been used to tempt her out of the cave, and the celestial jewels. He married *Kono-Hana-Sakuya-Hime*, the daughter of the mountain god, and set his court up in Kyushu. (See *Susanoo* for the origin of the sword.)

O-Kuni-Nushi

God of medicine and sorcery, son of the god *Susanoo*.

O-Kuni-Nushi cured a skinless hare, who rewarded the god by giving him a princess who had been promised to his brothers, all eighty of them. The eighty brothers plotted against O-Kuni-Nushi and killed him. He was resurrected by the goddess *Kami-Masubi* and took refuge in the Underworld. Here he met and fell in love with Suseri-Hime, daughter of Susanoo and O-Kuni-Nushi's own half-sister. The couple married. Susanoo was against the marriage and sent his son to sleep in a room full of snakes; he would have been killed were it not for a magic charm given to him by his new wife. Susanoo then moved him into a room full of poisonous insects, wasps and centipedes. O-Kuni-Nushi was saved from death by another charm given him by Suseri-Hime.

Susanoo thought up another plan. He took O-Kuni-Nushi out to a plain of dry grass and shot an arrow into the middle of it. Then he sent his son to search for the arrow. When O-Kuni-Nushi was surrounded by the tinder-dry grass Susanoo set the plain alight. The god was trapped on all sides by a swiftly advancing wall of fire. O-Kuni-Nushi heard a small sound; he looked down and saw that a mouse was trying to attract his attention. The little creature beckoned the god to follow and led him to an underground shelter. O-Kuni-Nushi took refuge in the dug-out and the mouse rushed away, only to reappear soon afterwards carrying the missing arrow. The two of them hid in safety while the flames passed over them. O-Kuni-Nushi emerged unscathed and coolly returned the arrow to Susanoo.

Susanoo was impressed and began to trust his son. They went home and O-Kuni-Nushi washed Susanoo's hair for him. Susanoo settled down to sleep while his long hair dried out. Seizing the opportunity, his wife and Susanoo's finest treasures (sword, bow, quiver and harp), O-Kuni-Nushi hastened to escape. But first he took Susanoo's long hair and tied it to the rafters of the house.

Loaded with their treasures, the divine couple crept away. But as they passed a tree a trailing branch swept across the strings of the harp. The resounding chord awoke the dozing Susanoo. He leapt up energetically, and pulled the whole house down on top of himself. O-Kuni-Nushi and his wife kept on running and by the time Susanoo had disentangled himself from rafter and tiles, they were well up the slope that leads out of hell. Susanoo had to confess that he was beaten. He called up to O-Kuni-Nushi and made him promise that he would make Suseri-Hime his Number One wife. He instructed O-Kuni-Nushi to use his new weapons against the eighty troublesome brothers, so as to ensure his supremacy over them. He also told the god that he would become lord of the whole world.

O-Kuni-Nushi returned to earth and became its overlord.

Omiwa
The god worshipped by *O-Kuni-Nushi* as his protective deity.

O-Wata-Tsumi
Sea god; the most important of several Japanese sea deities. Also called Shio-Zuchi, 'old man of the tide'.

O-Wata-Tsumi was the foremost of the aquatic divinities created by *Izanagi* when he bathed in the river after his trip to hell. He was ruler of all fishes and other living inhabitants of the oceans. His assistant and messenger was a sea monster called Wani.

O-Wata-Tsumi once gave control of the tides to *Hikohohodemi* in order to ease the latter's return to a trouble-free life on earth.

As his daughter was seen in dragon shape, it is possible that O-Wata-Tsumi also used to take that form.

(See *Izanagi* and *Hikohohodemi* for a fuller version of these stories.)

O-Yama-Tsu-Mi
Mountain god.

When the baby god of fire, *Ho-Masubi*, was cut up by his father *Izanagi*, eight mountain gods were formed. Of these O-Yama-Tsu-Mi was the first and most important. He was god of all mountains; the others were responsible only for specific parts, viz., foot, slopes, steep slopes, sides, lower slopes. There were also two gods for the minerals found on mountains. There is an association between fire and high places, volcanoes being especially venerated. Fire aspires to rise and the distorted heat haze it creates is somehow linked to the dizziness experienced on mountain heights.

Sae-No-Kami
Collective name for the guardian gods of the roads. They were gods who protected men from misfortune.

Sakyamuni
Japanese name for *Buddha* (see Indian section) whose family name was Sakyas.

Sengen-Sama
Goddess of the holy mountain Fujiyama. Her shrine is at the summit and provides a vantage point for those worshipping the rising sun.

Shichi-Fukujin
The seven gods of happiness. These are *Bishamon* (war and happiness), *Benzaiten* (love), Ebisu (work and fishing), Daikoku (prosperity), Fukurokuju (health), Jurojin (long life), Hotei Osho (good luck). They are of various origins.

Shiko-Me
Female devils (see *Hisa Me*).

Shine-Tsu-Hiko
God of the wind.

Shine-Tsu-Hiko was born from the breath of *Izanagi*. With his wife Shina-To-Be he held up the earth. He also filled the empty space between heaven and earth.

Shitatera-Hime
Daughter of *O-Kuni-Nushi*. She married the god *Ame-No-Wakahiko* and they lived for eight uneventful years until the gods sent down a messenger in the shape of a pheasant (*q.v.*).

Soko-No-Kuni
'Deep land', or 'hell'. A depressing and dark place reached from the earth by a long, subterranean slope, and inhabited by grotesque creatures like the *Hisa-Me*. (See *Izanagi*.)

Suitengu
Child-god of the sea.

Suitengu is a composite god made up of the sea god *O-Wata-Tsumi*, the Hindu god *Varuna*, and the deified child-emperor, Antoku. The latter perished in the sea battle of Dannoura during the wars between the Taira clan and their enemies, the Minamoto. Suitengu protected fishermen, sailors and children suffering from illness.

Sukuna-Bikona
Son of the goddess *Kami-Musubi*.

Sukuna-Bikona arrived on the coast, drifting in a boat at the mercy of wind and wave. He helped *O-Kuni-Nushi* organize his kingdom and to build fortifications. One day Sukuna-Bikona disappeared as mysteriously as he had arrived.

Susanoo
God of thunder, rain, storms, snakes and agriculture.

As soon as he was born Susanoo began causing trouble. His father

Izanagi produced him by washing his nose after his escape from hell. Susanoo wanted to go to hell to visit his mother *Izanami*. He pestered his father so much that Izanagi chased him away. Susanoo then went to see his sister, the sun goddess *Amaterasu*. His bad behaviour caused her to flee to a cave, and he himself was driven away from the Plain of Heaven by the irate gods. As a punishment they shaved off his beard and moustache, pulled out all his fingernails, made him pay a huge fine, and then ejected him most unceremoniously.

Susanoo came down to earth where he wandered about making a noise and upsetting people. He was god of thunder, and therefore of rain and also of snakes. Snakes were linked in the popular mind with thunder. Susanoo's character was uneven. When he was good he wasn't too bad, when he was bad he was utterly impossible. His disasters and pranks may be put down to high spirits and lack of judgement; to lack of self-control rather than to malice.

Susanoo once came across two weeping people with a young girl. He discovered that the girl had had seven sisters, slain by a snake on seven successive summers. Susanoo arranged with the distraught parents that if he could save the girl's life she would become his wife. He turned the girl into a comb, which he placed in his hair. He put out many bowls of rice wine and waited. The serpent came sliding along, sniffing the savoury smell of the saki. It sipped, each of its eight heads from a different bowl. It drank all the wine. It felt happy, a little sleepy perhaps . . . . Susanoo leapt forward with his blade and sliced the snake up into many small chunks. As he was cutting up the body, he discovered a beautiful sword hidden in the tail.

Susanoo changed his wife back from a comb to her former shape and settled down with her. He sent the magic sword he had found to his sister Amaterasu, to make up for all the trouble he had caused her.

Susanoo and his wife had a son, *O-Kuni-Nushi*. But by the time O-Kuni-Nushi grew up and had adventures of his own, Susanoo was living in hell with another child of his called Suseri-Hime, who later became O-Kuni-Nushi's wife.

Take-Mi-Musubi
Companion and adviser to the sun goddess *Amaterasu*. It was Take-

Mi-Musubi who gave *Ame-No-Wakahiko* a bow and arrows to protect himself with when he went down to earth. This gift was to prove fatal to Ame-No-Wakahiko (*q.v.*).

Taki-Tsu-Hiko
Prince Cataract, god of rain. He was in the shape of a rock and prayers for rain were addressed to him.

Tsuki-Yomi
God of the moon.

Tsuki-Yomi was born from *Izanagi's* right eye. His name 'Moon-Counter' shows his connection with the calendar and with the measurement of time. His main temples are at Ise and Kadono where a mirror is kept in which the god may sometimes be seen by those practising divination. The moon disc is depicted with a hare pounding rice in a mortar. In Japanese, 'rice pounding' forms a pun with the word 'moon', and the hare seems to be a legacy from China where a rabbit is often shown in the moon.

Uke-Mochi-No-Kami (Waka-Uke-Nomi, Toyo-Uke-Bime)
Goddess of food.

Uke-Mochi-No-Kami was sent by the goddess *Amaterasu* to her brother the moon, *Tsuki-Yomi*. The goddess of food invited Tsuki-Yomi to a banquet, where she produced all the food out of her own mouth. The moon god was so disgusted that he was about to object; but he remembered his manners and waited. The goddess continued to bring more and more food up out of her mouth. Tsuki-Yomi's disgust turned to a sense of feeling insulted. But still he waited, as yet more food appeared in this novel way. Finally anger got the better of good manners, and Tsuki-Yomi leapt to his feet and killed Uke-Mochi-No-Kami.

Aditi
'The unfettered', goddess of the sky, the past and future, and also mother of the Adityas, that is to say the gods *Mitra* and *Varuna*. Reputed mother of *Agni*, the fire god. Hindu.

Agastya
Son of *Varuna* and *Urvasi*. He was an ascetic, sage and the protector of the god *Rama*. His hermitage was on Mount Kunjara. An extensive Tamil literature records his achievements, not the least of which is his supposed longevity. He is supposed to retain human form to this day. Hindu.

Agni
Hindu god of fire. Also known as Pramati ('precaution'), a word with the same meaning as the name *Prometheus*.

Agni appeared in several forms. He was described as having his face smeared with butter, with wild hair, many swift tongues and sharp golden teeth. He was also portrayed as a red man with three arms, seven legs, black eyes and black hair. He rode on a ram, flames spouted from his mouth. and from his body shone seven bright rays of light.

Agni's birth was multiple and miraculous; he was born from water in the shape of a calf, from the sky in the form of an eagle, and from dry firesticks, *aranis*, as a glutton with a flame-tongue who devoured his parents as soon as he was born. He was also said to have been discovered either by the priest Arthavan or by the *Angiris*, who were *rishis* or sons of the gods.

Agni had three characters according to the direction in which he was born facing. To the east he was the fire for offerings to the gods; to the south for offerings to departed spirits; to the west for domestic cooking and other offerings. When shown with two heads Agni personified domestic and sacrificial fire; he was always accompanied by a ram. The correct offering to Agni was *ghee*, or clarified butter.

Apart from being a god of fire, Agni had other duties to perform. As lightning, he split the clouds to produce fructifying rain. As the fire of the sun, he was a messenger of the gods. He was also a supporter of the sky, for he created columns of smoke which were said to prop it up. He was the mediator between heaven and earth, for he presided over sacrifices and the burning of the dead.

Agni despised no one, however poor, and was willing to be a guest in every home. He was invoked to obtain food, prosperity and worldly goods. His sacred attributes were the axe, the fan, the torch, and the sacrificial spoon. Regarded as beneficent by men, Agni was often feared by the gods. He was powerful enough to take over from *Varuna* the kingship of the Pitris ('fathers'). The nymph Swaha visited Agni in disguise for six nights and from this union was born the god of war, *Karttikeya*. (See *Bhrigus*.)

Angiris

Angels who presided over sacrifices. They were named after Angiris, king of the Manes or Pitris ('fathers'). They were also called *rishis*, 'sons of the gods'. Hindu.

Ardhanarisvara

A composite deity made up of one half of *Siva* and the other half of Siva's *shakti*, or female power. It was divided down the middle; its torso displayed one female breast and its high-domed head represented the lingam, or male power, of Siva. Hindu.

Asparas

Heavenly and lascivious nymphs who were companions of the *Gandharvas*, gods of the air. Originally water spirits, they were later regarded as tree nymphs, *vrikshakas*. Hindu.

Asuras

Generic name for the race of demonic wizards and Titan-like evil spirits who were the perpetual enemies of the *Devas*, or gods. Hindu.

At the beginning of things the Asuras chose the path of falsehood and lies, and as a result prospered and grew rich. They also became greedy, eating up the offerings they were supposed to sacrifice. The result of their actions was to lessen their strength. Despite this they sometimes received power from the Devas and on occasion managed to defeat them.

Tempted to help the Devas churn the Sea of Milk, the Asuras

grabbed the liquid of immortality when it emerged from the sea. Before the Asuras could drink the magic liquid, *Vishnu*, the god of love, changed himself into a beautiful woman and tripped lightly and seductively towards the demons. The Asuras gazed on the fascinating apparition with unconcealed delight. Vishnu swayed closer, the demons stared harder. Suddenly Vishnu snatched the drink of immortality and whirled away. He gave the drink to the Devas who swallowed it and became strong again. They chased away the Asuras. (For a detailed description of the churning of the Sea of Milk, see *Vishnu/Kurma*.)

Asvins (Nasatyas)
Hindu gods of healing, administering to gods and humans alike.

The Asvins were golden-coloured twins on horseback who ushered in the dawn by making a path for her through the night clouds. As gods of healing, they cured blindness, lameness and old age. They were protectors of love and champions of marriage.

The Asvins have a peculiarly knightly flavour, and are the nearest thing to our ancient ideals of chivalry. They were excluded from heaven because their birth was too humble. One day they observed the young wife of an old *rishi* bathing in a pool. They urged her to choose one of them as a husband instead, for they were young. The girl (named Sukanya) replied that she loved her husband. The Asvins then said that they would make the *rishi* Syavana youthful again so that Sukanya's choice would be among three young men. They gave Syavana eternal youth. His wife chose him to continue as her husband, and he was so delighted with his new-found youth that he convinced *Indra* to allow the chivalrous Asvins to be regarded as gods and to be given the holy drink *soma*. The Asvins are personifications of the Morning and Evening Stars. (See *Saranyu*.)

Atri
Son of *Brahma*. Atri was a renowned sage, and it was said that *soma*, the holy drink, sprang from his eye. Hindu.

Bali
A Hindu demon.

116

Bali conquered heaven and earth and reigned over them as king. He was approached by a dwarf who modestly requested but three step's length of earth to have as his own. Bali agreed. The dwarf, who was the god *Vishnu* in disguise, instantly grew to divine proportions and stepped across the whole universe in two strides. Vishnu took his third step by placing his foot on Bali's submissive neck and pushing him down into the Underworld for the duration of eternity.

Bali was later slain by the god *Indra* in battle. A flood of gems poured from his mouth instead of blood. Indra hurled a thunderbolt at the demon's body and his flesh became crystal, his bones diamonds, his blood rubies, his eyes sapphires, his marrow emeralds, and his teeth pearls.

Bhrigus

The 'shining ones', born of flames; aerial storm gods who communicated between heaven and earth. Hindu.

The Bhrigus descended from Bhrigu, a wise man. He met and fell in love with a woman, Puloma, who was betrothed to a demon. Secretly Bhrigu wooed Puloma, won her and married her. He hid her away. The aggrieved demon went to *Agni*, the god of fire, and asked where the woman was hidden. Agni told him and the demon retrieved his promised bride. Bhrigu was furious when he found out and cursed the god bitterly. Agni replied that he had only told the truth, and pointed out to the wise man that he was the mouth of the gods and that according to the terms of Bhrigu's curse he was now under a compulsion to eat up everything on the earth. Bhrigu hastily changed his curse, saying that in future everything that went into the flames of Agni would be purified.

Bhrigu was once deputed to discover which of the three gods, *Brahma, Siva* or *Vishnu*, was the most deserving of worship and honour. He decided to test the gods by being rude to them. He approached Brahma without the usual signs of respect. The god reprimanded him and then forgave him. Bhrigu sought out Siva and repeated the test. Siva erupted in a fury of anger and Bhrigu had to soothe him with flattery and abject apologies. He then sought out Vishnu. He found the god sleeping and roughly awoke him with a kick. Vishnu sat up at once, but his only concern was

117

that Bhrigu might have hurt his foot. He fussed over the wise man and even massaged his foot for him. Bhrigu realized that he had found the answer he sought.

Bhutas
Group of ghosts or goblins who haunted cemeteries. They were dangerous spirits and so were included in the ritual of the Five Great Sacrifices. They were pacified by scattering grain in the direction of the four compass points, and in the centre. Hindu.

Boddhisattvas
Buddhist gods.

They are spiritually advanced persons whose virtue entitles them to divinity. But instead of merging with the godhead, they have consciously chosen to remain in the cycle of reincarnation in order to help those souls who lag behind in spiritual achievement. Of the many myriads of such souls, the Boddhisattva Avalokiteshvara is typical. His name means 'lord of complete enlightenment', and he devotes himself to helping the suffering. He is said to have a thousand arms, so that no one who appeals for his help goes unaided. The Chinese have transformed him into a goddess, identifying him with *Kuan-Yin*, the goddess of mercy.

Brahma
Father of gods and men, creator of the universe and first god in the supreme Hindu triad: Brahma, *Vishnu, Siva.*

The Great Unknown formed a seed; from this grew an egg from which emerged Brahma. He was called Narayana, 'he who dwells in the waters', for when he was conceived nothing else existed.

Brahma is depicted as having four faces, as being dressed in white and riding on a swan or peacock, or seated on a lotus. His consort, Sarasvati, emerged from his side. He saw that she was beautiful and gazed at her wonderingly. Sarasvati was modest as well as beautiful; she stepped to one side to avoid his gaze. Immediately a second face appeared on that side of Brahma's head, so that he could continue to look on her. She stepped away again, another face grew. And again, producing a fourth face. Sarasvati rose up and yet another, the fifth face, appeared on top of Brahma's head. This last face was later destroyed by the fierce heat of the third eye of the god Siva.

Brahma, though given outward shape, name, attributes and stories, can best be regarded as the personification of an attitude. Thus his devotees worship him in many forms, from pure abstraction down to primitive animism. (See *Bhrigus*.)

Brihaspati (Bramanaspati)
Teacher and chaplain of the gods. Hindu.

Master of magical power and the priesthood, and master of created things, Brihaspati was often confused with *Agni*, the god of fire. He was the husband of the goddess *Tara* who was abducted by *Soma*. This incident caused a war among the gods. (See *Soma*.)

Buddha
The Divine Teacher; an avatar, or incarnation, of *Vishnu*. Siddharta Gautama of the Sakyas, known in Japan as *Sakyamuni*.

Buddha, The Enlightened One, was born miraculously into the royal family of the Sakyas. He lived an enclosed and indulged life in a guarded palace whose rich gardens were surrounded by strong walls. His father saw to it that he lived a life of unalloyed pleasure, for he did not want to lose his son. After many years of this life, Siddharta expressed a desire to see the outside world; his father arranged for him to visit a nearby town, which had been cleaned, repaired and adorned so that his eyes would never fall on anything which might distress him. But by chance Siddharta came upon an old man. The shock was great for he had never seen advanced age before; he learnt with horror that all living things grow wrinkled and impotent before they die. Siddharta had never heard of death, nor of pain, sorrow, famine or disease. After this incident his father doubled the number of palace guards. He arranged a marriage in order to take his son's mind off what he had seen. Siddharta became a father.

One night, unable to sleep, Siddharta wandered through the harem. He saw the dancing girls, sleeping off their excesses. Some snored, some dribbled down their chins, some lay openmouthed, some talked in their sleep or ground their teeth and muttered drunkenly. The contrast of what he saw now to the

119

memory of their disciplined, alluring dance movements struck the young prince with the force of a revelation. It was like looking into a pit of corpses. Siddharta made up his mind to leave the palace and seek the real world. To aid him, the gods sent the guards into a deep sleep. Siddharta and his groom, Chandaka, left the palace, the gods lifting the hooves of his favourite horse, Kantaka, so that they would make no clatter on the marble terraces.

Out in the real world Siddharta cut off his long scented hair, changed his rich robes for the working clothes of a passing huntsman, dismissed his groom and horse, and sought out a group of holy men. In the monastery, he changed his name to Gautama.

Gautama found after a while that the monks were not able to satisfy his urgent spiritual needs, so he became a wandering beggar. He began to practise terrible self-torture, hoping to gain merit thereby. Before long he discovered that asceticism was as much of a trap as worldliness. He turned from his privations by accepting food from a young woman. His followers and companions left him in disgust. Gautama then travelled to Bodi-Gaya where he sat under a tree in meditation. The meditation grew into a profound experience. The demon Mara tried to distract Gautama by sending to him his seductive daughters; but they had no effect on the young prince. Mara then sent squads of disgusting and deformed spirits who hurled themselves on the seated figure. But they failed to move him or to interrupt his meditations. Finally Mara tried his ultimate weapon, a fiery disc capable of splitting mountains; but the sharp missile turned into a garland of flowers and hovered reverently over Gautama's head like a halo. Mara fled, not a little annoyed. The prince remained steadfast and the next morning he achieved blissful enlightenment. He saw clear to the root-causes of suffering, and knew how it was to be avoided; namely by reaching a state of desirelessness. In the weeks of meditation which followed Gautama realized that he could either enter Nirvana or stay on earth to help his fellow men, renouncing for a time his absorbtion into ecstatic awareness. Mara wanted him to leave earth but *Brahma* implored him to stay.

Buddha decided to remain and began preaching his doctrines of mercy, non-violence, destruction of passions and desirelessness.

The religion founded by the Buddha spread over Asia, finding a more permanent home in Sri Lanka, Indonesia, Burma, China, Japan and south east Asia than it did in his home country, India. Buddha is also regarded by Hindus as a Hindu deity.

Daksha
One of the *Prajapatis*, or lords of creation. Hindu.

Daksha had many daughters, of whom twenty-seven were lunar goddesses married to *Soma*, god of the moon. Daksha thought that Soma was favouring one of his daughters, Rohini, more than her sisters. To punish Soma he infected him with consumption. His other daughters objected strongly to losing their husband so Daksha made the illness periodic and not permanent. This accounts for the weakening of the moon's powers every month.

Another of Daksha's daughters, the beautiful *Sati*, fell in love with the god *Siva*. Daksha was annoyed for he didn't like Siva. He arranged a betrothal ceremony during which his daughter would choose a husband from among the assembled suitors. He was careful not to invite Siva. At the ceremony Sati looked about her and realized what her father had done. She took the garland which was to be placed about the chosen bridegroom's neck, and tossed it into the air. Miraculously Siva materialized, with the garland about his neck; the sign that he had been chosen by Sati. Daksha was outmanoeuvred for the time being, but he loathed Siva for his part in rituals of destruction and later found an excuse to go to war against him.

Devas
Hindu gods of the celestial powers.

Their name derives from *dyaus*, 'the bright sky', from which they were supposed to have come. They were the opposite of the *Asuras*, the demons.

Durga
'The inaccessible', an aspect of *Jaganmatri*, the Divine Mother who was wife of the god *Siva*. Hindu.

Durga forms a triad with the goddesses *Uma* and *Parvati*. This triad may be compared with the Celtic *Morrigan*. Sometimes aspects of the goddess *Kali* (the basic form of all three members of the triad) intrude into the individual aspects, as in the case of Durga Pratyangira, where Durga is depicted with vampire-like teeth and a flame-decked hat. In this guise she has four arms which carry the trident (weapon of Siva), sword, drum and bowl of blood. These four objects bear a startling resemblance to the four symbols of the Tarot cards. In the Lesser Arcana of the cards we find the wand, sword, cup and dish, which are the originals of the clubs, spades (*spatha*, sword), hearts and diamonds of modern card packs.

Durga is often shown mounted on a lion, for the story is told of a great battle in which she fought. The gods were once threatened by a savage demon called Mahesasura. Durga rode against the demon on her lion, with each of her ten arms (the number varies from story to story) wielding a weapon of the gods. The demon changed itself into a bull, then in mid-battle into an elephant, and finally into a monster with a thousand arms. As the battle raged, Durga's face remained serene and untroubled. In the end, she killed the demon.

Durga is a very popular goddess in Bengal, providing a national focus for a country that is both ancient and new. Her *puja* or sacred festival takes place in the autumn and provides the chief festival of the Bengali year.

Gandharvas
Hindu gods of the air, the rain-clouds and the rain.

The Gandharvas were described as shaggy, semi-animal creatures smelling of damp earth. Other descriptions say they were men with birds' wings and birds' legs, or men of pale and effeminate beauty. The Gandharvas were skilful horsemen and musicians, and served the *Devas* as squires. They were also connected with marriage and birth, for it was said that they were really souls trying to be born onto earth. (See *Asparas*.)

Ganesa (Ganesh, Ganapati, Gajana-'elephant-face')
Elephant-headed Hindu god of wisdom, literature and worldly success. Ganesa is thought to derive from an animistic deity,

possibly a Dravidian (aboriginal) sun god.

He is a propitious god, promising success, prosperity and peace and is invoked before any sort of enterprise. His pot-belly symbolizes a pitcher full of prosperity, a sort of abdominal cornucopia.

Ganesa is said to have been the son of *Parvati* and *Siva*. His task in life was to guard his mother and he took his job seriously enough to refuse admittance to Siva himself whilst his mother was taking a bath. Siva angrily struck off his son's head, and then relented, as fathers do. He promised Ganesa that he should have the head of the first creature who happened along. An elephant, the wisest of animals, appeared and became the involuntary donor in the first successful head transplant in history.

Ganesa was a glutton. One evening, having stuffed himself to capacity, he decided to take a post-prandial ride on his favoured mount, a rat. Along the moonlit road they chanced upon a large snake and the startled rat bolted, throwing the gross Ganesa. Ganesa fell heavily; he hit the ground so hard that his stomach burst open. Gathering up the remains of his self-esteem, his ample guts and the snake, Ganesa wittily used the reptile as a belt and tied himself up together again. Howls of derision shattered the peaceful scene; it was the moon who had witnessed the whole incident with great relish. Ganesa lost his temper and angrily looked about for something to throw at his tormentor. Finding nothing suitable, he ripped off one of his own tusks and hurled it at the moon. He added a vindictive curse that every so often the moon would lose its power of giving light.

Another explanation of his missing tusk is that he plucked it out in his enthusiasm to write down the Mahabharata, the Hindu religious epic. He was after all the Hindu god of literature. Would that all in the literary world were as kind, gentle and well-meaning as Ganesa.

Ganga
Goddess of purification of the river Ganges; her name means 'swift-goer'. Hindu.

Ganga was identified with *Parvati* and was depicted either as a crowned mermaid whose forehead was marked with ashes, or as a white queen enthroned with lotus and lute. Devotees who look on the Ganges, and touch and drink its waters, are cleansed from sin; those who ritually bathe in its stream are guaranteed acceptance into heaven.

Hanuman
King of the monkeys. Hindu.

Hanuman was famous as a helper of the god *Rama* and organized the building of a bridge from India to Ceylon (Sri Lanka). While riding along in the sun one day, Hanuman's shadow fell on the sea. It was seized by a sea monster who used it to drag Hanuman down into the waves. Hanuman, in an attempt to escape, increased his monkey shape to enormous proportions. The sea monster immediately did the same. Hanuman thereupon reduced himself to a small size and dived into the monster's body. While the monster hesitated in surprise, Hanuman cunningly slipped out of its ear and made his escape.

Much the same sort of thing happened again to Hanuman. This time it was the mother of Rahu (a sun-munching demon) who caught the monkey-king by his shadow. Hanuman made himself tiny and entered the demoness's body. Then he swelled himself up violently, bursting the demoness apart.

Hari Hara
A composite deity who represented an attempt to join together the gods *Vishnu* and *Siva*, love and terror. His left side was Vishnu and his right side Siva. Each side had the attributes appropriate to its god: the hair-knot, trident and tigerskin of Siva, and the tiara, disc and robe of Vishnu. Hindu.

Indra
Hindu god of war and fertility.

A powerful Brahmin once had a son who was a model of virtue. This son had three heads, one for studying, one for taking in food, and one for keeping a lookout. Indra grew jealous of the boy and formed a passionate hatred of him. The boy was studious, peaceful and pure. He was so holy that the whole of creation admired him and waited on him. Indra, god of war, was ignored.

He selected the most seductive girls and sent them to tempt the holy youth. Their obvious charms and skilful words were doomed, for the boy remained unmoved, undistracted from his studies and holy contemplation. Indra was deeply annoyed and, abandoning any further attempts at subtlety, blasted the boy with a thunderbolt. He cut off the boy's three heads and flights of doves emerged from the sacred corpse.

The boy's father conjured up a mighty demon named Vritra and sent him against Indra. Vritra was massive, his head reached the sky; he fought Indra, overcame him and swallowed him. The other gods came to Indra's rescue and managed to make Vritra open his mouth long enough for the god of war to escape. The god *Vishnu* proposed a truce. Vritra accepted on the following agreed terms: Indra promised never to attack Vritra with any weapon of stone, wood or iron, or any weapon wet or dry, and never to attack him by day or night. Indra waited impotently for revenge. He met Vritra at dusk on the sea shore, and realized that it was neither day nor night. Desperately he looked about for a weapon not covered by the terms of the truce, when suddenly a column of foam arose from the sea. Indra saw that the foam was neither totally wet nor totally dry, so he seized it and hurled it at the demon. Vritra fell dead, for the foam had contained the irresistible power of the god Vishnu who had created the column to help Indra.

That story indicates many of the characteristics of the god Indra. He was warlike, intemperate, selfish, full of aristocratic pride unalloyed by any idea of fairness or justice. And he was strong. Indra is the prototype of the Aryan race which invaded and subjugated India. His cognomen Parjanya may be compared to that of the Slavonic god *Pyerun*, and he is also called Svargapati, 'father of the shining place' (heaven), Meghavahana, 'cloud-rider' and Vajri, 'thunderer'. Indra is an embodiment of aggressive action, the god of the warrior aristocracy; he controlled the thunderbolts, rode in the sky either in his chariot or on the elephant Airavata (a product of the churning of the Sea of Milk), and was served by the *rhibus*, genii who are skilled at handling horses. His celestial abode on Mount Meru was full of dancers and musicians. Indra was capable of reviving those slain in battle, and with his arrows and thunderbolts he could tear open the clouds to make rain. Some claim that he was the twin of *Agni*, the god of fire. His wife is sometimes Indrani and sometimes Urvara, the fertile land.

Indra was once weakened by a curse put on him by the *rishi*, Durvasas. In order to obtain the drink of immortality and so regain his strength, he organized the famous churning of the Sea of Milk (see *Vishnu/Kurma*). But Indra was not omnipotent, and time and again he was saved by the intervention of Vishnu and others. (See *Bali* and *Surya*.)

Jaganmatrı
'World-mother', another name for *Durga*. Hindu.

Jalandhara
An *Asura* or demon. Hindu.

Jalandhara was a miraculous child, created at the request of *Siva* by the union of the goddess *Ganga* and the sea. In his infancy he flew on the winds, tamed lions and performed many similar prodigies. When he grew up he was given a kingdom and a wife named Vrinda.

Jalandhara was part of a massive scheme of deception and double-dealing arranged by Siva. The god *Indra* had taken advantage of an unguarded moment of Siva's to rob him of a great quantity of divine power. Now, as Siva had intended, Jalandhara grew strong and proud and had the hardihood to challenge the gods. He overthrew them in a great battle in which he came near to slaying *Vishnu*, and beat the gods out of heaven.

The defeated gods, ragged and scarred from the fray, sought the help of Siva, unaware of his plotting. Siva advised the gods to put all their talents and power into one weapon. They collected together all their fiery hatred and anger and Siva added to them his flames of wrath. It is not known if Siva's conscience had been at work or if he had suddenly realized the seriousness of the trouble in which the gods found themselves, but from now on he was on their side against the victorious demon. The weapon forged by the combined power of the gods was so blindingly bright that Siva was obliged to hide it from sight under his arm.

Meanwhile, back in heaven, an amorous Jalandhara was laying

heavy siege to the honour of the gorgeous *Parvati*, wife of Siva. While he was so engaged Vishnu took the opportunity of assuming the demon's outward shape. Thus disguised he approached Vrinda, who, thinking it was her husband Jalandhara, did not deny him his desires. Vishnu performed his 'husbandly' role with panache. When Vrinda discovered the truth of her seduction she took it to heart; she cursed Vishnu and expired of grief.

When Jalandhara heard of the death of his wife he hurried home to prepare his revenge. A vast and bloody battle was the result. At its climax Siva, who had some cause to hate the demon, considering the attempted seduction of his wife, threw the fiery disc containing the combined powers of the gods and sliced off Jalandhara's head. The resourceful demon sprouted another one. Siva clipped it off in the same fashion, and in the same fashion Jalandhara replaced it. Siva called on the goddesses to help. They reached the battlefield in the guise of ogresses, and drank up Jalandhara's spilt blood until he was weakened enough to be utterly defeated. The gods were now able to regain possession of their rightful kingdom, the heavens.

Kali (Kali Ma)
The 'black mother'. Hindu goddess of nature; ogress wife of the god *Siva*.

Kali is a particularly grisly creature: her skeletal body is bedecked with skulls and serpents, her earrings are made of corpses and her only clothing, a girdle, is composed of severed hands. Kali's face is stern and blood-smeared, her eyes red, her tongue protruding.

Kali once fought the demon *Raktavija*. Every time the demon was wounded and a drop of blood fell to the earth, there sprang up in its place a thousand giants. The only way in which Kali could overcome the demon was to drink each drop of blood as it fell, until his veins were drained. Drunk with battle rage, Kali threw herself into an ecstatic dance, making the earth quake. Her husband Siva asked her to stop but in her blind madness Kali cast him down and trampled on him, from which it is said that the world of nature is rooted in the world of spirit.

Despite her horrific appearance Kali is widely venerated; there seems to be something basically attractive about her. Men who have claimed to have seen her in visions describe her as being placid and delightful, motherly and fine. This is quite the reverse of the public image of the killer goddess.

It was Kali (sometimes called Bhowani) who inspired the cult of *thagna* or, more familiarly, *thugee*. The members of this murderous and secret cult, Thugs, made it their sacred duty to waylay innocent travellers and strangle them with knotted cloths. The word *thagna* means 'to deceive', and the cultists lived openly in the community as respected and orderly citizens. They were not a band of desperate and hunted outlaws, but prominent and well-liked men who lived double lives. The secret part of their life consisted of initiation into the cult, bloodless killings to prove that they were prepared to do anything for their goddess, and the search for enlightenment through ritual, self-tested by many different methods leading to complete self-control.

There can be no doubt that what began as a serious religious attitude was made into a method of personal gain by the unscrupulous. The cult was abnormally active during early Victorian days in India, although the British did their best to suppress the murderous side of it. Priests, holy men, women (for Kali was a goddess) and certain kinds of merchants were exempt from being chosen as victims by the Thugs.

Kali stands for energy, both creative and destructive. Her cult is linked with Tantric activities, which aim at enabling men to rise above their sexual nature by gaining full control over themselves. In her positive aspect she is named *Durga*, or Kumari, or *Parvati*. The city of Calcutta is named after her.

Karttikeya
Hindu god of war.

Karttikeya was created by the god *Siva* who once looked into a lake with his fiery third eye. Six children emerged from the water and were looked after by *Parvati*, the benign aspect of Siva's wife. Parvati was a very loving mother; she embraced the six children so energetically that by mistake she squeezed them all into one body. But the six heads remained separate.

Karttikeya is said to have been derived from an ancient god of war named Muruhan; he is also called Subramanya and Skanda.

This last name is a rendering of the Greek Alexander (the Great) and probably comes from the impact made on the Indian mind by the military successes of that fateful genius. (See *Agni*.)

Krishna

The most famous avatar, or incarnation, of the Hindu god *Vishnu*. He is important enough to be considered a god in his own right.

Born into a royal family in North India, Krishna was hidden away as soon as he was delivered. An uncle of Krishna's had been given a warning that one of his sister's children would assassinate him, so the uncle had made it his business to murder all his nephews and nieces as soon as they appeared. Krishna was brought up among cowherds. In common with all miraculous children he performed the usual feats of amazing strength, killing snakes and demons, uprooting trees, overturning ox-carts and other merry pranks.

Krishna had an infectious sense of humour; he persuaded the cowherds to worship a mountain instead of the god *Indra*. The irate god responded with torrential rain so Krishna held up the mountain on a single finger, using it as an umbrella against the downpour. Krishna played pranks; he stole the clothes of a group of bathing maidens and spied on them as they came out of the water. The sound of his flute drew sighs and eager glances from women of all ages, for Krishna was the epitome of erotic delight. Women would eagerly seek him out in field and forest, town or riverside. When dancing with groups of girls Krishna would multiply himself so that each girl would imagine that she alone was dancing with Hari Krishna, 'Krishna, stealer of hearts'.

Krishna is always depicted as dark-skinned and his name indicates 'black' or 'dark'. It is suggested by some that he is a residual memory of a much earlier god of the darker-skinned original inhabitants of India.

Krishna, apart from being a god of erotic delight, was skilled in warfare. He helped the five sons of Pandu, the Pandavas, in their war against the Kurus, their hundred cousins. Krishna acted as charioteer to a Prince Arjuna; his dialogue with him forms the 'Song of the Blessed One', the Bhagavad Gita. Arjuna had doubts about killing people; Krishna replied that it was only bodies that were killed, souls are eternal and cannot be destroyed.

Krishna met his own death by accident. Seated in meditation in the forest with his heel exposed, a hunter's wayward arrow struck him on the ankle. That ankle was the sole vulnerable spot on his body. (See *Lakshmi*.)

Kuvera or Kubera
Hindu god of wealth; alias Dhanapati, 'lord of riches'.

Kuvera was originally an earth god; since jewels and gold are found in the earth he became linked with the idea of wealth. A half-brother of *Ravana* and friend of *Siva*, Kuvera was a fat dwarf with three legs, eight teeth and one eye. He was carried about on the back of a man and lived in a palace on Mount Kailasa. Like the god Siva, he was associated with the creative force of sexuality.

Lakshmi
Hindu goddess of love and beauty.

Lakshmi was born from the churning of the Sea of Milk, one of the fourteen precious things which that event produced. She was the wife of *Vishnu* and although very popular, for she brought good fortune and prosperity, she had no separate cult of her own. Lakshmi always appeared perfumed, beautifully dressed and adorned. Also known as Sri, she was reincarnated as *Sita* and as Rukmini, consort of *Krishna*. (For the Sea of Milk story see *Vishnu/Kurma*; see also *Uma*.)

Manasa-Devi
Serpent goddess popular in Bengal. She was the sister of the great serpent who upheld the sleeping *Vishnu* on the primal waters. Hindu.

Maruts
Hindu storm and air gods.

A warlike pair of divine brothers who drove the clouds about, shook mountains with their energetic noise and often smashed down forest trees. They were active and aggressive and are often associated with the Rudras (see *Rudra*).

Mitra

This Vedic solar deity is far more indistinct and distant a personality than his Persian and Roman counterpart, *Mithras*. God of oaths and contracts, he formed a pair with the god *Varuna*. Known as the Adityas, or sons of *Aditi*, they used magical powers to maintain universal order; an order which they did not create. They are guardians and witnesses and are always present, for Mitra is the sun and Varuna is the moon. Neither god is allotted human shape. Hindu.

Nagas

An evil race of snakes who live in an underworld kingdom called Patala. Hindu

In southern India several of the Nagas are regarded as gods and accordingly worshipped. One of their kings is named Takshaka and rules over a kingdom which is adorned with precious stones. The Nagas are seen by many royal families as their ancestors. Statues of snake-gods have uncleared land around them, the idea being that if you give them enough space of their own they won't intrude on yours. Though dangerous and evil, there are many instances of snakes being helpful to the gods. *Vishnu* used one to sleep on and to perform the function of a rope for the churning of the Sea of Milk, and Gautama *Buddha* was sheltered from a storm whilst meditating by the hood of the great cobra, Musilinda.

Parvati

Hindu mother goddess, daughter of the Himalaya mountains, wife of *Siva*.

One day while seated naked on Siva's lap, Parvati was interrupted in her pleasure by some visiting *rishis*, holy men. The goddess was very embarrassed and Siva declared that if anyone disturbed them in future, he would turn the intruders into women. This pleased the bashful Parvati and caused an abrupt halt to the sniggering of the rishis.

Parvati was also known as *Uma* and *Durga*. (See *Jalandhara* and *Karttikeya*.)

Pisakas
Evil Hindu deities who are especially dangerous to the dead.

Prajapati
Hindu lord of creation.

Originally an abstraction allied to the smith god *Visvakarma* and signifying creative ability. As such he was a characteristic of both *Savitri* and *Soma*. He is a father figure; the gods and demons are his children. Some consider him to be *the* supreme being, others think of him as one among many.

Prisni
Hindu goddess of the earth and darkness, mother of the *Maruts*.

Her name means 'speckled' and hints at her connection with the image of the dappled cow, symbol of abundance and giver of life-enhancing milk.

Puchan
Hindu god of meeting.

Puchan was responsible for marriages, journeys, roads and the feeding of cattle. He was a psychopomp, conducting souls to the other world. He protected travellers from bandits and wild beasts, and protected men from being exploited by other men. He was a good guide god, leading his adherents towards rich pastures and wealth. He carried a golden lance, a symbol of activity.

Purusha
A mystic dwarf god; the 'Primordial Person' or 'Cosmic Man'.

Purusha has no eyes but sees, no feet but moves, no ears but hears. He knows everything but no one knows anything much about him. No bigger than a thumb, he still manages to encompass the whole earth. Hindu.

Rakshasas
Hindu evil spirits.

These magical half-divine creatures indulged in the most harmful of activities and encouraged both men and gods to do likewise. Their curriculum included lust, gluttony, deception, violence, and everything else along those lines. They used their magic negatively; they were shape-shifters and possessed extraordinary powers of levitation and locomotion. Yet they were under the heel of fate and had no choice in the matter. It was their destiny to be horrible to gods and men. As a sort of recompense for this ineluctable sentence the Rakshasas lived in an exquisite city specially built for them by the god of craftsmen, *Visvakarma*. (See *Ravana*.)

Raktavija

A general of the demon army; a fearsome giant of Titanic aspect. Raktavija was defeated only when the horrible *Kali* disabled him by drinking his blood. Hindu.

Rama

A Hindu hero-god; an avatar, or incarnation, of *Vishnu*.

Born into a royal family, Rama had to leave because of the plotting of his step-mother. His wife *Sita* went with him despite the dangers of jungle and wilderness. But *Ravana*, the demon king of the *Rakshasas*, tricked Rama away in pursuit of a phantom deer, and abducted Sita. She was held captive in Sri Lanka until her prison was discovered by a helpful eagle. His ally *Hanuman*, king of the monkeys, checked that she was still alive, then Rama gathered together an army and set out to rescue her. He tried to convince the ocean to divide and allow his army to cross over it, but it refused. Rama was helped by Nala, son of the smith god, *Visvakarma*, who instructed Hanuman's monkeys on how to build a bridge. They worked so hard and well that the bridge was erected in five days.

Rama's forces crossed to Sri Lanka and joined battle with the demons. Rama and Ravana came together like two lions. Rama took aim with his arrows and shot off Ravana's heads (he had ten), but they grew again. Then Rama selected a magic arrow made by *Agastya*; he shot it at the demon king. The arrow pierced Ravana's chest and passed through his body, returning to Rama as obediently as any well-trained dog.

Having slain Ravana, Rama would not welcome back his wife until her purity had been publicly demonstrated. He did not want there to be any rumours that she had been abused by the monster. The despairing Sita built a funeral pyre and climbed alive into the flames; the flames refused to hurt her and, taking the shape of a divine being, raised her aloft. After such a dramatic confirmation of his wife's purity Rama was satisfied and took her back.

Ravana
A fallen angel; the demon king of the *Rakshasas*. Hindu.

Having disgraced himself in heaven, Ravana was given the choice of returning to earth three times as *Vishnu's* enemy or seven times as his friend. On reflection he realized that Vishnu was very good at despatching his foes speedily so he chose the first alternative, reasoning that as the god's enemy he would spend less time on earth than as his friend. (He obviously regarded living on earth as a punishment.) He was therefore incarnated as the demon Hiranyakashipu. Vishnu incarnated himself as the lion-man and speedily gave Hiranyakashipu his quietus. The fallen angel then returned as Ravana and abducted *Sita*, faithful wife of *Rama*, another incarnation of Vishnu. When Rama caught up with him Ravana admitted that he had abducted Sita in order to get himself killed, which was not very flattering to Sita. (Another version of this story appears under *Rama*.)

Ravana's third expiatory incarnation was as a prince named Sisupala. The boy was born with four arms and three eyes. On the point of rejecting him, his parents were stopped by a mysterious voice which proclaimed that the child was favoured, and that his destined slayer was already alive. They would discover the future killer's identity for if Sisupala sat on his knee the extra limbs and eye would disappear. Soon Vishnu/*Krishna* came visiting. When the baby sat on Krishna's knee his third eye closed for ever and his surplus arms fell off. Sisupala's mother made Krishna promise that if ever her son offended him, he would forgive him.

Many years later at a public ceremony Sisupala brought the proceedings to a halt over a disputed point of precedence. There

134

was an angry argument and Sisupala insulted and threatened the worthy old men and honoured guests. Sisupala was told of the prediction concerning himself and Krishna, but that only angered him the more. He redoubled his insults and threats until they were past forgiving. At last Krishna's divine weapon, the magic disc, rose into the air and split the raging Sisupala from helmet to sandals. Thus perished the third and final incarnation of Ravana. (See *Vishnu/Narasimha.*)

Rhibus
Hindu craft gods, equestrian and solar deities.

The Rhibus were sons of Sudhanvan, 'the good archer'. Their function was to look after the harness and weapons of the *Devas*, the gods, and make chariots for them. They were squires of the god *Indra*. The Rhibus are typically Aryan, involved with horses and warfare and the whole aristocratic warrior traditions of the invaders from the north.

Rudra
Ancient Vedic god of the dead and prince of demons; the original of *Siva*. Hindu.

Rudra fed on the corpses of men slain in battle. He was a skilled archer, his arrows bringing disease and death to men and animals alike. Because he had the power to infect he also had the power to heal, and so was god of healing herbs and Pasupati, lord of animals.

With *Prisni*, goddess of darkness, he fathered the Rudras, *genii* of the storm winds who are also known as the *Maruts*. His consort was Rodasi and she accompanied him in his chariot. Rudra is described as having a red face and a blue neck. The sacred Hindu writings The Upanishads make mention of him having 'eyes on all sides, faces on all sides, arms on all sides, feet on all sides'. It was also claimed that Rudra dwelt in the hearts of men and was no bigger than a thumb. His devotees believed that he was the supreme god and creator of all things.

To gain the favour of Rudra the correct sacrifice was a bull, which had to be killed outside the village boundaries, on waste land belonging to no one; for Rudra was dangerous. Most gods are worshipped to encourage them to approach mankind; Rudra was worshipped in order to keep him away. His cult was overgrown by that of Siva.

Saranyu
Hindu goddess of clouds. Mother of the kindly Nasatyas or *Asvins*.

Sati
The good wife. The focus of all the many nameless mother goddesses which abound throughout India. Hindu.

Sati is of the greatest antiquity. Also known as Ambika, 'the source of life', she is shown as a calm-faced woman dressed in girdle and necklace with a child on her knee. Later she was identified with the daughter of *Daksha* who was one of the *Prajapatis* (lords of creation). In common with other mother goddesses in other parts of the world, Sati was relegated to a secondary place. She was a devoted and loving consort of *Siva*.

Savitri (Savitar)
A king of heaven and god of active power. Hindu.

Savitri is the principle of movement which causes all things to move and work. He makes the sun shine, the winds blow, the tides ebb and flow, the plants grow. Savitri has golden eyes, golden tongue and golden hands. He rides in a chariot of gold pulled by white horses. He blesses all things and gives them freedom to express themselves after their own fashion.

Sita
'The Furrow', famous as the faithful wife of *Rama*. Hindu.

Sita was abducted by the demon king *Ravana* and taken to Sri Lanka until rescued by Rama and the armies of *Hanuman* the monkey-king. To prove her purity she walked into flames, which failed to burn her, thus confirming her claim. (See *Lakshmi*.)

Siva (Shiva)
God of the cosmic dance; member of the supreme Hindu triad, along with *Brahma* and *Vishnu*.

Siva is a complex god with many conflicting attributes and names. He is Lingodbhava, the phallic deity; *Rudra*, lord of beasts; Pashupa, protector of cattle; Bhutapati, father of demons; Tryambaka, accompanied by three mother goddesses; Digambara, 'clothed in space' or 'sky-clad'; Nataraja, king of the dance. Siva indicates benevolence, but the name was propitiatory for he was dangerous, destructive and lethal. Round him collected all the negative deities of the Dravidians, the original inhabitants of southern India. Siva is not a *bhagavat* ('blessed one'), but an *isvara* ('a master'). He is the leader of all those who have no place in society: outcasts, vampires, demons, ascetics. Although destructive he is also merciful; although a phallic god he is also an ascetic. Siva combines contrasting characteristics and so points the way to an underlying principle of unification.

Siva wears a tiger skin and a snake collar; his hair is tied in the knot of the ascetic and adorned with the crescent moon and trident. He is shown with his third eye open, or this is indicated by three lines on his forehead; he has a variable number of arms, usually four. Siva rides on the bull Nandi, and so holy is he that even his mount has become a god.

As Nataraja (dance-king), Siva fills the whole cosmos with his joyful dance called *tandava*. He dances and dances until the cosmos is brought to the point of annihilation; it has to be destroyed in order to be reintegrated into the absolute. Siva's intoxicating and revelatory dance was often the cause of conversion of heretics and enemies. It is finally creative, for it expresses the otherwise inexpressible.

Siva has always had a wide and popular following and many stories are attached to him. He swallowed the poison produced by the churning of the Sea of Milk, thus saving the world (see Vishnu). In memory of this he is often depicted with a blue throat. He took a leading role in the various battles of the gods.

When the goddess *Ganga* descended to earth in the shape of the holy river Ganges, it was Siva who absorbed the otherwise destructive shock of the falling water by receiving its force on his head. For seven years the mighty Ganga wandered about in Siva's hair, seeking an outlet. Siva finally allowed it to flow onto the earth, but first he divided the great stream into seven channels to lessen its impact.

Siva, locked in a trance, is often unapproachable, and so his active force, *shakti*, is personified in the goddesses, *Parvati, Uma, Durga* or *Kali*. As Uma, Parvati ('she of the mountains') was responsible for opening Siva's third eye. Their physical union was a symbol of spiritual wholeness and forms the basic approach of the Tantric cult, which utilizes controlled sexuality to achieve ecstatic insight. (See *Ardhanarisvara, Daksha* and *Hari Hara*.)

Soma
Hindu moon god.

Probably the strangest of Vedic gods, Soma (Persian: *Haoma*) was originally an hallucinogenic drink made from *ephedra vulgaris*. As well as an actual drink it was also the symbolic nectar, an ambrosia which fortified the gods, giving them immortality and power. Soma appears in different forms, as a plant, a giant, a poet, a human embryo, a bird, a bull and, more importantly, the moon. He was born from the churning of the Sea of Milk (see *Vishnu/Kurma*) and because of a curse put on him by *Daksha* he wanes, but always recovers, regaining his brightness and strength.

Soma was not without faults. Proud of his strength he carried off *Tara*, wife of *Brihaspati*, chaplain of the gods. He refused to return her and a war broke out. Soma was helped by the demons, the *Asuras*. Finally *Brahma* intervened and forced Soma to release Tara. When she returned home it was to find more trouble. Brihispati took one look at her shape and turned her out, declaring that he would have nothing to do with her until her child was born. No sooner had he spoken these words than the child was instantly and miraculously delivered. The baby boy was so beautiful that both Soma and Brihaspati claimed paternity. Tara had to admit that the child had been fathered by Soma, who delightedly embraced the infant and took him off. The child was later to be the founder of a dynasty of lunar spirits. His name was Buddha, not to be confused with the later and more famous Gautama.

Surya
Hindu sun god.

Surya was of a dark red colouring with three eyes and four arms.

He was married to Sanjna, daughter of the divine smith *Visvakarma*. His wife found his presence too dazzling. Exhausted by his brightness she slipped away, leaving the goddess of shade, Shaya, to take her place. Curious to relate, Surya did not notice the difference for a number of years. Eventually he found out and learnt the reason for Sanjna's departure. So that she would be able to bear his glittering appearance he agreed to let her father, Visvakarma, shave off one eighth of his substance. From these shavings of the sun the divine artificer made a variety of useful things – a disc for *Vishnu*, a trident for *Siva*, a lance for *Karttikeya*, and various weapons for *Kuvera*, god of wealth.

With *Indra* (weather) and *Agni* (fire), Surya (sun) forms a Vedic triad of gods. His chariot was pulled by seven horses, which made up for the fact that it only had one wheel. Devotees of Surya often worship him whilst bathing in sacred pools or holy rivers.

Tara
Goddess wife of *Brihaspati*, chaplain of the gods. Her name means 'star'. Hindu.

Tara was abducted by *Soma*, the moon-god. A war was fought for her recovery, and after her return she gave birth to Soma's child. Tara was regarded by the Tantric sect as the aboriginal Great Goddess, the oriental equivalent of the Mother-Goddess of the Middle East. The Tantric sect specialized in the control of human sexuality to achieve spiritual enlightenment. The name Tara is used as an epithet for most Hindu goddesses.

Tvashtar (Tvashtri)
As Savitar Visvarupa he is the moulder of all forms. He was an aspect of the same power seen in *Prajapati*, *Puchan* and *Savitri*. He is the principle which gives life to all things. He created the thunderbolts of *Vishnu* and the moon which was the cup containing *Soma*. He was the grandfather of *Yama*. Hindu.

Uma
Hindu corn goddess and mother goddess. Also known as *Parvati* and *Durga*, among other names.

Uma is called Uma Haimavati, 'daughter of the Himalaya

mountains'. It was said that when it rained, vegetables and corn emerged from her body. All over India there were and still are many local earth goddesses; they are all basically the same concept but have a variety of names, which are reflected in the many aliases of Uma, Parvati, Durga, and *Lakshmi*.

Urvasi

Goddess of success in love affairs; she was an *apsaras*, a heavenly nymph. Hindu.

Urvasi and her consort Pururavas were connected with fire-making rituals: the sticks that were rubbed together to make flames were named Urvasi and Pururavas and their child, fire, was called Ayu.

Ushas

Hindu dawn goddess.

Ushas is reborn every morning and rides in a chariot pulled by cows or by red horses. Beautifully adorned and delightful to look on, she drives off the darkness of night and awakens the gods and all other living creatures.

Varuna

Hindu god of cosmic law and order; linked with *Mitra* (*q.v.*).

Varuna was one of the great *Asuras*, a creator of the cosmos. Often confused with *Indra* and *Agni*, his name means 'the coverer', that is to say, the sky. From being an organizer of cosmic order, Varuna developed into a constant observer and judge of the actions of mankind. Nothing escaped his searching gaze.

Varuna's generative powers are seen in the ancient habit of horse-sacrifice, the horse being the essentially Aryan symbol of creative power and life-force. The god's elevated position linked him to the idea of kingship. A strange sidelight on his character is that he received the souls of those who died by drowning.

Vishnu

Hindu god of love.

The early Vedic Vishnu was not personified; he was then the

principle of light which pierces the entire universe. Epithets applied to this principle are: Ananta, 'infinite'; Hari, 'stealer of souls'; Mukunda, 'liberator'; Kesava, 'hairy' (because of the solar rays emanating from his head). As a solar god, Vishnu is said to have crossed the universe in three strides (see *Bali*). He lives in heaven and is a conqueror of the darkness. His comrades are the *Maruts*, the storm and air gods.

As his worship became popular Vishnu acquired an outward form. His skin is described as dark blue, he is dressed in yellow, and with his consort *Lakshmi* rides on the back of Garuda, king of the birds.

As Vishnu lay sleeping on the coiled cobra of a thousand heads which floated on the primal waters, a lotus grew from his navel, bearing in its flower the god *Brahma*, creator of the world.

Vishnu visited the world in the shape of several famous avatars (shapes, incarnations) in order to save it from danger. The main avatars are described in the following:

Matsya The fish. The first man, Manu, found a small fish in his hand whilst washing. He put it in a vessel of water. In a day it grew too big for the vessel, so he put it in a lake. In a day it grew too big for the lake, so he put it in the sea. The fish warned him to take two of each living thing, and specimens of all manner of seeds, and put them in a boat with his family. Just as Manu did so, the sea came flooding over the land intent on destroying everything. Manu saw a huge fish with golden scales. It was *his* fish, *Vishnu*, come to save him from the flood.

Varahavatar The boar. When the flood covered all the land, the demons came swimming along, dived under the waves, stole the earth and took it away. Vishnu took on the shape of a boar, plunged into the waters and with his keen sense of smell located the stolen earth. He killed the demons guarding it, then pulled it up out of the water by means of his tushes. The earth emerged in the shape of a goddess.

Kurma The turtle. The *rishi* Durvasas had cursed *Indra*, and as a result all the gods began to lose their strength. Vishnu devised a plan. The gods were to take a mountain, Mount Mandara, and the great snake called Vasuki and use snake and mountain as a rope and stick with which to churn up the Sea of Milk. Vishnu promised that a drink of immortality and fourteen other precious things (including animals, weapons, even goddesses) would be produced as a result. The gods, *Devas*, should get the assistance of the demons, *Asuras*, by promising them a share of the proceeds. The demons agreed to help and took hold of one end of the great snake. The gods took hold of the other, coiled it about the mountain and began pulling back and forth; the mountain whirled and the churning of the Sea of Milk began. Soon the mountain became red hot, so Indra sent rain to cool it down. Then a new difficulty arose; the mountain, poised on the sea-bed, began to bore into the earth's crust. Vishnu turned himself into a turtle, swam down and supported the end of the mountain on his back.

The next problem was that the snake, Vasuki, unused to such dizzying motion, emitted streams of venom. *Siva* came to the rescue and drank the poison, thus saving the world. Eventually the Sea of Milk coagulated and many wonderful things were produced, not the least of which was the promised drink of immortality. The demons, always a devious lot, grabbed the liquid as soon as it appeared. Vishnu turned himself into a nubile young lady and while the demons were busy ogling him, snatched the liquid away from them and ran off. The gods had their drink, regained their strength and chased off the demons.

Narasimha The lion-man. The demon Hiranyakashipu turned the gods out of heaven and declared that from now on only he would be worshipped. But it so happened that he had a son who was a devout follower of Vishnu. The boy, whose name was Prahlada, continued to worship the god. His irate father tortured him to no avail. Then he determined to kill Prahlada. He tried magic, steel, fire, poison and even wild beasts, but failed to harm the gentle youth who responded by trying to convert his father. He declared that Vishnu was present in all things. Hiranyakashipu mocked this idea, and to disprove it he derisively took a kick at a pillar in his palace (much as the famous Dr Johnson was to do later to refute a philosophical idea). But far from making his point Hiranyakashipu sealed his own fate. For Vishnu, in the form of a lion-man, leapt out of the pillar and savaged the demon to death. (See *Ravana*.)

Vamana The dwarf. The demons had once more gained ascendancy over the gods; this time it was the fault of a character named *Bali*. The god Vishnu took on the form of a dwarf and appeared to Bali with a modest request to be given as much of the earth as he could cover in three steps. Magnanimously, the demon conqueror agreed. Vishnu reassumed his usual superhuman size and covered the whole universe in two strides; with the third he sent Bali down to an eternal and well-earned rest in hell.

Parashu Rama 'Rama with the axe', a variant of *Rama*.

Kalki (Kalkin) This avatar has not yet happened. He or it is variously described as a horse, or as a man on a horse, or as a horse-headed man. This future incarnation is destined to punish and destroy the wicked ones and to start a new and creative golden age. The image of the horse, a specifically Aryan animal, takes us back to the solar mythology implicit in all Vishnu's activities; it is also a link to prehistoric horse-worship, the horse symbolizing the power of the sun.

A number of avatars of Vishnu appeared in human form, the most notable being *Buddha*, *Krishna* and *Rama*. Because of their significance as gods in their own right they have been allocated separate entries in this book. (See *Hari Hara*, *Jalandhara*.)

Visvakarma
The divine artificer, craftsman and smith. Hindu.

Visvakarma cut off an eighth of the sun *Surya* so that his daughter Sanjna could go on living with him. He used the trimmings to make weapons for the gods. It is said that Visvakarma made everything in the universe from an unknown tree. He was also responsible for the maintenance of everything. Creator of differences in matter, he was the active principle which made things hold their shape. Visvakarma was in no way sectarian; he created palaces for demons as well as for the gods.

Yaksha and Yakshi
Fiendish attendants of *Kuvera*, the Hindu god of wealth.

Yaksha and Yakshi lived in the Himalayas, where they guarded fabulous treasures and had little to do with humans. Sometimes they appeared as terrifying, sometimes alluring.

Yama
Hindu god of the dead.

Born of the sun and his wife, Yama had a twin sister named Yami. Despite his sister's earnest and incestuous desires, Yama did not weaken. The twins were always together but remained chaste. Yama, the first man, was also the first man to die. He became king of the land of death and judge of men; after death he reunites friends and relatives. His kingdom is in the south and is a stormy part of heaven. It is there that the gods, *Devas*, and the fathers, Pitris, collect to drink *soma*, the precious liquid that made them invulnerable to a second death. Yama is called Pitripati, 'father of fathers'; Sraddaheva, 'god of funerals'; Samana, 'the leveller'; Dandadhara, 'the beater or punisher'. He owns a black thunder horse, his favoured means of travel. (See Chinese god *Yeng-Wang-Yeh*.)

Europe

GREEK ■ ROMAN ■ CELTIC ■ NORDIC
SLAVONIC ■ FINNISH

Adonis

(*Adon, Adonai*, 'lord'). God of vegetation and re-birth.

Adonis was the central figure in a widespread nature cult. The Greek version relates how a boy was born to an incestuous union between Princess Myrrha and her father, the King of Cyprus. The King had declared that his daughter was more beautiful than *Aphrodite*, so that jealous goddess caused Myrrha to fall in love with her father and seduce him when he was drunk. The King was so horrified by his sin that he tried to kill the resulting child, but Aphrodite hid him in a chest and deposited him with *Persephone*, goddess of the Underworld. With feminine curiosity Persephone took a look inside the box, saw the child, and fell in love with him. She decided to keep him. Time passed. Aphrodite demanded the young man back, for she too was rather keen on him. Persephone refused; the dispute raged. *Zeus* was called in to arbitrate. He decided that one third of the year the boy should have to himself, one third should be spent with Persephone, and one third with Aphrodite.

Adonis, the beautiful, is linked with the Middle Eastern god *Tammuz*, whose death was mourned in the autumn; and then in the spring, when certain red flowers bloomed and rivers ran red, he was remembered with mixed sorrow and joy. (See *Adonis*, Middle East section.)

Aeolus

God of the winds.

Aeolus was more of a caretaker than a dynamic force. He was appointed by the goddess *Hera* – the winds were her messengers. He lived on a floating island, and had six sons and six daughters; each son being married to one of the daughters. Another close-knit divine family. Aeolus tried to be helpful to Odysseus by giving him all the winds, except one, tied up in a leather bag. The only one that was not incarcerated was the west wind, the one Odysseus needed to help him home. But disaster followed. Odysseus' suspicious comrades opened the bag when he was asleep; the angry winds poured out and drove the ship off course.

Alphito
Originally a barley goddess of Argos.

Her name indicates whiteness; the whiteness of barley, the whiteness of bones in the dark earth, the whiteness of certain lethal diseases. So, little by little an unhealthy tinge crept over Alphito's image until she became a pallid and fearful hag; fit to threaten wicked children with, fit to lure men to their doom.

Aphrodite
Goddess of love and beauty.

When *Cronus* emasculated his father *Uranus*, he cast the severed organs into the sea. White foam, *aphros*, collected round them, and from this was born Aphrodite. She first came ashore on Kythera, and later crossed to Cyprus. Her epithets included Cyprian, Paphian, Anadyomene ('born of the salt waves'), Pelagia ('of the sea'), Dione ('of the bright sky'), Pandemos ('of common love'), Ouranos ('of heavenly love'). In her black aspect she was numbered among the Erinyes and called Androphonos ('killer of men'), Melainia ('black one'), and Epitymbidia ('she upon the graves'). Worshipped by prostitutes as Aphrodite Hetaira and Aphrodite Porne, she was also known as Kallipygos ('beautiful buttocks'), Hera ('mistress'), Enoplios ('armed'), Morphos ('shaped'), Ambologera ('postponer of old age'), and Genetyllis ('of childbirth').

Originally worshipped in her Greek form in Cyprus, Aphrodite is an obvious version of *Astarte* and *Ishtar* (*q.v.* Middle Eastern section) As befitted the goddess of love, she was an enthusiastic companion of the male gods. Married to *Hephaestus*, she also consorted with *Ares* (the result was highly embarrassing for both; see *Ares*), *Poseidon*, Pygmalion, *Adonis*, *Dionysus*, Anchises, Nerites, and Phaeton.

As well as pleasure, Aphrodite caused suffering. Pygmalion fell in love with a statue; Nerites was turned into a shell; Adonis died and was resurrected every year; Anchises had his eyes stung by bees for seeing the goddess naked, and was lamed by *Zeus* for boasting of his time with her; Phaeton was abducted to be the guardian of her shrine; Ares became an object of ridicule; and her child by Dionysus was born with a *membrum virile* of enormous size. There were thorns in her bed of roses.

A love-gift, in the form of a shining wreath, which Aphrodite gave Dionysus (*q.v.*) had an interesting later history. The generous Dionysus passed it on to Ariadne, again as a love-token. Ariadne in her turn gave it to Theseus, and it lit his way through the darkness of the labyrinth in his search for the Minotaur. (See *Venus*.)

Apis
Name of divine Egyptian bull, said to be linked to Epaphos, son of *Io*.

Apollo
God of prophecy, music and medicine.

Greatest of gods after *Zeus* and *Athene*, Apollo was born on Delos (originally Ortygia, 'isle of quails'). He was fed on ambrosia and nectar, food of the gods, and it was so good that his childhood lasted only four days. He set off immediately to kill the serpent that the jealous *Hera* had sent to torment his mother, *Leto*. The reason for Hera's jealousy was that Zeus, her husband, was the father. Apollo killed the python (serpent, dragon) at the shrine of Delphi, which he took over as his oracular shrine. In his temple there was the Omphalos, the navel of the earth. The oracular priestess of Delphi was known as the Pythia. It is said that Apollo's first temple there was built for him by a swarm of bees out of feathers and beeswax. Apollo was connected with the idea of light, but was never a sun god. He is shown with bow and lyre, a gift from the precocious baby *Hermes*. Apart from being famous for prophetic powers Apollo was also a pastoral god, caring for herds and flocks. As Kitharodos ('lyre singer'), he was leader of the Muses.

Apollo loved boys and maidens alike, many of his affairs ending unhappily. He accidentally killed his lover Hyacinthos with a stone discus, and from the slain youth's blood arose a blue flower, the hyacinth. Another of his lovers, Kyparissos, had unintentionally killed a much-loved pet stag. Wishing to die or mourn forever, he turned to Apollo for help. Apollo turned him into a cypress tree.

150

Apollo's first love was Daphne. She was later responsible for the death of Leukippos ('white stallion'), another of her lovers. Like Kyparissos she went to Apollo for help, and he turned her into the laurel, which became his favourite tree. Apollo mated with Dryope in the form of a snake and with Kyrene in the shape of a wolf. The son of this last affair was Aristaeus, inventor of the beehive, oil-press, cheese-making and snares. Coronis ('crow maiden') bore him *Asclepius*, god of healing.

Apollo was a tolerant if not a forgiving god. His cult discouraged killing for vengeance and encouraged lawful expiation of crime for all classes of society. Apollo himself urged Orestes to kill Clytemnestra as just punishment rather than revenge. When he himself caused the deaths of the sons of Niobe (causing her perpetual grief), he allotted the years they had not lived to Nestor, husband of Niobe's daughter, Chloris.

Apollo was a paragon, youthful, wise, beautiful, strong and just.

Ares
God of war, son of *Zeus* and *Hera*.

Ares, who originated in Thrace and Scythia, was not popular with the Greeks who looked on him as a god for other people. He did not deserve much honour for he was obstinate, hating, bickering, wicked, and untrustworthy. He was fond of nothing but strife, anger and furious blood-letting. There was nothing noble about Ares; he was therefore disliked by gods and men alike. He is a personification of the savage side of war; the father of Deimos ('terror') and Phobos ('hate').

Even Ares' love affairs ended in disaster. He dishonoured his brother *Hephaestus* by a relationship with the latter's wife, *Aphrodite*. Hephaestus set a trap for the lovers. He prepared a fine bronze net and told Aphrodite he was off on a long journey. As soon as he had left, Ares and Aphrodite began their sport. Hephaestus crept back in and let down the net over them, trapping them so they could not move. Then all the gods came trooping in gleefully to watch. Ares and Aphrodite were publicly humiliated.

Ares had the distinction of being the first god to be tried for murder, although he was acquitted (he had slain Halirrhothius, son of the sea god *Poseidon*, for raping Alcippe, Ares' daughter). The location of the trial was the hill of Ares, the Areopagus, which later was to become the place where murder trials were conducted.

Arethusa
Goddess of springs and fountains.

Arethusa was one of the *Hesperides*, who looked after the golden apples in the land beyond the setting sun.

Argos
Argos had a hundred eyes all over his body. Fifty of them watched while the other fifty slept; and vice versa. Because of this non-stop vigilance he was set by *Hera* to guard the priestess *Io* (*q.v.*), who had been turned into a cow by *Zeus* to disguise her. But *Hermes* charmed him to sleep and cut off his head. In his memory, Hera set his eyes in the tail-feathers of her favourite bird, the peacock.

Artemis
Goddess of fertility; patroness of young girls, virgin huntress, mistress of beasts and wild things.

Artemis helped women in childbirth, and though usually benevolent could just as easily bring destruction, striking suddenly from afar. Her Ephesus image is many-breasted. Usually she is depicted as an athletic, rather severe young lady, armed with bow and arrow. She chose to live in Arcadia, where a band of chaste and hardy nymphs shared her outdoor life. Those who treacherously succumbed to the pleasures that only men can supply were mercilessly shot down, as was the nymph Callisto. (Though another version merely changes the poor girl into a bear, along with her illicit child, and places them in the sky as the Great Bear and the Little Bear.)

Artemis was a dangerous goddess; even to look on her meant death, as Actaeon found to his cost. He stumbled upon the goddess as she was bathing, and was torn to shreds by his own dogs, even though it was hardly his fault. The only male person whom Artemis ever looked on kindly was Orion, but before anything could come of it there was an unfortunate accident. Artemis and Apollo were trying to best each other in archery. Apollo challenged her to hit a distant object out at sea. Artemis shot at the small point and pierced Orion through the head; for it was he, having a refreshing dip in the salt waves.

Another version relates that Orion accompanied Artemis on a hunting trip and mistakenly touched her. For such presumption, even if it was an accident, she ordered a scorpion to sting him to death.

Artemis was also responsible for the summary punishment of many minor errors on the part of other humans; a forgotten sacrifice here, a word out of place there, was enough to bring ruin on whole dynasties and lay waste entire countries.

There is the suggestion of a bear cult about the figure of Artemis; it had its centre at Brauron, Attica (see *Artio*, Celtic goddess). Once a savage she-bear had to be disposed of in Athens; to make amends for this killing (even though it seems justified) small girls were dedicated to her, and she became their protectress. (See *Diana*.)

Artemis of Ephesus
A fertility goddess of Ephesus.

Though probably the same as *Artemis* the huntress she gives a totally different impression, being many-breasted and welcoming, a typical Mother Goddess of the Middle East complex. Identified with *Diana*, she is the 'Diana of the Ephesians' whose followers St Paul had cause to remember.

Asclepius
God of healing.

Son of the god *Apollo* and a nymph named Coronis, Asclepius was saved from being burned on his mother's funeral pyre by his father's swift intervention. Asclepius was fostered by the centaur Chiron, who tutored him in the arts of hunting and medicine. He was such an apt pupil of medical science that he was able to revive the dead. This sparked off the fury of *Hades*, god of the dead, who claimed that he was being cheated of his lawful prey. Hades complained to *Zeus*, who agreed that Asclepius had overstepped the bounds of accepted practice. He terminated Asclepius' career with a well-aimed thunderbolt.

This made Apollo, Asclepius' father, not a little distraught. Since there was nothing Apollo could do to Zeus, he sought out the Cyclopes who had manufactured that particular thunderbolt and revenged himself by slaughtering them. Those who deal in armaments are just as guilty as those who use them.

The cult of Asclepius was active at Cos, Epidaurus and Pergamus. Those seeking a cure from the god would sleep in his temple. There the god would visit them in a dream and tell them what course of treatment to undergo. The grateful patients would throw gold into the temple fountain and hang votive offerings, small metal models of that part of the body they wished to be cured, on the temple walls

Athene
Warrior-goddess; protectress of Athens; goddess of architects, sculptors, spinners, weavers, horses, oxen, and olives. Also goddess of prudence and wise counsel.

Athene is defensive rather than aggressive, and is shown helmeted, wearing the *aegis*, carrying shield and spear and sometimes the image of a *nike*, or winged victory (see *Nike*). Warned that his children by his first wife, Metis, would be wiser than he was, the great *Zeus* swallowed her when she became pregnant. Result, a terrible headache. To relieve the pain *Hephaestus* split open Zeus' head with his axe; out came Athene, fully armed. She was to be her father's favourite, causing jealousy among the other gods on Olympus.

Athene took the Greek side in the Trojan war, favouring heroes such as Odysseus. Other heroes she helped were Hercules, Perseus and Bellerophon. Like *Artemis* she was a perpetual virgin. Like Artemis she punished a rash man who blundered into the place where she was bathing. This time the man was Tiresias and his punishment was to lose his sight; in recompense he was given the gift of foretelling the future. He could count himself lucky it wasn't the vengeful Artemis he disturbed, but the noble lady Athene.

Few were bold enough to try and molest the goddess' honour;

but one who did was Hephaestus (*q.v.*). He tried it on, as it were, during a fitting session for some armour he had made her. However, having a bad limp, he was at a disadvantage when it came to a chase. He discovered that Athene could out-run and out-fight him, and his attempted rape came to nought.

Athene was skilled in the arts of peace no less than those of war. She taught men how to tame horses and hitch them to chariots, she gave help in the building of the ship Argos, she invented the potter's wheel and made the first turned vases. She was also good at weaving and embroidery, a skill that came in handy for making veils and such for the other goddesses. Once, a mortal named Arachne dared to challenge her skill. Arachne wove a wonderful tapestry depicting the loves of the gods. It must have been a work of huge size, considering the activities of Zeus alone. Athene had to admit the tapestry was perfect. All the passions and deceptions were exactly portrayed. Angrily, but with a hint of poetic justice, she condemned Arachne to go on spinning into eternity, drawing the silk from her own body to supply the necessary material.

Atlas

A Titan who took part in the revolt against the Olympian gods and was punished by being made to stand forever on the edge of the world, bearing on his back the heavens.

His daughter Maia was mother of *Hermes*, his daughter Electra was mother of Harmonia, and his daughter Taygete was mother of Lacedaemon; *Zeus* being responsible for all three children. Atlas was father of the *Hesperides* When Hercules came to get the apples, Atlas helped him; while he was away Hercules performed his task of holding up the heavens. He gave Atlas the first and only rest he ever had.

Our map books are named after him because an early atlas had a picture of the Titan on its cover, holding up, not the heavens, but the earth.

Atropos

One of the Moerae (Latin, Parcae) or the fates who decided the destiny of each individual. Clotho spun the thread of life, Lachesis measured it out, and Atropos cut it. Against them there was no court of appeal.

155

Attis
A vegetation god; a Phrygian deity and close companion of *Cybele* adopted by the Greeks.

It was said that *Ishtar* (Middle East goddess – *q.v.*), the earth mother, swallowed either an almond or a pomegranate seed, by this means conceiving her son, Attis. It was also said that he was the son of Cybele, who may indeed be identified with Ishtar.

Attis was driven mad by his mother's demented love for him, and so castrated himself under a pine tree. This was remembered in his annual festival when a pine was decorated and then cut down. Attis was served by a eunuch priesthood, the Galloi, who would cut their arms in a frenzy as a public sign of mourning and a symbol of Attis' castration.

The Phrygians called Attis 'Papa', and worshipped him as a vegetation god; Cybele they named 'Ma'. He wore the Phrygian cap or *pileus* (see *Cabiri*), and is linked with the other vegetation gods of the Eastern Mediterranean, *Tammuz*, *Adonis* and even *Mithras*, though their exact relationships are hard to define with any certainty. Just how much conscious borrowing of attributes and stories there was between the cults is difficult to unravel.

Bendis
Goddess of the moon in Thrace.

An orgiastic cult devoted to her spread southward, becoming less frenzied in the civilized atmosphere around Athens.

Boreas
God of the North Wind.

Boreas was the most important of the four wind gods. He was winged and had two faces; one to see where he was going and one to see where he had come from. Anciently depicted with the lower parts of a serpent, he was the male counterpart of *Eos* and was a notorious abducter of maidens, one of whom, Oreithyia, gave him two sons, Kalais and Zetes. These two sailed with Jason on the good ship Argos; they alone were able to defeat the dreaded *Harpies*, chasing them up into the sky. Boreas was a friend of the Athenians and wrecked a Persian fleet for them.

Other notable wind gods were Zephyros (west), Notos (south) and Apheliotes (east).

Britomartis
'Sweet virgin', alias Dictynna; a goddess of chastity.

Britomartis was raised to the rank of goddess by chaste *Artemis* in recognition of her persistent chastity. She had been pursued by Minos all over Crete. Minos was obviously serious, for it is said the chase lasted for nine months. Eventually Britomartis was cornered on a sea-cliff (some say Mount Dicte, but that is a trifle distant from the sea for the story to work). Her skirts caught up on a myrtle bough. There seemed to be no escape. As Minos came on apace, Britomartis did what every sane nymph would do in the same circumstances; she threw herself down into the sea. Providentially she was saved by some honourable fishermen, who dragged her up in their nets and took her to safety, honour, and a place among the Immortals. Her name Dictynna comes from the Greek for 'fishing net'.

Cabiri
A mysterious quartet of gods; *qabirim*, 'powerful ones'.

Sons of *Hephaestus*, the Cabiri were dark and deformed. Their phallic cult was centred on Samothrace and was linked with an ithyphallic *Hermes*. The Cabiri were associated with magic, being described as 'great gods' and linked sometimes with the earth, sometimes with the sea. They wear the *pileus*, a pointed cap, which was also worn by *Attis*, *Mithras* and personifications of Liberty. Somehow the cap represents a secret tradition and survives today in our pictures of pixies, goblins and 'little people', who are degenerate scions of a divine dynasty. (See *Dactyls*.)

Castor
See *Dioscures*.

Chaos
The empy space which pre-dated the arrival of the elements and then the gods. It means 'gaping', a void, an emptiness rather than our sense of turmoil.

Charities
A triad of Aphrodite-like goddesses.

They are shown as three naked and beautifully formed women, two facing forward and one facing backward, sometimes with their arms around each others' necks. Their names were Aglaia ('glorious'), Euphrosyne ('joy') and Thalia ('abundance'). In some parts of ancient Greece there were only two Charities, representing the waxing and waning of the moon. The Charities may be seen as the opposite to the Erinyes (see *Eumenides*) and as the originals of the *Graces*.

Charon
Ferryman of the Underworld.

Charon punted souls over the waters to the kingdom of *Hades*. His fee was one obolus; the coin was usually placed in the dead person's mouth before the funerary rites.

Cottus
One of the Hecatoncheires, giants who each had a hundred arms and fifty heads. They fought for *Zeus* against *Cronus* and the Titans.

Couretes
Sons of the *Dactyls*.

The Couretes were divine youths who danced before the birth-cave of *Zeus* on Mount Ida, shouting and clashing their weapons and shields. This was to conceal the crying of the new-born Zeus from his father *Cronus*, who was fond of children, especially his own, for breakfast or supper.

Cronus
Father of the god *Zeus* and son of *Uranus* ('heaven') and *Gaia* ('earth').

Though divine, Cronus was not worshipped. He castrated his father with a sickle in order to free himself and all the other children from their enforced stay in Gaia. Uranus foretold that Cronus himself would be overthrown by one of his own sons.

Cronus and his wife, *Rhea*, had many children, and to avoid his prophesied doom Cronus would swallow the babies soon after birth. Gaia advised Rhea to wrap a stone in swaddling clothes and substitute it for her next infant. She did so and Cronus swallowed the stone, thinking it was the baby, Zeus. The child was brought up in a cave on Mount Ida. When he was old enough to do battle, Rhea managed to persuade Cronus to vomit up all his children. Zeus then led his siblings in open rebellion against the tyrant. Ten years hard fighting followed, until the victorious Zeus imprisoned Cronus and his cronies in Tartarus. Then began the glorious epoch of the Olympian gods.

Cybele
Goddess of the earth and caverns; a Phrygian deity, she was worshipped on Mount Ida.

As goddess of the natural earth, Cybele's domain included wild beasts; thus she is represented accompanied by lions. Her priests, the Galli or Corybantes, were noted for their noisy dancing and self-mutilation.

The Greeks adopted Cybele along with the god *Attis*. They made Attis more important than he was, depicting him as a handsome youth for whom the goddess had a great passion. She forbade him to marry anyone else, but he disobeyed; his punishment was to be turned into a fir tree. An alternative story tells how *Zeus* was jealous of Attis' success with the goddess and sent a wild boar to savage him to death.

Cybele herself was merged with the native Greek goddess *Rhea*. She was married off to Gordius, the famous knot-maker, and their son was Midas, who, considering his later history, was a most unlucky child.

Dactyls
Divine beings.

When *Rhea*, the wife of *Cronus*, was in labour she supported herself on her hands, and her fingers dug into the earth. This action brought forth the Dactyls ('fingers'), divine beings who assisted at the birth of *Zeus*. They were related to the mysterious *Cabiri*, and learnt the craft of blacksmithing from Rhea. They were magi, tutors of Orpheus, inventors of magic formulae used at Ephesus, and the founders of metre (including of course the *dactylic*). Pliny records Cretan thumb-shaped stones described as *Idaean dactyls*, and so Jung feels justified in calling the dactyls 'Tom Thumbs' or 'Thumblings'. If we accept a link between the Cabiri and our 'little people', then why not a connection between the Dactyls and our Tom Thumb? The thumb is an obvious phallic symbol.

Danae
Mother of the hero Perseus.

Danae was not divine but she is worthy of inclusion here on account of the method used by *Zeus* for her seduction. Zeus was always on the lookout for new disguises to deceive *Hera*, his wife. In Danae's case he took on the shape of a shower of gold. This story is typical of the poetic imagination with which the Greeks described their gods. How different from the prosaic and practical approach of the stony Romans!

Demeter
Corn goddess, queen of the fruitful earth.

An ancient and popular goddess who symbolized the eternal mother. Her daughter had been abducted by *Hades*, god of the Underworld. Demeter went in search of her and encountered a lustful *Poseidon*. Knowing only too well what was on his mind she fled and turned herself into a mare, mingling with the horse herds of King Oncus. Poseidon thereupon became a stallion and followed her into the browsing herd, where he sought her out and succeeded in performing in an equine state what he had failed to achieve in human form. Demeter was naturally furious and went into her aspect of Demeter Erinys. She only got rid of her anger by washing it away in the River Ladon, after which she became Demeter Lousia ('washed'). But she could not wash away Poseidon's success and gave birth to two offspring, Arion, a stallion with a black mane, and a daughter. This daughter was very special; she had a secret name which might not be mentioned outside the Mysteries. She is known instead simply as *Kore*, 'the girl'. This Kore is identified both with Demeter herself and with her daughter *Persephone* before her abduction by Hades. Demeter, Kore, and Kore-Persephone are three aspects of the one goddess.

However, back to the story. Demeter travelled about looking for her daughter. At Eleusis she was so kindly received tha⁺ she bestowed the gift of immortality on the son of the king She massaged him with ambrosia, the wonderful food of the gods, and held him over the fire to burn off his mortality. The startled queen came across her and Demeter was forced to reveal her true identity; in addition to the gift of immortality, she promised that at Eleusis she would reveal the mystery of the earth's fruitfulness to the faithful. Meanwhile the earth was suffering famine, for Demeter had stopped the crops growing until her daughter was returned to her. To save an impending crisis, *Zeus* arbitrated the dispute. He sent *Hermes* to fetch Persephone; but the wily Hades slipped some pomegranate seeds into her mouth just before she left his kingdom, making their marriage tie eternal, for the pomegranate is the fruit of death. Once more Zeus had to intervene. He decided that Persephone should live with Hades for one third of the year, and spend the remaining time on earth with her mother.

Demeter gave the gift of corn to those men who had helped her, and instituted the Eleusinian Mysteries. These Mysteries, the secret of which has never been revealed, were celebrated in February each year (The Lesser Mysteries) and in September every five years (The Greater Mysteries). No one truly knows what they were all about, or what the liturgy actually said. From various hints it has been guessed that processions, ritual ablutions and religious dramas were incorporated. There was a process of initiation on which devotees were permitted to embark; only initiates were admitted to the central mysteries, whose teachings remain a secret to this day.

Dionysus
God of wine, vegetation, pleasure, civilization. Orphic supreme god; alias Dithyrambos, 'double birth'.

While Dionysus' mother, Semele, was still pregnant, she was tricked by the vengeful *Hera* into asking to see *Zeus* as he really was. Zeus had already agreed to grant Semele whatever she asked for, so he had no choice but to show himself in all his fiery splendour. No mortal could bear to look on Zeus, for the divine flames which emanated from him could set fire to earthly substance. Semele, and the palace in which she stayed, were enveloped in raging fire. Zeus caused an ivy plant to sprout quickly and shield the unborn child from the flames; then he took the foetus into his own thigh, whence it was born as Dionysus in due time.

The child was farmed out to his aunt, Ino. She too fell victim to Hera, and became insane. Dionysus was taken to Nysa where nymphs, Sileni, Satyrs, and Maenads all had a hand in his education.

The young Dionysus discovered the vine and made the first wine. He began his travels, spreading the knowledge of viniculture and having many adventures. One day, walking on the seashore, he was captured by pirates and taken onto their ship. They recognized his regal bearing and hoped for a fat ransom. But when they tried to tie Dionysus up, they found that the knots came loose by themselves and the ropes fell off him of their own accord. The ship's pilot tried to make his mates release the captive, but they refused. Suddenly they discovered that the ship was ploughing through a sea of wine; a vine actually appeared to cover the sail; ivy swiftly wound itself up the mast. Dionysus himself assumed the shape of a savage lion. The pirates panicked and, throwing themselves into the sea, became dolphins. Only the pilot was saved.

On Naxos, Dionysus encountered Ariadne, who had been deserted by an ungrateful Theseus. Dionysus was able to 'comfort' her in the approved fashion. (This sequence of events has been described differently elsewhere – see *Aphrodite*.) After travelling the mainland and the Greek islands, Dionysus visited Phrygia, Cappadocia, Syria, Lebanon, India, Egypt and Libya. He returned home a true cosmopolite, hedonistic and wearily effete. He had picked up bad habits on his travels; orgiastic practices from the cult of *Cybele*, softness and luxury from the east.

Back home his influence was not appreciated. His followers. the Bacchantes, Satyrs and Maenads (mad women), were unruly, drunken and noisy. At length Lycurgus, King of Thrace, could stand it no longer. With Cromwellian fervour he rounded them all up and clapped them in prison. Dionysus responded by making Lycurgus' mind unbalanced. In this state Lycurgus came across his own son and thought the lad was a vine, the plant whose fruit had caused all the disorder. He took an axe and, as he thought, cut down the 'vine'. The troubles which beset Thrace did not cease until Lycurgus was trampled to death under the hooves of wild horses. This high-handed treatment did not silence Dionysus' critics. Pentheus, King of Thebes, managed to capture the god himself and lock him up in prison. Dionysus exerted his influence from behind locked doors. He picked on Pentheus' mother and her friends, a group of respectable, if staid, matrons. Under his influence they became Maenads, a rabble of demented, furious, noisy and lascivious creatures. Pentheus followed the mob of hell-raising old ladies out of town. He caught up with them and tried to reason with them. Well, one thing you don't do is try and reason with a Maenad, even if she is your mother. They turned on Pentheus and tore him limb from limb with their bare hands.

A dramatic liturgy grew up about the cult of Dionysus. This developed into dramatic festivals in the spring Dionysia, leading to more widely applied drama; much as our own Morality Plays took on a more general, secular tone.

Dioscures

Or Dioscuri. The collective name for *Castor* and *Pollux*, young sons of *Zeus*.

Their mother, Leda, was married to Tyndareus of Lacedaemon. Zeus visited her in the shape of a swan and she produced two eggs; each egg contained a boy and a twin sister. Though twins of a sort, the boys had different paternities. Pollux was considered to be the true divine child and so was immortal. It was an ancient tradition that, of twins, one was natural and one had a divine father.

Castor and Pollux sailed in the Argos with Jason to win the Golden Fleece. After that they had many warlike adventures, until Castor was killed by the Aphareids during a quarrel over loot. Zeus was deeply moved by the sorrow this killing caused to

Pollux, and he granted Castor immortality. There are two traditions about how this was done. Some say that Castor and Pollux were each alive on alternate days, a rather awkward arrangement one would have thought; others claim they live on as stars in the constellation Gemini.

Dryades
Tree nymphs.

Crowned with oak leaves and armed with axes, the Dryades punish those who harm the woodlands; for trees, especially oaks, are sacred to them.

Echidna
Monster goddess.

Daughter of Tartarus and *Gaia* and mother of Chimaera, the *Harpies*, Cerberus, the Lernean Hydra, the Nemean Lion, Orthos the double-headed dog, and also of the Sphinx. As befits the mother of such monsters, Echidna was half-human and half-serpent. She was gigantic and insatiable. Her human part was not unattractive; she was charming and bright-cheeked. Her monster part was terrible and lethal.

Echo
An oread, 'a nymph'.

Echo helped cover *Zeus'* indiscretions among her female friends by chattering and singing to *Hera*, diverting the latter's attention from her roving spouse. But Hera was no fool; she guessed what the game was and took away Echo's power of speech. All the nymph could do was repeat the last syllable of words spoken near her. Echo fell in love, but being unable to voice her thoughts was spurned by the one she adored. She faltered and died of grief. Her bones petrified and only her voice was left, hopelessly repeating the ends of the words she heard. The object of her love, Narcissus, was himself punished for spurning her. The gods decreed that he should fall in love with his own reflection. He happened to catch sight of that in a pool of water; seized by love, he remained there, staring into the pool, until exhaustion and then death overtook him.

164

Empousae
Demonesses and emissaries of *Hecate*.

The Empousae each had one ass's leg and one leg of brass. Some regard them as derived from the Lilim, devotees of Adam's alleged first wife, Lilith. They are also linked with the Lamiae, attractive witches who would waylay, seduce and then suck the blood of unwary travellers.

Eos
Goddess of the dawn; alias Aurora.

Sometimes Eos came on wings, sprinkling out the dew from an urn she carried; sometimes she rode on Pegasus, holding aloft a blazing torch. Sometimes she rode in a purple chariot, clad in a yellow robe. She was mother of the winds and such a delectable creature that jealous *Aphrodite* turned her thoughts towards mortals, to keep her away from the gods. Eos once kidnapped Orion, fated to die by the hand of *Artemis* (*q.v.*). She had many amorous adventures and then fell for a mortal, Tithonus, in a final sort of way. She asked the gods to give her lover immortality. They were quick to oblige, but Eos was horrified when she realized that she hadn't also requested eternal youth for Tithonus. Despite forced feeding on ambrosia, Tithonus slid into middle age, old age, then total decrepitude. He became so grotesque that Eos locked him away out of sight. At last the gods took pity on the poor fellow and turned him into a cicada.

The most significant of Eos' children are Phaeton, guardian of the temple of Aphrodite, Phosphorus and Hesperus, who are the morning and evening aspects of the planet Venus. (See *Boreas*.)

Eros
God of love.

There seems to be a deal of disagreement as to the parentage of Eros. For a mother choose between *Iris*, *Ilythia* or *Aphrodite*. For a father choose between *Hermes*, *Ares*, and, of course, *Zeus*. We mistakenly think of Eros as a chubby, winged infant determined to cause havoc with his bow and arrows. But Eros was a dangerous force; a force that could move men and women to self-sacrifice. It was both homosexual and heterosexual attraction, sometimes physical, sometime psychological. Always dangerous. This element of malice has been watered down into a coy playfulness by men who have no stomach for the reality of the force the Greeks called 'eros'. By so doing, they have deprived us all of a dynamic concept.

Ether

Primeval principle which symbolized finite things and which organized cosmic matter from the shapeless elements into the gigantic egg from which *Phanes* (*q.v.*) was to emerge. After the creation of Phanes (sometimes called Eros but not the same as Cupid), Ether became the light of heaven as distinct from *Chaos*. Ether was the child of Erebus and *Nux* ('night').

Eumenides
Or Erinyes; the Furies.

Their name means 'kindly ones', which is what people wished they would become. The name is placatory, for they were the Erinyes, older by far than the Olympian gods. Their skins were black, their hair was made of snakes, they wore soiled grey robes. Three in number, the Eumenides were often identified with the Moirai. An intolerable stench issued from their breath and their bodies, a poisonous discharge dripped from their eyes, they waved brass-studded whips, flaming torches and snakes. Not surprisingly, they were virgins.

Their names were Allecto ('unending'), Tisiphone ('retaliation'), and Megaera ('envious fury'). To their credit, they defended the interests of mothers and would not tolerate any flouting of the laws of blood relationship, as Orestes discovered.

Gaia
Goddess of the earth.

Pre-Olympian, source and sustainer of all life, deep-breasted mother of all. Gaia mated with her son, *Uranus*, to produce the Titans, the Cyclops and Hecatoncheires. Even after the rise to supremacy of the Olympians, Gaia was worshipped by men and gods. She presided over marriages, nursed the sick, and was foremost among oracles; for the great divination centre of Delphi was hers before the arrival of *Apollo*. From the earth of Delphi issued the mysterious pneuma, which caused men to prophesy. Gaia is represented as a gigantic female figure. To obtain her attention to your wishes, it was first necessary to offer fruits at her shrine. Sacred oaths were made in her name and sealed by animal sacrifices. (See *Cronus*.)

Ganymede
God of rain.

Ganymede was so beautiful that he was abducted by an eagle and carried up to Olympus to be the cup-bearer of the gods. (See *Hebe*.)

Gorgons
Children of Phorcys and Ceto: Stheno, Euryale, and Medusa.

Medusa was a Gorgon, and originally beautiful. She was the lover of *Poseidon* (often identified with Phorcys). Because the two of them spent a night in the temple of Athene, that goddess made Medusa ugly, with pop-eyes and snakes for hair. Her merest glance could turn men to stone. She was killed by the hero Perseus. Medusa's sisers were equally attractive! (See *Graiae*.)

Graces
Goddesses of joy and gratitude.

Their number and names varied in different areas of ancient Greece but it is generally accepted that there were three of them. They were called Aglaia, 'the shining one'; Thalia, 'the flowering one'; Euphrosyne, 'the one who makes glad'. The Graces were originally personifications of the benign rays of the sun. Not only did they make mankind happy but they also supervised the budding and fruiting of all manner of plants. In addition, they performed the task of handmaidens to the goddess of love, *Aphrodite*, helping to adorn her before she set out on a new seduction.

The Graces were anciently shown in long dresses and crowns, but in later times (about 200 B.C. onwards) were gracefully naked with their arms draped across each other's shoulders. They danced to entertain the gods on Olympus.

Graiae
Grey goddesses who guarded the cavern of the *Gorgons*.

Their names were Enyo, Pemphredo and Deino. They were associated with war and fortune-telling. Although born beautiful, the Graiae had grey (sometimes white) hair; colours associated with death. It was said that they had but one eye and one tooth between them. By purloining the eye as it passed from hand to hand, Perseus was able to bargain with the unlucky ladies and discover the way to the Gorgon's hideout.

Hades
God of the Underworld and wealth; the invisible one; alias *Pluto* ('riches'); alias Aidoneus.

Son of *Rhea* and *Cronus*, Hades was delivered from the darkness of his father's belly and allotted control of the Underworld. An easy transition, obviously. He rarely left his domain and was on the whole a faithful husband to his wife, *Persephone* (see *Demeter*). A two-sided character, Hades was the mysterious and terrifying god of death, and also the benign and generous god of wealth. To attract Hades' attention it was usual to strike the ground with hand or rod, and do him honour by offering a black-fleeced sheep.

There were differing theories as to the location of Hades' kingdom. The earth was seen as a flat surface surrounded by a vast tract of water called Ocean. Beyond this lay the Afterworld, a gloomy wasteland dotted with dark and fruitless plants. However it was proven by intrepid navigators that there were indeed lands and people beyond the sea. Perhaps these lands were not as bright and sunny as Greece, but it was all quite habitable. So Hades' kingdom had to be relocated and a suitable place was found, under the earth, connected to this world by various caverns, such as those at Epirus, Heraclea Pontica, and Colonus. Rivers which flowed underground were also considered highways, or low-ways, to the infernal regions. Understandably there was no accurate map of Hades, but it was thought of in the following way.

First one passed through the groves of Persephone (the original wasteland moved downwards); then came the gates of Hades, which were guarded by the monster dog Cerberus who greeted incoming souls kindly but would not let any of them return. (Cerberus could be appeased with honey cakes or music.) There were a number of rivers to cross, Acheron, Cocytus, Phlegeton, Lethe and Styx. Lethe, 'the river of forgetfulness', was the boundary between Tartarus, which was not a pleasant place, and the Elysian Fields, which weren't too bad, considering. The divine ferryman, *Charon*, would take you over Acheron for an obolus. There was also a trench going down into Hades which acted as a channel for the blood of the sacrificed black sheep, and the souls in Hades would go there for the occasional refreshing drink. There was nothing retributive about Hades. You lived on earth without being consulted about your birth; you died and went to Hades. And that was that.

Harpies
Storm goddesses or spirits.

An odious pair of creatures who wreaked misery among mortals. Born of Typhon, god of the storm wind, and Echidna, monster serpent goddess, the Harpies were first of all storm goddesses; irits who flew on the winds. Later their physiognomy was standardized according to the following pattern: they had beautiful hair, the face of an old hag, bear's ears, and a bird body with long hooked talons. It was their delight suddenly to appear and snatch food from tables, soiling with excrement anything they couldn't grab. Tormentors of King Phineus, who was blind, they were attacked by the Argonauts and put to flight by Zetes and Kalais, sons of the North Wind.

Hesiod gives them names, Aello and Ocypete.

Hebe
Goddess of youth.

Daughter of *Zeus* and *Hera*, Hebe was the eternally young girl, busying herself with domestic matters. She helped the gods to wash, dress, and adorn themselves. Her main task was to serve the gods at table with nectar and ambrosia. She was given to Hercules, the hero, as wife when he attained immortality. Hebe lost her job to *Ganymede*, god of rain, through her own clumsiness. One day the unfortunate maiden tripped while serving nectar and fell over, landing in an indecent posture. The gods were not amused.

Hecate
Goddessof the moon, magic, riches, wisdom, victory, flocks and navigation.

If you were a poor, stupid shepherd who had lost his way and had been beaten up, then Hecate was just the goddess you needed. Originally from Thrace, she was honoured on Olympus for her help against the Giants. Cousin to *Artemis* and sometime goddess of the moon, she became associated with magic and enchantment. Hecate defended children and was strongly connected with the hope of regeneration. She became queen of the dead and was much honoured in Asia Minor and Boetia. She would appear to men with her pack of hounds and favoured crossroads, tombs, and scenes of crime.

At crossroads there might be found statues of her, and these were triple statues. This is an interesting link with the many triads of goddesses and with the three-fold aspect: e.g. *Demeter*, as maiden, matron and hag.

Helios
God of the sun.

A minor deity, worshipped on Rhodes. Helios was most useful as a witness, for he saw everything. The Greeks never worshipped him in the way many cultures did; they were far too astute for that. (See *Hyperion*.)

Hephaestus
God of blacksmiths.

Originally a thunder god, Hephaestus' limp was said to make him walk awkwardly, imitating the zig-zag movement of lightning. Controller of the creative use of fire, he was patron of artisans, craftsmen, and mechanics. He is represented as a strong, bearded man, wearing a small conical hat and wielding a hammer and tongs. Son of *Hera* and *Zeus*, Hephaestus was unusually misshapen for a god. His ill-formed legs caused him to walk in a way which made the other gods howl with laughter. He was so ugly that Hera kept him out of sight. Hephaestus planned his revenge. He presented Hera with a splendid golden throne; but when she sat on it she discovered that she was trapped, for the throne was a cunning artifice. Hephaestus refused to let her out; refused even to leave his refuge until his wishes were granted. Foremost among his demands was that the gorgeous *Aphrodite* should become his wife. Once in Olympus, he was in fact a useful member of the society of gods; he created golden palaces for them, among other things. On earth he was helped in his workshops (generally situated near volcanoes; e.g. Etna) by the dwarfs, Sileni, Satyrs, and his sons, the *Cabiri*.

The very nature of Aphrodite should have made his marriage agreeable, but she was too good at her work. Hephaestus himself was not beyond censure; he had many children outside wedlock and was foolishly in love with the goddess *Athene*. He had assisted at her birth by striking Zeus on the head with his axe to relieve the latter's headache; Athene sprang forth fully armed. Hephaestus' rebuffed passion turned to rivalry, for both he and Athene were fire gods, and craft gods. Hephaestus was also something of a magician through his links with the Cabiri and with the *Dactyls*, who were possibly remnants of older, occult gods. Though lame he was an essential member of the community of gods, as indeed smiths were to the community of men.

Hera
Goddess of the sky.

Hera later lost her meteorological connections and became the personification of woman. Married to the most powerful of the Olympians, *Zeus*, her life was a continual domestic storm with the breaking of divine crockery and the slamming of heavenly doors. Represented as a noble and modest matron, Hera wears a crown. Her sacred bird was the peacock. Her worship was a powerful and ancient cult; both Samos and Argos claim to be her birthplace. She was usually worshipped in high places, her temples being built on the tops of mountains.

One day the beautiful Hera rescued a soaked cuckoo from a rainstorm. She put the bird on her lap and then found herself struggling with an amorous Zeus. Their children were *Hebe, Ilythia, Ares,* and *Hephaestus.* Hera was a faithful wife, in constant contrast to Zeus, who never stopped his infidelities. Her jealous watchfulness increased Zeus' trickery. Hera tried to chain him and failed; she tried to emulate his feat of giving birth unaided to *Athene,* and only managed to produce the monstrous Typhon. Hera's anger was turned onto the many females who consorted with Zeus (see *Echo, Io*). She dealt out death, pain, imprisonment, banishment, and many other neat strokes. Like making sure the whole Trojan race was wiped out because Paris had once thought *Aphrodite* more beautiful than she.

Hermaphroditos
Son of *Hermes* and *Aphrodite.*

Hermaphroditos was an outdoor type who roamed wild on Mount Ida. One day, when bathing in a lake, he was observed by the nymph Salmacis, who, dazed with love for him, threw herself on him in a passionate embrace. Poor Hermaphroditos, wanting none of that sort of thing, struggled in vain to get free. Salmacis called on the gods to make them one and their bodies merged, creating a creature that was neither man nor woman, yet both. An hermaphrodite. Before he was dragged down into the depths of the lake, the unfortunate lad called out a request that in future whoever bathed in those waters should lose their virility.

Hermes
God of travellers, trade and eloquence.

Originally a pastoral god watching over flocks and houses, Hermes became the god of travellers, his image being placed at junctions and crossroads. Travel and trade being closely linked, he then became a mercantile god, influencing profit. Extending the idea of profit, he took on the role of god of gambling, hazard and gaming. As sales patter is a necessary ingredient of trade, Hermes became the god of eloquence and a messenger. The Olympian gods used him in this capacity, and he was equipped with winged helmet and winged sandals. Hermes was also god of athletes and is credited with the invention of boxing and racing. He accompanied souls to *Hades*, being known as Psychopompos ('soul-conductor'). Other names for him are Logios ('wordy'), Diactoros ('messenger'), and Agonios ('judge of contests').

First Hermes was represented as a mature, bearded athlete; later, and this seems to have been a general trend, he became younger in aspect and was pictured as an *ephebe* (young athlete), carrying the *caduceus* (rod with twined snakes) and wearing winged sandals and *petasus* (winged helmet).

Born in Arcadia, son of Maia and *Zeus*, Hermes was a tricky sort of child, planning a robbery as soon as he was born. Quietly he clambered out of his cradle, put on a huge pair of sandals, and crept off to where a herd of cattle under the care of *Apollo* were penned for the night. He stole fifty heifers, making them walk backwards to confuse pursuers. He hid the animals in a cave after sacrificing the two fattest to the gods, skilfully skinning and butchering them. Then he crept back to his cave-nursery and feigned sleep. Apollo had a good idea of who was responsible for the theft, even though Hermes was only one day old. He searched the cave on Mount Cyllene, found nothing, and demanded to know where his cattle were hidden. Hermes swore on Zeus' head that he was just an innocent babe. Apollo picked him up and Hermes immediately did what babies do, all over Apollo's hand. They went to see Zeus, the furious infant running ahead with his swaddling clothes flying about his shoulders. When they reached Zeus the child ranted and raved at Apollo like a seasoned trooper, and swore many oaths of his own innocence. Zeus was hugely amused and the heavens rang with laughter. When he had recovered his composure, Zeus ordered Hermes to return the cows to Apollo. Hermes agreed, but resorted to more trickery. When all else failed he played the lyre, which he had invented. Apollo was enraptured by the sweet sound and willingly exchanged the cows for the wonderful instrument. He also secured for Hermes the job of Messenger of the Gods, and many other favours.

Hermes turned out to be the most pleasant and helpful of the gods. He was cheerful, charming, and always eager to assist; often finding ingenious solutions to the gods' problems. Not only the gods, but also heroes and ordinary men benefited from his kindness and obliging nature. Hermes had many children, by goddesses, nymphs, and mortal women. Foremost of these was the god *Pan*.

Hesperides
Goddesses who guarded the golden apples of the sun.

The Hesperides lived in gardens to the far west of Ocean, a place some thought of as the entrance to the kingdom of *Hades*. Some say they are the daughters of night, some the daughters of *Atlas*.

Hestia
Goddess of fire and the domestic hearth.

Every Greek town had its public hearth, sacred to her. Shrines of Hestia were commonly circular. Oldest of the Olympians, first-born of *Cronus* and *Rhea*, Hestia was restful, full of repose. She remained unmoved by the disputes and general brouhaha of Olympus, and stayed ever virgin. Hestia represented the quiet centre of existence, a central element in the life of home and city. Every sacrifice began with an invocation to her, for her worshippers understood how important she was.

Horae
Guardian goddesses of nature; rain goddesses; they looked after law, justice and peace, and protected young people.

There were three Horae – Eunomia, Dike, and Irene. They were full of poise and charm, and besides looking after the entrance to Olympus they entertained the gods by dancing for them, with the *Graces*.

Hyperion
A Titan, father of *Helios* ('the sun'), *Selene* ('the moon'), and *Eos* ('dawn'). Originally an important sky-father, Hyperion means 'the one overhead' or 'him up there'. Often confused with Helios.

Hypnos
'Sleep'; son of *Nux* ('night'), brother to *Thanatos* ('death'), and father of *Morpheus*, god of dreams.

A winged god, Hypnos had power over the Olympians as well as over mortals. He made people sleep by fanning them with his wings, or by tapping them with his wand.

Ilythia
Goddess of childbirth.

Ilythia brought both pain and relief; no child could be born without her presence. An ancient Cretan goddess, she is shown kneeling and holding a torch, for she brought light to the eyes of the new-born child.

Io
A priestess of the goddess *Hera*.

In order to have his way with Io, *Zeus* turned himself into a cloud. His wife, Hera, was soon hot on the trail, so Zeus turned Io into a white heifer to disguise her. He was persuaded to give Hera the heifer as a gift and the goddess, who had her suspicions, set *Argos Panoptes* ('all seeing') to watch the animal. *Hermes* charmed the giant to sleep with the sound of the flute he had inherited from *Appolo*. When Argos' hundred eyes were all closed, Hermes cut off his head. Hera sent a fly to sting and annoy the white heifer. To escape this persistent torture Io fled, swam the sea (which thereafter was named Ionian), and ended up in Egypt with her child, Epaphus. Later she was confused with the Egyptian *Isis* and her son with *Apis*.

Iris
Goddess of the rainbow.

Iris was the personal messenger of *Zeus*, who used her to transmit messages to men and gods. She carried the caduceus and had wings on her shoulders. Handmaiden to *Hera*, Iris also performed useful services to the other Olympians. Her cult centre was on Delos, and the proper offerings to her were dried figs and honey cakes.

Kore
'Girl'; alias *Persephone* (*q.v.*).

Leto
Alias Latona; goddess of night.

Mother of *Apollo*, Leto suffered terribly in bearing her child; for the jealous *Hera*, knowing that no child could be born without *Ilythia*, kept the goddess of birth away from her. For nine days Leto was racked with pain, until at last *Iris* managed to locate Ilythia and fetch her to the birthplace.

Melicertes
Adopted by the Greeks from the Phoenician god *Melkart* (*q.v.*), and worshipped in Corinth under the name Palaemon. The original boy on a dolphin.

Mnemosyne
A Titaness who bore the nine *Muses*. Inevitably, *Zeus* was the father.

Moros
God of destiny.

A shadowy figure supreme even to the Olympians. He was invisible, dark and unknown.

Morpheus
God of dreams.

He was the son of *Hypnos*, god of sleep, and therefore nephew of *Thanatos*, god of death.

Muses
Goddesses of springs, memory and poetry; daughters of *Zeus* and *Mnemosyne*.

Their numbers varied until they were fixed at nine. They were Clio, muse of history, Euterpe, muse of flute-playing, Thalia, muse of comedy, Melpomene, muse of tragedy, Terpsichore, muse of dancing and lyric poetry, Erato, muse of love poetry, Polyhymnia, muse of mime, Urania, muse of astronomy, Calliope, muse of epic poetry. Their oldest sanctuary was at Pieria in Thrace, but they were worshipped throughout Greece. Offerings to them were milk, honey, and cakes of grain and honey

Nemesis
Goddess of destiny; alias Adrasteia, 'the inevitable'

In early times Nemesis was a harsh, unremitting and irrational force; later she softened into a kind of bland acceptance of what must be. When the Persians invaded Greece, they brought with them a block of fine marble from which they intended to carve a victory monument. They met the Greeks at Marathon, and were badly beaten. The Greeks captured the block of marble and from it carved a statue of Nemesis. It was an elegant comment on the character of the goddess, as well as a wise gesture of propitiation.

Nereus
God of the sea; alias Proteus, Phorcys, 'the old one of the sea'.

Nereus was a shape-shifter and knew the future. If you could manage to take hold of him and keep clinging to all the different shapes he assumed, then he would answer any question you cared to put to him. Considered to be a just and kind god.

Nike
Goddess of victory.

Nike was daughter of the river nymph Styx and a Titan named Pallas. Her sisters were Bia ('violence'), Zelos ('jealousy') and Kratos ('force'). Nike was often used in sculpture to symbolize victory and was shown as a winged maiden holding aloft the wreath of victor's laurels (in reality, bay leaves). The term 'nike' is used to describe the small figures of the goddess often held by larger statues. The Romans knew her as *Victoria*.

Nux
'Night'. The goddess Nux sprang from *Chaos*, and among her own offspring were *Hypnos* ('sleep'), *Thanatos* ('death') and *Phanes* ('light') – the latter emerging from a vast egg formed by Nux and *Ether* ('air'), another of the goddess's children. Phanes and Nux later created *Uranus* ('heaven') and *Gaia* ('earth').

Oceanus
Ancieht sea god, ruler of the waters which surrounded the world of men.

Son of *Uranus* and *Gaia*, Oceanus married his sister, Tethys, and had six thousand children by her. Half of them were Oceanids, sea spirits, and half were rivers. When the Olympians came to power, he was displaced by the god *Poseidon*.

Pan
God of herds and male sexuality.

An Arcadian deity, his name means 'feeder of flocks' and has no apparent connection with the Greek word *pan* meaning 'all'. He was a bearded, horned man with the lower limbs of a goat. Often allied to or confused with the Satyrs, those lusty attendants of the god *Dionysus* (*q.v.*), Pan was a popular god; he was of the earth, of the folklore of ordinary people. Though a minor figure when compared to the mighty ones of epic and literary fame, Pan was probably closer to people's hearts than the Olympians.

He was the embodiment of male sexuality, of the free-ranging libido, his character expressed by the goat, symbol of unbridled fecundity. Among his more notable conquests were *Selene*, goddess of the moon, the nymph Pitys who ended her career as a pine tree, and the famous Syrinx. Syrinx was a nymph who would have no part of Pan; all she showed him was a clean pair of heels. Pan gave chase in the usual way and was on the point of seizing Syrinx and making a dishonest woman of her, when she called aloud for help to her father Ladon. Ladon was a river; he turned his daughter into a reed, thus foiling the amorous Pan. With commendable self-control the god sought solace in music; he cut some reeds and fashioned a new instrument, thereafter called the Syrinx, or pan pipes.

Pan was a god of extreme and rustic antiquity and he came to prominence among the Greeks in the following way. The renowned runner Pheidippides was jogging over the mountains to ask the Spartans for help in the coming battle against the invading Persians. Pan accosted him on the heights and demanded to know why the Athenians had not been honouring him for favours received. He hinted that if they acted better, he would help them in the battle.

178

When the Spartan contingent arrived at Marathon, the tiny Athenian army had scored a miraculous and devasting victory over the Persian hordes. The Athenians were canny enough to create a shrine for Pan on the Acropolis in recognition of his help.

Apart from being reponsible for the fertility of men and animals, Pan had a dark side. He was deemed to be the cause of the wild and unreasoning terror which seizes men and animals in high and lonely places. Moorlands, mountain sides, deep and gloomy woods seemed at times to affect people with a grim horror, an unexplained fear. Examples of that fear are not unknown even today; it is rightly called 'panic'. Pan, however, thought it was great fun. When not engaged in dalliance, he would lie in wait in some desolate spot in order to scare the wits out of any innocent traveller who might happen along.

Pan's parentage was obscure. The god *Hermes* was claimed as his father, but then the myth-makers had to account for Pan's undeniable goat characteristics: hooves, horns and such. The solution was to take a human or nymph (various names were suggested) and have Hermes assume the body of a goat for the necessary act. Apart from the gross male chauvinism implied in this arrangement, there were good precedents (see *Zeus*) in which the feelings, not to mention the physical discomfort, of the lady concerned were studiously ignored. Either that or ancient Greek nymphs were a good deal more adventurous than modern ones.

There is one more thing to be mentioned to Pan's discredit: he would insist on presenting young boys with musical instruments, thus condemning many a parent to hours of agony.

Persephone
Goddess of corn and the Underworld, consort of *Hades*.

Daughter of *Demeter* (*q.v.*), Persephone is sometimes called *Kore*, symbolizing the young corn, as Demeter symbolized the ripe corn. Though fond of *Adonis* (*q.v.*), she remained chaste. Her attributes were the bat, the narcissus, and the pomegranate. Persephone was given pomegranate seeds to ensure that she was permanently linked to the kingdom of death.

179

Phanes
'Light'; sometimes called Eros (not to be confused with the god of love).

First of all the recognizable gods, forefather of *Zeus*. Born from a vast egg formed by *Nux* ('night') and *Ether* ('air'), Phanes joined with Nux to create *Uranus* ('heaven') and *Gaia* ('earth'). (See *Ether*.)

Phoebe
A Titaness.

She was mother of *Leto* and so grandmother of the god *Apollo*, who took her epithet, Phoebus ('shining').

Pluto
Alias for *Hades*.

The name means 'riches', indicating the wealth of the earth in which Hades had his domain.

Pollux
See *Dioscures*.

Poseidon
God of the sea.

An Olympian whose name has the meaning 'master'. Poseidon once held sway over the earth and heavens, till supplanted by *Zeus*. One time god of earthquakes, fecundity and vegetation, he was also called Genethlios ('creator'). Horses and bulls, symbols of generative life-force, were sacred to him. Bulls, indeed, were sacrificed to him by being thrown into the sea, and horse races were held in his honour.

Poseidon was a son of *Cronos* and *Rhea*. He fought for the Olympians against the Titans, and his reward after victory was the illimitable ocean. Equal to Zeus by birth, he was less powerful than that god. As the master of lakes and rivers, as well as the seas, Poseidon was constantly in dispute with the gods who owned coastal areas. He was a possessive god, his waves constantly licking at the land, breaking off a bit here, a bit there. Poseidon was much given to oubursts of rage, which affected men as storms. He was thought of as an oldish fellow, driving a chariot. His amorous adventures were not entirely heterosexual. (See *Demeter* and *Gorgons*.)

Prometheus
'He who foresees', a demiurge, a god of creation.

One of the four sons of Iapetus. The others were *Atlas*, Menoetius, and Epimetheus. Prometheus is said to have made the first man from earth, water, and his own tears. When the Olympians were allotting portions of the sacrificial animal, Prometheus fooled *Zeus* into choosing the fat and bones. Zeus promptly withheld fire from men, so Prometheus stole fire from the forge of *Hephaestus* on the island of Lemnos; but Zeus had another trick up his sleeve. He created Pandora, a beautiful virgin, on whom the gods heaped all their gifts. Zeus, angered by the theft of fire, ensured that Pandora received from *Hermes* his treacherous qualities. Zeus gave Pandora a vase, or some say a box, full of destructive powers. Pandora was welcomed by Epimetheus, Prometheus' brother; as soon as she was among mankind she unstoppered the vase and all the sad afflictions of life flew out and covered the earth. A typically mean trick on the part of Zeus.

Rhea
The original Great Goddess; the Mother.

In the confused family relationships of the early gods, Rhea is sometimes described as *Cronus'* daughter, sometimes as his sister. What is not in doubt is that she was his wife as well; and every child she bore him was snatched away and swallowed by the father. Cronus hoped by this to avoid any threat to his authority, no doubt remembering what he had done to *Uranus*. To save the young *Zeus*, Rhea wrapped a stone in cloths and gave it to Cronus. He gulped it down unsuspectingly, and Rhea hid the baby until it could grow enough to challenge Cronus' supremacy. Originally an orgiastic Cretan Great Goddess, Rhea was an example of the widespread cult of the Great Mother, which took many shapes and names in the ancient Middle East. She was also mother of *Hestia, Hera, Demeter, Hades,* and *Poseidon.*

Selene
Goddess of the moon, sister of *Helios*, the sun.

Also called Mene, Selene fell in love with the young Endymion, embracing him secretly as he slept. Endymion requested immortality from the gods, and was careful to demand eternal youth as well. *Zeus* agreed, but added the condition that Endymion must sleep forever. The faithful Selene, driving across the night sky in her chariot, still visits the sleeping youth. Selene's only other recorded liaison was with the god *Pan*, who seduced her after luring her into a wood with a white fleece.

Thanatos
God of death.

Thanatos was sometimes a winged spirit and sometimes a black-robed man carrying a sword. Those he struck with his sword went to the kingdom of *Hades*, so Thanatos may be regarded as some sort of lethal recruiting officer. There was nothing obviously horrible or dramatic about him; he was a functionary, just doing his job. Thanatos was the son of *Nux* ('night') and brother of *Hypnos*.

Uranus
Son and husband of Gaia, the earth goddess.

Uranus sired the Titans, a race of giants. Then Gaia produced brood after brood of monsters, Cyclopes, and Hecatoncheires, creatures with a hundred arms and fifty heads apiece. Uranus was horrified by these monstrosities and shut them away. Gaia reacted angrily to this treatment of her children and planned revenge on her spouse. She sharpened up a wicked-looking sickle and whispered her plot to her children. *Cronus* was quick to see personal advantage in his mother's desire for revenge. When his father slept, Cronus used the sickle to castrate him. He then seized power and continued the work of procreation.

Zeus
God of the sky; lord of all high things, clouds, rain, winds, thunder, mountain tops. Founder of the Olympian dynasty.

182

Zeus was the supreme god; protector of laws, friend of the weak, champion of justice, omnipotent and omniscient. His sanctuary at Dodona in Epirus contained his sacred oak. Men would come from all over Greece to listen to the tree, for it was thought that Zeus spoke oracles in the rustlings of its leaves.

Zeus is represented as a powerful man of regal bearing, bearded and manly, robust and wise. He carries a sceptre and a thunderbolt. He was as proud, well formed and strong as a mature oak tree. Serene and majestic, he was the idealized ruler. He had style.

Zeus came to power by a *coup d'état*, banishing his grotesquely horrible father, *Cronus*, to eternal imprisonment below sea and earth. Having disposed of the tyrant and rescued his swallowed brothers and sisters, Zeus mounted a campaign against the Titans, his near relatives, and overthrew them in a mighty, earth-singeing battle. He then turned his forces against the giants, and then against Typhoeus, monster son of *Gaia* and Tartarus. When the giants were beaten and Typhoeus safely trapped under Mount Etna, Zeus was able to organize his court on Olympus and create a power structure responsive to his wishes.

Although a practical leader, Zeus was still a despot, moved more by anger than by justice, more by politics than by mercy. He was the divine version of the 'strong man'; the kind of leader some foolish humans still yearn after, despite the bloody lessons of recent history. Zeus epitomized the self-willed hero, active, golden, but ultimately selfish and incapable of moral growth.

The amorous affairs of Zeus are too numerous to recount. They are, on the whole, characterized by deceit, guile, and brute force; all existing in an aura of sadness, for neither Zeus nor any of his many ladies ever achieved a noble or worthwhile relationship. Zeus used and abused his divine powers for his personal ends. The ladies, many of them unwilling, were supposed to feel flattered at being used as sexual objects; and Zeus himself was always guiltily glancing over his shoulder in case the furious *Hera* should appear, divine rolling-pin in hand. Under these conditions Zeus' nobility soon dissolves into knockabout farce, as he changes from bull to snake, to swan, to golden rain, and even to a cloud, in order to have his way with the luckless females.

On the credit side, the stories of Zeus told by Hesiod and

Homer are wonderful flights of sustained poetic imagination, vivid, marvellous and masterly. Zeus was worshipped all over Greece, his influence reaching into every corner of the ancient world. He is paralleled in many Indo-European civilizations, from India to England. (See *Dionysus*.)

Angerona
Goddess of secrecy.

Ancient peoples acknowledged that the names of individuals, cities and nations were mysteriously powerful. For practical purposes there was an everyday name, but everything also had a secret name. If you could discover an enemy's secret name then he was powerless to resist you. Angerona was probably the custodian of the secret name of Rome. She is shown with her mouth bound and sealed, one finger placed on it in warning. We know little else about her or her cult. The secret has been well kept.

Bellona
Goddess of war.

Bellona's temple in Rome recruited its priests from gladiators; successful ones obviously. It was the place where foreign emissaries were met by the senate; which is indicative perhaps of what the Romans thought of foreigners. Before the temple was a certain pillar which was struck with a lance on the declaration of war. This tradition cannot have been unknown to ambassadors from other lands; the Romans were not novices in psychological aggression.

Bona Dea
Fertility goddess worshipped only by women. (See *Fauna*.)

Bonus Eventus
God of success in enterprise.

Originally a rustic deity, his brief was widened to include all manner of enterprises. Bonus Eventus became a popular city god with his own temple and a dedication on the Capitol.

Camenae
Oracular goddesses who were patrons of a sacred spring in a grove south of the Porta Capena (the gate which led to the Via Appia – the major approach road to Rome from the south).

Ceres
Goddess of corn.

Ceres' ancient cult was linked to that of Liber and Libera, earth deities. Her cult was Hellenized to the extent of merging with that of the Greek goddess *Demeter*. Ceres' festival was held in April, and she had a popular following.

Consus
God of seed sowing.

Consus' altar in Rome was buried in earth, being cleared only for two festivals a year. His cult was connected with horses, mules and asses. Races were held in his honour. During the festivals, the cult animals were given a rest and decked out in holiday garlands. An agricultural god, his worship was a good deal older than later gods of the city and state.

Cupid
God of love and son of *Venus*.

A weaker counterpart of *Eros*, he was not taken too seriously. Cupid was too 'soft' and lacked the powerful influence of the Greek god.

Diana
Goddess of fertility, childbirth, and wild places.

Later identified with the Greek *Artemis*, Diana acquired that goddess's attributes. Some hint of her former worship may be seen in the story of her temple near Lake Nemi, just north of Rome. It was a grove of oak trees, and the tradition went that any escaped slave who could challenge and slay the incumbent had the right to take his place. That included food, sanctuary and all the honour due to that position. It also included the risk of another desperate runaway arriving under cover of night and doing exactly the same thing to him.

Dis Pater
God of the Underworld.

186

His name Dis ('riches') appears to be a translation of *Pluto*, the Greek for riches and an alias for *Hades*. Not a popular god with the Romans, who didn't like to tempt death too much. They were far more interested in getting good value in this life. To that end they compiled a god guide of their own, the Indigamentum, which told them which god was responsible for what, what was offered and for what kind of sacrifice. They took pragmatic religion to its ultimate.

Egeria
Goddess of fountains and childbirth.

Pregnant women sacrificed to Egeria in order to ease the delivery of the expected child. She was worshipped along with *Diana*. She was also associated with the spring sacred to the *Camenae*.

Epona
Goddess of horses.

Epona was a Celtic deity adopted by the Roman cavalry. The Romans adopted gods from all over the place, but Epona seems to have been the only Celtic import. Perhaps they were more impressed by the skilful Celtic charioteers and riders than they officially admitted. (See *Epona*, Celtic goddess.)

Fauna
Goddess of fertility, female counterpart to *Faunus*.

Alias *Bona Dea*, Fauna's festival was celebrated by women only. Men were strictly excluded from what appears to have been a secret orgiastic celebration. In 62 B.C., one Publius Clodius had the temerity to dress himself up as a woman and infiltrate the secret rites. What made things worse was that the rites were being held in the house of the then Pontifex Maximus, who happened to be Julius Caesar. The scandal assumed the proportions of a political crisis.

Faunus
God of crops and herds, an oracular deity.

Faunus' temple, the Lupercal, was named after the grotto where

Romulus and Remus were suckled by the she-wolf. His festival, the Lupercalia, was one of purification and involved the sacrifice of goats and dogs. His priests, naked except for freshly-skinned goat hides, would whip women who wished to become pregnant with thongs of goatskin.

One day the god Faunus spied on Hercules and Omphale who lay together in a cave. As they slept, Faunus sneaked in, intending to take advantage of the nymph. But unknown to him the two lovers had exchanged clothes; a peculiar sort of prank. Faunus felt what he thought was Omphale's soft dress. Eagerly he proceeded with his plan. He soon discovered his error when a bewildered Hercules awoke. The hero's language is not recorded, but the event left a deep enough impression on the unfortunate Faunus for him to order that in future his priests must appear half-clad to avoid any possibility of error as to their gender.

Februus
Etruscan underworld god, equivalent to *Dis Pater*. February, the month of the dead, is his sacred month.

Feronia
Goddess of spring flowers, associated with *Flora*.

At her shrine were held the ceremonies for the manumission of slaves.

Fides
God of good faith.

Fides was responsible for verbal contracts; a sort of safeguard for the honest.

Flora
Goddess of fruitfulness and flowers.

Helped by *Robigus*, she defended corn from red mildew, and with the assistance of *Pomona* she looked after fruit trees. Flora's festivals were in April and May. She was the favourite goddess of courtesans.

Fortuna
Goddess of fate and chance.

Fortuna was an ancient civic deity and her aliases include Primigenia ('first-born child of Jupiter'), Muliebris ('of married women'), and Univirae ('once-married'). Her attributes were the sphere, the ship's rudder, the cornucopia, and the wheel. She brought men both evil and good, and was popular with high and low. The Emperors had an image of her in their bedrooms, both as a warning and as an encouragement (and also, one suspects, to have something to blame). Her image was powerful enough to last to this day. Wheels of fortune are to be found in casinos and church fêtes alike. The tenth card of the Major Arcana of the Tarot pack shows her wheel, still turning.

Fortuna advised her worshippers by making them draw oak billets at random from a jar. On the billets were written words of advice. People still open books at random to seek answers to questions; it used to be Virgil but more commonly now it is the Bible.

Genius
Protective god of individuals, groups and the state.

A sort of guardian angel. As well as every person, every place had its own guardian, *genius loci*. The Emperors turned their personal *genii* into public objects of worship.

Janus
God of doorways, gates, harbours, travel, daybreak – things which had the sense of beginning or going out.

As Janus Pater he was thought of as the creator and took precedence even over *Jupiter* in prayers. He is depicted as having two faces, signifying past wisdom and future knowledge. The first month of the year is his, and also the first day of each month. His temple was in the Forum; in times of war its gates were open, in times of peace they were closed. Because of the warlike nature of the Romans there are only eight recorded closings of the gates from the time of King Numa (715–672 B.C.) to the fourth century A.D. The temple was built on a spot where Janus was reputed to

189

have saved Rome from a sneak attack by Tatius and his Sabines. The god caused boiling water to gush out of the ground onto the invaders.

Juno
Goddess of light, childbirth, marriage.

Protectress of Roman matrons, Juno became protectress of the whole state, responsible for its well-being and prosperity. Her temple is ancient, having been built just after the foundation of Rome. Her festivals, the Matronalia, were held in March. During the festivities the woman of the house was the leading figure. She received presents and served her own slaves at table, confirming the provident and protective aspects of motherhood.

Juno had several aspects and her images had different attributes. One of her titles is Regina, queen, and she forms the Capitoline triad of gods with *Jupiter* and *Minerva*. Peacocks and geese are sacred to her, and she was associated with the moon.

During a Gaulish attack on Rome (*circa* 390 B.C.) her sacred geese raised the alarm. As a result, she gained the title Juno Moneta ('warning'). Later a mint was founded near her shrine and its coins acquired the epithet *moneta*, from which we get our word 'money'.

Equivalent to the Greek goddess *Hera*.

Jupiter
God of the sky (which includes sun, moon, winds, rain, thunder).

A warrior god, Jupiter was protector of youths and of the Roman state. He had many epithets: Liber ('creativity'), Dapalis ('sowing'), Terminus ('boundaries'), Optimus Maximus ('biggest and best'), Conservator Orbis ('preserver of the world'), and even Pistor ('baker'). This last title came from his advice to the beleaguered Romans to throw bread down onto their Gaulish attackers, to prove they had no fear of being starved into surrender. He shared the ancient Quirinal temple with *Juno* and *Minerva*, and the famous games were held in his honour. His images show him to be a more solemn and self-conscious copy of the great *Zeus*.

Jupiter had three thunderbolts. He could hurl the first at his own discretion, the second could only be used with the consent of twelve other gods, and the third required the permission of superior and hidden gods before it could be released. It is rather like a modern head of state consulting with his ministers before escalating armed intervention, and is typical of the Roman attitude of mind, essentially pragmatic and politic.

Lar
God of the house.

Originally a field protector, Lar shared the hearth with the *Penates* and *Vesta*. He is depicted as a happy youth and was honoured on all significant family occasions. Brides offered him sacrifice and money on entering the house. Rams were sacrificed to him after funerals as purification offerings. He lived quite happily along with numerous other household gods.

Lara or Mania
A talkative nymph whose tongue was cut out by *Jupiter*, who had had enough. Lara became a frightful bogey, used to scare children into obedience. She was the mother of the *Manes*.

Larvae
See *Lemures*.

Lemures
Ghosts of the dead.

The Lemures returned to wreak mischief and terror among the living. The ghost of Remus returned, not unreasonably, to complain about having been murdered, so Romulus instituted a festival in his honour to pacify him. It was called the Remuria, later corrupted to Lemuria.

The festival rites were performed by the father of each household. Barefooted, at midnight, he would snap his fingers, wash his hands, and fill his mouth with black beans. He would then toss the beans over his shoulder while chanting a banishing spell. After more ritual hand-washing, he would strike a brass gong and command the spirits to depart.

Liber and Libera
'He (or she) who germinates.' Fertility deities (male and female) linked to the earth goddess cult.

Their festival, the Liberalia, was celebrated on the 17th March. On that day, honey cake was sold in the streets by old women wearing ivy wreaths. It was also the day on which Roman adolescent boys assumed the *toga virilis* – symbol of reaching adulthood.

Liber Pater
God of human and agricultural fertility, linked with *Dionysus*. Derived from the *Liber/Libera* pair of deities.

During his festival, the Liberalia, adolescents donned the *toga virilis* for the first time. It was a sign of their reaching adulthood. Liber Pater became associated with Dionysus and was therefore guardian of vines.

Libitina
Goddess of funerals.

An ancient underworld deity linked to *Proserpina*. A coin had to be taken to her temple on behalf of each person who died. Funerals were arranged by *libitinarii*.

Maia
Goddess of fertility, associated with *Fauna*.

Her festival was the first of May when the priest of the fire god *Vulcan* offered her sacrifices. Maia gave her name to the following month.

Manes
Spirits of the dead.

On the foundation of every town, a hole was dug and covered with a stone. This symbolized the way to the Underworld. The stone was removed three times a year to appease the spirits and to allow them access. Early blood sacrifices to the Manes probably gave rise to gladiatorial combats, whose ritual origins were lost when blood-lust, politics and showmanship took over. Festivals of the Manes were in February, the month of the dead, and included a holiday from both business and religion. The tombs of the dead were decorated with flowers and food offerings.

The term *Manes* derives from an obsolete word for 'good', and its use for potentially dangerous spirits can be compared to the Greek term for the Furies, *Eumenides* – 'kindly ones'.

Mars
God of war and agriculture.

Officially less powerful than *Jupiter*, Mars' cult was the dynamic religious expression of the Roman mind. Like his people, he was first a farmer, then a soldier. Son of *Juno* and a mystic flower, he fathered Romulus and Remus on Rhea Silvia (she had little say in the matter; he approached her when she was sleeping). Sacred to him were the woodpecker, horse and wolf; also the oak, fig, laurel and dog-wood trees, and the humble bean. As god of war, Mars was honoured before and after battle and shared in any loot. His temple held sacred spears and the Ancilla, twelve sacred shields. The first shield was a divine gift to Rome, a pledge for the security of the city. The wily King Numa (715–672 B.C.) had eleven identical shields made to confuse potential thieves. The Ancilla were guarded by special priests, the Salii. One wonders how many of them knew which was the original shield? Indeed, did anyone know?

Mars gives us the name March, the month in which his festivities took place. His altar on the Campus Martius was purified every five years at census time. His agricultural aspect was honoured in the month of May; for he was also god of Spring.

Mercury
God of merchants.

To the Greek image of *Hermes*, with caduceus, winged hat and winged sandals, the practical Romans added a purse. Mercury arose later in Roman history as a civic god to take care of the mercantile aspects of a prosperous Empire. He was very popular. His sacred bird was the cock.

193

Minerva
Goddess of war, schools, commerce and artisans.

Minerva's Etruscan origins show influence from the cult of *Athene*, and also aspects of an ancient Italic goddess of handicrafts, Menerva. She was popular among craftsmen, doctors and musicians; and became one of the triad of the Capitoline Hill with *Juno* and *Jupiter*, a state goddess of the first rank.

Mithras
God of regeneration, vegetation and the sun.

If Mithraism had succeeded in overwhelming Christianity in the early years of our era, and for a time that was a possibility, then the world would be a very different place. The worship of Mithras, a version of the Indian god *Mitra*, had aspects which were especially attractive to the military mind. It had a wide and enthusiastic following among the legions and was carried all over the Roman Empire, including Britain, where a Mithraic shrine has been unearthed in London.

Originally Persian, the intercessor between *Ormazd* and mankind, Mithras promised his adherents worldly success and joy in the afterworld. What more could any man want? The religion was secretive, restrictive, hierarchical and exclusive in the sense that only men were entitled to take part in its mysteries. It contained much symbolism and a deal of soldierly play-acting. It was a combination of rugger club, smoking room, officers' mess and amateur dramatic society, all with Masonic overtones. No wonder it lasted a very long time, with some of its lore still apparently surviving in Syria and India.

The carefully screened candidate faced a rising gradation of initiation rites, each with its own ritual and stage directions. These degrees were named The Crow, The Secret, The Soldier, The Lion, The Persian, The Runner of the Sun, The Father, and The Father of Fathers. There were also additional degrees, as yet secret, ending with the King of Kings; a degree which could only be held by those of royal blood. This last degree was usually occupied by the Shahinshah of Persia (Iran).

Mithras himself is usually depicted as a young man wearing a short tunic and a Phrygian cap; he is in the act of driving a short sword into the neck-vein of a bull he has subdued. This symbol of man overcoming the dynamic sexual forces within himself merges with teaching derived from the Iranian cult of dualism; it contains an apocalyptic element in which, finally, the good are separated from the bad. There are many more similar Zoroastrian doctrines which combine to make an introverted and complex theology.

Among the rituals of the cult of Mithras was the Taurobolium, in which the initiate was placed under a grating on which a bull was sacrificed. The initiate, drenched with blood, identified himself with the slain god. It was at the same time a regenerative washing; the initiate emerged as if from death, reborn to a new life. There were also mock battles symbolizing the soul's fight with negative forces, a ritual communal meal, and all manner of theatricals in underground caverns (or rooms designed to look like caverns) with jolly fellows dressed up as demons, wild animals, kings and such. There were unveilings of hidden statues, the beating of drums, baptisms with honey, and trance-like states induced by hallucinogens. These goings-on were the more effective by being generally unavailable except to the few.

Apart from all that and a definite magical odour (astrology, cabbalistic numerology, 'words of power' et cetera), Mithraism had a side that was genuinely mystic. It has been likened to a psychic training system involving self-mastery, transmutation of sexual energy into psychic power, and the creation of what some schoolmasters still call 'character', which is nothing less than the conviction that you are right despite what any lesser mortals might suggest to the contrary. In fact it produced thoroughly 'worthy' people; so much so that Tertullian in the third century A.D. holds certain Mithraists up to slack Christians as good examples of fidelity and self-denial.

One can see in the appurtenances of Mithraism the germ of many a secret society and occult rite, many an exclusive cabal, and also the theme of muscular righteousness that is the basis for certain private schools and clubs. The idea of a religion that is only available to a selected few is more than merely arrogant; it is self-defeating. Hence the demise of Mithraism as a genuine spiritual expression. (See *Mithra* in the Middle East General section.)

Neptune
God of the sea.

Most of Neptune's attributes and power derive from the great Greek *Poseidon*. Originally worshipped on a small scale as insurance against drought, he became the unwitting incumbent of a vast maritime empire. The Romans were not what you might call natural sailors. They didn't have the Greek or Carthaginian feel for the sea. But they learnt quickly when it was to their military advantage. And they simply had to have a god of their own to make their naval supremacy authoritative.

Ops
Goddess of the harvest.

Ops looked after the crops owned by the state and later acquired aspects of the Greek goddess *Rhea*. The wealth with which she was associated was first of all in produce, later in more portable opulence.

Orcus
God of death; an alias of *Pluto*.

Pales
Goddess of flocks (was originally male).

An ancient divinity, her festival coincided with the date of the foundation of Rome. The festival, the Palilia, was one of purification. Houses and stables were sprinkled with lustral water supplied by the Vestals. Pales gave her name to the Palatine Hill, which gives us our word for the large and splendid houses of lords temporal and spiritual: palace.

Penates
Gods of the larder.

The Penates looked after food and drink, and were therefore of great importance to the family. They were two in number and shared a somewhat crowded hearth with *Vesta* and *Lar*. Their attachment was to the family rather than to the building, and so they moved with the family. There was also a cult of Penates on

196

the state level. Objects sacred to this cult were in the care of the Vestals.

Picus
God of agriculture (his name means 'woodpecker').

Woodpeckers were sacred to *Mars*, and birds of omen. A woodpecker brought food to Romulus and Remus. The plethora of minor gods, deriving from local deities, was indicative of the Roman ability to take the best of whatever was available, and make use of it.

Pomona
A minor Roman goddess. Her especial duty was towards fruit trees. She had no festival. (See *Flora*.)

Portunus
A god of harbours.

Of great antiquity, his festival was in August. Portunus was very much in the shadow of the mighty *Janus*.

Proserpina
Roman name for the Greek goddess *Persephone*.

Quirinus
Sabine god of war.

Connected with the Quirinal Hill, Quirinus was incorporated into Roman religious life as a state god, showing that there could have been nothing novel or upsetting about his cult. Absorption rather than suppression was the Roman attitude to foreign or conquered cults. It took the revolutionary Gospel of Christ to alter their minds. (See following entry.)

Robigus
God of red mildew.

His cult was organized by the priest of *Quirinus*, who performed propitiatory rites during April, and sacrificed sheep and a red-haired dog. (See previous entry and *Flora*.)

Rumina
Goddess of nursing mothers.

Rumina's shrine was under the *ficus ruminalis*, 'the fig of suckling'. Milk was offered at her shrine, not the usual wine.

Saturn
God of workers and vine-growers.

Driven from heaven by *Jupiter*, Saturn hid in Latium ('place of hiding'). He was responsible for prosperity and abundance. His famous festival was the Saturnalia (17-23 Dec.), a time of merry-making and feasting (some derive Saturn from *satur*, 'gorged' or 'stuffed'). All normal life stopped; law courts, schools and businesses were closed, and even warfare was interrupted. Slaves were allowed to do and say what they liked; for a time. Things were turned topsy-turvy; masters waited on slaves at table, with a Lord of Misrule misdirecting the revels. This was the origin of the similar mediaeval celebrations surrounding the election of a boy bishop for a short period. Another curious survival of this can be seen in the British army, when the officers of the regiment serve Christmas dinner to the men.

Saturn was an important enough god for his temple to be used as a depository for the state treasury and archives, and for the standards of legions not in the field.

Silvanus
God of forests and woods.

Silvanus patronized the clearing of land for farming, and so became the guardian of farming. He was propitiated by sacrifices of cattle. He is often identified with *Pan*, an object of terror for children and pregnant women. Early on he must have been the personification of the dangers of wild country. Even today many country folk have an unreasoning fear of overgrown and dark woodlands; unreasonable for such places are far safer than roads and towns.

Tages
Etruscan divine child who brought the skills of divination and

augury to the people. He arose out of a furrow, newly ploughed by a farmer called Tarchon.

Tellus Mater
Ancient earth goddess.

During her festival pregnant cows were sacrificed and the ashes of the unborn calves used later for the purification festival of the goddess *Pales*.

Venus
Goddess of spring and fruitfulness, protector of gardens, herbs, fruit and flowers.

Later identified with *Aphrodite*, supposed mother of Aeneas, by tradition ancestor of the Romans. Worshipped as Venus Genetrix, she also must have acquired Aphrodite's power over sexual love. Nowadays everyone assumes that love is her primary domain.

Vertumnus
God of fruit trees.

The name means 'changer', and he was a shape-shifter. Vertumnus was the seducer of the goddess *Pomona*, who had resisted all the other rural gods. He changed into a worker, then a vine-grower, then a harvester. It didn't work. Then he successfully allayed her suspicions by changing into an old woman. A deceit worthy of that cunning Greek, *Zeus*. Unlike Zeus, Vertumnus seems to have been contented with this one success. A god of small ambition.

Vesta
Goddess of domestic and sacred fire, the 'shining one'.

Vesta was worshipped privately in each house, and also publicly as a state goddess. At home she lived by the hearth, and the first of all food and drink was offered to her. Publicly she had a temple near the Forum where the Vestal Virgins looked after a sacred flame; the hearth, so to speak, of the entire nation. Apart from mothers, who were allowed to bring offerings during the

Vestalia festival, Vesta's sanctuary could only be entered by the Vestals. These priestesses were recruited from patrician families and served in the temple for thirty years, maintaining chastity. Punishment for breaking the vow of chastity was final: the fallen Vestal was walled up in a tomb, alive. Her guilty partner was whipped to death in the Forum. In well over a thousand years only twenty Vestals were so punished.

The Vestals were highly honoured in Rome. They were always accompanied in public by a lictor, a symbol of state authority, and if any condemned man chanced to meet a Vestal, he was immediately set free. (See *Lar* and *Penates*.)

Victoria
Goddess of victory.

Originally a Sabine goddess, Vacuna. A rural deity turned military The Roman answer to the Greek goddess *Nike*.

Vulcan
God of fire, sun, thunderbolts.

Vulcan was a dangerous god, originating from volcanic fire, and had to be placated. So live fish were offered to him by being thrown into flames, a rare treat for a fire god. Older than *Jupiter*, Vulcan was rather elbowed out of the centre of the divine stage. Later he was associated with *Hephaestus*, the Greek god of blacksmiths. Not a convincing role, for Vulcan was never an artificer.

Angus of the Brugh

A god of youth. Alias Oengus of the Bruig; alias mac Oc ('young son').

Son of the *Dagda*, Angus had a dream of a beautiful girl and fell in love with her. He grew ill and began to waste away as he searched the land for her. At length he came to Loch Bel Dracon and saw the girl. Her name was Caer Ibor-meith (Caer Yewberry) and she was tied with a silver chain to the hundred and fifty maidens who were her companions. Angus also discovered that Caer was a shape-shifter; one year she was a beautiful maiden, the next a white swan, and so on. Angus waited for the new year (1st November, the Celtic feast of Samhain); Caer changed to a swan. Angus called to her and when she approached, he too changed into a swan. Three times round the lake they flew, chanting a sleep-spell. Everyone slept for three days and three nights while Angus and his paramour flew to the safety of his palace, which stands in the Otherworld. It is represented on earth by Bruig na Boinne (which we know as New Grange, Co. Meath), for Angus' mother was *Boannan* or Buana, goddess of the river Boyne. Angus lived in the sidh ('burial mound') of Bruig na Boinne apart from a stay at Bri Leith (near Ardagh, Co. Longford) where he was fostered by the god *Midir*.

Arawn

God of Annwn, the Underworld.

Arawn offered to change places with *Pwyll*, prince of Dyfed, for a year and a day so that he could get rid of his rival Hafgan.

Arianrhod

Celtic goddess whose name means either 'silver wheel' or 'high fruitful mother'.

Arianrhod was the daughter of Don, mother of *Lleu Llaw Gyffes*. Earlier she had been one of the Three Virgins of Britain. Her palace is Caer Arianrhod, the Celtic name for the Aurora Borealis. In the adventure of Gwydion and Lleu Llaw Gyffes, Arianrhod's palace is described as being on Anglesey.

Arthur

It has been suggested that the Arthur of our myths is an eueheme-rization of a lost Celtic deity, possibly connected with a bear cult. Unhappily there is little real evidence to support this. In the early tales Arthur is a shadowy figure, less interesting and colourful than his 'knights'. But there had to be a king, a patron. Perhaps some dimly-remembered old god was wheeled out, dusted down and given new clothes. Perhaps.

Artio

Goddess of bear cult worshipped by Continental Celts in the area of present day Bern, in Switzerland. (See *Artemis*, Greek goddess.)

Badb, The

Celtic goddess of war; bird-shaped, red-mouthed, sharp-counte-nanced.

The Badb was one of the trio of war-goddesses known as the *Morrigan*. In common with her sisters, she appears sometimes as a foul hag, sometimes as a sexually alluring girl, and sometimes as a bird. She is often described as exulting over the severed head of the hero Fergal, for it was her duty to preside over the battlefield as Badb Catha, 'battle raven'.

The hero Cuchulainn once saw the Badb as a red woman wearing a red cloak. She rode in a chariot drawn by a one-legged red horse. The horse was attached to the chariot by a pole which passed through its body and emerged from the forehead, where it was fixed with a peg. With her was a man who drove forward a cow by means of a forked hazel switch. Cuchulainn asked their names. The Badb answered in riddles. Cuchulainn angrily leapt onto the chariot but it disappeared instantly, leaving only the Badb in the shape of a bird.

Other characteristics of the Badb were her ability to alter the outcome of battles by the use of magic, her lust for men as well as gods, her shape-shifting, and her affinity with water. She was sometimes encountered at a ford, washing the armour and weapons of those about to die in battle. She and her sisters are the possible inspirers of the raven army of Owain in Arthurian legend, the originals of Morgan le Fay. There are many triple goddesses in Celtic and in other pagan systems. Some people think of them as three aspects of the same thing – as the waxing, fullness and waning of a star, or as youth, maturity and old age. (See *Danu* and *Macha*.)

Balor
God, hero and monster, King of the Formorians.

Balor was slain at the second Battle of Moytura by the resplendent god *Lug*, a supposed descendant of his. Lug sent a slingstone into Balor's single eye with such force that it scattered his brains to the four winds, continued on its course, and killed no fewer than twenty-seven unfortunate Formorian warriors who had been tardy in taking cover. Balor's corpse was hung on the sacred hazel which thereupon dripped poison and split asunder. (For a description of the Formorians see the *Dagda*.)

Banba
Eponymous goddess of Ireland, found in a trio with Fotla and Eriu. They opposed the invading Milesians with magic. Like the *Morrigan,* this triad also had bird characteristics.

Belatucadros
'Fair shining one' – Celtic god of war, often equated with *Mars*.

A horned god whose cult was active in Cumbria, Belatucadros was worshipped by civilians as well as by soldiers.

Belenus
Alias Belinus, god of the Celts. His name means 'shining'; he was probably a solar or fire divinity.

Belenus was worshipped in North Italy, Gaul and Britain. He was equated with *Apollo* by the Continental Celts and his name is seen in Beltain, one of the four main festivals of the Celtic year. On the eve of May Day the Beltain fires were lit and cattle were driven between them in a purifying rite, the flames having a therapeutic significance. More inscriptions to Belenus survive than to any other Celtic god, proof of his widespread following.
    The Druids, the priests of Belenus, were an intellectual order

whose teachings were orally transmitted. Though not far advanced from shamanism and spiritism, there is evidence to suggest that they were attempting to regularize the haphazard plethora of Celtic local divinities into some sort of order. This attempt stopped when the invading Romans destroyed both priesthood and holy places with systematic savagery. The *nemeton*, or holy groves, were put to the axe, the priests and all their families slaughtered. The Romans realized that the Druids represented the driving force behind Celtic power. Their only answer to them was the sword. Evidence of this tragedy is to be found in the writings of Tacitus. He of course calls the slaughter of women and children 'heroism'. After using the sword the Romans then turned to the mightier pen and allocated foreign and inappropriate names to the native Celtic gods. A vigorous if primitive culture died with the Druid priesthood.

Boannan

Goddess of the river Boyne and sometime consort of the *Dagda*; mother of *Angus of the Brugh*. Other Celtic river goddesses are Siannan (Shannon), Sabrina (Severn), Sequana (Seine), Deva (Dee), Clota (Clyde), Verbeia (Wharfe), *Brigantia* (Braint, Brent).

To honour the healing properties of water the Celts threw votive offerings of art objects, weapons and money into springs, wells, rivers and lakes. Major sites such as Llyn Cerrig Bach and La Tene have become significant sources of all manner of artifacts for our archaeologists. There still exists a strange human compulsion to throw pins and coins into 'wishing wells', while nearly every well and spring in Celtic areas retains a magical aura, though generally Christianized.

Bodb

Irish goddess of battle.

After the Battle of Moytura in which the *Tuatha De Danann* fought and drove off the Formorians (see *Balor*), Bodb recounted the heroic struggle and gave a prophecy of doom.

Bran

'The Blessed'; a hero god, whose name can mean 'raven'. Benedigeit Bran, brother of the mighty *Manannan mac Lir* (known in Wales as *Manawydan ap Llyr*).

An Irish tale tells how Bran, son of Febal, was lured away by a beautiful spirit-woman to the Land of Women, which the spirit described in glowing terms as the paradise, the Otherworld. Bran set sail with twenty-seven companions. At sea he met a god driving a chariot; it was Manannan, who turned the sea into a flowery plain, the fishes into flocks, the leaping salmon into frisking calves.

After this encounter they sailed on and reached the wonderful island. Bran was afraid to land, but the leader of the women threw him a ball of twine which stuck to his hand. By this means the ship and all its crew were drawn to the shore. The adventurers were led across the Land of Women to a great hall where there was 'a bed and a wife for every man', and an unlimited amount of food. The magic island was inhabited entirely by comely women and Bran and his companions began a life of sweet pleasure. After what he thought was a year of this life, Bran and his men returned to Ireland. As his ship neared the shore people collected on land; they called out, asking his name. Bran replied: 'I am Bran, son of Febal.' The people replied: 'We know him not, but wait, one of our ancient stories is called the Voyage of Bran...'

A strange feeling seized the adventurers, but one of them, eager for home, leapt ashore. The instant the man's foot touched the land his body collapsed into a heap of ashes, for not one year, but many hundreds of years had passed, and the voyagers were as dead men. Bran called out his stories to the people on shore, then turned the ship away and left for ever; nor is anything known about him since then.

The Welsh have their own tales about Bran. The Mabinogion tells us that Bran was slain in a holocaust which few of the inhabitants of Ireland and the invading Welsh hosts survived (see *Branwen*). Bran was killed by a poisoned dart in his foot, but before he expired he ordered the seven Welsh survivors to strike off his head and carry it to the White Mount in London, where they were to bury it facing France. He predicted that they would be a long time on the road, feasting in Harlech, living at Penfro, more than fourscore and seven years in all; and all that time his uncorrupted head would keep them company. The seven did as they were bidden, finding deep contentment at Harlech and then at Penfro. Time dissolved. Then one day Heilyn, son of Gwyn, opened a door that had remained closed till that moment; the door looked towards Cornwall. The appointed time had come, for their happy minds were instantly flooded with the memories of all their sorrows and losses. They set out immediately for London and buried Bran's head on the site where now stands the White Tower. As long as the head is concealed, no misfortune will cross the sea to Britain.

Ravens, like crows, were sacred birds to the Celts and there are still ravens in the Tower of London. It is said that if the ravens leave then the White Tower will fall into ruin; a symbol of the destruction of Britain. Of the eight ravens presently in the Tower, five come from Wales, one from the Isle of Man, one from Cornwall, and one from Scotland. Wales, Man, Cornwall and Scotland are all Celtic.

Branwen
Daughter of Llyr (*Lir*).

Euhemerized as a princess, Branwen is named as one of the Three Matriarchs of Britain. It was her brother Efnisien who caused the friction at her wedding to Matholowch of Ireland. This developed into open warfare, and after terrible slaughter (in which *Bran* was slain) there were but seven survivors among the Welsh invaders and five others alive in the whole of Ireland. These five were women and they all happened to be pregnant. They hid in a cave and all bore sons. When the sons were of age each of the five women took one of them for a husband, founded the five provinces of Ireland, and set about restocking the empty land with people.

Bres
Divine leader of the *Tuatha De Danann*.

Bres was half Tuatha and half Formorian. He succeeded *Nuada* and married *Brigit*, daughter of the *Dagda*. His rule was an unhappy one, for Cairbe, chief bard of the people of Danu, satirized him so effectively and mercilessly that the wretched Bres came out in boils all over his face. After that there was nothing for him to do but abdicate.

Brigantia
'High One'; pastoral and river goddess.

Brigantia was intimately connected with flocks and cattle, having been reared on the milk of a white, red-eared cow, a beast of the Otherworld. The mighty queen Cartimandua worshipped her, and together queen and goddess are good examples of the honour and respect shown to the female sex by the Celts, who looked upon women as the sacred progenitors of the race and as repositories of all that was honourable. The Celts gave their women freedom, power and status. In many ways they regarded them as superior to men. Nor did this admission of the truth in any way lessen their manliness; even the Romans grudgingly conceded the valour and skill of the Celts on the battlefield. The oppression and even slavery of women which is practised by our culture was unknown to the Celts. Freedom of their women was not a cosmetic operation either; women were queens, political leaders, landowners, warriors and priestesses.

Brigantia is depicted in various ways: crowned on top of a globe, which is the symbol of victory; armed, wearing the Minervan breast-plate; bare-breasted in the company of the war god and the ram-headed serpent. She was connected with water, which has therapeutic associations. The rivers Braint and Brent are named after her, not to mention the powerful nation of the Brigantes.

Brigit
Goddess of poets, healing and fertility. Worshipped in Gaul, Britain and Ireland.

Daughter of the *Dagda*, Brigit had two sisters who were goddesses of smiths and laws. Christianized as St Brigit or St Bride, her popularity in both pagan and Christian times is attested by the many sites bearing her name. The Welsh mediaeval chronicler, Giraldus Cambrensis, reports that a sacred fire was kept burning at her shrine at Kildare. She is sometimes equated with *Brigantia*.

Caridwen
Celtic corn goddess; wife of Tegid Voel, Lord of the Lake.

Caridwen had two children; one was the most beautiful girl the world had ever seen and the other was the ugliest boy that ever there was. To make up for his hideousness, Caridwen determined to give her son the gifts of inspiration and knowledge. She collected magic herbs and set them to brew in her cauldron for a year and a day. She ordered a child, little Gwion son of Gwreang, to watch the fire and stir the cauldron. At the end of the appointed time three drops of the brew splashed onto his little finger; the boy licked off the hot liquid to cool his finger and instantly became filled with knowledge and inspiration. The first thing he realized was that Caridwen intended to kill him for having tasted the magic brew concocted for her son. He fled and she gave chase, screaming after him in the guise of a fearful black hag.

Little Gwion used his new power to change himself into a hare, so that he might run faster. But Caridwen turned herself into a greyhound. Gwion leapt into the river and became a fish. Caridwen dived after him in the shape of an otter. He flew up into the air as a bird, and the hag followed him as a hawk. Gwion flew into a barn, turned himself into a grain of wheat, and hid among all those scattered about the threshing floor. Caridwen then became a black hen, scratched about on the floor and gulped down the grain of wheat.

Caridwen resumed her human shape and found that she was pregnant; nine months later she gave birth to Gwion. He was so beautiful that she could not bring herself to kill him, so she sewed him up in a leather bag and cast him into the river. The bag caught on the fish weir of Prince Elphin who, on opening it, saw the beauty of the child and exclaimed, 'Radiant brow!' And so was Taliesin named –Taliesin ('radiant brow') was to be the greatest and wisest of all the bards.

Caridwen, whose name means 'white grain', was also the patroness of the arts of poetry. She was connected with the sow-goddess and with Albina, eponymous goddess of Albion; she was the 'white goddess' of Robert Graves. Caridwen lived at Caer Sidi, a mythical palace in the stars represented by a spiral. She was also linked to the cat cult by her gift to the people of Arvon of a kitten which grew up to be the Palug Cat (Cath Palug), one of the Three Plagues of Anglesey. Caridwen had connections also with wolves and some have claimed that she was the centre of a cult dating from the Neolithic era. One of her names was Hen Wen. 'old white one'.

Cernunnos
Gaulish horned god, representative of virility. A stag god who wears the torc (neck-ring) and is accompanied by the ram-headed serpent and a stag.

A very popular Celtic god, it is thought that Cernunnos' cult was encouraged by the Druids in an attempt to establish national gods rather than a plethora of local spirits. He is deeply rooted in Celtic consciousness, and his cult was a prime obstacle to the Christian church and was vigorously suppressed. He was probably the nearest the Celts got to a universal father figure in the fractured and indistinct system of worship they pursued.

The stag was, according to the Celts, the oldest of animals and played a major role in their imagination as an Otherworld creature, luring hunters through the tangled forests into the land of the gods, allowing itself to be eaten and resurrected. Cernunnos was most probably a composite deity. Originally Gaulish, his worship was prominent in areas settled by the Belgic tribes who imported his cult into Britain. Cernunnos, or a deity similar to him, is probably the god originally worshipped in the surviving Abbotts Bromley horn dance, and also possibly in certain Scottish dances where arms are raised above the head in imitation of a stag's antlers.

Coventina
Goddess of springs and waters.

Coventina is depicted floating on a leaf, with a water plant in one hand and a flowing cup in the other. Large numbers of coins, bronze offerings and even a human skull have been recovered from her Carrawburgh shrine, near Hadrian's Wall in the north of England.

Creiddylad
Alias Cordelia; a Celtic goddess and daughter of Llyr (*Lir*).

Creiddylad is said to have buried her father in a vault intended for Janus under the river Sore at Leicester (*Leir-cestre*). Gwyn son of Nudd and Gwythyr son of Greidawl fought each other for her love. First one then the other captured her. Arthur decided the contest by sending Creiddylad back to her father and declaring that the two men should fight each other every May Day until doomsday. Shakespeare used Creiddylad and Llyr as Cordelia and Lear.

Dagda, The
Irish earth and father god.

Leader of the *Tuatha de Danann* (children of the goddess *Danu*) the Dagda had a wife with three names, Breng ('lie'), Meng ('guile'), and Meabel ('disgrace'), and she bore him three daughters, all called *Brigit*. The Dagda was the son of Eladu ('knowledge') and is said to have lived in New Grange, Co. Meath. Three descendants of his, Brian, Iuchar, and Iucharbar, married the three royal owners of Ireland – Eire, Fotla and *Banba*. The Dagda as an earth god possessed the Undry, a vast cauldron of plenty. He controlled the seasons, which circulated to the sound of his harp. Others of his children are *Angus, Ogma, Midir*, and *Bodb*.

The Dagda is known as the 'Good God', not in any moral sense but meaning the god who is good at everything; a master of all trades. Names for him include Ruad Rofhessa ('red one of great knowledge') and Eochaid Ollathair ('Eochaid the Great Father'). The Dagda was both a death dealer and a healer. He had a mighty club so huge that eight men could not carry it; if dragged on the ground it made a furrow as deep as a frontier ditch. The club had to be mounted on wheels for ease of movement. With it the Dagda could kill nine men at one blow, and by applying the other end could bring the slain men back to life.

The Dagda became a grotesque figure of fun; he ate so much that he became gross and unwieldy, his waddling walk causing huge merriment. His cauldron was equal to his great appetite, for it held eighty gallons of milk and eighty gallons of meat and fat. His spoon was big enough to hold a man and a woman. He owned a magic pig in his sidh ('burial mound'); no matter how many times the pig was eaten it still appeared whole the next day, ready and eager to be eaten again.

The Dagda's sexual appetite was also superhuman. Every 1st November was a busy day for him; it was the Celtic New Year and on that day he was said to mate with the *Morrigan*, the raven goddess, who straddled a river for the occasion, with one foot on each bank – a coital position making up in imagination what it lacked in comfort. He also mated with *Boannan*, the goddess of the Boyne, on that day. Position unspecified.

It was on the 1st November that the Formorians forced the Dagda to consume huge quantities of porridge, which they ladled from an enormous hole in the ground. The Dagda ate all they could produce and even licked the sides of the vast vat. He rounded off the feast, which had been designed to incapacitate him, by having sexual intercourse with a Formorian maiden. The Formorians were a race of sea monsters who struggled for supremacy against the Tuatha De Danann in the two great battles of Moytura. Half-human and half-monster, they had each one hand, one leg, and three rows of teeth. Their leader, *Balor*, who had one eye in the centre of his forehead, was the grandfather of the god *Lug*.

Danu
Celtic mother goddess. In Ireland the mother of a brood of gods, the *Tuatha De Danann*.

Danu is an aspect of that great mother goddess of whom *Brigit* is another example. Mother of Brian, Iuchar and Iucharbar, she is also known as Anu or Ana, which signifies 'plenty'. In Kerry two peaks are called the Paps of Anu. She is connected with Aine of Knockaine, a moon goddess who looked after crops and cattle. Danu sometimes figures in the maleficent trinity of Ana, *Badb* and *Macha*, the *Morrigan*. (See the *Dagda*.)

Dian Cecht
God of healing.

After the second battle of Moytura, Dian Cecht murdered his own son, Midach, out of jealousy. Midach had been getting too good at curing people and so represented a threat to his father's reputation. It was Dian Cecht who designed and fitted a silver arm for the wounded *Nuada*. An ancient Irish legal tract, The Judgements of Dian Cecht, lays down the obligations towards the sick and wounded. The aggressor is made responsible for paying the bills incurred in curing the man he has hurt. Wounds were measured by grains of corn, so even the smallest wound had its price.

Dian Cecht healed the wounded gods by plunging them into a magic bath. He could replace eyes, using optical organs from cats. However, this operation had disadvantages, for the transplanted eye would sleep during the day and at night would be constantly awake, alert at every movement and sound, responsive to every squeak of even the smallest of mice.

Dian Cecht also slew Meiche, son of the *Morrigan*. Meiche was cut open and three hearts were found inside him. These hearts were in the form of snakes' heads and would have grown and emerged to ravage Ireland. Dian Cecht burned the hearts and threw the ashes into the river Barrow; the corrosive remains seethed up in the water and 'boiled to rags all living things therein'.

Epona
Goddess of horses.

Giraldus Cambrensis, the Welsh mediaeval chronicler, reports a royal coronation ritual from Tyrconnell in which the king crawled naked on all fours up to a white mare. After a symbolic copulation between king and mare, the animal was slaughtered and butchered. A broth was made from the meat and the king bathed in the stuff before drinking some of it. The worship of Epona was adopted by Roman cavalry units who had been much impressed by the horsemanship of the Celts. The cult was taken to Rome itself. Epona is depicted riding on a mare, sometimes with a foal. Her image was found on helmets and above the stables of cavalry barracks. The great white horse of Uffington in Wiltshire is more than likely connected with her cult. (See *Epona*, the Roman goddess.)

Goibniu
God of smiths.

One of the *Tuatha De Danann*, Goibniu made weapons which never failed for his comrades. He presided over the prestigious Otherworld feast, *fled Goibnenn*. He was one of the Tri Dee Danann, 'three gods of *Danu*'. He seems to have been concerned primarily with weapons, leaving more intricate work to *Dian Cecht*.

Govannon
Welsh equivalent of the smith god, *Goibniu*. He was also said to be a brewer. (Smithing is thirsty work!)

Gvenn Teir Bronn
'Gwen of the three breasts', goddess of motherhood.

Although described as the mother of an early Welsh saint, Gwen is evocative of a group of goddesses who all bore three sons and so were appropriately equipped to nurse them.

Gwydion
Magician god of the Welsh.

Self-appointed guardian of *Lleu Llaw Gyffes*, Gwydion healed the hero god when he was badly wounded. Lleu's mother *Arianrhod* had put a taboo (*ges*) on her son marrying any ordinary woman. So Gwydion made him a woman out of flowers, Blodeuwedd; but she didn't turn out too well after all, betraying her husband in his absence.

When Pryderi introduced the first pigs from the Underworld, Gwydion tricked him out of them by exchanging them for twelve horses, twelve greyhounds, and twelve shields which he had magically formed out of toadstools. It was Gwydion who successfully guessed the name of *Bran* in the Cad Goddeu, the Battle of the Trees. With his brother Gilfaethwy, Gwydion was responsible for the rape of Goewin, daughter of Pebin. The brothers were to suffer an unusual and shameful punishment at the hands of *Math Mathonwy* (*q.v.*).

Hooded Spirits
A triad of Celtic deities whose mysterious cloaked and hooded

forms appear on altars. They had associations with healing and fertility.

In the area of the Dobunni (Gloucestershire) the spirits are associated with the local war god in his healing capacity. Their names, stories and attributes are shrouded, like their bodies, in impenetrable mystery. Archaeologists know them as *genii cucullati*. Why give a Latin name to gods so obviously Celtic?

Lir
Irish sea god; in Wales he was known as Llyr.

Lir lived on the coast of Antrim. His most notable son was *Manannan* (Welsh, *Manawydan*). Lir was unconnected with the main families of Irish gods, but was a local god of considerable repute. An Irish saga called The Fate of the Children of Lir is devoted to his offspring.

Lleu Llaw Gyffes
Welsh hero god and equivalent to *Lug*. The Welsh traditions about him are so vibrant and imaginative that they are worth an entry on their own.

The story runs thus: *Arianrhod*, daughter of Don, was appointed as footwarmer to *Math Mathonwy*, a royal appointment reserved for virgins. Arianrhod's uncle *Gwydion*, the magician, had raped the previous holder of the job. Alas, Arianrhod turned out to be pregnant and the child was adopted by Gwydion. Arianrhod cursed the infant, declaring that it should have no name until she herself gave it one; a thing she swore never to do. She thereby condemned the lad to shame and ignominy. Gwydion made a beautiful ship out of dulse and sea-girdle, and from seaweed made fine leather. He disguised the nameless boy and himself as shoemakers and sailed to Caer Arianrhod, on the coast of Anglesey. From the palace Arianrhod and her maidens could see the fine ship and the skilful craftsmen on it, working away at the golden leather.

Arianrhod was enticed on to the ship and as she arrived a wren settled on the deck. The boy aimed at the tiny bird and hit it on the leg with a stone. Delighted with his skill, Arianrhod declared

214

that the fair one ('Lleu') had hit the wren with skilful hand ('Llaw gyffes'). Gwydion straightway declared that she had given him a name, Lleu Llaw Gyffes. The furious Arianrhod put another curse on the boy: he should never bear weapons until the day she herself strapped them on him, and there was precious little chance of that.

Gwydion left with the boy, fuming at the injustice of Arianrhod. But his guile had not escaped him; he once more disguised them both, and they gained entrance to the palace. That night, by means of magic, Gwydion made it seem that the palace was under surprise attack. In the dark, and terrified that her home would be sacked, Arianrhod armed the stranger to help defend the place. Gwydion could not resist revealing the trick. Arianrhod put one more taboo on the unlucky lad: that he should marry no mortal woman.

Lleu now had a name and weapons, but no wife. So Math Mathonwy and Gwydion got together and made him one out of flowers. Blodeuwedd was her name.

Later, in Lleu's absence, Blodeuwedd met and lusted after Gronwr Bebyr, Lord of Penllyn. Before too long they were in bed, enjoying each other enthusiastically. The adulterous lovers plotted to do away with Lleu. Blodeuwedd knew that Lleu had magical protection and so she tricked him into describing the one circumstance in which he was vulnerable to death. And more than that, saying that she wished to know the circumstance exactly, she coaxed him into actually reproducing the vulnerable posture. Gronwr, hiding nearby, rushed forward and stabbed Lleu with a poisoned spear. Lleu, in lethal agony, shrieked horribly, rose into the air as an eagle, and flew off.

Gwydion had to use his magic powers to track down Lleu, change him back to human form, and heal him of his deep wound. Lleu sought justice for the wrong done him, and Gronwr agreed to accept one blow in retaliation. Gronwr, well versed in Celtic deceit, arranged matters so that he would receive the blow standing behind a huge rock. But Lleu was in no way put out by this trickery; he gave a mighty blow with his spear, which pierced the stone and split Gronwr's spine in two. Blodeuwedd was turned into an owl, and banished to cry plaintively in the darkness.

Lug

Celtic hero god. Alias Lugh, Lleu, *Lleu Llaw Gyffes* ('bright one of the skilful hand'), Samildanach ('many-skilled'), Find ('fair -haired one').

One day Lug arrived at the court of the *Dagda* and demanded admittance to the glorious company of gods. The doorkeeper asked him what he could do. Lug started to enumerate his talents, but for each of his skills the doorkeeper declared that they already had an expert among the gods. Lug replied that they didn't have anyone who was good at everything. He was admitted and soon led the gods to victory over the monstrous Formorians. In the battle Lug wore marvellous armour from the Land of Promise; his golden shield and helmet of invincibility had been given him by *Manannan mac Lir*. He met *Balor*, king of the Formorians and supposedly his grandfather, but that didn't stop Lug from dashing his brains out.

Lug was the greatest and most popular of the Celtic gods. He has given his name to Lyons, Loudun, Laon, Leon, Leiden, Leignitz, Carlisle and Vienna (Find). Shrines to him are widespread, including examples in Spain and Switzerland. His feast was Lugnasad, a harvest festival, so important that the Romans found it expedient to rededicate it to Augustus; Lugnasad became August 1st. A fortnight before and a fortnight after this date the Celts held games in his honour. Lug was the archetype of the hero, young, golden-haired, strong and glorious.

Macha

Goddess of war, one aspect of the triple *Morrigan*.

Macha's name means 'crow' and she fed on the heads of men killed in battle. There is widespread evidence that the Celts were head-hunters. Warriors would hang the heads of their enemies on a nail outside their houses as proof of their skill. The gate of Bredon Hill fortress and the sanctuary of La Roquepertuse were decorated with severed heads. And Macha was offered captured enemy heads.

In addition to forming part of the Morrigan, Macha herself is sometimes described as being tripartite – Macha wife of Nemed, Macha wife of Crunnchu, and Macha the Red. She is characterized by her active sexuality and dominance over males through cunning and sheer physical force. She also had animal characteristics and was reputed to be a lamia. Macha wife of Crunnchu (an Irish peasant) ran a famous race against the fastest horses in the land, despite the fact that she was pregnant and near her time. She came in first but at the winning post gave birth to twins, and promptly perished. Emain Macha ('twins of Macha'), a great mound, is named after that event. Macha was honoured at the famous feast of Lugnasad (August 1st – see *Lug*). It has been suggested that she was originally a mother goddess and only later acquired a warlike reputation. (See the *Badb* and *Danu*.)

Manannan mac Lir
God of the sea and of fertility. In Wales, *Manawydan ap Llyr*.

Manannan mac Lir ruled the ocean beyond which lay Tir nan Oc, 'the land of youth'. Dressed in splendid armour, he sailed in a boat which needed neither sails nor oars to propel it, for it responded to his wishes, taking him wherever he pleased. His magic pigs were food for the *Tuatha De Danann*, for when eaten they would be wondrously restored. He gave his name to the Isle of Man and to Mona (Anglesey). Separate from the main family of gods, he is of great antiquity and is frequently connected with stories of rebirth. His worship seems to have been restricted to the insular Celts, who considered him an expert on weather forecasting and a skilled sailor.

Manannan mac Lir was an illusionist and shape-shifter, a psychopomp and a supernatural father, begetting children on other men's wives. As late as the seventh century A.D. he was credited with fathering a king called Mongan. Mongan is supposed to have been fostered in the Land of Promise. Pagan tradition was so strong that the story was believed, despite the Christian environment. Mongan is reputed to have been helped into Heaven by Colum Cille (St Columba).

A curious legend tells how Manannan made a bag from the skin of a crane who had once been a woman. In it were kept a variety of cult objects: a magic shirt, a knife, the girdle of *Goibniu*, the shears of the King of Scotland, the helmet of King Lochlainn, the bones of the magic swine of Asail, and the spine of a whale.

When the sea was full the treasures could be seen; when the sea was in ebb the bag appeared empty. *Lug Longarms* owned the bag until his death; the bag eventually passed down to the hero Finn.

Apart from magic pigs, Manannan also owned magic cows and a seafaring horse called Acallamh na Senorach ('speech of the ancients'). He also had a pack of hounds; they chased a boar into a lake and were all drowned, hence Loch Con, Lake of Dogs.

Manannan gave chosen mortals a preview of the Otherworld by conducting them there for a time. He was a handsome fellow dressed in a green cloak, a satin shirt with silver brooch, a gold headband and gold sandals. His elegance reminds us that the Celts were exceedingly fond of fine clothing and ormanents. They were always well groomed and well dressed, the men as richly adorned with jewels and gold as the women, and even the poorest of them were fastidiously clean and neat.

Manawydan ap Llyr
Welsh version of *Manannan mac Lir.*

Manawydan was one of the seven survivors who took *Bran's* head to London. He married Rhiannon, mother of Pryderi. Pryderi and Rhiannon gave Manawydan the seven *cantrefs* (counties) of Dyfed. But soon a strange enchantment was cast upon Dyfed; there was a peal of thunder and a mist and all the people disappeared, the houses and farms and courts remaining desolate. Manawydan, his wife Rhiannon, Pryderi and his wife Gilfa went in search of a livelihood and worked as saddlers in Hereford. Their work was so good that the local cordwainer's guild lost their customers, and so drove them out. They went to London and worked as shoemakers, until one day Pryderi and Rhiannon disappeared in another sudden clap of thunder and curling mist.

Manawydan and Gilfa returned to the desolate lands of Dyfed with a bag of seed corn. Manawydan planted it. One day, near harvest, he discovered that one of his fields had been ransacked; every ear of wheat had gone, leaving the naked stalks. This also happened to the second field, so Manawydan kept watch at night over the third field. He heard a scampering noise and saw hundreds of mice climbing the stalks and biting off the ears. He gave chase and managed to catch one mouse that was heavier and slower than the others. He put the animal into his glove and took it home. There he decided that justice must be done. He declared his intention of hanging the mouse as a thief and set about making a small gallows. A ragged priest appeared and offered to buy the mouse; Manawydan refused. Then came a well-dressed cleric with another offer of more money; he too was refused. Finally a bishop came offering a huge bribe for the life of the doomed rodent. Then the truth came out. The bishop had been wronged by both Pryderi and Rhiannon and so had put the enchantment on the land of Dyfed. He had also captured the two protagonists. The mice who had devastated the wheat fields were in fact the bishop's soldiers, servants and court ladies; and the fat mouse which Manawydan was about to kill was the bishop's wife, heavy with child. Manawydan exchanged the mouse for Pryderi and Rhiannon, and the bishop lifted the enchantment.

Math Mathonwy
Welsh god of sorcery.

Math Mathonwy struck the brothers *Gwydion* and Gilfaethwy with his wand and turned them into deer. This was a punishment; the brothers had raped the royal foot-warmer, a girl called Goewin. Math declared that the brothers would stay in their animal bodies for a year and, to their great shame, would mate with each other and produce a hind. After a year had passed, Math turned their issue into a boy and condemned the brothers to spend another year as a sow and boar. At the end of that year they gave forth a piglet. The piglet was turned into another boy and the brothers were changed into a wolf and she-wolf. After a further year they produced a wolf cub. Math, seeing that each had played the part of a female and given birth to offspring, decided that they had been shamed enough and allowed them to become men again. (See *Arianrhod* and *Lleu Llaw Gyffes*.)

Medb
Goddess of war.

The *Morrigan* used magic to influence battles, but Medb actually took part in the fighting. She was a formidable enemy, for she could run faster than the swiftest horse and the sight of her made men's eyes grow dim. Strong warriors would be seized by a vapid inability, their skill, strength and cunning running away like water from a broken bowl. Her name means 'drunk woman'; she was sexually insatiable, having many children and vast numbers of lovers.

Medb combines mother and warrior in a specially Celtic way. The honour paid to her, and indeed to all women, was tinged with wry humour, never descending into the heavy Teutonic seriousness characteristic of later English chivalry. According to the story in the Tain Bo Cualnge, the great final battle was about to be joined. With consummate timing, Medb declared an urgent desire to relieve herself. There being no convenient woods nearby, her husband of the moment, one Fergus son of Roech, obliged the goddess by sheltering her with his shield. Being a goddess, even such a mundane act was performed with superhuman gusto. The quantities of water she passed were so huge that three streams were formed, each of enough force to drive a mill.

Fergus himself was quite a capable sort of chap. Medb normally required thirty men a day to satisfy her appetite, but when Fergus was around she made do with him once a day. Fergus, on the other hand, needed a daily ration of seven women for his sexual satisfaction. Only Medb and another goddess named Flidais could each satisfy him individually.

Midir
A chieftain god of the Underworld.

Midir is described as living both at the sidh ('burial mound') of Bri Leith in Co Longford and on the isle of Man. On Man his castle was guarded by three cranes, whose croaking call warned away any travellers who happened to pass too close. Midir was fostered by *Manannan mac Lir* and in his turn fostered *Angus of the Brugh*. This system of fostering out the sons of royalty and the nobility was a Celtic habit and part of the complex interrelation of allies and subjects. Fostered youths were hostages of a sort, but treated as honoured guests and brought up with due deference.

Morrigan, The
Goddess of battle; 'Great Queen'.

Forerunner of the Arthurian Morgan le Fay, the Morrigan was an extremely unpleasant lady, hag-like and with a demonic laugh. Her name is used as a collective term for a triad of war goddesses, as well as for her as an individual. She appears as a hag, or a crow, or sometimes as a seductive maiden. Having failed to seduce the hero Cuchulainn, her lust for him turned to hatred and in his hour of greatest peril she attacked him in several different shapes – as an eel, a wolf, and a red-eared heifer. Cuchulainn, who was busy fighting off his mortal enemies at the same time, was severely wounded, but he still managed to give the Morrigan grave hurts. After the fight he met an old hag milking a cow; he begged a drink from her and in exchange gave the old woman his blessing. Too late he realized that the hag was the Morrigan in disguise; his blessing had healed her wounds. (See the *Badb*, *Danu* and *Macha*.)

Nuada

Former leader of the *Tuatha De Danann*. Alias Nud, Nodens, Lud and Llud Llaw Ereint. His epithet is Argetlam ('silver hand').

At the first Battle of Moytura, Nuada had the misfortune to have his arm cut off. This gave *Dian Cecht* the chance of pioneering the field in bionics; he designed and fitted a fully operable arm made out of silver. Nuada owned an invincible sword which he used in the second Battle of Moytura. By now *Lug* had arrived on the scene to lead the 'Tuatha De' in battle, for Nuada had forfeited the leadership when he lost his arm.

Nuada is closely associated with healing and with water; his name is connected with the meanings 'wealth-bringer' and 'cloud-maker'. On the banks of the river Severn, at Lydney, are the remains of a temple complex dedicated to him, a site of major importance. Small votive limbs have been found here. The place was a healing centre; people would go to stay there and it was said that they were visited in sleep by Nuada's sacred dogs, who healed them. Women who were barren left pins in the well, in the hope of having children.

A site like Lydney (Ludd-ney, Ludd being the same as Nudd) throws the literary myths into sharp focus; suddenly we realize that the actors in the divine drama were actually worshipped as gods. There is no reason to doubt that many other similar sites exist, still undiscovered, in the English countryside.

Llud Llaw Ereint ('Llud of the silver hand') was the Welsh equivalent of Nuada. Comparisons may also be drawn with a Cornish saint, Melo, who had a silver hand and a silver foot.

Ogmios, Ogma
God of eloquence, inspiration and language. His epithet, Grianainech, means 'sun face'.

The Gaulish Ogmios was depicted as an old man dressed in a lion skin. From his tongue ran fine gold chains which were attached to the ears of several eager and attentive followers. Ogmios' lion skin was also an attribute of the Greek hero Hercules. The Celts honoured inspired speech above brute force. To them speech, not silence, was golden.

There are ancient Breton gold coins which show human heads attached by cords to a larger head; a fine compliment to Ogmios, whose words shine like gold. The Irish Ogma is credited with the invention of the ceremonial Ogham script. Used on the edges of stones, the script consists of groups of straight or angled lines, elegant to look at and easy to carve.

Partholon
Ancient leader of the *Tuatha De Danann*. Races were held in his honour. The succession of leaders indicates a shift in the importance of various gods.

Pwyll
Sometime god of the Underworld; known as Pwyll Pen Annwn ('Pwyll head of Annwn').

Annwn was the Underworld, normally ruled by *Arawn*. Pwyll married Rhiannon, a fertility goddess whose son Pryderi was a future king of the Underworld. The Underworld was distinct from the Otherworld, which is described in various ways: Tir nan Oc ('land of youth'), Mag Mell ('field of happiness') or Tir fo Thuinn ('land under the waves'). The way to the Otherworld was through a sidh, or burial mound, or it could be reached through magic mists and mysterious forests, if the right guide was at hand.

Tailtiu
Goddess of the earth.

Tailtiu was married to Eochaid mac Eire, king of the Fir Bolg, the aboriginal inhabitants of Ireland. During their relationship there was an era of peace and prosperity in the land, before the invasions of the Formorians, *Tuatha De Danann* and Milesians.

Tuatha De Danann
The main family of Irish gods.

Their name means 'tribes of the goddess *Danu*' but is more usually translated as 'children of the goddess Danu'. It is often shortened to Tuatha De, 'the children of the goddess'. The Tuatha De arrived in Ireland which was already occupied by the Fir Bolg (probably derived from the Belgae). They fought them and defeated them at the first Battle of Moytura. In the second Battle of Moytura the Tuatha De fought under the leadership of the god *Lug* against the Formorians, a monstrous race who were probably remnants of ancient gods. After these battles the Tuatha De ruled Ireland; that is to say their worship supplanted that of the former gods. (See the *Dagda*.)

Aegir
God of the sea; personification of the strength of the ocean for good or ill.

To appease Aegir's wrath Saxon pirates would offer him a tenth share of their captives, choosing the victims by lot and throwing them into the sea. The pirates had no fear of bad weather after that; in fact they rejoiced in it, for it gave them a chance of surprising their enemies.

Aegir gave feasts for the gods and so is sometimes called 'Alebrewer'. His nine daughters were the collective mother of the god *Heimdall*; the father was Ruad Rigdonson. Rigdonson's three ships had stopped making headway on their voyage, so Rigdonson dived down to investigate. He found that each ship had three of the daughters of Aegir hanging on to its keel. The sea maidens captured this bold man and took him down to their hall, where he was compelled to spend a night with each. Then he and his ships were allowed to go, after promising to return. Rigdonson broke this promise, so the sea maidens (whose names all mean 'wave') pursued him, and, it is said, cut off the head of his child and flung it after him.

Aegir was married to *Ran* and was later overshadowed by *Njord*.

Aesir
The race of gods founded by *Odin*. They fought a feud against the *Vanir*, another family of gods.

Alaisiagae
War goddesses (see *Valkyries*).

Alcis
Twin gods of the sky, sons of the Sky Father.

Mentioned by Tacitus as being worshipped by the Naharvili tribe near Breslau. All traces of their cult, images and traditions are lost, though they seem to be connected with other notable divine twins (e.g. the Greeks *Castor* and *Pollux*).

Alfheim
The realm, beyond Asgard (home of the gods), where the fair elves lived.

In the eleventh century A.D. the rural Swedes were still sacrificing bulls to the elves, pouring the blood over mounds thought to be the homes of the little people. The elves, being light and fair, were sun creatures. Nearer our own times in that same country it was the habit of rural folk to pour milk into cup marks cut into certain stones. This also was a libation to the elves. This practice of leaving milk for the elves has persisted into living memory in both Britain and Ireland. Doubtless it still happens in certain areas.

Andvari
A dwarf.

Andvari possessed a great treasure which was taken from him by *Loki* to pay the ransom for killing *Otr*. This treasure was to be the ruin of the house of Hreidmar, and the doom of Sigurd.

Angrboda
'Grief Boda'; a giantess on whom *Loki* fathered monstrous children, among whom were *Hel*, *Fenrir*, and the Midgard Serpent.

Baldur
'The beautiful'; an heroic god, son of *Odin*.

Wise as well as handsome, Baldur was married to the goddess *Nanna*. He was invincible because all things had vowed to the goddess *Frigg* that they would not hurt him. But Frigg had not made the mistletoe swear the oath, for she thought it too young to understand. Baldur's invulnerability was the cause of great delight among the gods, who would bounce axes and spears off him for sport. *Loki*, the mischief-maker, gave the blind god *Hoder* a sprig of mistletoe to throw, and guided his hand. Baldur was slain by the missile, his death a tragedy which showed the gods that not even they were to be excused from Wyrd ('fate'). Attempts have been made to link Baldur with other dying gods (*Osiris*, *Tammuz*, *Adonis* – q.v. Middle East) but he is not a vegetation god, nor was he ever resurrected. In fact Loki went to great trouble to keep Baldur in the kingdom of *Hel*, and all efforts to save him failed.

Boe
According to the chronicler Saxo Grammaticus, the son of *Odin* and Rinda. He avenged the death of *Baldur* by killing *Hoder* in battle.

Bor
Son of Buri and father of *Odin*, Vili, and Ve.

Bragi
God of poetry.

Bragi's name means 'poetry' and 'leader'. His wife *Idunn* guarded the apples of immortality, the food of the gods which kept them ever young

Donar
God of thunder

Called High Thunderer, Donar was the predecessor of the mighty *Thor*. His sign is the swastika which appears on graves and cremation urns in Anglo-Saxon England. Donar was associated with hammers and oaks. Sacred to him were holy groves and individual trees which the early Christian missionaries felled with great delight.

Elli
A mysterious woman who wrestled with *Thor*. The god was unable to get her off her feet; instead, to his surprise, Thor himself was forced down on to one knee. And then he discovered her name: Old Age. (See *Utgard-Loki*.)

Fafnir
A dragon god, son of Hreidmar.

Fafnir's brother, *Otr* (an otter), was killed by *Loki*, who had to pay compensation by covering his skin with gold. The treasure caused dissension among Fafnir and another brother, Regin. Fafnir turned himself into a dragon so that he could keep all the treasure for himself. Later both brothers were slain by the hero Sigurd (Sigfried). (See *Otr*.)

Fenrir
Or Fenris Wolf; offspring of *Loki* and *Angrboda*.

Fenrir was bound by the god *Tyr* who lost a hand in the process of taming and binding him. His chain was made by dwarves from the roots of a mountain, the noise of a moving cat, and the breath of a fish; it was as thin as silk, yet none could break it. Bound in this chain until the *Ragnarok*, he is destined to break loose, slay *Odin* and be himself slain

Fjorgynn
Mother of the god *Thor*, her name was used as a synonym for earth.

Forseti
Son of the god *Baldur* and divine giver of good laws.

An inhabitant of Asgard, home of the gods, Forseti owned a hall called Glitnir which was made of gold and silver. He was a great arbiter of disputes, a sort of divine ombudsman.

Freyja
Goddess of sex.

Freyja's father was *Njord* and her twin brother was *Freyr*. Apart from matters of love, she had some power over the dead and rode in a chariot drawn by cats. Her husband was Od; when he disappeared she wept tears of gold for him. She has given her name to many places in Scandinavia.

Freyja had incestuous relations with her brother Freyr, though originally they were probably just one and the same god. Four dwarves had made a wonderful necklace and Freyja got possession of it by sleeping with each in turn. This ornament, the Brisingamen (or Brosingamene, 'necklace of the Brosings'), is the symbol of her sexuality and is possibly linked with 'brisingr', a rare word for fire. It is not known if the ornament was worn as a girdle, necklace or tiara, but it is generally referred to as a necklace.

Freyja had the ability to fly birdlike over great distances; this ability was probably invested in some wing-like garment, for we are told that *Loki* occasionally borrowed it. She was patroness of a kind of witchcraft called 'seithr', in which a sorceress went into a trance in order to answer questions about the future. Such women, known as Volva, were itinerants. They seem similar to the shamankas of recent times in northeast Europe and north Asia. There was also a connection with a horse cult, for the seeresses were reputed to be able to turn themselves into horses, either to encompass the murder of a rival or in order to enjoy unbridled carnality.

Half of all those slain were Freyja's due, the other half going to *Odin*. Freyja belonged to the *Vanir*, the godly family who governed fertility, and her epithets include Gefn ('giver'), Mardoll ('sea'), Syr ('sow'), and Horn ('flax'). Freyja's worshippers undoubtedly practised orgiastic rites similar to those of *Isis* (Middle East goddess) and *Cybele* (Greek goddess), rites which drew horror and loathing from contemporary and later Christian chroniclers. Freyja also looked after women in labour. (See *Frigg*.)

Freyr
God of fertility, son of *Njord*, twin brother of *Freyja*.

One of the *Vanir*, Freyr gave men sunshine and rain, the products of peace, joy, and relaxed happiness. His cult included human sacrifice and some sort of religious drama in which men dressed as women and mimed and danced to the sound of bells. He was associated with the horse cult, and animals dedicated to him were kept near his shrines. In Hrafnkell's Saga the mistaken riding of a horse dedicated to Freyr brought slaughter and misery to many men. Freyr is also closely linked with the boar, a cult animal of the Nordic and Teutonic peoples as well as the Celts. Boar figures were worn on helmets which went under names such as Hildigoltr ('battle pig') and Hildisvin ('battle swine'). The boar symbol was protective rather than aggressive and was used to strengthen one's defences. The old English poem Elene, which deals with the Empress Helena and the conversion of her husband Constantine, described the latter as being under pagan protection before his vision of the cross of victory: 'He started from sleep covered with his boar-helmet'. (We note in passing that Helena was the daughter of King Coel, whom we all know as Old King Cole.)

Freyr also had a wonderful ship, Skidbladnir, which was big enough to hold all the gods but which when not in use could be folded up and put into a small pouch. Like *Manannan's* ship it could travel anywhere at will.

The image of Freyr was carried about from place to place on a cart, receiving gifts and sacrifices and ensuring fertility for each place it visited. In the eleventh century A.D. a fugitive named Gunnar Helming joined such a procession in Sweden. The cart became stuck and was abandoned by all except Gunnar, who was Norwegian, and the beautiful young priestess who was supposed to be the god's wife. It is reported that Gunnar sheltered in the cart, a sacrilegious act, and that he wrestled with the spirit of the god until accepted. What really happened will never be known, but what we do know is that the cart appeared at its next stop. People there were surprised to see a living man in place of the usual wooden image of Freyr. Pleased that the god should condescend to drink and eat like a human, they, at his request, commuted their sacrifices into gold and treasures. The cart continued its journey to the admiration of the ignorant. Proof that the man was indeed Freyr, the fertility god, was not lacking; the peasants noted that the beautiful priestess was now vastly pregnant, and the anxious farmers saw with satisfaction that the weather was perfect and that a good harvest was assured. The man-god was honoured and his fame spread even as far as Norway, where the king, Olaf Tryggvason, suspected the truth. He sent a pardon to Gunnar Helming, who thereupon loaded himself and his wife with gold and slipped back home in secret.

Frigg
Goddess of fertility; wife of *Odin*, queen of Asgard, mother of *Baldur*.

Frigg had magic powers and could foretell the future. She and her husband often supported rival human claimants for help, and Frigg was not above using trickery to get her own way. She is depicted as weeping; weeping for her son Baldur. Baldur had had dreams of doom, so Frigg exacted oaths from all things not to harm him. She left out the mistletoe, thinking it was too young to understand. *Loki* disguised himself as a woman and, chatting to Frigg, discovered the omission, with dire results for Baldur. When Baldur had been slain and led to *Hel*, Frigg called on all living things to weep for him. If everything wept then he could be saved. Every created thing except a single giantess shed tears for Baldur. The giantess refused to weep; not surprisingly, since she was really Loki in disguise.

It is generally considered that Frigg, so closely allied to *Freyja* must have shared her identity. Both are fertility goddesses, both can assume bird shape, both are depicted weeping. And Frigg was not entirely the respectable matron; it was rumoured that she had indulged in illicit relations with Vili and Ve, the brothers of her husband Odin.

Garm
The hound of the Underworld; at the *Ragnarok* he will break free and kill the god *Tyr*. He is probably an aspect of *Fenrir*.

Gefjun
Alias Gefion, the goddess to whom virgins went after death.

Gefjun was sent by *Odin* in search of some land. King Gylfi of Sweden promised her as much land as she could plough in one go. The cunning Gefjun sought out a virile giant and had four sons by him, changing the beefy youths into four mighty oxen. With the strength of these beasts to help her, she ploughed a huge furrow from sea to sea, creating the island of Sjaelland (Zealand) from the Swedish mainland. She went to live on that island with Skiold, a son of Odin. She has some connection with the goddess *Freyja*, and her name is linked with the sea and with 'giving'. She also obtained a wonderful necklace by the simple expedient of sleeping with its owner, in this case a handsome young man.

Heimdall
'The white god'; guardian of the bridge Bifrost.

Heimdall was posted at the bridge to prevent the giants from crossing over into Asgard, home of the gods. Son of nine sea maidens, his ears were so sensitive that he could hear grass growing on the earth and wool growing on the backs of sheep. His horn, Gjallarhorn, could be heard through all the many-layered worlds of the gods, giants, heroes, men, dwarves and spirits. It will arouse the gods at the *Ragnarok* for the last battle, the twilight of the gods. Heimdall doesn't fit in too neatly with all the other Nordic gods, but one can probably place him among the *Vanir* family rather than the *Aesir*.

Hel
Goddess of death; ruler of Niflheim, land of mists.

The daughter of *Loki*, Hel received the souls of those who died of disease or old age into her palace of mist and darkness. It was secured by high walls and strong gates. Not even the god *Baldur* could be rescued from there. It was Hel who promised to let Baldur loose if all things would weep for him. Despite *Frigg's* attempts to save her son, Baldur remained behind Helgrind, the gate of Hel. (See *Frigg*.)

Hermod
Son of *Odin*.

Hermod rode his father's eight-legged horse, *Sleipnir*, into the realm of *Hel* to look for *Baldur*. He rode over the Gjallarbru, 'the ringing bridge', where the maiden Modgud, who guarded it, told him that Baldur had passed across, as had five troops of warriors. No one has explained this inconsistency: warriors slain in battle usually went to Asgard, the home of the gods, to feast in Valhalla (see *Odin*).

Hoder
The blind god who killed *Baldur* with a sprig of mistletoe. (See *Loki*.)

Hoder was Baldur's rival for the hand of *Nanna*. The chronicler

231

Saxo Grammaticus' version of the death of Baldur has Hoder wounding the young god with a magic sword which he obtained from the dwarf Mimingus, the wound causing Baldur's death three days later. Hoder was himself slain by *Boe*, son of *Odin* and Rinda.

Hymir
A giant.

Hymir accompanied *Thor* on his famous fishing trip to hook the Midgard Serpent. He spent the whole trip in fear and trembling, and when Thor tried to pull the serpent up out of the sea, cut the line in panic. Perhaps Hymir was still sore at Thor for eating two of the three oxen he had prepared for breakfast that morning. Hymir is said to be the father of the god *Tyr*.

Idunn
Goddess who guarded the golden apples of youth for the *Aesir* gods. She was the wife of *Bragi*, god of poetry.

One day *Loki* got into a fight with an eagle that had demanded an unfair portion of the god's dinner. They came to blows and the eagle carried Loki off. He let him go only on the promise that Loki would steal the golden apples from Idunn. Loki, who was a persuasive sort of fellow, lured Idunn out of her home, and the eagle, who was really the giant Thiazi in bird form, carried her off along with the apples. Deprived of their magic food, the Aesir began to age rapidly. Things became so serious that they promised to put Loki to death unless he returned both Idunn and the apples. Loki borrowed *Freyja's* bird shape and flew to Thiazi's place. The giant was out. Loki changed Idunn into a nut and carried her back in his claws. He was hotly pursued by the returning Thiazi, who had reassumed his eagle shape. After a chase which would have done credit to Hollywood, Loki arrived at Asgard, the home of the gods. A moment later Thiazi turned up and flew right into an ambush. The gods had made a huge pile of wood shavings which they ignited as soon as Loki had passed. The leaping flames singed Thiazi's wings and he made a forced landing right in among the gods, who killed him stone dead before he knew what hit him. Idunn and the precious apples were safe, and Loki was forgiven.

Ing
Founder god of the Anglo-Saxons and founder of the royal dynasty of Berenicia.

Both the Swedish royal line, the Ynglings, and the Vandal royal dynasty claim Ing as an ancestor; as indeed did the local kings of northeast England. One of the *Vanir*, Ing is connected with *Freyr*, and is most probably an aspect of that earth and fertility god.

Kvasir
Wisest of the Nordic gods; he was created from the spittle of both the *Aesir* and the *Vanir*, the two great divine families.

When *Loki's* mischief had grown too damaging for the gods to bear, they looked for a suitable net in which to bind him. Kvasir inspected the ashes in Loki's grate and from them deduced that a net had been burned. He worked out that Loki had destroyed the net because it was of the special pattern which was a danger to him. Kvasir reconstructed the design of the mesh from the ashes, and the gods were able to make a similar net which would catch and hold Loki.

Kvasir's name is connected with Kvas, 'strong beer' or 'crushed fruit'. He was slain by two malicious dwarves who mixed his blood with honey to make the mead of inspiration. Anyone who drank of the mead could thereafter compose poetry and utter wise words.

Logi
The personification of fire.

The opponent of *Loki* in that god's competition against the giants of Utgard. Loki was set to race Logi at eating. Loki ate up all his meat swiftly enough, but Logi went on and consumed the bones and the great food-trough as well. Later it was revealed that Logi was in fact fire. (See *Utgard-Loki*.)

Loki
God of mischief

One of the greatest, most active, and certainly the most unpleasant of all the gods. Yet in many ways Loki was an attractive personality. He was vengeful, sly, destructive and evil, but also handsome, sociable and possessed of a sense of humour. He was the father of *Hel*, *Fenrir* and the Midgard Serpent, whom he fathered on the giantess *Angrboda*. Loki played a prominent part in the myths and adventures of the gods; he was a magician and shape-shifter, and was at home among giants, monsters and men. He accompanied *Odin* on his travels, helped to build the world of men, and was instrumental in the construction of Asgard, the home of the gods. Loki's contribution to the last cause happened like this: the gods had convinced a cunning giant to build a wall round Asgard to secure it from attack. The giant said that if he finished the task in one winter he must be given the goddess *Freyja* as a reward. As the gods thought the task would take many years they agreed, but to their amazement the work progressed with unbelievable speed. The giant had a wonderful horse who worked on the wall all night. Spring was but a few days away and the wall was nearly finished. It was Loki who, as it were, stepped into the breach. He turned himself into a mare and approached the giant's hard-working stallion. With many a prance and backward look the mare lured the eager horse away from its work; far away. Spring arrived; the giant was unable to complete the task in time to claim the glittering prize for which he had striven. *Thor* returned to the wall and paid the giant by splitting his skull. As for the mare, she produced a strange foal; it had eight legs and was to be the special mount of Odin, winning fame under the name of *Sleipnir*.

That was one of Loki's helpful acts; many others he performed were vindictive and without good reason, such as cutting off the golden hair of the goddess *Sif*, the murder of *Otr* and *Baldur*, and the abduction of *Idunn* and the apples of immortality.

When the gods had had enough of his tricks they fashioned a special net and bound him up. Snakes were specifically employed to drip poison onto him as he lay helpless. Though Loki deserved his punishment, he was not evil in a simple, obvious way. He had many attractive qualities, a ready wit, resourcefulness, and a sardonic humour which was aimed at himself as much as anyone.

Mimir
God of wisdom.

Mimir's spring bubbles up below the giant root of the tree Yggd-rasil, the tree which holds up the worlds. The spring is full of the waters of wisdom, so desirable that *Odin* gave an eye for a drink of them. Mimir was sent to the *Vanir* gods as a hostage along with the silent Hoenir. The impenetrable silence of Hoenir annoyed the Vanir so much that they cut off Mimir's head and sent it back to the *Aesir*. It seems an incredibly unfair thing to have happened; after all it wasn't Mimir who annoyed them. The Vanir probably thought that Hoenir's massive silence hid information of real value. However, Odin sang spells over Mimir's head and it re-vived, and was able to converse with the gods and give them secret knowledge. Compare this event with the story of the head of *Bran*.

Nanna
Goddess-wife of *Baldur*.

Some suspect Nanna of being an aspect of the Great Mother, the Earth Goddess of the Middle East. She shared the funeral pyre of Baldur, but it is not certain if she died of grief or committed *suttee*. She is presented as a quiet, colourless, mousy sort of woman with none of the vivid impact and solid earthiness of the Middle-Eastern complex of Mother-Earth goddesses. She is res-ponsible for an anti-climactic and thoroughly domestic action in the midst of high drama. The god *Hoder* makes the perilous journey to the kingdom of *Hel* to trace Baldur. Baldur sends back the magic ring Draupnir (see *Sif*) with Hoder. Nanna, who is with Baldur, sends back 'some linen'.

Nehallennia
Goddess of plenty; her cult flourished on Walcheren Island in the North Sea.

Nehallennia's cult is connected with seafaring and also with the fruitfulness of land and sea. The cornucopia, horn of plenty, is one of her attributes. She was a local goddess who acquired classical significance through the presence of the Romans, who were not slow to recognize the military importance of the estuary where Walcheren is situated.

Nerthus
Goddess of earth.

Nerthus' image was carried about on a cart and none but priests were permitted to touch it. When not in use the cart was stored in a sacred grove on an island. Wherever the cart went, peace broke out. Tacitus, who despite his name was never silent for long on any subject, declares that after use the wagon was washed in lake waters by slaves, who were then drowned for having touched a sacred object.

The processional rites surrounding the cult of Nerthus bring to mind aspects of the worship of the Phrygian goddess *Cybele*. One of the tribes who worshipped Nerthus was, according to Tacitus, called Angli. Nerthus remained in the Anglo-Saxon consciousness for a good long while, for we have old English charms which mention Mother Earth along with Christian prayers. We may be certain that the worship of Nerthus was brought from Frisia by our English ancestors, and that its suppressed beliefs, habits and images supplied the basis for later witchcraft.

Another fascinating survival of the worship of the earth goddess is the type of carvings known to archaeologists as 'sheelas', from the Irish 'sighle na gcioch' (*sheela-na-gig*). These carvings, found prominently displayed on Irish and English churches, show naked female figures in an attitude of display. They possess enlarged sexual attributes. There are nearly a hundred such figures extant, proving beyond a doubt the survival of Nerthus-connected beliefs well into mediaeval times, despite the suppression of women by the Roman Church.

Njord
God of sea and ships.

A *Vanir*, father of *Freyr* and *Freyja*, Njord controlled the winds, fishing, voyages, and brought wealth to men. Though masculine, he seems to be identical with the goddess *Nerthus*, translated from earth to sea. Skadi came from the mountains to marry him but they didn't make a go of it, since neither was willing to leave home. Skadi, an athletic sort of girl, soon returned to the mountains where she delighted in hunting on skis with her bow. For the coast dwellers of the Baltic and North Sea, ships were an important link with the world of the dead, just as they were essential equipment for life. Ship burials, tombs in the shape of ships, the idea of sailing from life into death, all these are powerful emotive images to the seafaring folk of the north. Ships are also linked strongly with wealth, for the sea provided harvests both of fish and plunder.

Some have seen the sex change of Nerthus into Njord as a mirroring of changed social conditions, and the growing importance of men. Perhaps, but changes in divine sexuality are nothing new. It is interesting to note that the earliest divinities who inhabited human consciousness were thought of as female. The first tentative steps in man's journey to the Divine were in all probability inspired by women. We should not belittle their contribution, both past and present, nor obstruct their future. (See *Aegir*.)

Odin

Alias Othinn, Woden, Wotan. God of battle, death and inspiration. Chief of the *Aesir* family of gods, he was the 'All-Father', the one-eyed god of wisdom, the omnicompetent god of battles, god of hanged men.

When not armed for battle, Odin wears a slouch hat, eyepatch and cloak, and rides about the earth visiting gallows and slaughter fields. Son of Bor, he was brother to Vili and Ve; they helped him slay Ymir, the old giant, and the troop of frost giants of whom the sole survivor was Bergelmn From the blood and bones of old Ymir the three brothers fashioned Midgard, the place where mortal men live. From two trees they made man and woman, endowing them with feelings, understanding, soul and the ability to move about. Then the brothers created the treasures of the gods, night and day, sun and moon. They built Asgard, home of the gods, and there Odin had a hall, Valhalla, which housed the throne from where he could see all the created worlds.

On Odin's shoulders perched two ravens, Hugin ('thought')

and Munin ('memory'), who were able to fly to the ends of creation to fetch him knowledge. In Asgard was Valhalla; the feast-hall of dead heroes. All day long the heroes would fight; in the evening the dead were revived, the wounded healed, and the golden company would sit down to a feast of roast pork and mead, the supplies of which never failed. What more could any man want?

Righteous men were not forgotten. In Asgard was the hall, Gimli, which was set aside for their use. Neither their activities nor the menu are specified, but they doubtless did what is pleasing to righteous men. Whereas Valhalla probably looked and sounded rather like dinner time in a junior school, Gimli, one supposes, had an Athenaeum-like calm.

Heroic, aristocratic, stern, Odin was the paragon of Nordic authority; battle was his main concern, warriors his companions. He was responsible for poetry and inspiration, but it must have been of a particular kind for there is little of the contemplative or even of the ethical about the Aesir and *Vanir*. Might was right. Odin taught horse-handling, tactics, command and control, techniques of fire-power. Yet he was in no way omnipotent; he and all the other gods were subject to Wyrd ('fate'). Wyrd was a force stronger than winter, weather, kings or armed warriors.

Let it be recorded that there was a deceitful side to Odin; many a saga declares that he was not to be trusted. He is described as untrue, foul, unsafe. When it pleased him he could abandon his brave worshippers and give the victory to their enemies, who were plainly cowards. This was not purely Christian propaganda either; pagans were even more scathing than monkish chroniclers about Odin's treachery and duplicity. His cult was marked by sacrifices, hangings from trees and gallows; hardly a heroic way for the god of battles to treat even his enemies. So the worship of the war god stopped short of the sanctification of righteousness. The doyens of mediaeval chivalry, which was in reality a hideous sore on the side of the Church, could have learnt something from that, had they the humility.

Otr
'Otter', son of Hreidmar, killed by the god *Loki*.

The killing was the flashpoint of a series of conflicts, fights, treasure stealing and such, which gave rise to the changing of *Fafnir* into a dragon, and the whole Sigurd (Siegfried) business. These later events form the basis for the mediaeval German epic poem The Nibelungenlied, for the operas of Wagner, and for the pagan heroism which is an indelible part of German national consciousness.

This is the story behind the slaying of Otr: Loki and *Odin* were sauntering along a river bank one day when they saw an otter munching on a freshly-killed salmon. Loki threw a stone, killing the animal. He boasted that he had made a double catch, and skinned the otter. That night they lodged with Hreidmar and the unhappy man, recognizing his son's skin, threatened to take the gods' lives as payment. Loki agreed instead to cover the otter skin with gold; he bullied the dwarf *Andvari* into giving up his hoard and succeeded in covering the skin. The final whisker was covered with a special gold ring that Andvari had desperately tried to retain, declaring it would bring destruction on whoever possessed it. Loki wasn't too concerned since the gold now belonged to Hreidmar. Loki and Odin got off with their lives, but the family of Hreidmar was torn apart by the jealousy caused by the gold (see *Fafnir*).

Ragnarok

'Destruction of the powerful ones'; the word used to describe the coming apocalypse of Norse mythology.

In this future time, a time of 'fire and ice', the forces of evil will be unleashed to destroy the gods. The evil ones will also destroy Midgard ('Middle Earth', home of men) and Asgard (home of the gods and heroes). A more familiar operatic equivalent to the term Ragnarok is the phrase 'twilight of the gods'.

Ran

Goddess of the sea; wife of the god *Aegir*

Ran netted drowned seamen and took them to her subaqueous halls. If drowned men appeared as revenants at their own funeral feasts, it was proof that they had been given a good welcome by Ran. Ghosts at banquets remind us of the apparition of the Green Knight in the Arthurian legend, and of Banquo's appearance in Macbeth. Ran is Kipling's 'old grey widow maker' in the finest of modern poems about the Norse. Ran means 'ravisher', and those she ravished could find good treatment at her hands if they came to her with a gift of gold. That is why gold was carried by sailors, often in the shape of earrings so that it was safely accessible; as a sort of insurance, not against death, but for their reception after death in the halls of Ran.

Ran and Aegir had nine daughters, whose names all meant 'wave'. They were alluring maidens who would entice young men into their beautiful arms, softly embrace them, and then suddenly drag them down to their watery grave.

Ratatosk
A vindictive squirrel who ran up and down the World Tree, Yggdrasil, chattering rumours and mean gossip. Not a god by any means but worthy of inclusion for his beautiful name.

Sif
The goddess wife of *Thor*.

Sif had golden hair of great beauty. Just for a joke *Loki* cut it all off. A prank to the god of mischief. Thor, however, was not amused; and he had a large hammer, which he said he would use if Loki didn't replace the hair. Loki visited two clever dwarves he knew and got them to make hair out of gold. Not just a golden wig, but real gold hair that grew. The dwarves, flushed from their success, went on to make other wonderful things, like *Freyr's* folding ship and Odin's great spear, Gungnin, which stirred up warfare and decided the outcome of battle. This activity led to a sort of competition among dwarf craftsmen, instigated by Loki. He bet his head that no treasures created could outshine those three artifacts – hair, spear and ship.

As the dwarf competitors sweated at their forge some inkling of their cunning, and fear for his head, must have reached Loki. The dwarves, intent on their task, were tormented by a fly which buzzed round their heads in an annoying fashion and stung them at critical moments. It was of course Loki trying to foul their efforts.

Despite the fly, the dwarves produced a golden boar, a ring and a hammer. The golden boar could run faster than any horse and its bristles lit up the night; the ring, Draupnir, dropped a litter of eight other gold rings every ninth night; and the hammer, Mjollnir, would hit anything at which it was thrown with unfailing accuracy and then return to the hand of the thrower. The only defects the gods could see was that Mjollnir was a trifle short in the handle; the fly had stung the dwarf craftsman on the eyelid at a critical time. This small fault was not enough to prevent the gods declaring that Mjollnir was the best artifact of all, and so Loki was given for judgment. The exultant dwarves wanted to cut off his head, but the god declared that he had wagered his head, not his neck. The dwarves settled for sewing up Loki's mouth instead.

So Sif, with her one talent, was the cause of many wonders and not a few troubles.

Sigyn
Goddess wife of *Loki*.

Despite Loki's vindictive nature there must have been something attractive about him, for he had a wife who remained loyal to him throughout his troubles. When the long arm of enraged justice finally fell on Loki he was, quite literally, bound over to keep the peace. He had the additional torture of snake poison constantly dripping onto his face, just to underline the fact that he wasn't too popular among the gods. Sigyn, whose love was not lessened by adversity, performed the merciful task of collecting the dripping poison in a bowl which she held above Loki's face. The only problem was that when the bowl was full, she had to leave Loki for a short while. So the god of mischief was punished, but not unmercifully.

Sleipnir
The eight-legged horse of *Odin*.

The giant who built the wall around Asgard, home of the gods, was helped by his stallion. Loki assumed the guise and odours of a mare on heat and lured away the stallion, to save the goddess *Freyja* from being lost to the giant as part of a wager. The result of distracting the stallion was Sleipnir, a fit mount for Odin, god of battles. (See *Loki*.)

Thor

Formerly *Donar*, alias Thunor; god of thunder, the sky, weather, and the crops which depended on the weather.

Thor was a huge, red-bearded, irascible and loud-voiced fellow. He wore a girdle of strength, iron gloves, and carried the wonderful hammer Mjollnir ('the mill'), which was both a missile and a hand weapon. He was widely popular and worshipped well into Christian times, for archaeology shows us that miniature Thor's hammer amulets were manufactured in silversmiths' workshops alongside crosses and crucifixes. (See *Sif*.)

Thor was the complete man of action, direct, uncomplicated and strong, with a renowned appetite for food and drink. Popular among thralls and peasants, he controlled the weather and the crops, and also trading voyages affected by the weather. Men swore sacred oaths on holy rings kept in the shrines of Thor. His images were used for making holy fire, and probably had stones or metal embedded in their heads from which such fire was struck. The origins of this practice no doubt derive from the story of his battle with the giant Hrungnir. The giant had a huge whetstone and a shield. Thor hurled his hammer and the giant replied by throwing the whetstone. The stone shattered, but one lump of it buried itself in Thor's skull and was never removed.

One is reminded of another piece of weapon left in a warrior's skull. In that case it was a fragment of sword left in the headbone of the Morhold by Tristan of Cornwall. Yssylt discovered the identity of the fugitive Tristan as her uncle's slayer, and conceived a violent hatred for him. It took a potion to change the hatred to love. Perhaps there was a connection between the Thor story and that of Tristan; the motif seems too good not to plagiarize.

Tiwaz

Germanic god of battle, originally a sky god.

The worship of Tiwaz, which involved human sacrifice, was conducted in forested places. All the worshippers were bound with cords, and if one had the misfortune to fall he was obliged to find his way out by rolling over and over; he was not allowed to get up and walk out. Tiwaz was one-handed, suggesting a link with *Tyr* who lost a hand chaining *Fenrir*. Tiwaz was concerned with justice, law and the binding of solemn oaths. Unlike his successor *Odin*, he was innocent of guile and deceit. As an ancient sky god, Tiwaz was formerly responsible for many of the functions later performed by Odin, *Thor* and others.

It is thought that another name for Tiwaz was Irmin, which links Tiwaz to the Irminsul, a mighty pillar which symbolically held up the whole universe. A temple and sacred wood of that name were later destroyed by Charlemagne.

Tiw, the English form of Tiwaz, was an important sky god. His memory is retained in many place names (e.g. Tuesley, Tyesmere, Tifield, Tysoe), as well as in 'Tuesday'. Like his continental counterpart he was succeeded by Woden, the English form of Wotan or Odin.

Tyr
A battle god, identified with *Tiwaz*.

Alone of all the gods Tyr had the courage to bind the wolf Fenris (see *Fenrir*). He lost a hand doing it. By the time the stories were written down, the one-handed god was outclassed by *Odin* and *Thor*.

Ull
A minor god who deserves scant mention. He is described as an inhabitant of Asgard (home of the gods) and was famous for archery and skiing.

Utgard-Loki
A supernatural giant.

Asgard, home of the gods, was not the only supernatural realm in Norse mythology. There were several, one of which was Utgard, ruled by a giant, Utgard-Loki, otherwise known as Skrymir ('big boy'). He is not the infamous *Loki*, god of mischief, although the two of them did meet. Loki and *Thor* were on their way to a competition against the giants of Utgard. In the dark they came across a vast sleeping giant, and hurriedly took shelter in a nearby building. The building was enormous and they discovered a large side passage where they felt safe. The two gods spent the night there while the huge building shook and vibrated with the giant's snores. In the morning they discovered that the building was in fact Skrymir's glove. The passage in which they had spent the night was the thumb of his immense gauntlet.

It was during the competition in Utgard that the two gods encountered *Logi* and *Elli* (*qq.v.*).

Valkyries
O.E. Waelcyrige – 'Choosers of the slain'; alias *Alaisiagae*.

The nearest Norse equivalent to the *Morrigan*, these females were the helpers of the god of war. They influenced the outcome of battle and conducted the slain to Valhalla, where they also served mead. They had human counterparts, for we hear of priestesses sacrificing captives. Such priestesses were condemned by Archbishop Wulfstan of York (1002-1023) in his famous Sermon to the English. He brackets them with witches, 'and her syndan wiccan and waelcerian', in a superbly orotund paragraph of denunciation that rings as true nowadays as it did nearly a thousand years ago.

Armoured, horsed, spear-waving and maleficent, the Valkyries ride out of Teutonic gloom to terrify and scourge; they pour gore over the countryside from great troughs, ride by on wolves, or scull a ghastly boat through rains of blood.

Njal's Saga describes their visit before the battle of Clontarf in 1014. They were seen weaving men's intestines on a loom weighted with severed heads, its heddle-rods were spears, the shuttle was an arrow, and for a beater they used a sword.

As time went on the Valkyries became more dignified and, regrettably, a trifle pompous. Wagner did them a great deal of damage, aided by stage-designers and the fact that a large voice needs a large body to live in. Today their downfall is complete, and the commonly accepted image is of a strapping woman with straw-hued plaits, a pair of saucepan-lids chained over her ample bosom, and a voice not unsuited to the parade ground.

Vanir
Name of the family of Norse fertility gods. They were complemented by the *Aesir* with whom they sometimes feuded. Among their number are included *Freyr*, *Freyja* and *Njord*.

Weland
God of smiths; alias Volundr, Wieland or Wayland.

Weland seems to have survived in oral tradition as more important a god than archaeology would lead us to believe. Like Robin Hood he seems to fit naturally into the English countryside, as does a hedgerow or coppice, overshadowed, unnoticed but essential.

The verse Edda tells us how King Nidud stole Volund's sword and ring, hamstrung him (which accounts for his limp), and marooned him on the island of Saevarstod. Volund avenged himself by enticing the king's children onto the island. He killed the sons, raped the daughter, and then made his escape on wings, which, Daedalus-like, he had contrived himself. He was revered by our Germanic ancestors as a supreme craftsman. It is said that a horse with a cast shoe left with a coin at one of his haunts will be miraculously shod on its owner's return. He was thought to have been responsible for the mighty stone remains that the English found scattered over Britain when they arrived there. These structures were obviously the work of gods or giants; even today the famous Neolithic long barrow of Wayland's Smithy in Berkshire attests that belief, as does the earthwork known as Grim's Dyke (Grim is *Odin*).

Weland is depicted on the famous Franks casket in the British Museum; he is holding tongs and his kilt reveals a defect in his leg. He has many attributes in common with smith gods from other cultures. This is not surprising. The slow spread of technology on a person to person basis, the resultant freemasonry of specialists (which is seen today even among modern scientists), would assure a similarity of attributes in the responsible deity.

Bannik
God of the bath.

Bannik was a wizened little character with wild white hair and a long straggly beard. He lived in the bath-house or *banya*, which was usually separate from the main rustic dwelling or *izba*. Every fourth bathing session in the *banya* belonged to Bannik, by ancient custom, and at these he would entertain his spirit friends from out of town and his devil comrades from the forest. If a human were foolish enough to enter the bath-house while Bannik and his guests were there he would be lucky to get off with a mere drenching in boiling water; more likely he would be badly beaten or even strangled. All humans who used the *banya* would leave a little water for the god as an offering. Bannik was possessed of oracular powers; in order to consult him about the future you had to sit in the doorway of the bath-house with your naked back facing inside. Then you asked your question. If Bannik scratched your back the answer was negative, if he stroked it then the answer was positive

Bogatyri
Under Christianity many of the old Slav gods were still secretly worshipped by the peasants. Or they were turned into mythological heroes whose stories kept alive old attitudes. These heroes were known as the Bogatyri. Many of them were personifications of rivers such as the Don, Volga and Dneipr, and we can assume they were originally the gods of those rivers. Numerous folk heroes may also be traced to local deities. The transformation was done with such style and intensity that the heroes now occupy a place of their own in Russian folklore.

Byelobog
The white god (*byeli*, white; *bog*, god), the positive half of a dualist theory of the spiritual.

Byelobog was balanced by *Chernobog* (*chernyi*, black), the black god. They were personified opposites: good against evil, light against dark, creation against destruction, day against night. Byelobog was a venerable old man with a white beard; he was dressed entirely in white clothes and appeared only in the day time.

Chernobog
The black god; the opposite in every way to *Byelobog*.

Dazhbog
God of the sun.

Dazhbog lived in a golden palace in the east, in a land of eternal summertime, a land filled with everything that men could possibly want. Every morning Dazhbog mounted his chariot of diamond, pulled by white horses breathing fire. He was born afresh every dawn as a young and handsome king, and drove across the sky ageing as the day went on, till at sunset he was old and ready to die. In the court of Dazhbog were two pretty maidens called Dawn and Evening, a wise old counsellor called Moon, courtiers called Planets, and dashing young equerries called Comets. The Comets were the god's messengers, streaking across the sky.

In some stories Moon (*Myesyats*) is a young maiden of great and serene beauty. At the beginning of summer she and Dazhbog are married, but in winter he abandons her to move south. He is reunited with his wife in the spring. Their children are the stars. Even in the best regulated households there are occasional disagreements; when the sun and moon conflict there are earthquakes, which are felt by mankind.

Dazhbog was a god of happiness and destiny; he was a fair judge and peacekeeper, punishing evil and rewarding good.

Domovoi
Guardian spirit of the house (*dom*).

Domovoi was seen in many forms: as a small hairy man, as half-animal and half-human, as an animal, or as an object such as a truss of straw or bundle of twigs. You could hear him about the house, in the creakings and groanings as the wooden structure responded to changing temperatures. He was a powerful character, so if you heard him it was best not to look in his direction but to turn your eyes away. There was more than one Domovoi; they were fallen spirits, chased down from heaven by the Great God because of their misdeeds and rebellious natures. Hundreds of them fell down to earth, landing all over the place like rain. Some descended on houses, barns and farmyards. These Domovoi were influenced by the proximity of man and became less aggressive and more civilized. Their comrades who fell on fields, woods and waste ground remained wilful and lawless.

Like the *Lar* of the Romans the household god of the Slavs moved with the family, but he had to be tempted away from a place he had got used to. In the *izba*, or dwelling, the *chelovek* ('fellow' as he was called) lived near the stove, always the best place to be in a Russian house. Old-fashioned Russian stoves were massive affairs of brick or mud on which it was possible to sit, and where older, weaker people frequently made their bed. In contrast to this favoured position the 'fellow's' wife, *Kikimora*, lived in the cellar. They were both useful spirits to have around for they warned the family of coming disasters, such as spilt milk and death.

Dvorovoi
God of the courtyard.

For some reason Dvorovoi simply detested animals with white coats. He was the sworn enemy of all white dogs, cats and horses. He didn't much care for white hens either but they were protected by their own god and so could afford to ignore him. Men could influence Dvorovoi in two ways, with punishment or with bribery. The god could be won over with bread and pieces of sheep's wool. To punish him you had first to take a thread from a dead man's shroud and tie it to a stick to make a whip. Then if you went into the yard and thrashed about with it, you would be sure to hit Dvorovoi. Alternatively you could take a pitchfork and pin him to the fence with it. However Dvorovoi was not entirely help-less, as is shown in the following story:

A beautiful young peasant girl, Katya, had been orphaned and had inherited her parent's house. As she went about her tasks she was conscious of being helped by an unseen spirit. As the years passed she grew capable of seeing him; he was a handsome young man, and he had fallen in love with her. Flattered by his attentions, Katya invited him to live with her. He plaited her hair and made her promise never to unbraid it. At length Katya realized that her lover was no lover at all; he was a spirit and incapable of physical affection. She began to yearn for a real man, not a mere shadow. She met Stefan, a good-looking peasant lad. By now she was no longer young but was still attractive. In time-honoured fashion she and Stefan found themselves in a copse one evening. Stefan, realizing that Katya had a lot to offer besides her inheritance, proposed marriage.

On the night before her wedding, Katya prepared herself. She came in from the *bunya* (bath-house) in a warm and relaxed mood, thinking of Stefan. She undid her hair and ran a brush through it. It had grown very long. Then she lay down to sleep. In the morning the neighbours came knocking, but there was no reply. Worried, they broke into the house and discovered Katya still in bed. Her long hair was twisted and knotted about her throat. She had fallen victim to the jealousy of Dvorovoi and had been strangled with her own hair.

Kikimora
Female household divinity of the Slavs, sometimes described as wife of *Domovoi*.

Kikimora lived in the cellar and helped about the house. Good housekeepers would get her seal of approval and their tasks would be lightened by her assistance. Lazy housewives would, however, be persecuted by Kikimora; she would spoil food, break crockery, lose small objects and wake the children at night by tickling them. To come to peaceful terms with the goddess you had to make fern tea and wash all the kitchen implements in it. Kikimora specialized in looking after the household poultry; she is depicted as having chicken's legs and a long beak-like nose.

Kupala
Goddess of water, magic and herbs.

In common with many people, the ancient Slavs believed that water had magical properties. Worship was accorded to sacred springs and rivers, and Kupala was the personification of the deity inherent in water. Her worship involved ritual washing and the offering of flowers, which were cast onto the surface of water. Strangely it also involved fire-rites, for fire was considered to have much the same purificatory properties as water. Kupala's worshippers would run round fires and leap over the flames in order to purify themselves. Effigies of the goddess were either burned or thrown into pools.

Closely linked to the cult of Kupala was the whole lore of magic plants and herbs. Foremost among these was the fern, which if collected under the correct circumstances had great power. Magic herbs could give men all manner of skills – the power of thought-reading, of taming demons, breaking up metals, discovering buried treasure, acquiring beautiful women, wealth and power over kings. But there were risks involved; in order to gather the right herb at the right time a man had to display nearly superhuman nerve and determination in the face of grave dangers, both physical and psychic. He had to meet and overpower spiritual forces and, most of all, overcome his own fears and inbred assumptions.

Leshy
God of the forest.

Leshy had human shape but his blood was blue, and this imparted a curious tinge to his flesh; his eyes and beard were green. To make recognition easier for ignorant mortals, the god wore his shoes on the wrong feet, and he had no shadow. When walking about Leshy would adapt his size to the surrounding growth: among trees he was as tall as they were, in the grass he was blade-high. Leshy stayed off land owned and worked by men; he loved the wild places, the forest and waste land. Here he was supreme, and should any humans venture into his territory he would lead them a merry dance through the thickets and undergrowth. Peasants, travellers, woodsmen and hunters would all be led astray. Not that Leshy was malicious; he carried out his deceptions in a light-hearted manner, with a smile on his lips. Humans had one infallible way of defeating the god, and that was to imitate him: to put their clothes on back to front, and wear their shoes on the wrong feet. No matter what you looked like when you emerged from the forest, at least you had got there.

In some areas there were whole tribes of Leshies. Every spring they would run through the woods, yelling and screeching with the sheer pleasure of being alive and powerful. Every autumn, like the leaves, they died.

Mati Syra Zemlya

Goddess of the earth. Mati Syra Zemlya is not a name but a title which has the meaning 'moist mother earth'.

The worship of the earth as the productive force of all life seems inevitable in all agrarian cultures. The Slavs were no exception. Prayers were addressed by them direct to the earth and libations were poured onto it in a way very similar to that performed by our not-too-distant Anglo-Saxon ancestors. Mother Earth was conscious, and just and oracular. Anyone who had the ability to interpret her language could understand her. There was no need for a priest or wise man as intermediary; any peasant who dug a hole with his hands and listened intently could hear things. The earth was often called as a witness to solemn agreements and oaths; a common method was to place a handful of it on your head while taking a vow. To do this was a most solemn undertaking, for Mother Earth could not be cheated.

The cult of Mother Earth dated from very early times, but never developed into a personalized system such as existed elsewhere (e.g. *Isis*, *Ishtar*, *Ceres*). Among the Slavs no nationally accepted or definitely named goddess ever appeared; it seems that the arrival of Christianity inhibited its development into a well-organized theogonic system. However, 'Mati Syra Zemlya' was worshipped well into this century; the cult was expressed mainly by women, which is as it should be, women having always been the main inspirers and supporters of mankind's religious awareness.

Some experts think that the worship of the mother goddess originated in the Don basin about 30,000 B.C., for there are extant a number of figurines of that period and provenance. If these idols, who display exaggeratedly feminine attributes, had names we do not know them; but there can be no doubt as to their significance. Created some 23,000 years before the Neolithic agrarian revolution, they represent both a striving after something beyond the apparent and a curious foreshadowing of ideas which later agriculture underlined. Even scavengers and gleaners had an idea that the earth was the productive element; settled arable habits brought the fact of fecundity to the front of men's minds. The early idols, rather inappropriately and ineptly termed

'Venuses' by archaeologists, had no faces.

Myesyats
God of the moon.

Sometimes a young maiden, sometimes an old man, the moon was the companion of the sun (*Dazhbog*). The shift in gender is not unusual, the important thing is that the moon itself is a deity: the moon is the god rather than there being a god *of* the moon. Our habit of separating things into parts, of dissecting natural phenomena, is a fairly new sort of barbarism. If we believed that divinity resided in the soil, for example, we would be unable to steep our fields in toxic chemicals and then justify the crime by economic arguments.

Polevik
Spirit of the field.

Polevik's appearance varied with the topography. Sometimes he was all in white, sometimes he had grass instead of hair, or he was a dwarf or an earth-hued man with eyes each a different colour. Drunkards who slept off their excesses in the fields were likely to be attacked and murdered by Polevik, who was very jealous about the sanctity of his acres.

Poludnitsa
'Noon-girl', a North Russian field goddess.

Poludnitsa was a tall comely maiden dressed in white. She saw to it that no one worked at midday; anyone who broke this rule and was found labouring when they should be resting would have their hair savagely pulled by the goddess. Apart from being some sort of shop-steward, Poludnitsa would also lure children into the tall corn and make them lose their way.

Pyerun (Piorun, Perun, Peron)
God of thunder among the central and eastern Slavs.

Pyerun's name is probably linked to Parjanya, an epithet of the Hindu god *Indra*. He was a war god armed with the thunderbolt; as the thunderbolt was the ultimate weapon he was therefore lord of the universe. Pyerun was very much an exclusive deity, the god of the fierce warrior class; he had no priests and his rites were carried out by princes and military leaders. His character was possibly influenced by the arrival of Norsemen, who crossed the Slavic lands to settle in Kiev and provided the Byzantine Emperor with an elite force, the Varangarian Guard. As late as the Fourth Crusade the tradition of North European mercenaries serving in Constantinople was still active. It is reasonable to speculate that these mercenaries had arrived there by the old river routes and that they saw in Pyerun the image of their own Nordic god *Odin*, called Grim by the English.

Rusalki
Water and woodland goddesses.

Originally Rusalka was a young girl who had perished by drowning. Such unfortunate maidens became water spirits and lived in streams, pools and rivers. They took their nature from their surroundings. Soft and sunny southern rivers had nubile and attractive Rusalki, while those of the chilly northern streams were stern, cruel and, who knows, frigid. But cold or welcoming their object was the same, and that was to seize men and drag them down into the water to their doom. When not drowning men the goddesses indulged in other aquatic amusements, like ripping fishing-nets, breaking weirs and sabotaging millwheels. From time to time the Rusalki would emerge from the water to dance in the forests, and where they trod the grass grew sweeter and thicker. Men had some defence against their playful wickedness: a useful antidote was to carry a leaf of the absinthe plant. The Rusalki hated the absinthe and would exert every ounce of their energy to absent themselves from its proximity.

Svantovit
God of war.

A god with a Baltic provenance, Svantovit was shown, in a Galician statue, as being gigantic, four-headed and holding a bull's horn filled with wine, a sword, saddle and bridle. In his temple a white horse was kept and revered as the mount of the god, and as a means of divination. The ideas of horse and warfare are closely linked. The horse symbolized the warrior aristocracy and its humbler and more useful functions took second place.

When used for divination, Svantovit's horse was driven by the priests through a sort of slalom of spears stuck in the ground. If it knocked any over there would be bad luck in the coming year. The shrines of Svantovit were decorated with his war banner and were the gathering places of the ruling military class. He was god of all other gods and several war deities are probably aspects of his overwhelming power. He was also considered to be father of the sun, father of fire, and father of abundance. He is a reminder of the days when war was pursued for profit and glory.

Svarog
God of the sky.

Svar comes from a Sanskrit root meaning 'bright, clear, shining'. It is also seen in the word *swastika*, the ancient sun symbol, whose true meaning of light and hope has been so inhumanly perverted in our own times. Svarog, 'the bright one', was the sky itself, later personified into a god. Svarog became a supreme being and as such it was natural, or supernatural, for him to father children. These were *Dazhbog* (the sun) and Svarogich (fire). Svarog therefore may be regarded as father of the gods. Though not as noticeable or flamboyant as the sun, he was nonetheless ever-present, forming a kind of scenic backdrop to the other gods.

Vodyanoi
Water god.

Vodyanoi was a very dangerous spirit who inhabited all kinds of water and especially mill races and ponds. He appeared in many shapes, some tempting, some horrific. His main object in life was to lure humans to the water and drag them under. The unfortunates would then become slaves in his underwater palace. During the day Vodyanoi rested; but at sunset he would rise to the surface and snatch whoever he could find. He was of a destructive nature and would damage mill-sluices. To appease him millers would often seize a stranger who had arrived after dusk and throw him in as an offering to the god. Vodyanoi could appear in the form of a fish, a floating log, a moss-covered monster, an old man with green hair and a beard, or even an attractive naked woman washing her hair at the water's edge. Whatever his guise his character remained the same, dreadful.

Volos
God of the beasts.

Protector of the flocks and herds, Volos was often confounded with *Pyerun*. With the arrival of Christianity (*circa* 900 A.D.) he was rusticated and eventually became absorbed into the cult of St Vlas (St Blaise). In other parts of Christendom Blaise took care of people's throats; in Russia he looked after their flocks. When disease hit their livestock the Slavs would tie a sheep, a cow, and a horse together by their tails. An ikon of St Vlas would be shown to the sick animals and then the sacrificial trio would be pushed over a ravine and finished off with stones. Despite the presence of St Vlas it was a placatory sacrifice to Volos, ancient god of animals.

Yarilo
God of love.

His name is derived from a word with the meaning 'passionate' or 'uncontrolled'. Yarilo, god of human generative power, is connected to spring-sown corn, for in summer there were funerary rites celebrating his death, or harvest. Those who have perused The Golden Bough will instantly recognize the threnody, the women intoxicated with sorrow loudly bewailing the death of the beautiful young god, symbolized among the Slavs by an effigy made of the new straw. The cult of Yarilo caused the Orthodox Church no end of worry; it was too deeply rooted in the Slav consciousness to be easily ignored, a powerful expression of their sexuality. In spring the most beautiful girl of the village would play the part of Yarilo. She would be dressed in white and adorned with flowers; where possible she would be mounted on a white horse. Her accompanying handmaidens would wear flowers and dance over the newly sown fields, singing traditional chants about the fertile powers of the god. Yarilo himself is described as being young, handsome, and dressed in white. He carries flowers and sheaves of corn, rides on a white horse and is always barefoot.

Zorya
Goddesses who guard the universe.

There are sometimes two and sometimes three and they are all connected with the idea of dawn (Zorya is linked to *Aurora*). They are Morning, Evening and Midnight. When there are two, Morning opens the gates to let out the chariot of the sun and Evening opens them again to welcome the sun home. The Zorya are guardian goddesses of the universe, for they watch over a fearsome hound who is chained to the constellation of the Little Bear. When the hound breaks loose from its chain the end of the world will come.

Zvezda Dennitsa and Zvezda Vechernyaya
Goddesses of the Morning Star and the Evening Star.

These goddesses derive their importance from the brightness of their heavenly body, the planet Venus. Dennitsa is the equal of all the other gods, for it is she who tends the horses of the sun; her evening aspect is the herald of the moon.

Ahto (Ahti)
Chief god of the waters of the ancient Finns.

Ahto lived with his family under a sea cliff. He was served by the water spirits, the Vetehinen, and Tursa the sea monster. Since the great *Lemminkainen* was also called Ahti, it is thought that he was a derivation or even an aspect of the sea god. Ahto is described as having a beard made of moss.

Akka (Mader-Akka, Rauni)
Goddess of the harvest and female sexuality.

Akka was often represented by a triangle or a six-sided polygon. She was the wife of the god *Jumala* and as such was the feminine side of the supreme deity. The mountain ash was sacred to her and from that tree she got the name Rauni. She was called Maan-Eno by the Estonians. Akka was responsible for the fertility of the fields and ruled the harvest. She helped her husband in his act of creation; he created the souls of men but she created their bodies.

Antero Vipunen
A mythical Finnish giant who slept in the earth with trees growing on him. He had the magic songs which the great *Vainamoinen* needed to complete his ship. Antero Vipunen only parted with the songs after cruel punishment from the eager hero-god.

Hiisi
Finnish god of evil.

Hiisi's songs and spells were sung by *tjetajat* or wizards. Finland has long had a reputation as a land of skilled sorcerers and necromancers. Their particular style of working is closely allied to the shamanism of the north, the use of sacred drums and the habitual trance-like states induced by monotonous chanting. Hiisi joined with other evil spirits to direct *Vainamoinen's* axe against himself; Hiisi being responsible for making the axe slice through the hero-god's veins.

257

Ilma
Finnish god of the air.

He is notable for having fathered *Luonnotar*, the mother of the hero god *Vainamoinen*. Luonnotar was instrumental in the creation of the world.

Ilmarinen
Smith god of the Finns.

Ilmarinen undertook the forging of a talisman called the *sampo*, demanded by the sorcerer Pohja in return for the hand of his daughter. The smith god collected together the following things: the point of a swan's feather, the milk of a sterile cow, a grain of barley, and wool from a fertile ewe. During the forging process many wonderful objects appeared: a golden bow, a golden plough, a ship, and a cow with golden horns. But Ilmarinen rejected all of these marvels and worked patiently at the furnace until the mysterious, never-described *sampo* emerged.

But the *sampo* did not guarantee Ilmarinen happiness; he married Pohja's daughter, but she was soon killed by evil bears. He saw how the *sampo* had brought prosperity to the land of the sorcerer, and so he and the hero *Vainamoinen* set out to win back the talisman. After many adventures the *sampo* was shattered, and Ilmarinen and Vainamoinen recovered only fragments of it. (See *Vainamoinen*.)

Jumala (Mader-Atcha, Ukko)
Sky and thunder god of the Finns.

Jumala was also the creator of men's souls, his wife creating their bodies. He was invoked as the supreme god only after all the other gods had been called upon in vain. The oak tree was sacred to him and he ruled all that happened in the sky; he held it up, caused the clouds to gather and made the rain descend. He is depicted as wielding a jagged stick, symbolic of thunder.

It is curious to see how the most diverse cultures produce similar attributes, recognizing such connections as oak tree and thunder. This may derive from the fact that certain trees react differently to being struck by lightning. The smooth bark of a beech will direct the energy down to the earth; but the broken, chunky skin of the oak will take the charge inward, where its fierce heat causes the sap to vaporize. An explosion results, and the tree bursts like a faulty boiler.

Kalma
Goddess of death. Her name means 'corpse-stench' and she was the owner of a monstrous animal who at her behest would seize and devour humans with a speed that left them gasping.

Kipu-Tytto
Goddess of illness. This unpleasant lady lived in Tuonela, the Finnish hell. (See *Tuoni*.)

Kuu
The moon in Finnish mythology. Kuutar 'the shining' was daughter of the moon.

Lemminkainen
Hero-god of the epic Kalevala, Elias Lonnrot's synthesis of Finno-Ugric myth.

Lemminkainen is possibly a development of the sea god *Ahto*. When a baby he had been ritually washed in order to make him a magician, a scholar, and a successful hero. By nature he was cheerfully amoral, genially turbulent and merrily aggressive. He made mistakes, as such a character would. He foolishly tried to kill the swan which floated on the black and infernal river of Tuonela, the Underworld; the result was that he was torn into shreds by the son of the god of the dead, *Tuoni*. His mother had to gather up all the pieces and put him together again; she revived him by the use of magic. Lemminkainen met the hero-god *Vainamoinen* after they had both gone to the land of Pohja to look for wives. They joined forces and fought against the goddess *Louhi*. As well as personal courage and audacity, Lemminkainen challenged the forces of darkness with spells and incantations.

He dispersed Louhi's sorcerers with his own particular brand of wizardry and good humour. (See *Vainamoinen*.)

Louhi
Goddess of sorcery and evil.

It was in Louhi's house that the necromancers gathered to sing their songs of darkness. She ruled the land called Pohja, located in the north. When the hero-god *Vainamoinen* wished to marry her daughter she bargained with him: he had first to make the mysterious magical talisman called the *sampo*. Although Vainamoinen achieved this difficult task, the goddess deceived him and allowed her daughter to marry the smith god, *Ilmarinen*.

When *Lemminkainen* attacked Pohja, he was defeated by the superior magic of Louhi. He and Vainamoinen joined forces and succeeded in winning back the *sampo*. The evil goddess unleashed all sorts of horrors on to them, but they managed to escape. Louhi's magical powers were so great that she could conjure the sun and moon into captivity. (See *Vainamoinen*.)

Loviatar
Goddess of disease.

Swarthy-faced and crinkle-skinned, Loviatar was certainly not the most attractive of women. She mated with the Wind and gave birth to nine monsters, each personifying some horrific disease. She lived in the Finnish underworld of Tuonela and her parents were *Tuoni* and Tuonetar, god and goddess of the dead.

Luonnotar
'Daughter of Nature', she was actually daughter of the goddess of air, *Ilma*.

Luonnotar lived in heaven but was unmarried, even though she was nubile and not unwilling. Determined to cease being a virgin, she dived into the sea and floated on the surface. The wind embraced her and the sea mated with her. For seven hundred years Luonnotar floated; she had no choice since the land had not yet been created. Then a duck landed on her knee, which protruded from the billows, built a nest there and laid eggs. Luonnotar floated on until she felt hot in the sun; she adjusted her position and the eggs slipped off her knee and broke. Their lower halves became the earth, their upper halves became the heavens, their yolks formed the sun and their whites the moon. Luonnotar landed at last and made a few alterations to the earth; she levelled the coastlines, dug straits and built headlands. Her pregnancy lasted thirty years, much to the discomfort of her son, the great *Vainamoinen*. Vainamoinen eventually lost his patience and emerged by his own efforts.

Naaki
Spirit of the waters.

Every morning and evening Naaki emerged from the waters and walked on the earth. He was a shape-shifter and was dangerous, for he caused the death of men by drowning them. Before bathing in the lakes of Finland it was advisable to recite the appropriate spell or to throw in a placatory coin. Some Finnish lakes are said to be bottomless, and are ways to the underwater kingdom of the god *Ahto*. Naaki is the best known of his attendants.

Tuoni
Lord of Tuonela, the Underworld; god of death.

Tuoni's wife, Tuonetar, and his various horrible daughters lived with him. His kingdom was protected by a black river on which swam a beautiful swan. The god had a son who was an accomplished sorcerer and who tore to bits the hero *Lemminkainen*, after the latter had attempted to kill the swan of Tuonela. When the hero-god *Vainamoinen* visited the Underworld he was offered beer crawling with worms and frogs, and his way was blocked by an iron net. Vainamoinen only escaped from the place by changing himself into a slim serpent and slipping through the net.

Vainamoinen
Hero-god of the epic, Kalevala – Elias Lonnrot's synthesis of Finno-Ugric myth.

Vainamoinen's mother was *Luonnotar*, the Virgin of the Sky. He remained in her womb for thirty years until he became bored and forced his way out. He set about clearing the forest and tilling the soil and then went in search of a wife. Having been promised the daughter of the sorcerer Pohja (in some versions it is the daughter of the goddess *Louhi*), Vainamoinen persuaded the smith god *Ilmarinen* to forge for him a mystic talisman called the *sampo*, to give in exchange. The smith succeeded but the daughter of Pohja forsook Vainamoinen and married Ilmarinen instead. Shortly afterwards the daughter was killed by bears, and Ilmarinen informed Vainamoinen that the *sampo* he had made was the source of the immense and new-found wealth of the kingdom of Pohja. The two gods decided to go and steal it for themselves. They were joined by the merrily amoral hero *Lemminkainen*. On the voyage, they caught a huge fish from whose bones Vainamoinen made a five-stringed musical instrument. With this instrument he sang a song of enchantment, which made the people of Pohja fall asleep.

The gods crept into the land and stole the *sampo*, but the foolish Lemminkainen could not resist a mocking song of victory; this awoke the sorcerer, who conjured up a crashing tempest. The howling winds and thudding waves nearly over-whelmed the gods' ship. The tempest tore the musical instrument out of Vainomoinen's hands and the waves swallowed it up. The *sampo* was pulverized by the impact of the storm. The gods escaped, but Pohja mounted a series of magical attacks on them. Vainamoinen overcame these assaults and, having completed his mission, built himself a ship and sailed off into the sunset.

Vainamoinen was a creative personality, fighting evil, solving problems and involving himself with the good uses of the super-natural. He was reputed to have brought the benefit of fire to mankind. The sky god *Jumala* had struck the first fire from his fingernail with his sword; he gave it to a goddess of the air to look after but she dropped it. It fell to earth and was swallowed by a trout, which was swallowed by a salmon which was swallowed by a pike. Vainamoinen caught the pike and cut open the layers of fish. The fire escaped and after setting the forest ablaze was caught by Vainamoinen and imprisoned in a metal jug.

Middle East

EGYPTIAN ■ MIDDLE EASTERN GENERAL
■GNOSTIC

Aah
One of several names for the god of the moon (see *Thoth*, *Khons*). He was depicted as a man wearing the moon symbol, which was a combination of the full moon and the crescent.

Amenhotep
Amenhotep was a renowned architectural genius and sage of the 18th Dynasty. Because of his extraordinary talents and achievements he was raised to the rank of god. Very few commoners were granted this distinction, for normally only Pharaohs were considered suitable human material for deification. (See *Imhotep*.)

Ament (Amenti)
Goddess of the land of the west.

A native of Libya, Ament became goddess of the Underworld; for the west was another way of saying death. It is an idea still current in our phrase 'gone west'. She is depicted as an attractive young princess seated beside Ra-Harakhty (see *Horus*). Her emblems are the hawk and the feather. The feather means 'Libya' and therefore 'west'. Ament lived in a tree near the World Gates and offered approaching souls refreshment of bread and water. Whoever accepted this hospitality became an associate of the gods and was obliged to follow them, never to return. Ament is occasionally replaced in this task by other goddesses: *Nut*, *Hathor*, *Neith*, *Maat*.

Ammut
A demonic goddess who attended the Judging of the Dead; she was given the condemned souls to devour. She was a horrible-looking concoction, a cross between a crocodile, lioness and hippopotamus.

Amun (Amon, Ammon, Amen)
Originally the local god of the city of Thebes (Nut Amun).

As the city grew from a village to a powerful metropolis so Amun, whose name signifies 'hidden', grew in importance. He ousted the Theban god of war, *Mont*, and went on to be regarded as chief god of Egypt, 'King of the Gods'. Originally he might have been a wind or air god; later he was given several powers and attributes. As an ithyphallic god, either standing or enthroned carrying a whip, Amun was god of fertility. At Karnak he was considered to be incarnate in a sacred ram which was kept in that temple. Another symbol of sexual power, the goose, was also sacred to him. From being worshipped as a god of generative power to being worshipped as an agricultural deity responsible for the growth of crops was but a short step for Amun. He then rose to be the patron of the Pharaohs, and because of the inevitable connections between royalty and the sun, became linked to the great god *Ra*. As Amun-Ra he became supreme among the gods and ruler of the *Great Ennead* (*q.v.*).

During the reign of Akhenaten, the worship of Amun, like that of all the other great gods, was severely curtailed. (The story of this extraordinary episode is told in the entry under *Aten*.) On the death of Akhenaten the new king, the boy Tut-ankh-aten, changed his name to declare his allegiance to the neglected but now ascendant Amun; the youthful monarch is known to us as Tut-ankh-amun.

Thebes, home of the god Amun, developed into a state within a state, a rich and powerful inner kingdom ruled by the high priestess of Amun and staffed by men of nobility and genius. The god's fame extended well beyond the boundaries of Egypt; Ethiopia was virtually a vassal state to the city of Thebes. To the west, in Libya, his cult was the centre of public religion, lasting well into Classical times as the cult of Jupiter Ammon. Even Alexander the Great thought it worthwhile consulting the oracle of Amun. He received a favourable reply and assumed the title, Son of Amun.

Apart from Thebes, which grew so important that it was simply known as 'the city', Amun was worshipped all over Egypt, and his magnificent temples at Luxor and Karnak are among the finest remains of antiquity. Amun formed a triad with his wife *Mut* and his son *Khons*.

Anhur (Anhert,Onouris)
A sky god associated with *Shu*.

Anhur is shown as a man with one or both arms raised. He wears four straight feathers on his head and sometimes holds a spear. His name is interpreted as 'skybearer', or 'he who leads that which has gone away'. He was a warrior, and was invoked against both human and animal enemies whom he chased in his chariot. Apart from being a personification of war, he was also regarded as the creative power of the sun. Sometimes he is shown holding a string by which he leads the sun; this to recall the story that when *Ra's* eye wandered away it was Anhur who went to fetch it back. He was a popular god in the New Empire with cult centres at Sebennytus and This.

Married to the goddess Mehit, Anhur was a generally benign god, warlike in order to be helpful. His festival included a playful mock combat between the priests and people, who hit each other with sticks in honour of their saviour god.

Anta (Anat)

Considered by the Egyptians to be a daughter of *Ra*, Anta is an aspect of *Ishtar*.

Anubis (Anpu)

Funerary god of embalming and of tombs.

Anubis is shown as a jackal-headed man, or as a jackal. With the god *Thoth* (*q.v.*), his duty was to weigh the heart of each dead soul against a feather, the symbol of truth. The apparatus was a sort of lie-detector for the dead man to protest his innocence of various crimes; if he lied then the balance would respond, his heavy heart would sink on the scales. Anubis was responsible for the evisceration of the dead body, which during the embalming was assumed to have the ritual identity of the god *Osiris*. Anubis 'the faithful' had assisted *Isis* in the original embalming which became the pattern for all subsequent ones.

Jackals were frequent grave-robbers, so on the principle that like can defeat like, Anubis was honoured as a protector of the dead. His cult centre was Cynopolis or modern El Kes. His father was Osiris and his mother *Nephythys*. (See *Maat*.)

Anuket (Anqet, Anukis)
Divine wife of the god *Khnum*.

Anuket can be recognized by her feathered head-dress. She was associated with the Nile Cataracts, especially Aswan. Her favoured places were Seheil and Elephantine Island. Her name indicates 'hugging' or 'clasping', as if she were pressing the river between its banks, squeezing it between rocks and islands.

Apep (Apophis)
Demon enemy of the sun.

Apep was a huge snake, symbolizing darkness, storm, night, the underworld and, of course, death. He did nightly battle with the sun god *Ra*, and every night was defeated in order that the sun could shine again upon the earth. Apep, who lived in the depths of the celestial Nile, had the occasional near-success during eclipses when he swallowed the boat of the sun god, sometimes wholly, sometimes partially; but he always regurgitated it. Ra was protected by another serpent, *Mehen*, who is shown defending the sun god by coiling itself round the deck-house of the boat.

Apep was often bracketed with the dark god *Set*; as evil a pair of villains as anyone could wish to meet. The children of Apep attacked the god *Shu* (*q.v.*), causing his illness and eventual abdication.

Apis (Hap)
A bull god who wears the solar disc and royal *uraeus* (coiled cobra).

Apis was the sacred animal of *Ptah*, who in the form of celestial fire mated with a heifer. At Memphis a real bull was kept and was regarded as the incarnation of both Ptah and *Osiris*. When each bull died his successor was recognized by certain marks on his body. The bull at Memphis was popular and much-visited, for he was considered a powerful oracle and visitors drew various conclusions from his behaviour. Honoured in death as in life, the bulls of Memphis were embalmed and mummified and kept in a vast subterranean complex at Zaqqara. As Osiris-Apis he was the original of the new god *Serapis*, worshipped in Ptolemaic times.

Astarte

This Canaanite goddess, though an importation, was considered to be a daughter of *Ra*. Numbers of foreign gods and goddesses joined the existing crowds of native Egyptian deities. All were made welcome and given a home; even the gods of enemies were honoured.

Aten

God of the Pharaoh Akhenaten.

If you had asked any Ancient Egyptian priest about the god Aten you would have been fortunate to get a coherent answer. Even if the priest could have overcome his rage, wounded pride and bitterness, it would still have been difficult to understand his description. In fact there is really only one man who would have been able to give you even an approximate idea of Aten: the eccentric king Akhenaten, originally known as Amenhetep IV.

By the 18th Dynasty, *circa* 1400 B.C., the power base of the Egyptian state had already moved from Heliopolis, home of *Ra* the Sun god, to Thebes, home of the god *Amun*. To satisfy the need of the Egyptian kings to be identified with the solar deity, he was now called Amun-Ra.

There had been some move to get back to the pure solar idea of Ra when all of a sudden Amenhetep IV, a physically and emotionally odd sort of character, created a religious cataclysm by declaring that all the many Egyptian gods were false; including the all-powerful Amun-Ra. Henceforth the only god to be worshipped, solely and supremely, was to be Aten. The stunned priesthood watched amazing scenes of official revolution. Temples were closed down, priests and priestesses turned out, all references on monuments, tombs and civic buildings to 'gods', especially the name of Amun-Ra, were brutally obliterated by hammer and chisel. Lightning had struck at the heart of Egypt, leaving it paralysed.

The idea of monotheism, of one god eternal, transcendent and uncreated, was alien to a people who saw gods in every natural phenomenon about them. Their minds were simply not on that wavelength. But that is what the king ordered them to believe. He called his abstract god after the shining solar disc of

Ra, the *aten*. To this god he composed hymns, rituals and new ceremonies. The dissident king changed his name from Amen-hetep ('Amun is content') to Akhenaten ('it is well with Aten'). He deserted Thebes for a brand-new capital city, Akhetaten ('the horizon of Aten'); for which he departed lock, stock and sarcophagus as soon as it was finished.

The new god was depicted as the sun from which descended many rays, each ending in a hand which caressed the royal family. The changed attitude even affected sculpture; Akhenaten was carved as he really was, not as an ideal. And he really was a strange looking man; a bony equine face with sensitive features, a thin body with a bulging paunch. The king neglected state affairs for the constant rituals and ceremonies of his god; as a result things went badly on the frontiers, the north-eastern boundary especially was prone to pressure as Hittites, Habiru and dynasts took advantage of Egypt's internal troubles.

The worship of Aten lasted exactly as long as the life of the king; and not a minute longer. Aten's priests had all been syco-phantic time-servers, and were swift to drop the new and disturb-ing worship. The truth is that Akhenaten was a man out of his time who, because of an accident of birth that made him king, had the power and authority to express and publicize his per-sonal beliefs on a scale never before or since achieved by a mere mortal. On the road-map of religions, the worship of Aten was a cul-de-sac.

Atum (Tum, Tem)
Evening aspect of the sun god *Ra*.

It was a common trait of ancient thought to see the same thing, in this case the sun, take on different personalities according to its outward appearance. Thus the crescent moon has a different personality from the full moon, and the planet Venus in the morning is not the same as in the evening. Atum was the sun, Ra, but in his evening aspect. Worshipped at Heliopolis, he was shown wearing the *pshkhent* or double crown of Egypt. This was composed of the squat red crown of Lower Egypt and the tall white crown of Upper Egypt. Progenitor of the human race, Atum was con-sidered to have lain dormant in the primeval waters of Nun long before creation. He fought with the *Apep*-serpent in the form of a male cat. His sacred animal was the bull. He is shown carrying the symbol of life, the *crux ansata*.

Auf (Efu Ra)
An aspect of the sun god *Ra*.

Auf was a ram-headed god who wore the solar disc and travelled at night through the Underworld waterways in order to reach the east in time for the new day; however, he still had to fight off the creatures of the Underworld. Demons and gods towed his boat along while Auf stood in a deck-house, over which was coiled the serpent *Mehen* who warded off the dangerous *Apep*. The boat of night was crewed by the gods *Hu*, *Saa* and *Wepwawet*.

Ba Neb Tetet (Banebdedet, Baneb Djedet, Banaded)
Ram god.

When the two gods *Horus* and *Set* were making the heavens ring with their wranglings over precedent, it was the ram-god Ba Neb Tetet who sensibly suggested to the gods in council that they should write a letter to the goddess *Neith* and ask for her opinion. His suggestion opened the way for discussion and arbitration which finally settled the dispute. His character, one of peace and level-headedness, has been sadly perverted in sensational 'occult' fiction, for Ba Neb Tetet is the benign original for a travesty called the 'goat of Mendes', who is supposed to be some sort of diabolic spirit. Satanists have got everything else wrong, so is it really surprising that they cannot tell sheep from goats?

At Mendes was kept a sacred ram, worshipped as the incarnation of *Ra* and *Osiris*. Originally a local god, Ba Neb Tetet was given the solar disc and *uraeus* (coiled cobra) and brought into the main-stream of religious life.

Bastet (Bast)
Cat-headed sun goddess.

The town of Bubastis was the cult centre of this solar goddess represented as a woman with a cat's head, or simply as a cat. The goddess holds a *sistrum* or rattle. She was identified and confused (which is much the same thing) with both *Mut* and *Sekhmet*, the lion-headed goddess. Bastet wore an *aegis* or shield in the form of a semi-circular plate, embellished with a lion's head. She was goddess of pleasure and inevitably became one of the most popular deities. In her temple were kept sacred cats, who were supposed to be incarnations of the goddess. When they died they were carefully mummified. The Egyptians found something to worship in just about every animal they had: dogs, cats, lions, crocodiles, snakes, dung-beetles, hippos, hawks, cows and ibises.

Bes
A guardian god.

A god of a far different order from the serene and poised figures of the official pantheon. He was a plump, bandy-legged, hairy, rude dwarf with a wicked gleam in his pop-eyes, his tongue resolutely stuck out at the follies of mankind. Bes was a foreign god, an import from the land of Punt (Libya). He was a swaggering, jolly, mock-gallant pigmy, fond of music and clumsy, inelegant dancing. He was a popular proletarian god who was adopted by the middle classes; he was considered a tutelary god of childbirth and, strangely enough, of cosmetics and female adornments.

Bes chased away demons of the night and guarded men from dangerous animals. His image was carved on bedposts, bringing a touch of coarse geniality into the boudoir. He eventually became a protector of the dead and, amazingly, competed with even the refined and magnificent god *Osiris* for the attentions of men.

Bes' only clothing appears to have been a leopard skin tied round his shoulders and an ostrich feather stuck in his uncombed hair. (See *Bes*, Middle East General section.)

Duamutef (Tuamutef)
A funerary god, son of *Horus*.

Like *Anubis* he was jackal-headed and concerned with the dead. The stomach was Duamutef's sphere of influence, the preserved viscera in question being removed from the body, preserved in spices and placed in a jar on which was a model of Duamutef's head. The viscera were preserved as being essential parts of the mummified human. (See *Hapy*.)

Geb (Keb, Seb)
Earth god.

After *Ra* had created *Shu* and *Tefnut*, the two new deities mated and produced Geb ('earth') and his sister *Nut* ('sky'). Despite their relationship Geb and Nut soon became locked in a firm embrace. They had four children, *Osiris*, *Isis*, *Set* and *Nephythys*, then returned immediately to their embrace. Ra thought it was about time they desisted but they quite naturally paid him no attention. Ra then ordered Shu ('air') to slip between them and forcibly separate the enraptured pair. Nut was pushed up into an arch, resting on her toes and fingers while Geb was thrown down, his sprawling limbs becoming the uneven, hilly earth. This scene is depicted in many paintings: Nut is a slim, elongated maiden, the half-kneeling Shu holds her up with both arms, while the dark-skinned, ithyphallic Geb lies beneath them both.

Geb was a god without a cult; he was given the world to rule. One day he and a group of friends rashly opened a box in which was kept Ra's *uraeus*, the divine cobra. The snake's poisonous breath killed Geb's companions and severely burned Geb. The god was healed by the application of a magic lock of hair belonging to Ra, and ever after that was careful to mind his own business. After a long and uneventful reign he handed his power over to his son Osiris and retired to heaven. There he occasionally assisted the god *Thoth*, sometimes as a magistrate, sometimes as an envoy.

Geb's generative power is shown not only in representations of him as an ithyphallic man, but also in the story that he once had the shape of a gander. He mated with a goose to produce an egg, the sun. Many cultures regard the earth as female; Geb is an interesting exception.

Great Ennead, The
These nine gods were the foremost deities of the Egyptian pantheon. They were the close family of *Ra*, the sun god, and formed a sort of protective dynasty about him. They were also called the

Great Ennead of Heliopolis, and that city was for a long time the religious capital of Egypt. As its name implies, it was the city sacred to Ra. The nine gods of the Great Ennead were Ra, *Geb, Nut, Shu, Tefnut, Osiris, Isis, Set* and *Nephythys*.

Hapi
God of the Nile.

Hapi was in male form with a large paunch and well-developed, almost female, breasts. He wore a crown of papyrus or lotus, and was shown carrying a tray of food or pouring water from urns. He lived near the First Cataract and was a personification of the waters of the Nile. Hapi was invoked according to need; he was a localized, animistic deity and never attained the superhuman stature of the great gods. He was responsible for food production, but as a passive rather than an active element. He may have been the waters of the Nile, but the all-important flooding was controlled by other forces.

Hapy
A funerary god.

One of the divine sons of *Horus* whose duty was to look after various parts of the human viscera after embalming. The ape-headed Hapy was guardian of the lungs and was assisted by the goddess *Nephythys*. The viscera were removed during the embalming process and sealed with preservatives in four jars, the lids of which were in the shape of the head of the appropriate god. These jars are often called Canopic jars (see *Mesta, Qebhsnuf, Duamutef*).

Hathor
Goddess of love, tombs and the sky.

Hathor is shown as a cow, or as a woman with cow's horns between which are the solar disc and two feathers. Daughter of *Ra*, she is considered an aspect of *Isis*, sometimes mother, sometimes wife of *Horus*. Every evening the sun god is enclosed in her bosom, from which comes the idea that she is a goddess of love. It is claimed that she brought forth the whole world including the sun, and that she was fond of assuming the form of the *sistrum* or rattle. The rattle drives away evil spirits and is used to accompany the dance; so Hathor is protectress of women and mistress of song, dance, leaping and flower garlands. She is also queen of the West, protectress of the necropolis of Thebes. Those who knew the right spells could ride on her back to the Underworld.

As lady of the Sycamore she waited in the Libyan mountains, in the land of the west, the furthest limit of the living; there she hid in a tree and would emerge to offer bread and water to passing souls. Alternatively she would hold the ladder to enable the good souls to clamber up it in safety to the heavens.

Hathor was a mother-figure; it was said that she nursed the infant Pharaohs who, along with her nourishing milk, imbibed divinity. Thus they became her children and reached the status of gods. Hathor's creative motherliness had another, darker side to it; for it was Hathor to whom Ra turned when he wanted to slay mankind. Hathor performed such terrible slaughter on earth that Ra was shocked into changing his mind. He tricked her by preparing vast quantities of beer which he coloured red with pomegranate juice. Hathor thought it was blood and eagerly drank it; she became intoxicated and was unable to continue the carnage. (See *Sekhmet*.)

Hathor's main temples were at Dendera, Edfu and Ombos.

Heket (Heqet)
Goddess of creation, birth and the germination of corn.

Heket was pictured as a frog, or a frog-headed woman. She is a midwife, assisting at the daily birth of the sun. An earlier theogony made greater claims for her, saying that with *Shu* as husband she gave birth to the gods. A goddess of very great antiquity, her cult never really got off the ground. (See *Khnum*.)

Horus
Sun god.

When *Osiris* was treacherously done to death by *Set* his body was finally discovered by *Isis*. Assuming the form of a hawk, she settled on his belly where her warmth revived Osiris' sexual powers long enough to make her pregnant. The child that was born was Horus, the hawk-headed solar god of Memphis. Horus is often indistinguishable from the great *Ra* and is god of the sky as well as the sun; hawk being synonymous with sky. He was widely and faithfully worshipped; his images are universal and he has many names and aspects. Horus was secretly brought up in the Delta swamps about Buto until he was old enough to challenge Set, his uncle and father's murderer. The battles with Set were long, fierce and inconclusive. They were verbal as well as physical. At last judgement was given in a formal trial in Horus' favour. (See *Neith*.)

Some of the major aspects of Horus are given below:

Haroeris (Har Wer) 'Horus the elder' or 'Horus the great'. This aspect has several different names attached to it. Horkhenti Irti ('Horus who rules the two eyes') was his name in Letopolis. The two eyes were of course the sun and the moon. In Pharboethos he was called Hor Merti ('Two-eyed Horus'). Horus in this aspect is described as being in constant battle with Set; Set tears out the eyes of Horus while Horus castrates Set. Even while struggling with his enemy Horus is called Hor Nubti ('Horus conqueror of Set').

Hor Behdetite This was the title of Horus at Edfu (Behtet); he is shown as a winged solar disc, a design placed over the porches of temples. This design also hovers over battlefields, more like a hawk about to stoop than a vulture, and the prey is always the god Set.

Harakhty (Herakhty, Heraktes) 'Horus of the horizon'. At Heliopolis, centre of the sun cult, he was linked with Ra in the form Ra-Harakhty, whose symbol was the rising and setting sun.

Heru-Em-Akhet (Harmachis, Harmakis) 'Horus who is on the horizon'. This is the name of the great sphinx of King Kephren at Gizeh, symbol of resurrection. Thothmes IV justified his claim to the kingship by saying that the god Horus had promised him the throne in return for clearing away the sand which had piled up about the sphinx. Many and strange are the tall stories told to justify the seizing of supreme power, and you would have to go a long way to find a better, more imaginative one than this. It has the additional strength of being impossible to verify or disprove. Thothmes deserved the throne for his wit if nothing else.

Hor-Sa-Iset (Harsiesis) 'Horus, son of Isis'. This minor aspect of the god was to become the supreme Horus, avenger of Osiris. The cult began as one of falcon-worship near Buto.

Heru-Pa-Khret (Harpakhrad, Harpocrates) 'Horus the child'. Depicted as a baby at the breast, or as a naked and dimpled godling on his mother's knee, or as an infant boy with big, innocent eyes, engaged in sucking his finger. When the Greeks, who were sometimes too clever by half, saw this particular image they jumped to the unfounded conclusion that the infant was making a gesture of silence. Impressed by such cleverness in one so young, they forthwith claimed him as the god of secrecy and discretion If only stones could speak.

Har-End-Yotef (Harendotes) 'Horus father-protector'. This Horus grew up to be a skilful warrior called Hartomes ('Horus the spearman') and engaged in long and arduous war with the evil Set; until the gods judged he should regain his inheritance, after which he was known as:

Har-Pa-Neb-Taui 'Horus of two lands' and *Heru-sam-taui* (Harsomtus) 'Horus, uniter of the two lands'. In this aspect he is a youthful god who wears the double crown (*pshkhent*) of the two lands of Egypt, thus representing the claim of Horus to rule over his father's kingdom. The Pharaohs used the title 'living Horus' to strengthen their own personal claim to both kingship and divinity.

Hu
'Authoritative utterance'; a personified abstract and one of the sun god *Ra's* attendants.

Hu travelled on the night-voyage with Ra and he had a place in the Hall of Two Truths, the judgement hall. Here there gathered forty or so of the more important gods to hear the cases of the dead, and to give judgement. It was an awesome scene, for the soul, in the presence of the gods, had to declare a long list of protestations of innocence while his heart was being balanced against the feather of *Maat* ('truth').

Hu had no independent sphere of influence as a god; he was a mere helper, in constant attendance on Ra.

Imhotep
God of learning and medicine.

A rare example of a commoner who reached the rank of god by sheer merit. Like the later *Amenhotep* of the 18th Dynasty, Imhotep was an architect and polymath. He was made god of learning and medicine and given *Ptah*, the artificer-god, as a father. Imhotep, whose name means 'he who comes in peace', was an adviser of King Zoser (Jeser, Djoser) of the 3rd Dynasty. It is thought that he was responsible for the design of the Step Pyramid of Zaqqara, and he is also credited with introducing the stone column. Imhotep's cult was centred on Memphis. He is shown seated with an open manuscript roll on his knees and with the shaven head of a priest.

Isis (Aset, Eset)
The greatest of Egyptian divinities, the embodiment of ideal motherhood and womanhood.

Sister-wife of *Osiris* and mother of *Horus*, Isis was the daughter of *Geb* ('earth') and *Nut* ('sky'). When her husband succeeded Geb as king of Egypt she became a tutelary figure to her subjects, teaching them to grind flour, spin and weave, cure disease. She regularized the affairs of men and women by introducing the custom of marriage. When Osiris was away on his journeys to civilize other nations Isis was regent, governing wisely and well. The murder of her husband plunged her into grief; she set off to search for his body. She recovered the coffin but *Set* got hold of the corpse and cut it into fourteen parts, which he scattered far and wide. Isis diligently searched for the fragments, found them and reassembled them. Then she embalmed the body, founding the rites of many later embalmings. Osiris was restored to eternal life.

279

Before Osiris had been dismembered Isis had managed to bring enough warmth to his body to make herself pregnant. With her son Horus she fled into the swamps about Buto, warding off dangers by use of her magical powers until Horus was old enough to regain his patrimony.

The cult of Isis originated in the Delta town of Perehbet and spread all over Egypt. It reached Rome and lasted at Philae well into the sixth century A.D. Her images show her as an attractive, mature woman. On her head is a miniature throne (the ideogram of her name) and the solar disc between the cow's horns of *Hathor*. In some cases vestigial cow's ears are all that remain to show her connection with that goddess. Sacred to her were the *sistrum*, the rattle, to ward off evil spirits, and a magic knot called Tat. She is shown in many attitudes: suckling the infant Horus, enthroned alongside Osiris, protecting her husband and the souls of the dead with her winged arms. Her magical powers were considerable; Isis was the only divinity ever to discover the secret name of *Ra*. She used a magic snake to torment him with its poison until he revealed his true name to her. Possession of the name would have given her power of life and death over Ra, and there is in this story a hint of an inner cult. The outer cult has been described in The Golden Ass by Apuleius.

Isis is a splendid example of the primeval mother goddess developed into a regal lady. She is positive and attractive, modest yet active, loving, faithful and humane, civilized and sensitive. Her name, linked to *Ishtar*, has charmingly been described as an onomatopoeic derivation of the sound of weeping, and indeed Isis is often shown with tears.

Josephus relates a story about the Roman priesthood of Isis during the time of the emperor Tiberius. A rich young nobleman named Mundus had fallen in love with a handsome woman called Paulina, a devotee of Isis. He offered her huge sums of money for her favours, but she refused. A woman servant of his bribed the priests of Isis who went to Paulina with the story that the god *Anubis* wished to lie with her. She was flattered and agreed. She was taken to the temple of Isis at night and left there alone. The young nobleman appeared, pretended to be the god Anubis and achieved through her devotion what his money had failed to purchase. A few days later he boasted to her of what had happened.

Paulina went to the emperor, who banished Mundus and had the servant woman and all the priests crucified. Isis' temple was destroyed and her statue thrown into the Tiber.

Khepra (Khepri, Khepera)
One of the many images of the sun god *Ra* was the scarab beetle. The Egyptians saw in its tireless moving of a ball of dung a parallel to the movement of the sun across the sky. They also noticed that small beetles emerged from similar balls and assumed that, like the sun, the scarab was a self-creating entity. Heliopolis was the cult centre of Khepra worship; the name Khepra means 'scarab' or 'he who becomes', with the added idea of continuing and eternal life. The god was shown as a scarab beetle, or as a man with a complete beetle instead of his human head.

Khnum (Khnemu)
God of fecundity and creation from the Cataract area.

Originally a local ram-god, his sanctuary was on Elephantine Island; he was visualized as a man with a ram's head and wavy horns. He guarded the source of the Nile, which to the Egyptians was the same as guarding the source of life. From a guardian god he developed into a demiurge (creator), and it was said that he shaped the world on his potter's wheel. As a potter shapes clay so does Khnum shape man's flesh; it is he who is responsible for the formation of the foetus in the womb.

In Nubia there was a ram-god called Doudoun with whom Khnum may be associated. The Egyptians married Khnum off to the goddess *Heket*, who was a frog.

Khons (Khonsu, Khensu)
God of the moon.

Khons was the son of *Amun* and *Mut* and with them formed the Theban triad of gods. He is represented as a royal child, wearing the side-plait and carrying the crook and flail. He is also shown as a falcon-headed youth whose head is surmounted by the lunar disc and crescent combined. In time he was regarded as a god of healing. Khons was thought of as the placenta of the king; a ghostly twin, a sort of royal guardian angel as distinct from the

281

king's normal *ka*, or etheric double.

To the Theban triad were raised the biggest and most imposing of Egyptian temples. Every new year was celebrated in a festival which included a ritual river voyage between the two great temples of Karnak and Luxor.

Maahes

Son of *Ra* and *Bastet* the cat-headed goddess. He was shown as a lion, or as a lion-headed man. He must have originated from Upper Egypt, for he is shown wearing the *atef*, the tall white crown of that area.

Maat

Goddess of truth and justice.

Maat's symbol, and the ideogram of her name, is the feather. Daughter of *Ra* and wife of *Thoth*, she was goddess of law and sat in the Hall of Two Truths to give judgement. There the hearts of men were weighed against her feather of truth (see *Hu*). Such was Maat's power that people were naturally interested in how they could please her. There was a healthy amount of fear behind this desire. It was said that a small image of Maat was more pleasing to the gods than piles of rich offerings; a little truth was more welcome than huge bribes. One has to wonder if the priests thought in the same way.

Maat was certainly the embodiment of the main moral force of Ra, for he loved truth above all else. He required an exact account of all a soul's earthly acts before admitting it to heaven. (See *Anubis*.)

Mehen

The divine snake whose coils protected *Ra* as he journeyed on his boat through the waterways of the kingdom of night. Mehen is usually seen draped in protective coils about the deck-house in which Ra stands. (See *Apep*.)

Mertseger

Funerary goddess of the Theban necropolis.

Friend of 'silence' or 'beloved of the silent one', Mertseger was identified with the highest mountain of the Theban necropolis, *Ta-dehnet* ('the peak'). She could be both benign and vindictive, and was variously described as having a snake's head, a woman's head, or a vulture's head.

A servant of the necropolis, one Nefer-abu, once did something which displeased Mertseger. He was stricken with illness; but his supplications to the goddess were successful and he was cured. Nefer-abu thereupon raised a *stela* to Mertseger, describing the event. The *stela* was as much a warning to others as a thanks-offering to the goddess, one suspects. Like many Egyptian deities, Mertseger was originally a local goddess who rose to prominence with the increased importance of her particular locality.

Meskhent
Goddess of childbirth.

Meskhent was sometimes represented as a woman with a head-dress of palm-shoots and sometimes as a brick with a woman's head. She appeared to women at the moment of childbirth and would predict the future of the newly-delivered infant. It was the custom in ancient Egypt for the expectant mother to sit, supported by two bricks, in order to give birth; hence the strange image of the goddess.

Mesta (Imseti)
One of the sons of *Horus* who guarded the human viscera after mummification. Mesta, shown as a bearded, mummiform man, was the protector of the liver. He was helped in this task by the goddess *Isis*.

Min (Minu, Menu)
Ithyphallic god of sex.

Min is another form of *Amun* and was chiefly worshipped at Coptos and Panoplis. He wears the plumed head-dress of Amun and holds a whip-like sceptre. He is also shown holding his erect phallus in his left hand. Though the Greeks identified him with *Pan* there is nothing Pan-like about him. Min is a proud, regal figure. His ancient symbol was the thunderbolt and he was sometimes considered to have been the creator of the world, or even as another form of *Horus*. Coptos became an important entrepôt for desert trading expeditions and so Min became the god of roads and travellers. As god of fecundity he was also god of crops, and the first sheaf of wheat was offered to him by the Pharaoh at harvest time. His sacred animal was a white bull while the games of Panoplis were held in his honour during the period of Greek influence.

Mont (Month, Menthu, Mentu)
A falcon-headed god of war whose cult was at Hermonthis (Armant).

Mont was favoured by the kings of the 11th Dynasty, who used his name as part of theirs. Sometimes pictured as a bull-headed man, he was reputed to incarnate himself in the bull called Buchis, kept in the shrine at Hermonthis. Mont also had solar characteristics (a bull often represents the heat and power of the sun) and for a while was supreme god in the south, until he was included in the Theban triad and demoted by the god *Amun* of Thebes. As war god he is shown with the *khepesh*, curved sabre. During the war against the Hittites, Rameses II found himself losing; he called upon Amun and rallied his forces to the counterattack. He successfully routed the Hittites and then declared that he was like the god Mont. The Greeks and Celts might have had gods who intervened in battles, but the Egyptians had a god on the battlefield; their king.

For all his qualities Mont was later dropped from the Theban triad in favour of *Khons*, the lunar god.

Mut
Sky goddess and wife of *Amun-Ra*.

Mut's name means 'mother' and she wore either a vulture head-dress or the *pshkhent* (the double crown of Egypt). She is linked with the cow (indicative of the sky), the cat and the lioness. Mut was a colourless sort of personality, her main claim to fame being her husband. The divine couple had no children; first they adopted *Mont*, then *Khons*. With Khons and Amun, Mut formed the Theban triad.

Nefertem (Nefertum, Iphtimis)

A young god of Memphis who was shown wearing the lotus flower on his head and bearing the *khepesh*, curved sabre. He was the son of *Ptah* and *Sekhmet*.

Nehebkau
Serpent god of the Underworld.

Looking like a serpent but with human arms and legs, Nehebkau lurked in the Underworld as a constant menace to gods and men. He was however a subject of *Ra* and would often give food to the dead. He is sometimes shown with two heads at one end of his body and another head at the other end.

Neheh (Heh)
Personification of eternity, used as a common decorative design on furniture. He is shown as a squatting man wearing on his head a curved reed and carrying symbols of life, like the *crux ansata*.

Neith (Neit)
Goddess of war and domestic arts, especially weaving.

A very ancient goddess and patroness of Sais, capital of Egypt in the 26th Dynasty (seventh century B.C.). Called Tehenut, 'the Libyan', her sign was two crossed arrows on a shield or animal skin. She wore the *net*, the red crown of Lower Egypt. Because the ideogram of her name was the shuttle, she was elevated to being goddess of the sky; it being claimed that she wove the world with her shuttle. It was also claimed that *Ra* was her son. Thus we see a local goddess acquiring the attributes of a member of the *Great Ennead*; in this case those of the goddess *Nut*. Later Neith was identified with *Athene* and *Isis*, had the alias Mehueret, and was thought to perform the duty of offering transient souls refreshment of bread and water. With *Duamutef*, a son of *Horus*, she protected the embalmed stomach of the mummy.

   In impossible cases the gods would turn to Neith for advice. Such a situation arose over the dispute and savage conflict between Horus and *Set* over the vacancy left by the murdered *Osiris* Neith acted as arbitrator in the hearing, telling the gods that they should give Horus his rightful inheritance and also give Set compensation of an amount equal to all his possessions. In addition he was to be given *Anta* and *Astarte* as his wives. It should be noted that both these goddesses were foreigners. No local interests would be offended by their alliance to the evil murderer of the great god Osiris. (See *Selket*.)

Nekhebet

A guardian goddess of Upper Egypt who looked after children and mothers.

Nekhebet was worshipped at Nekheb (El Kab; Greek: *Eileithyias-polis*). She was shown hovering over the Pharaoh in vulture-form, holding a fly-whisk and a seal. She protected and suckled the royal children. The Greeks identified her with their goddess of childbirth, *Ilythia* or Eileithyia.

Nephythys (Nebthet)
Goddess of the dead.

'Mistress of the palace', she wears on her head the ideogram of her name, Neb ('a basket') and Het ('a palace'). Daughter of *Geb* and *Nut*, Nephythys was married to her brother *Set*. They had no children. Nephythys seduced her other brother *Osiris* by making him drunk; their child was *Anubis*. When Set killed Osiris she deserted him in horror and helped *Isis* to embalm the murdered god. She and Isis are the protectresses of the dead; they are shown with winged arms, for in order to mourn Osiris they changed themselves into kites. Nephythys helped *Hapy* to guard the embalmed lungs of mummified people.

Nun (Nu)
The Egyptian name for an idea that appears in many cultures, the primal waters which were the source of all life.

Although personified as a bearded man waist-high in water, Nun is more of an idea than a god. Father of the gods, he existed before creation as a watery mass filling the universe. From him sprang *Ra* and then all of life. The Oseirion at Abydos had a subterranean water channel to represent Nun. Nun is also depicted holding aloft Manjet, the morning boat of the sun god Ra.

Nut
Goddess of the sky.

Nut united with her brother, the earth god *Geb*, in a tight and passionate embrace until separated by *Shu* ('air') on the orders of *Ra*. Ra was annoyed because Geb and Nut had come together without his knowledge or agreement. Expecting that there would be a natural result of their affection, he declared that Nut could not give birth to children on any day of any month of any year. The god *Thoth* came to Nut's help. He had been playing draughts with the moon and had won enough of the moon's light to make up five new days. Since these days were not on the official calendar, Nut was able to bear a child on each. She gave life to *Osiris*, *Isis*, *Set*, *Nephythys*, and *Horus* the Elder. (Horus is missing from the Ra version of the same event.)

Nut is represented as a slim-limbed girl; supported only on the tips of her fingers and toes, she arches over the fallen body of Geb, who sprawls with limbs awry and phallus erect. Nut is supported by the god Shu in some representations, and her star-spangled belly forms a canopy for the earth.

When Ra decided to go away and have nothing to do with men, he rose to the heavens on the back of Nut who had taken on the form of a cow. Nut grew rapidly to such an enormous height that it was feared her legs would snap, so to each leg was appointed a god whose duty was to stiffen and strengthen it.

Nut arches over the earth in an east to west direction, and it is said that Ra is reborn each morning from between her thighs.

Osiris
Originally a vegetation god closely linked to corn; later god of the dead, the supreme funerary deity.

Osiris was born at Thebes of *Geb* and *Nut* and succeeded to the throne on his father's abdication. He took *Isis* as his queen and set about teaching the Egyptians the arts and crafts of civilization. He showed them how to use grain for bread and grapes for wine. He started religion, built temples, composed rituals, carved statues. He taught them weaving and music, founded towns, and introduced codes of law. Having brought the Egyptians up to a reasonable standard of personal and social behaviour, Osiris set off to do the same for other nations. He was accompanied in these journeys by *Thoth, Anubis* and *Wepwawet*.

In his absence his kingdom was successfully governed by Isis. After the return of Osiris, *Set*, who had been growing more and more jealous of his brother's successes and popularity, invited him to a great banquet. During the feast a huge and beautifully-decorated coffer was brought into the hall. Set jokingly declared that the coffer would become the property of whomsoever it fitted. Osiris was invited to be the first to try it. Amidst general mirth he clambered inside and lay down. Immediately the lid was slammed on and nailed down tight. The banquet guests, who were all in the conspiracy, sealed the coffer with molten lead. Secretly, in the darkness, the coffer was carried to the Nile and dropped into the swift waters.

The coffer floated out to sea and eventually came to land at Byblos in Phoenicia. It beached near the roots of a tamarisk tree. The tree, as if sensing the presence of something divine, spread around the coffer magically, protectively. The tree grew rapidly to a huge size, so that the great box was entirely closed in its magic trunk. The local king, Malcandre, heard of the wonderful giant tree and had it cut down to be used as a column in his palace. The column gave off a sweet perfume.

News of this wonder reached Isis, who understood what had happened and set off for Byblos in disguise. There she was given the royal baby to look after by the queen, Astarte. Isis wanted to give the gift of immortality to the child and began to burn off its mortal being with magic fire. Astarte saw the flames, misunderstood what was happening and spoiled the spell with her anxious intervention. Isis then confessed her true identity and told them the reason for her visit. King Malcandre gave her the column and the goddess retrieved the coffer containing her dead husband. Returning to Egypt, she hid in the swamplands of Buto and managed to revive the body long enough for it to make her pregnant.

But Set, out hunting in the swamps, came across the hiding place and found the body. Furiously he dismembered the corpse into fourteen parts and dispersed them about the land. Isis searched for the pieces and patiently reassembled her husband. One part, the phallus, was missing, for it had been consumed by a Nile crab.

With the assistance of other gods and goddesses Isis embalmed the body, and Osiris was revived into eternal life. He retired to the Underworld.

Osiris, chief god of Busiris, had many incarnations and aliases. He was the corn and the vine, born every year and slain every year; he was the Nile which rises and falls, the rising and setting sun, the fertile land about the Nile threatened by the desert, Set. Shown as a mummy with a man's head crowned with the tall white cap of Upper Egypt, his crossed arms hold the flail and hook of royalty. His skin is shown with a greenish tinge. He is also the bull Onuphis, the ram of Mendes, the Bennu bird. One of his symbols is the *djed* pillar, a tree-trunk. It was considered to represent his spine and indicated stability; the stability of eternal life.

Ptah

God of artisans and artists, designers, builders, metal workers, architects and masons.

Sovereign god of Memphis, ancient capital of Egypt, Ptah is shown as a shaven-headed, mummified man. He was popular with the kings of the 19th Dynasty (Set I, Rameses II) and became the third most important god in Egypt. His priests claimed that it was Ptah who had made the world. He became famous for defeating the Assyrians; he ordered hundreds of rats to creep into the enemy camp and eat all their bowstrings. Married to *Sekhmet*, their son was *Nefertem*, and *Imhotep* was adopted as their earthly child after his deification.

Ptah is linked with *Apis*, the sacred bull. It was said that Ptah, in the form of celestial fire, mated with a virgin cow who gave birth to Ptah himself in the shape of a bull. Ptah is sometimes shown as a dwarf with misshapen legs, linking him with other lame smith-gods. He is also allied to *Tanen*, an ancient earth god, and to *Seker*.

Ptah-Seker-Osiris
A composite funerary god made up of the three gods who appear in his name. Sometimes he was a dwarf, sometimes a mummified man.

Qebhsnuf (Qebehsenuf)
One of the sons of *Horus* and visceral guardian. He looked after the intestines with the help of the goddess *Selket*.

Qetesh
Goddess of love.

This minor deity was probably an Asiatic import. The Egyptians regarded her as an aspect of *Hathor*. Pictured as a nude woman holding flowers and standing on the back of a lion, she is reminiscent of the Persian Anahita, or the Phoenician *Anat* who is also called Qadesh.

Ra
God of the sun.

Finding himself alone in the watery mists of *Nun*, the sun god Ra achieved the remarkable feat of making himself pregnant. He then gave birth to air, *Shu*, and moisture, *Tefnut*, by spitting them out of his mouth. Shu and Tefnut mated to produce the earth god *Geb* and the sky goddess *Nut*. These grandchildren followed their parents' incestuous example with such enthusiasm that they engendered four great-grandchildren for Ra. There were two of each sex, which was convenient, for *Osiris* mated with *Isis* and *Set* with *Nephythys*. They are known collectively as the *Great Ennead* of Heliopolis, the nine major gods of Ancient Egypt.

Ra had several aspects. As *Atum* he is a man wearing the double crown of Egypt; as *Khepra* he is a dung beetle tirelessly rolling its ball to hide in the sand – as tirelessly as the sun is moved across the sky. As Ra he is a falcon-headed man wearing the *uraeus*, the coiled cobra, and sun disc.

Every day Ra travelled from Manu, the hill of sunrise, across the sky in a boat called Manjet. As he travelled, he aged from boy to old man. At night he assumed a ram's head and transferred to the boat called Mesektet for his night journey through the waterways of the Underworld. The reliability of his sailings, the eternal validity of his season-ticket, were constant facts in Egyptian life.

Ra is said to have created man from his tears; a symbolic birth since, as we know, mankind is nothing but a problem to the gods. And sure enough there was trouble. Men were wicked, unruly and treacherous. Eventually Ra had had enough; he ordered *Hathor* to kill mankind. The goddess went about the work so efficiently and enthusiastically that Ra changed his mind. Aghast at the slaughter, he ordered her to stop. Hathor ignored him, and he had to resort to trickery to cease the carnage. Ra found men so distasteful that he took to sailing, assuming what is now known as a low profile; if that is possible for the sun.

Ra had trouble with his eye, the sun. Not only did it stay out at night, but it actually began to wander off on its own. The god had to send *Anhur* (some say *Thoth*) to bring it back. When the sun realized that its place in the sky had been taken by a rival, the moon, there were angry scenes. Ra had to play the diplomat and find places and suitable times for both of them.

There was a close interdependence between Ra and the Egyptian kings. The kings claimed not only relationship with the sun but also identity. Thus a Pharaoh was the son of the sun, and also the incarnation of it. Ra was the sun and the king was Ra. This identification was strengthened by royal titles in which the name Ra predominated, by the wearing of the golden cobra or *uraeus*, and by the practice of incest in the royal family. All this ensured stability for the king and for the priesthood of Ra.

Many lesser, local or foreign gods were solarized by assuming that they were the children of Ra; or by actual identification, as in the case of *Amun*. Such is the effectiveness of a strong and ruthless priesthood with a vested interest in political power. Ra was king of gods, and god of kings.

Renenutet (Ernutet, Renenet)
Goddess of harvest and the suckling of babies.

For the second function Renenutet was called 'Lady of the double granary'. While nourishing a baby she gave it its name, personality and future fate. She is variously depicted as a woman, or a woman with a serpent's head, or as a serpent wearing the solar disc between the horns of *Hathor*. She attended the weighing of men's hearts in the Hall of Two Truths along with *Shait*.

Renpet
Goddess of youth and springtime.

Mistress of eternity, she was linked with the general idea of time. She wore a palm shoot on her head.

Resheph (Reshpu)
The Egyptian version of the Semitic *Aleyin/Amurru*. Though originally a vegetation god (Canaanite *Osiris*), the Egyptians regarded him as a warrior and showed him weaponed and crowned with gazelle's horns.

Saa
The personification of intelligence. He is mostly known for the help he gave the sun god *Ra* on his boat during the night journey through the Underworld.

Sebek (Sobk,Suchos)
Crocodile god of Fayum (Crocodilopolis).

Sebek's worshippers thought of him as a creator god, emerging from the waters of chaos to lay his eggs of life on the bank. He was linked with the evil god *Set*. Sebek was guardian of royalty in the 13th Dynasty. In a lake near his temple a real crocodile was kept and regarded as the god incarnate. This animal's name was Petesuchos. He was much fussed over, and had golden rings in his ears and gold bracelets on his legs. He became a renowned tourist attraction and visitors would save food and wine to feed to him.

Seker (Sokar, Socharis)
God of the Memphis necropolis (Sakkara), one of many funerary gods.

Seker was often shown with a falcon's head. He was linked to *Osiris* and *Ptah* in the composite deity *Ptah-Seker-Osiris*. He was a guardian of the access door to the Underworld.

Sekhmet (Sakhmet)
Goddess of war and battle.

Sekhmet, 'the terrible one', had a lioness's head crowned with disc and *uraeus*, a coiled cobra. Wife of *Ptah*, she symbolized the destructive rage of the sun.

Sekhmet is linked to *Hathor* in the story of *Ra's* destruction of mankind. Hathor took on the shape of Sekhmet in order to attack men at Ra's order. The slaughter was so terrible that Ra asked her to desist; the goddess refused. Ra mixed beer and pomegranate juice, and left large amounts of the mixture about the battlefield. Hathor/Sekhmet thought the liquid was blood and delightedly swigged vast quantities of it. She became so drunk she was unable to continue the mayhem.

Although she was the malignant sun, Sekhmet attracted osteopaths to her cult. Despite her destructive bent she was happily married to Ptah, that most creative of gods.

Selket (Selchis, Selquet)
Guardian goddess of conjugal union.

Selket and *Neith* watched over the sky, the bedroom where *Amun* and his wife were busily engaged. Their duty was to ensure that the couple were not interrupted by anyone bursting in. Selket is pictured either as a woman with a scorpion on her head or as a scorpion with a woman's head. She helped *Qebhsnuf* guard the embalmed intestines in their funerary jar. Selket is another daughter of *Ra*.

Septu (Sopd, Sopdu)
War god.

'Smiter of the Asiatics', he was shown as a man with foreign features wearing two tail feathers on his head. He was also shown as a falcon wearing the same two plumes. Septu is a reminder that there was a constant intercommunication, constant movement among the nations, tribes and cities of the ancient world. Our regrettably inadequate methods of teaching history have resulted in many people regarding the past as a series of insulated corridors, receding each in its own direction into the darkness of ignorance.

Serapis
The national god of Ptolemaic Egypt.

Serapis was invented by Ptolemy I (Soter) by combining *Osiris*, god of vegetation and death, with *Apis* the bull-god. A very fine head of Serapis, bearded and with curly hair, was found in London in the temple of *Mithras*. Serapis wore on his head a *calathus* or *modius*, a corn-measure looking uncannily like a modern flower-pot.

At first sight it seems strange to find such a sculpture in such a place. The combined cult of *Isis* and Serapis was accepted in Rome where both Caligula and Caracalla were adherents; Serapis-worship was therefore most likely brought to Britain by the Romans. His worship is also tenuously linked to Mithraism, for both include the idea of the Underworld and have the bull as a central image.

Seshat (Sesheta)
Goddess of writing and letters and archives.

It was Seshat who measured time, calculated the best sidereal moment for laying the foundation stones of temples, kept the royal accounts and made audits of the loot captured by warlike expeditions. She was shown as a woman holding a pen, palette and sometimes a tally stick; on her head she wore a star, a crescent and feathers. In time the crescent grew into horns, possibly in imitation of those of *Hathor*; because of the associated ideas of writing: measurement: time: stars: sky, she would have been linked with Hathor the Heavenly Cow.

Seshat was married to *Thoth* and in many areas is his double. That does not mean that she was originally inferior; it could have been that Thoth acquired some of his attributes from her.

Set (Seth, Seti, Sutekh)
God of thunder and storm; the personification of evil in the battle against good.

Child of *Geb* and *Nut*, Set was a premature birth; he tore himself out of the womb as if eager to be born. To the Egyptians he was a disgusting sight, for his skin was white and his hair red; a horrible, unnatural colouring for a civilized human being. The Greeks identified him with their Typhon, a monstrous creature.

Set's misdeeds have been recounted in the entries on *Osiris*, *Horus* and *Isis*. He came to be identified with evil, drought, dryness, destruction, and all the other terrible things that the desert can inflict on mankind. He was responsible for heat, suffering, hunger and thirst. Worshipped at Kus and Ombos, Set became identified with Sutekh, god of the hated Hyksos invaders, who about 1650 B.C. drove the Egyptians southward and formed themselves a kingdom in the Nile Delta. The Hyksos themselves had been dispossessed by encroaching Hittite peoples. The Egyptians drove out the Hyksos but Set's reputation, never very good, was now utterly lost. His statues were smashed, his name forbidden in both writing and speech, his memory reviled.

Set was represented as an ugly pig-like creature with erect tail. Archaeologists call this concoction of evil the 'Typhonian animal'. Every month Set, in the shape of this creature, attacked and consumed the moon, which was the hiding place of Osiris, and also the spot where souls gathered together after death.

Shait
Goddess of destiny.

Shait was a sort of guardian angel who was born with each new person and lived a parallel existence. When the person died and the soul reached the Hall of Judgement, Shait was there to give a true account of all sins and good works. Against her evidence there was no appeal.

Shu
God of air and the atmosphere.

Husband of *Tefnut*, together they were the first couple of the *Great Ennead* of Heliopolis. She was called 'The Upholder', 'The Carrier'. At *Ra's* orders he forcibly separated the loving embrace of *Geb* and *Nut* and held Nut up to form the sky. He was a character of myth rather than a god with all the necessary temples, priests and such. Shu was king of the world after Ra. However, the children of *Apep* ambushed him in his palace. He beat them off but was left weakened and exhausted. He abdicated in favour of Geb, which after his treatment of him was the least he could do. After a noisy farewell party, a tempest which lasted nine days, he retired to heaven.

Tanen (Tathenen)
Ptah in an aspect of an earth god. During the dispute between *Horu* and *Set*, he was linked with Ptah as one entity.

Taueret (Taurt, Thoueris)
Goddess of childbirth.

Popular with the middle classes, this domestic deity had a most extraordinary look to her; she was a female hippopotamus with human breasts, lion's feet, and a scaled, crocodilian back. Standing upright, she had a sort of wig descending to her fat shoulders, and she carried a bundle of reed or straw in the shape of the hieroglyph *sa*. This hieroglyph was a sign of protection. Her ugly appearance belied her character, for Taueret was kind and helpful. Her protuberant belly probably gave rise to the idea that she was the protectress of childbirth.

Tefnut (Tefenet)
Goddess of moisture, especially of the atmospheric variety – dew, rain and mist.

Consort of *Shu*, Tefnut was depicted either as a lioness or as a woman with a lioness's head. There was a hint of the sun in her character; she is otherwise a mere attendant on her husband.

Thoth (Tehuti, Thout, Djehuti, Zehuti)
Great god of wisdom, magic, music, medicine, astronomy, geometry, surveying, drawing and writing.

Thoth's name means 'he of Djehut', which was a province in Lower Egypt. His cult centre was at Hermopolis (Ashmunen). He was depicted as an ibis-headed man or as an ibis- or dog-headed ape; on his head he wore the combined lunar disc and crescent. His priests claimed that he was the true universal demiurge who created everything by sound.

Thoth, despite all attempts to find him parents in the main-stream of the gods, remains outside the Osirian family. His achievements are great. He helped to revive the dismembered *Osiris*, he defended *Horus* and cured him from scorpion poison, he adjudicated in the dispute and afterwards cured the wounds which gods Horus and *Set* had inflicted on each other. He invented all the arts and sciences. His followers said that Thoth had certain books which contained all magic and all knowledge. He had locked them up in a crypt, and his priests claimed that they alone had access to them. Not without reason was Thoth called 'Thrice Greatest'.

After spending a busy time on earth Thoth became overseer of the moon. He was responsible for measuring time (the first month of the year was named after him); he was in charge of all calculations, archives, inventories of treasure and loot. He was historian, scribe, herald and divine judge. Thoth was called *Hermes* by the Greeks and is the original of Hermes Trismegistus ('thrice greatest Hermes'), the mystical figure behind many an arcane school of celestial philosophy; and for those who know, the god was the originator of the Four Laws of Magic (D.W.K.S.).

Thoth's festival was celebrated with figs and honey and his worshippers greeted each other with the phrase 'Sweet is the truth'.

Uajyt (Uatchet, Per Uadjit, Uazet, Uto, Buto)
Guardian goddess of Lower Egypt.

Uajyt's main shrine was at Buto (Per Uadjit, 'the dwelling place of Uadjit'). As sovereign of the Delta lands, she helped *Isis* hide with the child *Horus* in the swamps. She was a cobra goddess, winged and crowned with the red crown of Lower Egypt. Often identified with the *uraeus* serpent, she was guardian of royalty and an image of her was worn about the forehead, either alone or combined with one or both crowns of Egypt.

Wepwawet (Upuaut, Ophois)
'Opener of roads'; a god of the Underworld.

This wolf-headed god lived in the west and was guide of the dead. With *Anubis* he was worshipped at Lycopolis. When *Ra* floated on his boat through the regions of night it was Wepwawet who rode on the bows, guarding the way ahead. Wepwawet is found leading all manner of processions, religious, civil, scientific and warlike. Demoted from his godship of Abydos by *Osiris*, Wepwawet, a lord of the Necropolis, is often seen dressed as a soldier, for he accompanied Osiris on his travels to civilize (conquer) foreign lands.

Wepwawet is one of those useful sort of gods who keep quietly in the background and simply get on with their work, with the minimum fuss and the maximum efficiency.

Addad

Otherwise known as Addu or Haddad. God of the atmosphere, clouds and tempests; worshipped in Canaan, Babylon and Assyria.

Son of *Asherat of the Sea*, Addad was a rain-giver and thunder-bringer. He is shown as a lordly man wearing a pointed helmet with horns. These horns are not the protruding kind associated with romanticized Vikings, but are shown flat on the surface of the helmet, curving round its shape like wings at rest. The thunderbolt he wields is sometimes very similar to the three-pronged zig-zag of Classical sculpture. Addad's animal is the bull, symbol of strength and fierce creativity; and also capable of destruction.

North of Canaan, in what is now modern Syria, Addad was called *Rimmon* or Rammon, the Thunderer. The Hittites borrowed an alias of his, *Ishkur*, to denote their god of tempest and rain. Though we do not know this god's true name it seems he was close to Addad, for he was shown as a bearded man standing on a bull and carrying thunderbolts. As Lord of Foresight the god was considered a help to mankind by controlling floods. (See *Baal*.)

Adonis

Ancient Semitic god whose name Adon, Adonai means 'lord' (as does Baal). It was a title later changed into a name by the Greeks.

The Adonis cult is closely parallel to those of *Dumuzi*, *Tammuz* and *Attis*, but shows differences in detail. The origin and cult centre was Nega (Byblus, on the Syrian coast). This forested region had produced a god of forest growth called *Hay-Tau (q.v.)*, who is regarded as the prototype of Adonis. Adonis replaced Hay-Tau and also assumed roles played by the two opposed vegetation gods, *Aleyin* and *Mot* of Ugarit (Ras Shamrah). Adonis (the Greek form of *Adon*, *Adonai*) has several legends attached to his name. Born from a tree his great beauty caused friction between *Aphrodite* and *Persephone*, who both yearned for him. *Zeus* decided that the youth should spend half the year in the kingdom of Hades and the other half above ground. Another story has it that Aphrodite, who had fallen deeply in love with him, warned him not to go hunting. Adonis ignored the warning and was killed by either a boar or a bear.

The god's annual descent into the Underworld caused universal lamentations among his women worshippers, who repeatedly cried out his name. His festival came immediately after the harvest; he was identified with the corn and the death of the crop was his death also. Pots were planted with quick-growing fennel, wheat, barley and lettuce. The seeds germinated quickly and sprouted, but the plants soon died, symbolizing the transitory nature of the god. Some evidence shows that the death of Adonis was paralleled by a human sacrifice, which was offered to recompense the god for having been cut, threshed, dried, and ground up.

At certain seasons the river near Byblus, called by the Greeks Adonis (modern Nahr Ibrahim), is coloured red with particles of haematite washed off its banks. It was said that the red colour was the blood of Adonis, who had returned to the place of his reputed death to die once more for the good of the harvest.

Adonis was revered under the name Tammuz even in Jerusalem, where women wept by the north gate for him. Many years later there were to be more weeping women by the gate of the north wall. A different time, a new wall, but the same old sorrow looking towards Calvary.

Ahriman
Zoroastrian spirit of darkness and deception.

Ahriman is the enemy of *Ahura Mazda*, matching his good creations with evil ones. Against life he created death. Into the fruitful garden of Ghaon he introduced destructive pests and insects; into the sublime city of Muru he injected bad faith, misleading counsel and rumour. He sent wild animals into the pastures to attack the herds. Into men's prayers he insinuated seeds of doubt. Into wealthy mansions and palaces he smuggled sloth, luxury and inflation (he obviously had an eye to the future). Worst of all to the Zoroastrian way of thinking, Ahriman started the criminal habits of burial and cremation. Both earth and fire are sacred and must not be defiled with human flesh. The normal Zoroastrian funerary practice was to expose their dead on high towers to be disposed of by the vultures; the remaining bones were then stored in the main part of the 'tower of silence'.

All things considered, Ahriman was a wrecker on a massive

scale. He could call on the help of squads of demons, the *Daevas*, who did much of his petty hustling for him. Among these energetic trouble-makers we come across a familiar name, Indra. In order to cross to the other world the souls of the dead must use a bridge called Sinvat, a name which to us has an ominous but purely accidental ring. On the bridge lurked Iranian Indra, whose delight was to leap out of hiding and push unwary souls over the parapet into the swirling rapids far below. Among the living, Indra created doubt and moral uncertainty; the only thing he had in common with the great Indian god of the Vedas was his energy, and even that was used for harming mankind.

Two other interesting demons in Ahriman's camp were Sauru, linked by name to the Indian gods *Rudra* and *Siva*, and a character called Aeshma Daeva, who is none other than Asmodeus (who in the Book of Tobit was responsible for the deaths of the husbands of Sara).

Ahriman accounted for the deaths of Gayomart, the first man, and of Gosh, the primal bull. (See *Zurvan*.)

Ahura Mazda
The great and omniscient god of the Persians.

Ahura Mazda's regal supremacy can be seen as a parallel to the earthly power of the Persian royal family, with which he was connected. There are differing opinions as to the meaning of his double-name. Ahura has been linked to the Indian *Asura* (see Asia section) and to the Assyrian *Ashur*. It can be interpreted as 'divine being'. Mazda is linked with words meaning 'illumination', 'intoxication' and 'wisdom'.

Ahura Mazda was creator of all things and, unlike many gods, was far above human weaknesses. He was served by legions of archangels who helped him in his fight against the forces of darkness. The dualist interpretation of Mazda by Zarathustra is part of a complex theological development and should not be accepted too simply. There is indeed a struggle between light and dark, good and evil, positive and negative, but that is not the whole story. Zarathustra, the founder of Zoroastrianism, merged the two parts of Ahura Mazda's title to give us *Ormazd*, the essence of good and light, against whom was set *Ahriman*, darkness and evil. Ahriman is compounded from the words Angra Mainyu, which means 'negative thought'. Thus two opposed polarities were described and in between them lay the world, whose inhabitants are inevitably involved in the cosmic struggle. This is not pure dualism for Ahura Mazda was said to have created Ahriman, who is probably a descendant of an ancient underworld deity to whom *Mithra* is also linked. In the future, or rather in the end as far as humans are concerned, Ahura Mazda will defeat Ahriman and live on after him.

Aleyin
Phoenician god of springs and vegetation.

Aleyin is sometimes described as a son of *Baal*, sometimes as an aspect of Baal. He rides in the clouds accompanied by seven comrades and eight boars. Another name for him is *Amurru*, and under this name he was married to his sister *Anat*, then called Qadesh ('holy one'). His shrines were the scene of the mourning rites associated with most vegetation gods. Aleyin was the antagonist of the god *Mot*; they were both vegetation gods and so in competition with each other. The story of their struggle is recorded on the tablets discovered at Ras Shamrah. First Mot kills Aleyin, then Anat kills Mot; and this means that Aleyin is resurrected. After several other struggles Mot descended, defeated, into the Underworld.

Once the gods were building a temple in which both Baal and Aleyin were to be honoured. The god(s) *Kusor-Hasisu (q.v.)* offered to insert a window in the temple, but Aleyin refused. The reason for his refusal becomes apparent later in the story. They go to Baal for arbitration and Aleyin agrees to a compromise: instead of a window there will be a skylight. Kusor would be given control of the skylight and Baal agreed to open a fissure in the clouds above it. This meant that Kusor would regulate the rainfall. As Aleyin was god of springs there was an obvious conflict of interests here; but he agreed to Kusor being in control of the rain from the sky, for he saw that uncontrolled rain might easily lead to floods which could threaten his vegetation. Kusor thus became the regulator of the seasons.

Aleyin is said to spend six months of the year in the Underworld, the season when seeds lie dormant.

Allah
God of Islam.

The idea and reality of the one God experienced by Jews and Christians was transmitted by the Prophet Mohammed to the previously idolatrous Semitic peoples of Arabia. The Prophet put down his inspired rules of life in the Islam Scripture, the Koran. The new religion was centred on Mecca, towards which the prayers of the faithful are addressed. Islam arose at a period of history when the two other main religious trends of the area, Christianity and Zoroastrianism, were experiencing difficulties; difficulties over which the former was to triumph and under which the latter was to collapse.

Islam enshrines an uncompromising monotheism; it is racially inclusive and though it has strong religious leaders it does not have a hierarchical priesthood. Allah is a righteous God, His worship has no ambiguous symbolism, no altars, and in its pure form regards all its believers as equal.

Amahraspands
The Bounteous Immortals of Zoroastrianism.

There were six of them, originally aspects of *Ormazd*; they were later individualized. The Amahraspands guarded the elements of the universe and carried on battle with the demon hordes, their eternal enemies. Their names are Vohu-mano, Asha-Vashistra, Khshatra-Vairya, Spenta Aramaiti, Haurvatat and Ameretat.

Amurru
Another name for the god *Aleyin* of Phoenicia.

Also called God of the West (the place of the dead), Amurru was known to the Egyptians as *Resheph*. At harvest-time he appeared with his sister Qadesh (later *Anat – q.v.*) to sacrifice a stallion and an ass. This ritual was to reawaken the spirit of the vine, which the nibbling ass and browsing horse are assumed to have damaged. Ritually and imaginatively the horse and the ass

303

occupied the same place in the scheme of things and both can be used to symbolize the power of the sun, scorching and shrivelling the vine plant.

Anahita
Persian goddess of the waters and of procreation.

Anahita was widely venerated in the times of the Achaemenians (558-330 B.C.). An ancient image shows her naked except for necklace and anklets, and in the company of what appears to be a bull-headed lion. Under the later name of Anaitis she was a popular goddess in Asia Minor and the Mediterranean. Robert Graves, in his book The White Goddess, links Anaitis with a riot of goddesses ranging from Persia across Europe to Ireland.

Anat
An earth goddess.

Daughter of *Baal* and sister of *Aleyin*, this warlike goddess was responsible for the ritual murder of the god *Mot* (*q.v.*). By constant sacrifices she sustained the gods. Her worship was introduced into Egypt by the Hyskos (1650 B.C.), a mysterious race of 'shepherd kings' who set up a kingdom in the Nile Delta. After the expulsion of the foreign invaders her cult remained, centred on a shrine at Avaris. Anat was the consort of Baal-Sutekh and goddess of the dew, which she sprinkled over the earth (dew was poetically described as the 'fat of the earth'). She was also known by the name Qadesh, meaning 'holy one', and was linked with the lion. In a highly evocative description of her dealings with Mot, she first sets her dogs on his flocks, then kills him with a sickle, beats him with a flail, roasts him with fire, grinds him up and scatters the debris over the fields.

Annunaki
The seven judges of hell, children of the god *Anu*.

Regarded by some as the Sumerian 'fates', they are usually described as waiting at the gates of hell to judge the newly-arrived souls. At other times they sit before the throne of *Ereshkigal* (*q.v.*). When *Inanna* descended into hell to attend the funeral of brother-in-law Gugulanna, they caused her death simply by staring at her and speaking 'the word which torments souls'. The Annunaki, like Ereshkigal, had once lived in heaven, but were banished to hell for their misdeeds. They did not even retain their names, being collectively known as 'Great Ones', Annunaki.

Anshar
Sumerian god of the celestial world.

Anshar was born of the serpents Lakhmu and Lakhamu, and mated with his sister *Kishar* to produce the great gods. He is considered the male principle; Kishar, the female. He was the sky and she was the earth. He organized the gods in their fight against *Tiamat* and though deeply involved did no fighting himself, thus setting the precedent for all wise generals to lead from the rear. He was the father of *Ea*.

Anu
Heaven-god of Mesopotamia

With his horned head-dress Anu personified the ideas of rulership and royalty. Called An by the Sumerians, he was overlord of the gods, their father and protector. His authority waned as a result of the success of gods like *Enlil*. Anu was a remote, celestial god who was not interested in mankind and didn't bother much with them. His soldiers were the stars; part of the Milky Way (Anu's Way) was his personal road. His parents were *Anshar* and *Kishar*, his wife was Antu, and his children were the *Annunaki*. Despite his indifference to men he had a fine temple at Uruk, an unusual twin-towered ziggurat dating from 3000 B.C. As was the custom, the temple would have been in the charge of a priestess; temples of goddesses being commanded by male high priests. Frequent animal sacrifices performed several functions; the sacrifice itself was an act pleasing to the god, the entrails of the sacrificed beast were used for divination, and doubtless some of the more succulent cuts of meat found their way into the priestly stew-pot.

Anu, though transcendent and overbearing, was capable of helping others (as long as they were gods), for he took the part of the lesser deities when they went on strike over digging a canal for the god Enlil.

Apsu

The Babylonian Abyss; the waters which surround and hold up the earth.

A concept not unlike the Greeks' idea of 'Ocean'. From the mingling of sweet, salt and vaporous waters came the gods. Held underground by the powerful incantations of *Ea* (*q.v.*), the waters of Apsu nevertheless managed to break through in places, producing streams and springs.

After the birth of the gods Apsu was disturbed by their noise and complained to *Tiamat*, their mother. This complaint started a series of disagreements which led to violence. Internecine warfare among the gods followed and ended with the death of Tiamat herself

Aruru

Creative goddess of Sumeria.

In the Akkadian version of the Epic of Gilgamesh, Aruru created the wild man Enkidu from clay. Enkidu ate grass and drank from pools alongside the wild beasts. He was savage and strong, a primal beast. Gilgamesh lured him into submission with the bait of a temple prostitute; after seven nights and days with the woman Enkidu found that his former companions, the wild animals, shunned him. He turned to the semi-divine hero Gilgamesh for company.

Asherat of the Sea

Phoenician goddess of the sea.

In Ugaritic texts of the 14th century B.C., Asherat is mother of Baal Haddad (*Addad*). She was in fact mother of many of the gods, giving birth to seventy children in all. She shared the gift of wisdom with the god *Latpon* and was responsible for obtaining permission from the great god *El* for the building of the temple to *Baal* and *Aleyin*. She was the consort of El and from her are derived many examples of the mother goddess – *Ashtart, Astarte, Ishtar, Isis, Ashtoreth*. Asherat is the earliest goddess of whom we have written evidence, though images of a mother goddess survive from the dawn of human consciousness and were probably the first expressions of both art and religion.

Ashtart
'Of the sky of Baal'; the goddess of the planet Venus, the most beautiful and familiar planet to early astronomers.

This Phoenician goddess, who is probably linked to the Egyptian *Hathor*, was worshipped in Sidon and in Jerusalem, where Solomon built her a sanctuary (1 Kings II, vs 5-8). Philo indicates that she wore a bull's head (sign of Hathor) and says that the goddess discovered an aerolith (a fragment of a meteor) which she took to Sidon, where it was venerated as a holy object. Ashtart had a considerable following and was worshipped at Carthage under the name of *Tanit*.

Ashur
National god of the Assyrians; may be identified with the Babylonian or Sumerian god *Anshar*. God of fertility and war.

Ashur's symbol was the winged disc; he was depicted either as the disc itself, or as a king standing on a bull, or as a man surrounded by vegetation and accompanied by a female goat. This last aspect shows his power of fertility. The goat is an alternative symbol of generative power to the ubiquitous bull; it can survive in terrain hostile to other animals. Well into our own era the goat was worshipped as a symbol of life, and its characteristics – horns, hair and hooves – were added to the commonly accepted description of Satan.

Ashur's wife was Ninlil (see *Belitis*), linking him to *Enlil* of Babylon.

Asuras
Good spirits.

In Persia the Asuras were the good spirits who fought against the *Daevas* or devils. In India the roles of Asuras and Daevas were reversed; there the Asuras were evil and the Daevas were good. One man's meat is another man's poison.

Atar

God of the ancient fire cult of the Aryans which survived into the Mazdaism of the Persians.

Considered to be the son of *Ahura Mazda*, Atar was celestial as well as earthly fire. He brought men comfort, virility, their livelihood. He defended the world against evil and guarded the chariot of the sun on its daily journey.

Baal

Means 'lord' or 'master', and was a title rather than a name. The true name of many gods was a well-guarded secret. This secrecy was to prevent strangers addressing the god and winning his favour away from his normal worshippers. Men and cities also had secret names, knowledge of which could be dangerous in the hands of an enemy. So, many local gods of the Phoenicians are simply called Baal.

The greatest Baal dates from the Phoenician settlement of the Eastern Mediterranean coast, to which they migrated from the Negev. This Baal was an enemy of *El*, the greatest god of the time, and he was called Baal Tsaphon, 'lord of the north', and Baal Lebanon. It is thought that his real name was *Addad*, the weather god, which would mean that his mother was *Asherat of the Sea*. He is shown wearing the divine horned helmet and spearing the earth. A Ugaritic carving shows him grasping a tree which he is about to strike with a club. Both these images are quite evidently symbolic of lightning. Great Baal was the father of *Mot* and *Aleyin* and *Anat*. He finally fell foul of his enemy, El, who had created monsters which attacked and killed him. He was buried by Anat, who mourned his death.

There were several other Baals of note. The Baal most commonly met with in the Scriptures is Baal Shamim, 'lord of the skies', alias Beelsamin. It is probable that he had solar characteristics. The Baal worshipped in Tyre was originally a solar god who acquired nautical attributes as god of an important trading port. He was otherwise known as *Melkart*, 'king of the city', and as Melech. This last title is the same as Moloch, whose priests Elijah slew with such righteous fury. The Baal worshipped in Sidon was *Eshmun*, god of health. In Carthage, a colony of the

Phoenicians, they worshipped Baal Hammon or Baal Ammon, a Libyan god whom the Romans later adopted as Jupiter Ammon. He was a sky and fertility deity whose animal was the ram. The Carthaginian goddess *Tanit* (Ashtoreth, Ashtart) was given the title 'face of Baal'. Near the source of the river Jordan was the shrine of Baal Gad, a goat god. Not far away is Mount Hermon, otherwise Baal Hermon.

Another interesting Baal is the god of the tribe of Zebulon. These northern Semites had a god called Fly, or as we know him, Beel-Zebul, 'lord of Zebulon', often erroneously called Beelzebub.

Baalith

Goddess of love, the moon and the Underworld; trees (especially willows) springs and wells. She was the predecessor of *Ishtar*, sister and mistress of *Tammuz, Dumuzi* and *Adonis*. Baalith is a title of the Great Goddess.

Bel

A Babylonian god, a version of *Enlil*, Bel being just a title: 'lord' (see *Baal*). The familiar Apocrypha story of Bel shows us his great importance, for the god was every day offered by his worshippers forty sheep, twelve great measures of fine flour and six vessels of wine.

Beletersetim

Alias for *Belit-Sheri* the scribe of Arallu, the Mesopotamian Hades.

Belit-Illi

Goddess of childbirth; her name means 'lady of the gods'. Another name for *Nintu*, 'lady of childbirth', among the Mesopotamian peoples.

Each part of human life was regulated by some god or other. These gods could not change man's destiny, that was up to the supreme god (who at various times was *Anu, Enlil, Ea, Marduk*, Baal-Marduk); but the gods could warn men about their fate even if they could not reveal it.

Belit-Illi was important not only because she ensured a safe delivery but also because a man's fate was set at birth. Once a man had been born, his fate, like a recording clock, began ticking away. (See *Ninkhursag*.)

Belitis
Or Ninlil, goddess of fertility.

Belitis means 'lady'; she was consort of *Enlil* or *Bel*, 'lord'. Her symbol was a tree of stylized design with interwoven branches. (See *Ninkhursag*.)

Belit-Sheri
Female scribe and archivist of the Mesopotamian gods of the Underworld.

Belit-Sheri makes a brief appearance in the Epic of Gilgamesh. She is described as squatting in front of the throne of *Ereshkigal* (queen of the Underworld), reading from a clay tablet. She looks up puzzled when she sees Enkidu, who has travelled to the Underworld in a dream. She demands to know who has brought him there, and on that the dreaming man wakes up from his prophetic nightmare, aghast with terror.

Bes
A popular god worshipped in Egypt, and in Canaan and Carthage.

Bes was a grotesque little creature; an obese dwarf with fat, bandy legs, oversized bearded head, and a leopard-skin cloak wrapped about his dumpy back. He was a professional buffoon, fond of melodramatic dancing, risqué songs and mock-heroic posturing. He afforded the other gods much superior amusement. Originally a proletarian god, his sense of fun gained him many converts among the merchant class. Bes is a beautiful joke played upon the inadequate by a mocking Fate. What makes him really attractive is that he doesn't try to win our sympathies by any of the insincere attitudes of sadness and mental agony shown by modern clowns. He is a bloated, randy, drunken, pompous, honest to goodness old-style knockabout comic. (See *Bes*, Egyptian section.)

Daevas

The powers of evil in ancient Persia.

The Daevas were the demon hordes who helped *Ahriman* (*q.v.*) in his fight against all things good Their name is the same as that used for the Indian Vedic gods and is cognate with Latin: *deus, divus*. Their reversed position in Zoroastrian myth may be because of Zarathustra's reforms. Old and conquered gods frequently stay around as demons and devils. For each good spirit there was a demon working against him. Among the Daevas are several gods who are elsewhere revered as good, such as *Indra*. It is interesting to note that the *Asuras*, good spirits in Persia, are the demons of India.

Dagon

Or Dagan; god of Ashdod (in modern Israel), represented as half-man and half-fish.

The Philistines placed the captured Ark of the Covenant in his temple. The next morning the statue of Dagon was found lying on the ground, doing honour to the Ark. Josephus relates that this happened twice, and was followed first by an epidemic which decimated Ashdod, and then by an army of mice which consumed the growing crops. Later a conquering Israelite army burnt down Dagon's temple. Despite these reversals Dagon was later connected to the cult of *Apollo*. One reason could be that Apollo as Apollo Smintheus had the ability to drive away mice.

Damkina

Or Damgalnunna; alias Ninki, goddess wife of *Ea* – Sumerian god of sweet waters. Also known as *Ninkhursag*.

Demarus

According to the Greeks he was father of *Melkart*, god of Tyre. His name is certainly Greek and he was reputed to be the son of *Uranus* and 'a concubine'.

Djinns

Ancient Arabian spirits, the genies of the Arabian Nights. They were often monstrously ugly and misshapen but were not as malicious as the *Efrit* (*q.v.*). Djinns could be controlled by means of magic and ritual and like European elemental spirits could be ordered to perform otherwise impossible tasks for the human magician who possessed the right knowledge.

Dumuzi

Alias *Tammuz*, harvest god of ancient Mesopotamia; in Sumer, the god of vegetation and of the Underworld.

Dumuzi's titles include 'the shepherd' and 'lord of the sheep-folds'. He is a companion of Ningizzida (also his mother) and stands at the gates of heaven. An ancestor of the semi-divine hero Gilgamesh, he was the consort of *Inanna (Ishtar)*, who was one of the most popular Babylonian deities. When Dumuzi died (he had been a king of Uruk) Inanna sought him, but failed to bring him back from the Underworld where he reigned now as king. Unlike Tammuz, *Attis* and *Adonis*, he did not rise again. To ensure the continued fertility of the land the kings of Uruk, successors to Dumuzi, ritually mated with the goddess Inanna, represented by a priestess.

Ea or Enki

'House of the water'; god of sweet waters and wisdom, creator of mankind and patron of all the arts; chief god of the Mesopotamian city of Eridu.

Ea was god of the waters called *Apsu*, not of the bitter sea. He had great oracular powers and was frequently consulted by the gods as Lord of the Sacred Eye, Ninigiku ('he whom nothing escapes'). He was a vigilant and clever god who corrected the mistakes of the other gods as well as those of men. He was god of incantations and of skills and crafts. Ea was depicted either as a goat with a fish's tail, or in human form with water gushing from his shoulders or from a vase he carried.

Ea is said to have created man from clay with the help of the goddess *Aruru* and the power of his divine word. So when *Enlil* was bent on revenge against mankind it was Ea who urged restraint.

Ea was married to the goddess Ninki or *Damkina* and his

children were *Nanshe* and the great *Marduk*.

Efrit
Spirits of the ancient Arabians.

Arising out of a pervasive animism which saw spirits in every object, the Efrit were malicious and powerful shape-shifters who assumed a variety of forms in order to cheat mankind. One of them once offered to fetch the Queen of Sheba's throne to Solomon in less time than it would take Solomon to rise from his chair. It is not known if this offer included the exotic queen herself. (See *Djinns*.)

El
The supreme Semitic god who ruled Canaan for many years.

As father of the ancients and king of the elements, El ensured that the rivers which watered the East littoral of the Mediterranean continued to flow. His strength meant that he was represented as a bull; not the only god to be so described. Like the words Baal and Adoni, the image of the bull was a title, a description of power. It was applicable to goddesses as well. Doubtless the use of such images degenerated over the years until people, confusing the description with that which it described, worshipped the animals themselves. The prophets of old thundered righteously against the idolatry of the Canaanites, not just because it was idolatry but also because it attracted away their own people from God.

The word El means 'god', not 'the god' but 'a god'. El was firmly ensconced in the theogony of his time and place. Originally he was probably a god of the oak tree; he was thought of as a sun god as well, for he is described taking part in a procreation rite by plunging into the sea. He raised out his hands which became waves; he put the waves in the sky and created rain. After the rain five gracious gods were born to his wives. It is thought that this myth dates from the distant time when the Phoenicians lived in the Negev region.

Later, El is described as living in a pavilion by the sea-shore. *Elat*, the feminine form of his name, received worship in the port of Sidon. El's favourite son was *Mot*; another of his children

313

was the god *Latpon*. The goddess *Asherat of the Sea* was a close adviser of his. When the gods wished to build a temple for *Baal*, they sent *Hiyon* the craft god with a gift of a golden table and throne to sweeten El's disposition. Despite this, El created the monsters who later slew Baal .

Elat
Semitic goddess, the female form of *El*.

Ellat
A goddess of the ancient Arabians. Sometimes called Alilat, her shrine was at Taif and she herself was represented as a block of stone.

Enlil or Ellil
God of earth and wind.

A child of An ('heaven') and Ki ('earth'), he separated them and took the earth as his domain. Patron of the city of Nippur in Mesopotamia, Enlil supplanted *Anu* as chief god. He is sometimes known as *Bel*. As lord of the air and god of hurricanes, his chief weapon was the flood. Enlil was a personification of the forces of nature. He was also master of men's fates and was so import-ant that when the Babylonians adopted the Sumerian gods, they made him one of their great Triad. He was equated with *Marduk* and lived in the great mountains to the east; his consort was *Ninkhursag*, 'lady of the great mountains'. As father of the gods he begot the moon *Nanna* (*Sin*) and was grandfather of *Shamash*, Utu, and *Inanna* (*Ishtar*).

Enlil had an important role to play in the affairs of men, for it was his gift of strength that made things work; he was the ac-tive element in life, he made things happen. His importance is seen in an episode of the Epic of Gilgamesh. It was he who made the god *Humbaba* guardian of the forest. After Humbaba had been slain by Gilgamesh, Enlil redistributed the strength he had given the god to the barbarians, to the lions, and to the furious daughter of *Ereshkigal*. When time came for Humbaba's death to be paid for, it was Enlil who decreed that the wild man Enkidu should die and that Gilgamesh should live. Earlier on, when

Enkidu and Gilgamesh first met, the former had realized that Gilgamesh was no ordinary mortal but fit to be a king because of his extraordinary strength.

It was Enlil who was responsible for the flood which destroyed all mankind except the sage Utnapishtim and his kindred.

Ereshkigal
Queen of the Underworld in ancient Mesopotamia.

Ereshkigal was once a sky goddess and was abducted to the Underworld after heaven and earth had been separated. Her story has parallels with that of *Persephone*, but unlike the Greek goddess she did not return from the Underworld. Being a figure of terror, Ereshkigal is never directly described. After a sort of hellish *coup d'état* she accepted the god *Nergal* (*q.v.*) as her husband. Ereshkigal was sometimes described as the elder sister of *Ishtar (Inanna)*. A more satisfactory idea is that she represented the dark side of that goddess.

Eshmun
The god of health and healing in ancient Sidon.

The Greeks described him as *Asclepius*. It is easy to resent the Greeks for their robust Hellenization of everything they touched; but we should really be grateful to them, for much of our information about ancient gods comes from their insatiable curiosity about the beliefs of other people.

Eshmun is the real name of the god called Adoni by the Phoenicians; the same *Adonis* whom the Greeks adopted with reverent enthusiasm. The cult of Eshmun was taken to Carthage with several other Semitic deities. But the destruction of Carthage did not result in the total extinction of Eshmun, for apart from Adonis there is some evidence to suggest that he also inspired another great medical god, *Thoth*. Herodotus reports that the refugee priesthood of Thoth claimed that their cult was originally Phoenician.

Eshmun, 'he whom we invoke', was said to have revived the powerful god *Melkart* by holding a quail to his nose.

315

Fravashis
Ancient Persian guardian angels.

Ormazd created them as an essential part of the soul of each man. During the man's life the guardian lived as a sort of spiritual counterpart or reflection. When the man died the Fravash lived on.

Gibil
Alias Nusku; Assyrian fire god.

A son of *Anu*, Gibil was called governor of gods and men. His special task was to sit in judgement over the souls of men who in their lives had been unjust judges.

Gula
Ancient Mesopotamian name for the Earth Mother goddess; consort of *Ninurta*.

A daughter of *Anu*, Gula was responsible for healing and could also inflict illness. Her animal was the dog; an interesting if coincidental parallel to the dogs of the Celtic god *Nuada* (*q.v.*), the therapeutic deity of the great temple at Lydney in the west of England.

Haoma
A god and sacred herb.

Haoma is the centre of a ritual meant to drive away evil and welcome good. It was the origin of the *Soma* of the Indians and is linked to ambrosia, the drink of immortality of the Greek gods. The plant was crushed and its juice clarified and drunk to produce 'spiritual effects'. Its undoubted hallucinogenic properties may be likened to *amanita muscaria*, toad-skin, peyote, coca and hashish, all of which have been used for much the same purpose and most of which have succeeded in deceiving the gullible. There are undoubted medical benefits in some of these substances; coca seems to be used correctly, and the Yaquis approach the use of mescalin in a reverent and fastidious way. Hashish, on the other hand, was used cynically by Hassan of Sabah to acquire power and worldly wealth through his band of assassins, Hashishin.

There is no quick way of achieving spiritual insight through chemical means, but some people, brought up in the correct way with properly developed sensibilities, can doubtless be aided by certain preparations. Zoroaster considered that crushing the haoma was an act of piety. Pounding the plant symbolized the killing of the god; this sacrifice points the way to future immortality, which may by some be glimpsed fleetingly when the juice is reverently drunk.

Haoma, *ephedra vulgaris*, is described as a tree of life growing in the sacred waters of the spring Ardvisura. It is also described as growing in lake Vouru Kasha, while round it swims the fish Kar-mahi whose duty is to defend the tree from the god *Ahriman*. Haoma is *pharmakon athanasias*, 'the preparer of corpses'.

There is a possibility, by no means proved, that haoma may be linked to the Huma bird of the Persian sorcerers; this bird alone knows the location of the Fountain of Life, reputedly hidden in the Persian Mountains.

Hay-Tau
Phoenician vegetation god of Nega.

Hay-Tau was adopted by the Egyptians who merged him with their *Osiris*. The Egyptians say that Hay-Tau's brother had threatened to kill him so he fled to a valley of pine trees and hid his heart on the topmost twig of a pine. His wife, captured by Egyptian soldiers, somehow had the tree cut down and the god died. Several years later Hay-Tau's brother found him and the god miraculously came back to life, changed himself into a bull and returned to Egypt. Hay-Tau is regarded as the prototype for *Adonis*.

Hepat
Sun goddess of Arinna; she is shown standing on a lion, her emblematic beast.

Hibil-Ziwa
God of the Mandean heresy.

The Mandeans were originally a Gnostic sect claiming descent from *John the Baptist*. They believed that liberation of the soul

317

from its imprisoning material body was made possible through the action of Hibil-Ziwa, who descended into the Underworld and defeated the forces of evil. The rituals of the sect had to be carried out in exact detail, for it was prophesied that any mistake or deviation, no matter how small, would have dire consequences for priests and people alike. In the nineteenth century A.D. a sudden and mysterious plague wiped out nearly the whole sect! (See *Hibil*, the Gnostic god.)

Hiyon
Divine craftsman of Phoenicia.

Hiyon worked with his bellows, hammer and tongs to make images of bulls out of gold and silver. The bulls were to decorate the temple of *Baal*. We are familiar with these images from Biblical descriptions.

Humbaba
Alias Huwawa or Khumbaba; nature god of either Elam or Syria.

The doubt arises from various interpretations of the journey of the hero Gilgamesh. Humbaba was a gigantic, powerful creature of horrific aspect, for a carving shows that his face was composed of human entrails. He was king of the cedar mountain, guardian of the cedar forests. The great god *Enlil* (*q.v.*) had set him to watch over the cedar trees. Humbaba had phenomenal hearing; he could hear a heifer stirring in the forest sixty leagues away. He was attacked by Gilgamesh and the wild man Enkidu, and was only overcome when the winds and storms joined the struggle against him.

Hvare-Khshaeta
Chaldean sun god. He rode across the sky in a chariot drawn by swift horses.

Igigi
Common name for all the great gods of Mesopotamia. The Igigi lived in the sky, the *Annunaki* inhabited the earth and the Underworld.

Imdugud
Rain god worshipped in the area of Ur of the Chaldees (west bank of the Euphrates).

Imdugud was shaped like an eagle with a lion's head, and brought the rain which revives the earth after a long drought. His wings are the clouds. In about 3000 B.C., a man called Gudea claimed that the god appeared to him in a dream and told him to build a temple at Lagash. Gudea did so. There are extant small representations of Gudea so that we know at least what he looked like. (See *Ningursu*.)

Inanna
Earth and later moon goddess; Canaanite derivative of Sumerian Innin, of Ishtar of Uruk.

Inanna was preceded by Belili, wife of *Baal*. The Hebrews knew her as Tamar. The ancient Hebrews went out of their way to proscribe the habit of boiling a kid in its mother's milk. Such an act was a ritual practice of the worship of *Ishtar*; the Hebrews were thus forbidding people to honour the goddess. Inanna later became the horned moon goddess and ended up as Annis, the blue hag who sucked the blood of children.

Inar
Hittite god who destroyed a great serpent and its family. Inar put on a feast for the serpents, who ate so much that their bloated bodies could not fit back into their holes. Unable to escape, the serpents fell prey to Inar.

In-Shushinak
Elamite god whose main cult was at Susa, the city which was later to be the terminus of the great Royal Road of the Persian empire. He was master of heaven and earth and king of the gods. He could possibly be an interpretation of the god *Addad*.

Irra
An aspect of the god *Nergal*, given the task of inflicting disease on mankind at the request of the gods.

Ishkur
Sumerian name of *Addad*, rain god of the Hittites.

Ishtar
(*Inanna*, *Ashtart*, Ashtaroth, Ashtoreth, *Astarte*, Anaitis, *Anat*, Atar, *Isis*); the Mesopotamian goddess of love and fertility.

Ishtar's father was *Sin*, her brother *Shamash*. As was commonly the case, she controlled the negative as well as the positive sides of her particular domain. So as well as being the radiant, sweet and delightful goddess of sexual love, she was also the stern and cruel goddess of war. She was 'lady of sorrows and battles', as well as 'lady of heaven'. To the spiritually adolescent human mind, Ishtar rang absolutely true as the adored but cruel object of youthful desires. Male readers will recognize her instantly; those that don't had better beware. In all her aspects she is linked with the male vegetation god (*Adonis*, *Tammuz*, *Dumuzi*, *Attis*), and for his sake descended into the Underworld.

Her main shrine was in ancient Uruk (Erech), where sexual rites were performed as an offering to the gods. The part of the goddess was played by priestesses; the priest-king, who was their carnal partner, being slain in imitation of the death of the god.

Ishtar's passion caused men to become vulnerable; even animals were weakened and could easily be trapped or domesticated. The hero Gilgamesh was the centre of her attentions for a while. He spurned her with great courage, knowing that all her lovers came to a bad end; the lucky ones were killed, the others were changed into wolves, frogs or moles. By refusing her sexual advances the semi-divine Gilgamesh ensured his own death. Ishtar is therefore the original *femme fatale*; when she turned her burning eyes on you there was no escape.

Ishtar was worshipped in Babylon where a magnificent gate is named after her. She was identified with Ninlil, the consort of *Enlil*, and shown wearing a necklace of lapis-lazuli, carrying a bow and arrows, and treading on a lion. It was said that she was the cause of the death of Tammuz (*q.v.*); death seeming to come to all who experienced her love. She was also identified with the planet which we call Venus. The character of Ishtar is so poised and vibrant that it seems to us to be a distillation of a truth recognized by all cultures at all times.

Ishum
A fallen god. He was chief advisor to the goddess *Ereshkigal* and her ᴖonsort, the god *Nergal*, in the Mesopotamia Underworld.

Jehovah
See *Yahweh*.

Jesus of Nazareth
The Messiah, Christos 'the Anointed One', Son of God and Son of Man.

The Incarnation of God in the human body of Jesus of Nazareth marks an entirely new relationship between God and his created world. Jesus embodies the Logos, the Spiritual Word, and with the Holy Spirit joins with God to form the Trinity. Subsequent to the Incarnation came the unique teachings of the Messiah, the Crucifixion and the Resurrection, in which God overturned the whole of human history, freed the human soul from darkness and brought man into a new mystic relationship with his Creator.

Since the resurrection the world has been a different place from the aeons-old planet which hitherto existed; its very substance has changed, has been fused and permeated with an energy called Grace. Yet despite the deep mysteries it contains, the living Body of Christ, the Church, is freely open to all.

The details of the life of Jesus are too well known to repeat in this book. The Gospels are widely available and in those parts of the world where they are forbidden, Nature itself, suffused with the power of the Logos, will provide both support and instruction.

Kadi
Goddess of justice of Der. A snake with a human head, she was a derivative of Ki or *Kishar* ('the earth').

Ker or Q're
Pelasgian solar god of ancient Syria.

Ker had strong calendrical connections; every year he was shorn of his hair. Male adherents offered him their own hair, which they cut off in his honour. It is also claimed that hair was cut off and sacrificed to the god *Yahweh*. Hair symbolizes the rays of the sun, and also physical strength. Clipped hair has for many years been a sign of subservience, an indication that a jealous and authoritarian attitude is in control. For an army, or a religious cult, or even a nation to force individuals to have their hair shorn is a psychological attack and a sure sign of totalitarian attitudes.

Keret
Son of the great god *El*; king of Sidon.

There had been an invasion by the people of Zebulon, headed by their moon god, *Terah*. El ordered Keret to resist the invaders. Keret, on receiving his orders, shut himself into an inner room and burst into tears. He cried himself to sleep and had a dream in which he was told he would have a son. This dream gave him confidence, so he made an offering of wine, honey, blood and a lamb. He went out and led his armies against the hosts of Zebulon and the god Terah. And was beaten.

Returning from the battle Keret bought a wife and in due time she had a son. The boy was exceedingly beautiful and as soon as he was born he shouted out in a loud voice, 'I hate the enemy! I hate them!'

Kingu
God of the Mesopotamians, notable for helping *Tiamat* to fight against *Marduk* (*q.v.*). He was overcome by Marduk who sent him to the Underworld after draining off his blood. Marduk mixed the blood with clay and created the first men from the mixture.

Kishar
Female principle, sister of *Anshar*, the male principle.

Born of Lakhmu and Lakhamu, Kishar represents the earth. She and her brother mated to produce *Anu*, the great Mesopotamian god. She is also known as Ki, 'the earth'.

Kusor
Phoenician god of many talents; controller of the seasons.

Kusor appeared during the construction of the temple of *Baal* with his brother Hasisu (sometimes they are one composite god, Kusor-Hasisu). They had come to install windows in the temple, but there was violent disagreement from *Aleyin* (*q.v.*) who didn't want any. So they compromised on a skylight. Kusor was given the task of operating the skylight by which means rain was let down onto the earth. Thus Kusor became the controller of the seasons.

Described as 'Kusor the sailor', he was revered as a god of divination and incantation. He was also god of mechanical devices and invented the fishing boat, fish hooks and fishing lines, iron-working, and navigation. Phoenician success in maritime ventures doubtless contributed to his growing importance. The Phoenicians were energetic traders and daring seamen. Starting from relatively minor ports on the coast of present-day Israel, they monopolized the Egyptian trade and set up colonies, the greatest of which was Carthage. The Greeks identified Kusor with *Hephaestus*.

Lama
Sumerian goddess whose main function was to guide the worshipper into the presence of the particular god he was praising. In the same category of official functionary come the Lamassu, guardian spirits of Babylon.

Latpon
A Phoenician god of wisdom; son of *El*.

On the death of *Aleyin*, Latpon went to El to ask for a replacement for the god. El left it to *Asherat of the Sea* to appoint one of her sons. Latpon was the magician of Asherat.

Lugulbanda
God and shepherd king of Uruk.

Lugulbanda was protector of the hero Gilgamesh who was one of his adherents. Gilgamesh presented the god with the horns of the Bull of Heaven, which he had overcome. He had the horns plated with costly lapis-lazuli and hung them on the palace wall; the horns were large enough to contain six measures of oil.

Lugulbanda's cult included some sort of anointing ritual; he was worshipped in Uruk (Erech) for over a thousand years, and is the hero of two extant Sumerian poems. He was supposed to be the third king of Uruk after the great flood. His recorded adventures have many points in common with those of Gilgamesh, and it is possible that they influenced the composition of later versions of the Epic of Gilgamesh.

Mammitu

Mesopotamian goddess who watched over the destiny of newborn children.

Alias Mammetun, 'mother of destinies', Mammitu decreed the fate of men; but she would not reveal the date of a man's death. A whole industry was built up in Mesopotamia to try and discover the future of men; all manner of divinatory methods were used, mostly involved with the entrails of sacrificial animals with especial attention paid to the liver. Ceramic models of livers are extant with the surface divided up into areas, and the more meaningful characteristics noted and explained. Sacrificial livers were considered maps to the future. A firm belief in fate and predestination is the basis of such activities. The industry they founded is still going strong, and will continue so long as men remain ignorant and gullible.

Marduk

The great god of Babylon.

An agricultural god, he was also called Lord of Kings, Shepherd of Gods, Guardian of Law and Order, Great Healer, Great Sorcerer. Son of *Ea*, Marduk was the fertilising force of water. Depicted as a kingly figure with a scimitar, his main temple was in Babylon, and his power grew with that of the city.

Marduk came to the forefront of the gods by main force. The goddess *Tiamat* had threatened to do away with the gods, the *Igigi*, because of complaints received from *Apsu* about their noise. The gods panicked; Ea, knowing the strength of Tiamat, the dragon goddess, asked Marduk to accept the leadership for the coming war. Marduk agreed on the condition that he be given supreme authority for ever after; the Igigi agreed.

Marduk took his bow and a net. He loosed the strong winds against Tiamat, and caught her in the net of the hurricane. Tiamat opened her jaws to swallow Marduk, but he hurled the winds into the gaping mouth and the goddess could not bring them together again; the blast of the wind kept her mouth wide open. Marduk loosed an arrow which pierced Tiamat's entrails and split her heart. He then turned on her astonished army and captured them. Returning to the mighty corpse of the dragon goddess, he split the skull and severed all the blood vessels. He then filleted the body lengthways; one half he raised to form the heavens, the other half he left lying to make the earth.

Having got started on creating things, Marduk went on; he made a home for the gods, created the planets and stars, invented time, the seasons and the movement of the heavenly bodies. Then he took the blood of the enemy god *Kingu* and mixed it with clay to make men. With the help of the goddess *Aruru* he created seed for mankind. Peace reigned and each sphere was given a ruler; *Anu* for the sky, *Enlil* for the earth, and Ea for the waters. Marduk was loaded with honours and titles; at last his fame made him supreme, even to the powerful god Anu.

As controller of the destiny of men, Marduk was in possession of the clay tablets of Fate. Some say that his victory over Tiamat had won him the tablets, others that the storm-bird *Zu* had stolen them and Marduk had recaptured them.

Marduk kept an eye on the doings of the higher beings as well as those of men. The wicked deeds of the evil spirits had been interrupted at night by the moon god, *Sin*, whose brilliant light revealed their activities. The spirits succeeded in tricking *Shamash*, *Ishtar* and *Addad* into helping them eclipse Sin's light. Marduk took swift and firm action; he defeated the misled gods and gave Sin back his brilliance.

The supremacy of the city of Babylon led to Marduk being raised to prime position among the gods. From Esagil, his temple in Babylon, an annual procession in his honour wound out of the city to a rural shrine, where sacred dramas and the ritual marriage with his consort Zarpanit were enacted. As Bel-Marduk (Lord Marduk) he is shown enthroned with horned head-dress on the stele of Hammurabi, handing to the king the ring and sceptre of authority. He was protector of the king and the code of laws inscribed on the stele. Bulls and dragons were sacred to Marduk and his symbol was the spade. To the Amorites he was god of spring, sun, warming the earth and its seeds; of thunder, which presages fertilising rain; of herbs and of trees which grow for the benefit of man. In his temple his golden statue weighed fifty talents – by current values something in the region of twenty million dollars.

Melkart
God of Tyre, 'king of the city'; the Phoenician equivalent of the Greek Hercules.

Dying yearly, Melkart was revived by *Eshmun* (*q.v.*) by means of a quail. This charming story probably derives from the fact that when the birds return in spring the oaks are miraculously renewed. Originally a solar god, he acquired nautical characteristics because of his proximity to the sea and seafaring men.

The Greeks adopted him under the name *Melicertes* and gave him a parentage (mother, Ino of Pelion; father, Athamas), and the following story to explain his arrival in Greece.

Ino and Athamas had given refuge to the young *Dionysus*, who was trying to keep out of the way of the vengeful *Hera*. Hera unbalanced Athamas' mind and in a blind rage he tried to kill his own son. Ino (or Leucothera) leapt with the child into the sea to save him. The god Melicertes, now transformed into a Greek youth, was drowned and his body carried to the shore of Corinth by a dolphin. Here he was venerated as a god under the name Palaemon and the Isthmian games were held in his honour.

Out of all this the Greeks created a beautiful and haunting image, that of the boy on a dolphin; an image whose resonance still affects us in the strangest way.

Misor
This Phoenician god was credited with the discovery of salt. Misor was claimed as an ancestor of *Taautos (Thoth)*, the inventor of writing.

Mithra
Ancient Persian god of contracts and friendship. His cult grew

until under the Romans it became the main opponent of Christianity.

Rooted in Mazdaism, Mithra shows undeniable solar origins; he was allied to the sun, drove the sun's chariot and exhibited the qualities of the sun: strength, truth, knowledge. He is described as the sun's companion and they are depicted as two youthful gods, both with golden hair, wearing white tunics and wide trousers, and crowned with golden crowns. Mithra holds the golden shoulder of a young bull and this is indicative of his power over the animal, whose constellation (The Great Bear not Taurus) turns the heavens about.

Mithra carried the bull to a cave where he ritually sacrificed it. There are many interpretations of this act, but the most commonly accepted is that the killing of the bull fertilizes the earth with his blood and seed. Bull-killing and washing in the animal's blood played a part in Mithraic initiation, as it did in the cult of *Attis* and others. There was much that was secretive about the cult which absorbed Oriental and Greek philosophy, Babylonian myth and astrology, Magian rituals, and echoes of the cults of Attis and *Zurvan*. It also acquired an apocalyptic element and influences from the stern Gnostic teachings on morality.

Apart from the Taurobolium, the Mithraic cult, whose rites were practised either in real caves or temples designed to look like caves, was notable for repeated ritual washings and the taking of a communal meal. There is no doubt that the first is a residue of a solar cult (sun entering and emerging from sea), and the second a survival of the *Haoma* (*q.v.*) ritual. Early Mithraic ceremonies involved the offering of the sacred herb Haoma to the god by those who had painstakingly prepared themselves and had reached a reverent mental condition. Mithraism is also indebted to the cult of the dying vegetation god. Mithra wears a Phrygian cap, the *pileus*, a link with certain deities from whom our modern pixies may be descended. In later times his cult was nearly universal (see *Mithras* in the Roman section).

There are hints that Mithra was linked to a secret tradition even beyond that handed down to the initiates; he was said to be possessed of hundreds of eyes and to be part of a hidden triad of gods. (See Indian god *Mitra*.)

Mot
A harvest god.

Mot was the god twin of *Aleyin*, who fought his brother for the sexual favours of the goddess *Anat*. The two can be viewed as gods of the waning and waxing year. Mot, son of *El*, and spirit of the harvest, ruled the arid plains. He was killed twice, by Anat (daughter of the rain god and sister of the water god) and by Aleyin (son of *Baal*, otherwise *Addad* the weather god). He is ritually murdered by the arrival of rain. Mot was important because he ruled that part of the year when the sun ripened the corn, and was as necessary to the scheme of things as rain itself.

Nabu
Mesopotamian god of writing and destiny.

Nabu was son of *Marduk* and his main shrine was at Borsippa. His job was to receive the Tablets of Fate from his father and write down on them whatever destiny his father decreed for the coming year. He could at will alter the number of days allotted to men, making them more or less, and was therefore a useful god to know. As god of intellectual activity and literature, he and his wife *Tashmetrum* had developed the materials of writing from natural resources available in Mesopotamia. Clay from the alluvial plain was made into handy tablets, and cut reeds from the river bank were used to impress the cuneiform (wedge-shaped) script onto the malleable clay. Left in the hot sun, or dried in ovens, the tablets baked hard, forming a nearly indestructible record legible even after thousands of years. When our books have rotted to dust, when our electronic data-banks are cold and inaccessible, the ancient clay tablets will still be as clear as they have ever been.

Nabu is remembered in the name Nebuchadrezzar (nabu-kudurri-usur, 'O god Nabu, protect my frontier-markers').

Namtar
An evil Mesopotamian god who was an agent of *Ereshkigal*, queen of the Underworld; the negative aspect of fate, he was a bringer of disease to the earth.

Nanna

Moon god of Ur, the equivalent of *Sin*.

Nanshe

Mesopotamian goddess of springs and water-ways.

Daughter of the god *Ea*. Nanshe was worshipped in Eridu and Lagash, where her festival included a procession on the water (in boats of course). Her symbol was a vase in which swam a fish.

Nergal

Babylonian god and king of the Underworld.

Nergal was ejected from heaven and invaded the Underworld with fourteen demons. He blocked all the gates and made himself a complete nuisance until *Ereshkigal* (*q.v.*) accepted him as her husband and made him 'lord of the great dwelling'. During the great flood Nergal tore away the mast of the ship in which Utanapishtim, the Babylonian Noah, was sailing to safety. Utanapishtim escaped and was saved along with his family and specimens of all manner of animals.

Nergal is also a god of plague though he leaves most of the detailed work of that kind to his satellite *Namtar*. His symbols are a sword and a lion's head.

Ningursu

God of irrigation and fecundity.

Born of a she-goat, Ningursu was god of the Sumerian city-state of Lagash. He is shown in an ancient carving from Lagash as a bearded king, holding an eagle in one hand and a club in the other. By his side is a net full of human captives.

Nigursu appeared to a man, Gudea, in a fearsome aspect with instructions to build him a temple at Lagash. He seemed to be as tall as the sky with a god's head, the eagle wings of *Imdugud* and hurricanes for feet. He was flanked by a pair of lions. In another version of the story, it was Imdugud (*q.v.*) himself who appeared in the dream.

Ninkhursag

Alias Nintu, Ki, Ninki, Ninmah, Ninlil, Innini, Bau, *Gula*, Nin-karrak, Ga-Tum-Dug, *Belit-Illi*, *Belitis*. One of the four main Sumerian gods. (See *Damkina*.)

As mother goddess, earth goddess, Ninkhursag was the fount of all life; the creative principle which was later fragmented into many individual earth goddesses. As Ninlil she was wife of *Enlil*; as Ninki, she was wife of Enki (*Ea*). She is the original mother from whom all others come, and is similar to the Greek *Gaia*. Earthly kings were said to have been nourished at her breast, ingesting divinity with her milk.

Nintu or Nintud

An aspect of *Belit-Illi*, mother of the gods.

Ninurta

God of war, wells, canals and the South Wind; he was also a messenger.

Ninurta was derived from *Ningursu*. Son of *Enlil*, he was worshipped in Lagash. He was champion of the gods and depicted as wielding a club in the company of snakes. In Sumer and Akkad he was god of the constellation we call Orion. Because of his warlike character the whole of nature conspired to attack him. Even the stones joined in the fray. After a great battle, Ninurta was victorious; he blessed those stones which had helped him and cursed those that had fought against him. That is why some stones are worthless and others are precious.

Ninurta built dams to hold back the bitter waters of the Underworld, while in the Epic of Gilgamesh he helps to flood the earth by throwing down the dykes and breaking the dams. His consort was *Gula*, a goddess who helped breathe life into mankind. Their wedding feast was celebrated on New Year's day.

Nisaba

Babylonian goddess of grain, sister of *Nanshe*.

Ormazd

Zoroastrian god of light. The name was created by fusing Ahura with Mazda. Creator of life, Ormazd commanded the Benign Immortals in their fight against *Ahriman* (*q.v.*) and the forces of darkness. (See *Zurvan*.)

Rimmon (Rammon)
A Syrian weather god.

Called the 'thunderer', Rimmon was equated with *Addad*, *Adonis* and the Hittite Teshub. The pomegranate was sacred to him. The fruit was a symbol of life and death; it produced a red dye and was the only fruit allowed to be represented on the robes of the Hebrew high priest. It has a part to play in the story of *Attis*, and in the myth of *Persephone*. Never eaten by worms, the pomegranate was considered holy; it was probably the original fruit of many stories (apples of immortality, poisoned apples etc.) and an obvious solar symbol.

Sapas
One of those minor deities who exist merely to perform a function. Sapas was a Phoenician goddess and daughter of *El*. She was known as 'Torch of the Gods' and was a divine courier. She helped conduct the god *Aleyin* back from the Underworld.

Shamash
Mesopotamian sun god; in Sippar and Larsa he was also god of divination.

Son of the moon god *Sin*, Shamash was brother and husband to the divine *Ishtar*. Known for his wisdom, he was represented with a saw, with which he 'cut decisions'. Omniscient and all-seeing, his rays are thrown over the earth like a net.

Shamash lived in the mountains of the east. There, every morning, the great door of his palace was opened by scorpion-men. The god, armed with his saw, then mounted his chariot, kept waiting for him by his driver Bunene. They set off for their daily journey across the sky. At night Shamash entered another great door in the mountains of the west and travelled through the earth back to his starting place.

Shamash is shown as a four-rayed sun, or as a winged sun-disc. His sons were Kittum ('truth') and Mesharum ('justice').

331

The Arabic for sun is *shams*. Some think that the story of Samson reveals him to have been originally a sun god; certainly the cutting of the hair, with its attendant loss of strength, is a solar feature. The Sumerian name for Shamash was Utu.

Sin

Mesopotamian moon god; in Ur he was known as Nannar or *Nanna*.

Sin was one of the first rank of gods and formed the main triad with *Shamash*, the sun, and *Ishtar*, goddess of love. He was described as an old man with a long beard, and every night he sailed the sky in his boat. When the moon was full it was described as his crown, when it was crescent-shaped it was thought of either as his boat or his weapon. Sin was the enemy of evil spirits, the enemy of all those who would use night to cloak their wicked deeds. Once he was eclipsed by a rebellion fomented by evil spirits and was saved by *Marduk* (*q.v.*).

Sin was wise, secretive and full of good counsel. He was the measurer of time. Son of *Enlil* and Ninlil, his own children were Shamash and Ishtar.

Taautos

According to Philo, this Phoenician god was the precursor of the learned Egyptian god *Thoth* (*q.v.*); he is said to have designed the insignia of royalty.

Tammuz

God of the harvest of Mesopotamia, Akkad and Sumer.

Originally a tree god and son of Ningishzida (or Ningizzida, 'lord of the tree of life'), Tammuz' death was caused by the love of *Ishtar*, who sought him in the Underworld and fetched him from there to stand at the gate of *Anu*. Ishtar's absence on the long search had a negative effect on the reproductive ability of man and beast alike. As she was the personification of life-creating sex her absence could eventually have been fatal for human and animal existence. Tammuz was the personification of the annual death and withering of vegetation, and the late summer month of Tammuz was named after him (it roughly corresponded to our late June and early July). (See *Dumuzi*.)

The dying and rising god of vegetation forms a similar theme in the Middle East and Mediterranean world, and has given us *Osiris*, *Attis*, *Adonis* and *Mithras*. In most of them the description of the death of the god is a close parallel to what happens to corn at harvest-time. Apart from the fact that Tammuz grows and is cut down every year, he is a colourless, characterless sort of god. In that sense he is a function, a reflection of an external agricultural fact. The use of certain words such as 'dying' and 'resurrection' often form a misleading image of what these vegetation gods represented. Each of them must be seen in the context of their time and place and as necessary but minor attendants on their respective consorts (the earth goddesses), who were always more important.(See *Dumuzi*)

Tanit (Tanith)
The Phoenician moon goddess of Carthage.

Tanit is a development of the Great Goddess and so linked to *Ishtar*, *Ashtart*, *Astarte* and the rest. Her symbol of a circle inside a crescent, supported by a blunt cone, forms a moon sign similar to that of the Egyptian goddess *Hathor* (a disc between horns).

Tashmetrum
Goddess wife of *Nabu*; she helped him invent writing.

Telepinu
Hittite vegetation god.

One fine day Telepinu disappeared, taking with him all his possessions and powers. Very soon the earth sickened and dried up. The plants wilted. The anxious gods got together and tried to discover a way of making him come back. They searched for him in vain. Then the Mother of the Gods took a bee aside, giving it orders to find Telepinu and sting him into returning. The bee hummed off and soon the god was back where he belonged. Once more the earth flourished.

Terah
Moon god of the Zebulon.

The Zebulon were a Semitic tribe who became part of the people of Israel. Alias Etrah, Terah led the Zebulon in their conquest of part of the possessions of the Phoenicians by defeating the puerile *Keret* (*q.v.*). The Zebulon settled on the land between the Carmel range of hills and Lake Galilee, the area in which Nazareth is situated. Abram's father was named Terah. The chief god of the tribe was Baal-Zebulon, otherwise known as Fly. (See *Baal*.)

Tiamat

Goddess of the primal abyss, that chaos which gave birth to the gods of Mesopotamia.

Tiamat took the form of a dragon and her abode was the sea. The god *Apsu* was upset by the noise made by his newly-arrived companions and complained to Tiamat, who set about the task of disciplining the gods with great energy. She gave birth to lizards, dragons, sphinxes, hurricanes, mad dogs, scorpion-men, fish-men, lion-demons and centaurs. These creations were her storm troopers; she set the god *Kingu* at their head and pinned the Tablets of Fate on his renegade chest.

    The gods were scared off by the army and recruited *Marduk* (*q.v.*) as their champion. Using magic and winds, Marduk slew Tiamat and split her in half to make the heavens and earth. After the death of Tiamat and the rout of her hordes, peace and harmony ruled among the gods; the work of further creation could continue. (See the Gnostic *Leviathan*.)

Utu

God of the sun, the Sumerian equivalent of *Shamash*. Utu was also a god of fertility, judgement and law-giving.

Yahweh

One God of all the earth.

His true and holy name may only be spoken once a year by the High Priest in the Holy of Holies. 'Yahweh' and 'Jehovah' are interpretations of the four Hebrew letters *yod, he, vau, he*. Known to the Greeks as Tetragrammaton ('four letters'), it is a formula which signifies the One God.

    Like all other peoples, the ancestors of the people of Israel worshipped many and various deities. It was Abram whose genius first comprehended and declared that God was Indivisible, Omnipotent and Eternal. It was Abram who interpreted a totally new vision, that of a God who was moral and righteous, and who had chosen a small group of Semitic tribes to hold and pass on his promise of a new relationship between Himself and mankind. It was a supremely difficult task for the people of Israel to perform, surrounded and pressured by all the old forms and ideas of pagan godhood. From their struggles and their sufferings the new vision was preserved and extended by the prophets. Man could never be the same again for now he was set in a divine context, in an eternal contractual relationship with Yahweh.

Yahweh, with *Allah* and the Christian God, is arguably too intimately exalted to belong in the gaudy and exotic company who throng these pages. But God is to be found everywhere.

Zurvan

Persian god of infinite space and time of whom *Ormazd* and *Ahriman* (*qq.v.*) are but parts. His cult was a development of dualism. He was god of the four faces, which are Procreation, Birth, Ageing, Return to the Infinite.

The story goes that Zurvan desired a son; he sacrificed for a thousand years. Then a doubt crossed his mind, was personified and born as Ahriman. Because he appeared first, Ahriman was given control of the world for nine thousand years. All this time he must fight with *Ahura Mazda* (*q.v.*), who was created by Zurvan's holy acts of sacrifice and devotion.

Abathur

Otherwise called B'haq Ziva. He was an Uthra, or a divine being of the rank of angel.

Born and living within the World of Light, the Uthras, along with their *sh'kinas* (clouds of light – a surrounding area or habitation), are of varying ranks and of varying goodness or badness. Abathur, by contemplation of his own image, brought forth the divine being called *Ptah-il-Uthra*. The image he contemplated was that of himself reflected off black water. Abathur ordered his son to create a world in imitation of the heavenly world.

Achamoth

A Gnostic fallen god; a fallen aspect of the lower *Sophia* who was rejected, aborted and thrown out into the spinning void. His name derives from the Hebrew *chokmah* ('wisdom') and shows his link with the lower Sophia (*Gk:* 'wisdom'), an important divine principle.

Archons

These gods held an important place in Gnostic thought. There were seven of them, and they were the degenerated spiritual controllers of seven spheres which surrounded the earth. Their malicious nature made them enjoy their task of keeping mankind from reunion with God. The Archons ('rulers') were probably borrowed and refurbished Babylonian gods; though, in line with the Gnostic habit of blasphemy and deliberate denigration, they were given as names certain titles properly applied to God – *e.g. Iao, Elohim* and *El Shaddai*.

Gnostic theories, which differ with each sect, start from the basic assumption that man is the victim of a huge deception from which it becomes obvious that good is evil and evil is good. This precept is presented in terms calculated to offend and distress devout Jews, Christians and, later, followers of Islam. The Early Church in particular, remembering the words of Christ that he would be followed by many false gods and evil deceivers, made a clear and energetic stand against this often attractive heresy; or group of heresies, for there was never a central body of doctrine to Gnosticism, rather a concurrence of thought (not entirely free from a certain amount of plagiarism).

Gnosticism took its basic concepts and words from where ever it found them, from Oriental thought, Iranian and Babylonian religions, Judaism, and above all, Christianity. Its method is speculative and its vocabulary is abstract. (See *Elohim, Ialdabaoth, Leviathan.*)

Barbelo
Mother of the Archon *Ialdabaoth*. She is also called First Man, Male-Female, Original Spirit, and *Sophia*.

Barbelo was very like *Ennoia*, but was in fact the product of the first spontaneous divine reduplication, for she was produced by the *Spirit-Father*. She was the personification of his Thought. With the agreement of the Spirit-Father (otherwise known as 'The Abyss' or 'The Silence') she created the Aeons, more personified abstracts who busied themselves in worshipping Barbelo and the Spirit-Father. The Aeons were produced in pairs, thus giving them the ability and the chance to create issue of their own. The only divine being not produced at this time was the Only-Begotten Son or Christos who was a later creation of Ennoia. A special Gnostic sect was devoted to Barbelo. (See *Spirit-Father* and *Sophia-Prunikos*.)

Cain
In true Gnostic fashion, the first murderer, Cain, was considered a good spirit and therefore worthy of worship. A sect called the Cainites grew up around him.

Chroshtag
Gnostic divinity named 'The Call' who was sent by the Mother of Life to rescue her son 'The Spirit' or 'Primal Man' from his enemies. When freed the son returned to his mother as 'The Answer'.

Edem
Gnostic goddess who is the principle which causes evil. She herself is not necessarily evil.

Elohim or Eloaios

For the Gnostics this title of God became the personal name of one of the seven *Archons*. It was used in a pejorative sense, as a calculated insult to accepted attitudes of devotion. The Archons, rulers of their own spheres, actively blocked the attempts of men's souls to reach God; according to some Gnostic teachings, they were the creators of the world. They ruled fire and the winds and combined to control 'The Tomb', the Gnostic term for the human body. Elohim separated from *Edem* and was rehabilitated. He had been born with *Jave*, both of them the result of *Ialdabaoth's* rape of the virginal Eve. To add injury to insult he was referred to as 'cat-faced'.

El Shaddai or Esaldaios

A Gnostic *Archon*, a divine being of demonic nature.

Ennoia

A complex Gnostic goddess, the personification of thought.

Ennoia was the bearer of creative power, but cut off from her source she became a wandering and much-desired mother figure. Everywhere she went she caused strife by inflaming hungry passions. Everyone wanted to possess and enjoy her; even her progeny of spirits, refusing to let go of her, dragged her down from heaven to the earth. She appeared often in the bodies of women, clothed in flesh, including that of Helen of Troy, whose sexual treasure caused the mass slaughter of Greeks and Trojans. Throughout history she migrated from female body to female body, causing emotional, psychic and physical havoc among mankind. At last she became the inmate of a Tyrian brothel.

Simon Magus, the great charlatan and religious conjurer, was accompanied by a Tyrian prostitute whom he claimed was none other than the fallen Ennoia, by whose salvation Simon would save the whole world. This woman's name was Helena; sometimes allied to the Greek goddess *Selene*, by which name it was hinted that she was also the goddess of the moon. Simon was a master of persuasion, but he came to a sticky end in Rome; it is said that he fell to his death while attempting to fly without benefit of wings. Another version of his death relates that he blasphemously claimed that he was divine and would ascend to heaven to prove it. As the magician began to rise, St Peter, who was present, shouted out a curse and Simon came crashing to the ground.

Simon and the Tyrian Helena have both survived in our literature, for Simon used the name 'The Favoured One'; that is to say, Faustus. (See *Sophia-Prunikos*.)

Hibil
A Gnostic Uthra (a divine being of the rank of angel).

Otherwise recorded as Hibil-Ziwa, he was a saviour god who entered the flesh-mountain Karkun (Hell) in armour from which protruded dozens of blades and points. His sharp suiting made mincemeat of the insides of Hell, who, or which, prudently vomited him out again. We cannot pass on without noting the correspondence of this story to that of the famous English north country folk tale of the Lambton Worm. Young Lambton fished up a worm, threw it in a well and went on the Crusades. The worm grew into a vast and loathsome dragon which terrified the countryside. Lambton returned, had sharp blades soldered all over his armour and wrestled with the creature. The harder the creature wriggled and squeezed the more effectively it cut itself up into tiny bits, which the tide washed away before they had a chance to reassemble themselves. A man in spiked armour can be likened to the sun which puts to flight the dragon of darkness. (See *Hibil-Ziwa* in the Middle East General section.)

Ialdabaoth
The first Gnostic *Archon*.

Sophia conceived a Thought on her own and without the permission of the *Spirit-Father*. Because the latter had not been involved in its making, the Thought emerged malformed and ugly. Sophia wrapped the thought-child in a cloud of light to conceal it, and called it Ialdabaoth. Full of ambitious pride, Ialdabaoth created the other six *Archons* and a total of three hundred and sixty angels. But he withheld from these creations the power he had got from his mother. He went about bragging and boasting that he alone was the true god, the only demiurge or

creative force. His mother rebuked him sorrowfully but he refused to listen to her. Having glimpsed the reflection of the
Spirit-Father in water, Ialdabaoth became inspired by creative
ambition and conspired with the other Archons to create a man
in the Divine Image. Their creation was only partially successful;
they made what the Gnostics call 'psychic Adam', a man without
life. All their attempts to get him to breathe and move failed.

Sophia, who wanted to regain her power from her evil son,
took the problem to the Spirit-Father. He sent some disguised
angels to Ialdabaoth, advising him to breathe some of the spirit
(*pneuma*) he had got from his mother into the nostrils of 'psychic
Adam'. The result was a living Adam or 'pneumatic man'. Soon
after that, Adam was entombed in matter and put on earth. While
trying to extract the hidden power from him, Ialdabaoth created
Eve. He gave the couple strict orders not to eat of the Tree of
Knowledge. But Adam and Eve were advised by Christ to eat of
the fruit of the tree; they did so and became aware of their
ignorance and lack of spiritual life. They became spiritually
ambitious, wishing to reach up to the Spirit-Father. Ialdabaoth
had tried to hide Knowledge from them, for he knew that they
would turn away from him. He turned them out of Paradise.

Overcome with lust for the virginal Eve, Ialdabaoth forced
himself on her sexually. Eve gave birth to two sons, *Jave* and
Elohim. Then in an attempt to weaken Adam and drag him down,
Ialdabaoth implanted lust in him. The product of Adam and Eve's
first love-making was Seth, a dark character who would ensure
the furtherance of lust in the future world.

In the Barbeliotic sect, Ialdabaoth was linked to the Great
Adversary; among the Ophitic ('serpent') sect of the Gnostics, he
was recognized as the creative force or demiurge. It follows from
all this that the world and all its creatures were created by evil, a
doctrine held by the later heresies of the Cathars and Albigen-
sians. (See *Sophia-Prunikos*.)

Iao
A Gnostic *Archon*; he was called 'serpent-faced'.

Jave
Bear faced god of the Gnostics. Child of Eve and *Ialdabaoth*.

John the Baptist

In their attempts to attack and pervert Christianity the Gnostic sects came up with many peculiar notions. One was that John the Baptist was the true divine figure and that Christ stole his ideas from him and gave them out in a garbled form. Here is the true weakness of Gnosticism; it was a purely intellectual creation with no Divine backing. Its thought may have been free-ranging and complex, its imagination brilliant and its syncretic powers well-tuned and sensitive, but it had no basis in inspiration or revelation. It can be seen as a last-minute and forced flowering of pagan darkness in a world slowly emerging into the light of Grace.

Leviathan

The Ophitic cult of Gnostics places the seven spheres of the *Archons* within a vast, encircling serpent called Leviathan. The Mandean sect called this serpent Ur and regarded him as father of the Archons. Leviathan, inescapably linked to *Tiamat* of Mesopotamia and the Ophis serpent of the Egyptians, was regarded by the Gnostics as the father of the snake who appears in the Gnostic gospel Actae Thomae as the seducer of mankind.

Manda D'Hayye

'Knowledge of Life'; the saviour god of the Mandean sect.

Manda is the equivalent of the Greek *gnosis* ('wisdom'). He was created in the World of Light by 'The Life', or Great Mana, to counter-balance the attempts by the Uthras to make a world which was to be designed after heaven. He was sent down to spy on the Uthras and report back to the Great Mana. (See *Abathur*.)

Ptah-Il-Uthra

Mandean demiurge who made men outside the sphere of 'The Life' or Great Mana.

He put a hidden spirit (*pneuma, mana*) into Adam and Eve and then was stricken with remorse because the act had been a violent one, and was not according to the scheme of 'The Life'. The Gnostics regarded him as son of *Abathur*. His name tells us that he was derived from the creator god of the Egyptians, *Ptah*, that he was a god, Il (cognate with *El*), and that he was an Uthra, a divine being.

Ruha D'Qudsha
Chief demonic goddess of the Mandean Gnostics.

Ruha D'Qudsha was entirely evil. She gave birth to the planets and with their help set out to ensnare and degrade mankind, using sexual love and alcohol as her main weapons. Other forms of sensuality were also used; she is described as trying to entrap Adam with 'embracing', and with 'horns and flutes'. Gnosticism abhorred sexuality and all forms of sensual pleasure. Its aggressive, nearly paranoid, proto-Puritanism was allied with a cynical attitude of blasphemy, for Ruha D'Qudsha really means 'holy spirit'.

Sabaoth
Archon and ruler of the fifth sphere; he was son of *Iao* who was son of *Ialdabaoth*.

Sophia-Prunikos
An Aeon (see *Barbelo*) who like *Ennoia* conceived a Thought without the aid of her pair-companion or consort. She was the transmundane mother of *Ialdabaoth* and therefore the counterpart to Ennoia (*q.v.*), whose story and attributes are hers also. Sophia is personified wisdom, while the Prunikos part of her indicates her prurience. She is regarded as the mother of the God of the Old Testament, and is continually active in trying to prepare mankind for his coming salvation. This salvation will be the work of a Spirit sent by the holy Aeons. The *Archons* continually work against her by means of their false Spirit or Counterfeit. They also thought up an evil trap for man and all the other struggling beings such as demons, angels and gods. This wicked invention was none other than Fate, which binds all things.

The Gnostics usually thought of Sophia as being in two parts, the upper Sophia and the lower Sophia. The lower Sophia is the fallen aspect with all the resultant distress and problems caused by the fall. Usually the higher Sophia is called Barbelo, Virgin, Ennoia, and Holy Spirit. The lower aspect is called Sophia, Prunikos, and The Left. This dual framework was the starting point for a veritable explosion of speculation and differing theories, especially among the followers of the teacher Valentinus. The Early Christian authority Irenaeus comments that the followers of Valentinian speculation were not considered worthy unless they had invented something new to add to the labyrinthine ideas and theories of Gnosticism.

Spirit-Father

One perception of God, who is variously described, formulated and readjusted to fit into the constantly changing pattern of Gnostic thought. He was supposedly a perfect Aeon and was called Fore-Beginning, Fore-Father, Abyss, Great Father, Great Mana. This Aeon was pre-existent and had remained for countless millennia in perfect silence and rest. Part of him, *Ennoia* (also called Grace and Silence) conceived and gave life to Nous ('mind') and Alethia ('truth'); these in turn produced Logos ('word') and Pneuma ('life') who produced Andros ('man') and Ecclesia ('church'). These Aeons brought forth more Aeons solely in order to worship the father. The original group of eight Aeons, added to ten produced by Logos and Pneuma, added to twelve produced by Andros and Ecclesia, made up what is known as the Pleroma ('fullness'); fifteen pairs or thirty Aeons in all.

Of all the Aeons only Nous knew of the Spirit-Father, and he wanted to communicate his knowledge to the others; but the Spirit-Father forebade it. This disharmony caused *Sophia* to fall into a fit; she was besieged by varying passions, giving birth to all manner of emotions. She came to rest on the outermost reaches of possibility at the Limit, or Crux ('cross'). The Limit is a preserving aspect which gave to Christos his active role in re-establishing harmony in the Pleroma. Christos and Holy Spirit were emanated for a specific function and, later on, Jesus, another Aeon, was introduced in order to heal the external world beyond the Limit of the Pleroma. Christos formed the residue of the disturbance caused by the internal disharmony into an external world, giving shape but not life to the lower Sophia. The cross in question is not the Christian one but the Greek Tau cross (T-shaped). The upper bar is the line between the upper and lower worlds, and the vertical bar divides the psychic world from the material one. (See *Barbelo*.)

343

Oceania

Including AUSTRALIA ■ NEW ZEALAND
MELANESIA ■ MICRONESIA
■ POLYNESIA

Abere
Melanesian demoness.

A wild woman accompanied by girls, Abere was a seducer and murderer of men. Reeds would grow up around her to hide her from her intended victims. (See *Mesede*.)

Agunua
Primary serpent god of the Solomons; all others are aspects of him.

Agunua made all the fruit and vegetables but his brother scorched some of them, making them forever uneatable. He made a boy but the little fellow couldn't cope with the problems of life alone, so Agunua made a woman to do the cooking and tend the vegetable gardens. The first coconut from each tree is sacred to Agunua. In Oceania there is a widely held belief that there is a heaven specially for coconuts; and they deserve it, providing as they do food, drink, shelter, and fuel.

Aluluei
Micronesian god of knowledge and navigation; son of *Palulop*, the famous sea captain.

In one series of tales Aluluei is the father of *Longorik* and *Longolap*; in another he is said to have two brothers, Big Rong and Little Rong. They had always been rivals until Aluluei arrived. He had acquired wisdom while still in the womb, so his jealous brothers united against him. They killed him and cast his weighted body into the sea. His father, Palulop, brought him back as a spirit, protecting him with many shining, star-like eyes. At his father's urging, Aluluei began stealing his brothers' possessions. Then Palulop told his two older sons to build a large canoe with a hut on it, saying it would bait the thief. It did, too successfully, and they were astounded to see the canoe make off with only one man on board. Aluluei had enlisted the help of forty rats, and the obliging rodents were crewing for him. On board was also a tree and some sand. After sailing a while, Aluluei made himself an island out of the sand, planted the tree and erected the hut under it. He lived there quite happily.

Palulop had another son, *Faravai*, who visited the island and offered Aluluei food. This was found to consist of fish skins and coconut shells. Aluluei was so annoyed at his brother's parsimonious gift that when a storm blew up he didn't lift a finger to help him. Faravai was shipwrecked on Aluluei's island. Aluluei fed him – on fish skins and coconut shells. Faravai went fishing; as he began to fillet the fish he had caught, the relevant portions of Aluluei's anatomy began to disappear until the god of navigation was just a skeleton. This was Aluluei's way of teaching his brother food taboos.

Before letting him go home Aluluei demanded that Faravai should clean Aluluei's hair. Faravai was frightened, for he saw bright eyes gleaming at him out of his brother's locks. Aluluei told him that what he saw were stars; after a quick course in navigational astronomy Faravai was sent home in a canoe made of sand. After many adventures the canoe at last fell apart, and Faravai arrived home on the back of a turtle.

In Micronesia sailors would build a miniature hut on their outriggers and fill it with amulets and offerings to Aluluei. The god was thought to make his home on sandbars. Apparently he had two faces; one to see where he was going, the other, presumably, to see where he had been.

Ambat
Melanesian hero-god who taught men pottery and ritual.

Ambat is perhaps best known for having introduced commemorative figures (small clay models) for the dead. The oldest of five brothers, he saved them all from the ogress *Nevinbimbaau* who had trapped them in a deep pit. He led his brothers to safety along the root of a banyan tree.

Anulap
Micronesian sky god.

Anulap was a teacher of magic and knowledge, and founder of the Idan peoples of Truk Island. His wife, Ligoububfanou, was the actual creator of the islands, men and animals. He was the grandfather of the notorious *Olifat*.

Atea
Alias Atea Rangi or *Rangi*; Polynesian sky god.

The god *Tane* drilled holes in Atea to let in the light for men. Atea was the father of the great *Tangaroa*; his wife was *Papa*, the earth, mother of gods and men. Atea's generative force began all life.

Baiame
Australian sky god; father of the one-legged *Daramulun*.

Bunjil
Australian sky god.

Bunjil made two men out of clay while his brother, the Bat, made women out of water. He gave mankind tools, weapons, rituals, and initiation ceremonies.

Bunosi
Melanesian culture god.

A snake-child, Bunosi had gigantic coils big enough to fill a large house. Bunosi's parents evicted him so his sister, Kafisi, looked after him and accompanied the god on his travels. Bunosi rewarded her by creating fire and coughing up pigs and useful plants.

Daramulun
Australian sky god.

The one-legged Daramulun had many aliases, and many versions of his adventures are extant. During ceremonies, men swung bull-roarers to imitate the sound of his voice. Bull-roarers don't sound much like bulls; the noise they make is a deep, rather eerie buzz. Models of Daramulun show him with his mouth filled with quartz and with an exaggerated phallus. Sometimes he carries a stone axe, a suitable thunder weapon for a sky god. (See *Baiame*.)

Djanggawul
Australian founder deities.

In the Dreamtime (see *Ungud*) there arrived from Bralgu, island home of the dead, three Djanggawul. They were two sisters and one brother. They landed at the 'Place of the Sun' (Port Bradshaw in the Northern Territory) carrying a variety of ritual apparatus: a sacred bag, woven mat, and *rangga* emblems. As they went they thrust the emblems into the ground and produced springs of water, trees and yams. From the bag, the mat, and from the sisters came a constant stream of babies; the Djanggawul brother keeping the women constantly pregnant. These babies became the inhabitants of the lands they crossed and for them the Djanggawul left animals, plants and sacred ceremonies. All religious life was under the control of the two sisters until the brother stole from them the sacred apparatus. He also shortened their elongated genitals, depriving them of their former dual principle. They became like ordinary women.

The Djanggawul continued their journey towards the setting sun, still producing children and giving people the rules for, and necessities of, life. They are remembered by a ceremony in which women hide under mats; the men poke the mats with sticks in symbolic mating and the women wriggle like children in the womb. Then they come out from under cover, reliving the story of their ancestors' emergence from the mat of the Djanggawul and from the sisters' wombs.

Euro Brothers
Australian culture gods of the Aranda people.

The Euro brothers gave men spears, spear-throwers and the art of cooking on hot coals.

Fakahotu
Alias for *Papa*, the Polynesian earth goddess.

Faravai
Son of the Micronesian sea god *Palulop,* and part of the divine family which included *Aluluei, Rongerik,* and *Rongelap*. (See *Aluluei*.)

Gaingin
Papuan primordial beings who were larger than life. These beings, of various kinds according to different traditions, helped shape

349

the earth which was already in existence. As sky-beings they came from a sky-world and returned there when their work was finished. However there are two Gaingin still on earth: Bugal, the snake, and Warger, the crocodile.

Excessive rain means that the sky-beings are angry and during such a storm people, fearing that the sky-pole might break and let down the beings, stand ready to defend themselves.

Gidja
Moon god and totemic ancestor of the Australian Dreamtime.

Another term for Dreamtime (see *Ungud*) is *altjiranga mitjina*. With the meaning 'dream ancestor was' this phrase is a clue to the part played by Gidja in creation. He created the female sex by castrating *Yalungur* and was attacked by *Kallin Kallin* for his misplaced enthusiasm. Gidja was washed out to sea and ended up in the sky; he is now the moon. By making sex possible Gidja was man's true ancestor.

Great Rainbow Snake
Australian totemic deity of the Dreamtime (see *Ungud*). Many different names are used for this god in various parts of the continent: Galeru, Ungur, Wonungur, Worombi, Wonambi, *Wollunqua*, Yurlunggur, *Julunggul*, Langal, Muit, Yero, Taipan, Mindi, Karia, Kunmanggur.

The Great Rainbow Snake is the life-giver, living in deep pools, arching across the sky, shining from water drops, quartz, mother of pearl. In the Dreamtime he shaped the waterways of the land. He regenerated the earth and all living things, including man. To some he was the all-father, to some the great mother, while others said he was bisexual. That is not too important; the main thing is that he sends rain, which is life. Holding life and death in his power, the Great Rainbow Snake must not be offended. His sacred pools must not be defiled with human blood, for blood was his gift to man. Through this gift he controls all man's bodily processes, including that of procreation. If any of his rules were broken, for example if incest was committed, he would become angry and hurl his red knife at the guilty ones to the sound and fury of the thunderstorm.

Sympathetic magic is performed by sorcerers who manipulate quartz and mother of pearl, whose iridescence contains the watery life-force of the Great Snake. Worshipped all over Australia he has the majesty and power of the great gods, the stature of an *Odin* or a *Jupiter*. (See African god *Danh*.)

Ha'iaka
Sister of the goddess *Pele*.

Ha'iaka had been born in the shape of an egg and was carried by Pele under her arm when that goddess travelled to Hawaii. A minor goddess, she seems only to come alive when opposed by Pele.

Pele, the goddess of volcanic fire, wandering in the spirit trance, was attracted to a nearby island by the sound of a nose flute. On her arrival she assumed a human shape, for she saw a hula ceremony taking place. There she met a handsome young chieftain and for three days and nights their romance blossomed. Then Pele had to leave his bed, promising the young man that she would send a messenger for him. She chose her young sister Ha'iaka for the job, and gave her magic powers in order to overcome the supernatural problems she would encounter.

First of all Ha'iaka met some monsters of the variety known as Mo'o. She entangled them in a wonderful quick-growing vine. Then, as she was about to step onto a bridge, her magic powers alerted her. The supposed bridge was in fact the tongue of a monster. Ha'iaka would have walked straight into the creature's mouth. She avoided the 'bridge' and made another one out of her skirt.

But despite her determination she arrived too late; the young chieftain had expired from unrequited love. Ha'iaka saw his soul fluttering about like a butterfly and managed to catch it and return it to his body. They began the return journey, but were assailed by an army of spirits who were indignant that Pele should dare consort with a mere mortal. Meanwhile Pele, left behind to wait, began to grow jealous; she remembered that some foolish people thought her sister beautiful. As her imagination worked, she began to construct intricate webs of supposition. By degrees she grew more and more jealous. Then finally Pele literally blew

351

her top; she was after all a volcano goddess. Hot lava and thundering fire killed her sister's friend, Hopoe, and destroyed Ha'iaka's garden of lehua blossoms.

Because of her new magic powers, Ha'iaka knew what Pele had done. But she remained loyal to her mission and her sister. On the way back the two travellers met, after sundry hardships, a seeress called Pele-Ula (it was the goddess in disguise). The two ladies played a game of quoits, with the young chieftain as the prize. Ha'iaka won, and the handsome young man thereupon declared his undying love for her.

But Ha'iaka stayed true to her sister. She delivered the mortal to the brink of the volcano. Then she happened to glance down the slope and see her blackened groves; overcome by sorrow she embraced the young man. Just then, as luck would have it, Pele saw them. Once more she lost her cool. A furious outburst of jealous fire engulfed the pair. The mortal perished; but Ha'iaka's magic saved her. She managed to catch her lover's soul again and healed him a second time. Then they both returned to his island and, we may suppose, lived happily thereafter.

Hatuibwari
Serpent god of San Cristobal, in the Solomons. He had a human head, four eyes and four breasts.

Haumea
Hawaiian goddess of childbirth.

Haumea introduced natural childbirth; before then babies had been removed by section. She was called 'Tree-of-changing-leaves', indicating constant productivity. Haumea had the ability to transform herself from age to youth. In her care were wild plants; but Haumea was capable of negative action, withholding the growth of such plants in times of need. Much of her power was negated by the trickster *Kaulu*, who stole cultivated plants from the gods and killed Haumea.

Haumia
God of uncultivated plants.

At the time of the great separation of *Rangi* and *Papa* (*q.v.*), Haumia and his brother *Rongo* hid themselves inside their earth-mother (Papa) in order to escape the gusty anger of the god *Tawhiri*.

Hikuleo
Goddess of the underworld of Pulotu.

Hikuleo drove out the five creatures who had hidden themselves in the Underworld, but was not able to stop them from stealing yams and taro for the benefit of man.

Hina or Hine
Polynesian goddess of darkness and death created by the god *Tane* to be his wife, called Hine-Hau-One ('earth-formed-maiden'). She was mother of (and is) the great Hina, goddess of death, called Hina-Titama ('dawn-maiden').

Hina-Titama became the great goddess of darkness after she discovered that her husband was also her father. She is also called 'Hine-the-mitigator-of-many-things' and 'Hine-who-ate-from-behind-and-before', indicating that she had two faces. She was closely associated with the moon, being called 'Hine-who-stepped-into-the-moon'. One story has it that while sailing with her brother *Ru* she drifted off to see the moon, liked what she saw and decided to stay there, becoming 'Hina-the-watchwoman' and a patroness of travellers. There she makes tapa (bark-cloth), sheets of which can be seen on the moon when it is bright.

Another story says that once when she was making tapa, the noise of the beating of the bark to separate the fibres disturbed the rest of the mighty god *Tangaroa*. He sent a messenger to ask her to stop. Hina refused so Tangaroa ordered the messenger to hit her with her own mallet. The messenger performed the task so energetically that her spirit was knocked clean out of her body, and ascended to the moon.

This death-stroke tells us that Hina has a dark side as bringer of death to mankind. A widely told story of Hina concerns her seduction by an eel while she was bathing in a pool. The eel was slain but she kept its head, from which sprang the first coconut tree. By killing the god *Maui* during one of his more esoteric jokes she brought death to men.

Yet another explanation for Hina's journey to the moon was that she was so sickened by the noise and mess of her babies that she left the earth to seek refuge from the clamour and the smell.

Imberombera
Australian mother-creatress and consort of *Wuraka*.

Alias *Waramurungundju*, Imberombera came out of the sea from the direction of Indonesia. She made the landscape and from her body produced children, animals and plants. To each tribe she gave a language.

Inapatua
Aranda (Australia) myths tell us that the *Numbakulla* from the sky came down and made men out of Inapatua. Inapatua were shapeless creatures in whom could be seen the possibilities of human form.

Io
New Zealand Maori supreme being.

Io's knowledge was taught in the whares – schools where priests were educated. His aliases reveal his supposed nature: 'Io of the hidden face', 'Io the originator of all things', 'Io eternal', 'Io god of love'. He was known only to the priesthood, and was supreme above all other gods. There is no way of telling if his cult was a genuine esoteric one, hidden from view until the 1870s; or if it was an addition to Maori myth under the impact of Christianity.

Julunggul
One of the many names for the *Great Rainbow Snake* of Australia.

In the Dreamtime (see *Ungud*), the Great Snake lived with the other totemic ancestors and helped to shape the landscape, especially rivers and creeks. Particularly concerned with human fertility, he is himself bisexual. He produced spirit-children, and is closely linked with blood. Humans who have recently shed blood, for natural or cult reasons, fear to approach water, knowing that the Great Snake's creative power is matched by his destructive ability. His anger causes floods and disease.

Certain natural substances like quartz and pearl shell emanate his power. Sorcerers and wise men claim to be able to control this power by ritual manipulation of such objects. Julunggul has sacred pools; only sorcerers and healers dare to enter them. Julunggul's female side is seen in the stories of swallowing and regurgitation. (See *Wawalug*).

Jurawadbad

The snake man. His story was re-enacted by the Urbar, a cult in Australia.

Jurawadbad had been betrothed to a woman but she refused him his conjugal rights. She and her mother scorned him and insulted him. Jurawadbad went off and hid in a hollow log. His wife and mother-in-law came along, searching for food. They approached the log, which seemed a likely place, but aware of possible danger decided to look inside it first. Jurawadbad shut his eyes tight so that their brightness would not be seen. The daughter looked into the log and saw nothing but darkness. Then it was the mother's turn. Jurawadbad opened his eyes wide, so wide that they appeared to fill the log. The mother looked in and saw nothing but light. Thinking the log was empty, the two women put their hands into it. The snake man bit them, and they both died.

Kallin Kallin

'Chickenhawk', a totemic Australian deity.

Kallin Kallin was angry because *Gidja*, the moon, had castrated *Yalungur*, the Eaglehawk. Gidja had then put a bark baby into Yalungur's belly, making him a woman. In this way the female sex was created. Kallin Kallin's anger stemmed from the fact that Yalungur belonged to the same moiety, or social grouping, as he did. He waited to punish Gidja, and one day saw his chance. Gidja was crossing a bridge of vine. Kallin Kallin cut through the vine and Gidja crashed down into the torrent below. He surfaced and was swept away by the river out into sea, ending up in the distant sky where he remains to this day. Kallin Kallin had by this time worked out that because Yalungur was now a woman, she belonged to a different moiety. He promptly took her as his wife, founding the aborigine tradition of taking wives from a different community.

Kamapua'a
Polynesian hog man.

Kamapua'a had the ability to change himself into a hog, or a fish, or a plant. In his human aspect, he wore a cloak to conceal the bristles on his back. He wooed *Pele*, goddess of volcanic fire, but she scorned him, calling him, with some justification, a swine. They fought like dogs. Pele threw fire at Kamapua'a but Kamapua'a brought rain and fog to put it out. He caused herds of porkers to roam over Pele's lands, rooting up the earth. He was so successful in extinguishing the flames that soon only the sacred fire-sticks were left alight. Before they could be extinguished, the gods hurriedly intervened in the dispute in order to save man's cooking fire. They divided up the island of Hawaii Pele had the lava fields and Kamapua'a had the moist, windward areas.

Kambel
Melanesian sky god.

One day Kambel heard strange sounds issuing from a palm tree. He cut it down and people came out. Then a strange white object emerged from the palm, eluded his grasp, and rose into the sky. It was his son, the moon.

Kambel sent lizards to get him fire. One after the other they went, in order of size. Finally the smallest lizard managed to bring it back. Kambel roasted palm-pith and tossed it up into the sky, thus creating the clouds; and the clouds pushed up the sky which till then had been too close to the earth.

It was discovered that Kambel's son was guilty of incest with his mother. Kambel killed the boy. The boy had a dog, which complained bitterly about this summary treatment of his master. Kambel, fed up with the dog's whining protests, skewered down the animal's tongue with a cassowary feather, to prevent it telling Kambel's wife of the killing. To this day dogs cannot talk; they can only bark and howl.

356

Kapua
The divine tricksters or mischief-makers of Hawaii.

The Kapua were deities who used their supernatural powers to perform tricks. They were constantly engaged in amusing and sometimes destructive adventures. They were usually born in a non-human form and brought up by their grandparents; their superhuman powers enabled them to perform shape-shifting, extension and shrinking, as well as giving them great strength and incredible mobility. Some of their adventures are based on word play. Kawelo was mocked by men who punned on his name and called him 'son of a cock'; he swiftly replied that the cock roosts above even the chief's head.

Many Kapua exploits are of the Baron Munchausen variety. For example, Pekoi was able to string forty rats together by their whiskers by shooting a single arrow. They regarded themselves as above the normal rules of social conduct. They were often thieves like Iwa, who began his career of robbery while still in the womb. Later he was pitted against six master thieves in a contest to see who could fill a house completely with stolen goods in a single night. Iwa waited for the others to do all the work while he slept. He then woke up and stole all their recently acquired goods to fill his own house.

The trickster Ono is an example of multiple magic powers. He was born in an egg and fed on air. When slain, he brought himself back to life. He could stretch himself out as big as the sky, and then resume his normal size. Ono was also capable of breaking himself up into small pieces, and then reassembling himself.

Kaulu
Polynesian trickster god whose name means 'growth in plants'.

Kaulu stole cultivated plants from the gods, and killed *Haumea* by tossing her in a net. This is recalled in a yearly ceremony in which food is tossed in a net.

When Kaulu was born he looked like a piece of rope. His good brother put him on a high shelf out of reach of his evil brother, until such time as he acquired proper shape. Kaulu was fond of breaking things; he broke big waves into surf, and once broke a large dog into many little dogs. When his brother was swallowed by the king of sharks, Kaulu drank up the sea in order to rescue him. He then spat it all out again and his saliva made the sea salty.

Kaulu went to the gods' garden pretending to be a weakling. He pestered the gods to give him some plants. Eventually they became fed up with him and, believing he was weak, told him he could take whatever he could carry. The delighted Kaulu immediately dropped his pretence, gathered up every single plant in the garden, and marched away with them. In order to restock their garden the gods had to beg him for a specimen of each plant.

Kilibob
A trickster god.

In the absence of his older brother, Manumbu, the latter's wife persuaded Kilibob to tattoo her. Tattooing was usually performed on the genitals and therefore had erotic associations. When Manumbu discovered what had happened, he poured boiling water over his wife; she turned into a turtle and swam away. Then Manumbu asked Kilibob to help him build a house and carve its corner post. Kilibob carved a likeness of the unfaithful wife, and so his brother concluded he was guilty and decided to kill him. He waited till Kilibob was down in the post-hole, then dropped the massive post on top of him. Kilibob escaped by wriggling through an ant tunnel; he fled in his canoe to create new islands and people elsewhere.

Post-hole killings were not uncommon, for new houses were sanctified with blood. What usually happened was that the builders waited for the first stranger to arrive, killed him, and used his blood. Post-hole killings provided some justification for the murderers' action, the plea of ritual necessity being used to satisfy a personal grudge.

Koevasi
Melanesian snake goddess.

Koevasi was the ancestor of all the people of Florida Island in the Solomons. She supplied them with the necessities of life. Her speech was confused and halting, so when she gave the people their language each group heard something slightly different, and so each had its own dialect.

358

Kukalikimoku
Polynesian god of war. Red and yellow are his colours and he wears the crested feather helmet of Hawaii.

Kunapipi-Kalwadi-Kadjara
An Australian ogress.

Kunapipi used her daughters to ensnare young men whom she killed and consumed. She regurgitated them, but only bones appeared which meant they could not be revived. Regurgitation is usually a symbolic rebirth.

The mass disappearances became a problem, so Eaglehawk (*Yalungur*) went out to investigate. He caught Kunapipi and killed her. Kunapipi's dying shout entered every tree. Eaglehawk made a bull-roarer and swung it, giving her back her shout in the sound 'Mumuna'; this became her secret name.

In another myth Kunapipi was entrusted with nine children by some foolish person. She delightedly swallowed all nine whole and ran away. The men went out to search for her along the river bank. A certain murkiness in the water showed that she was there; then they saw her huge eyes break the surface of the water. The man called Lefthand speared her legs, and the man called Righthand broke her neck with his club. Kunapipi was still alive when they dragged her on land; but they killed her, cut her open, and recovered the children.

These stories are background to a revivification ceremony. Young men, trembling with fear, are taken to the ceremonial ground. They really believe that the Old Woman Kunapipi will swalow them up. They hear her voice, the bull-roarer, and are smeared with blood. After a symbolic swallowing they re-emerge and take their places in society as adults. (See *Wawalug*.)

Lightning Brothers
North Australian weather gods.

The Lightnings introduced the ritual of genital sub-incision They argued over a woman and the younger one was slain with an axe. Rock paintings of them show that they have no mouths; they have stripes on their bodies which represent rain, and possess horn-like projections on their heads.

359

Longorik and Longolap
Sons of the god *Aluluei*.

Their father gave them tuition in seamanship but the elder, Longo-lap, had just got married and his mind wasn't on his lessons. The brothers went out to cut down a tree to make a canoe, but every time they cut it, it joined itself up again. Longorik discovered that a small bird chirping nearby was really *Solang*, god of carpenters. Longorik asked for his help; Solang sent them off to the women who made sails while he built the canoe with the help of some ants. Longorik wanted to visit certain islands that his father had made. Aluluei agreed, but warned him about the dangerous spirits who lived there. He gave Longorik advice on how to evade their wiles: he was to wash in dirty water, and at night put bits of white coconut meat over his eyes so that the spirits would think he was awake and keep away. And he was to ask for Aluluei's magic stone.

Just as Longorik was about to depart, his elder brother appeared and insisted that he ought to be the first to sail the new canoe. He forced his younger brother out of the craft and set sail himself. Of course he had ignored all his father's instructions and had not heeded his words of warning. He arrived at his destination and did everything wrong. The cunning spirits crept in at night and walled him up at the end of the house. It fell to Longorik to rescue him. (See *Rongerik* and *Rongelap*.)

Lono and Laka
Lono was the Polynesian god to whom the first fruits were offered. Laka, his sister, was goddess of the wildwood. She was represented by a small cloth-covered block of wood.

Lono (Hawaii) is an aspect of Ono (Marquesas) and *Rongo* (New Zealand). He was god of agriculture in Hawaii, and god of singing in the Marquesas (his name means 'sound'). His colourful festival in Hawaii occupied five days of merrymaking, sports and wrestling, mock battles, processions with idols and feasts. The net of Maheola (in which *Kaulu* (*q.v.*) killed *Haumea*) was filled with food and shaken. If nothing remained caught in the net then a prosperous season was forecast. Lono founded the festival in the following way. He descended on a rainbow to look for a wife.

360

Having found one, he lived in conjugal bliss until he heard that she had been unfaithful to him; then he beat her to death. When Lono stopped to think about what he had done, he found he was truly sorry and instituted the games and feasts in her honour. Then he sailed away in a well-provisioned canoe, saying he would be back with a floating island loaded with goodies. When an unsuspecting Captain James Cook arrived, the island folk thought he was Lono.

Lowa
Micronesian creator god.

Lowa created the Marshall Islands by emitting the sound 'Mmmm'. He had a blood blister on his leg and from this emerged a girl and a boy; the first humans. Some say Lowa lived in the sea, others that he came from the sky.

Mahui-Ike
Polynesian goddess of fire and of the Underworld.

Mahui-Ike was tricked by the god *Maui* who stole fire from her. The familiarity of the Polynesian islanders with volcanic fire, bursting from the depths of the earth, will explain the linking of fire with the underworld. Volcanoes have female personalities (see *Pele*).

Makemake
Creator god of Easter Island; patron of the bird cult.

Makemake manifested himself as a skull and presided over the birds, driving them to a small islet to save their eggs from the gatherers. The first man to find an egg became 'Bird Man' for a year. His hair and eyebrows were shaved and he lived for twelve months in seclusion.

Mali
The Bat, elder brother of *Gidja*, the moon.

Mamandabari
Dreamtime (see *Ungud*) spirits of the Walbiri aborigines of Australia.

361

The Mamandabari introduced bull-roarers, sub-incision, pit digging, pole erection, fire and revelationary ceremonies. On their return home after distant wanderings, they were killed by wild dog-men.

Marawa
Melanesian spider god responsible for the introduction of death.

Marawa was the companion of the god *Qat*; he copied whatever Qat did but he always got things wrong. Qat made figures of wood; Marawa copied him but buried his figures in the earth and they rotted away. Qat was cutting down a tree to build a canoe. Every time he cut a chip, Marawa put it back again. But he had his uses. When Qat was being crushed in a hole, Marawa rescued him; and again, when Qat was stranded on a stretching tree (a tree that could be made to grow suddenly to an enormous height through magic), Marawa threw up to him his long white hair, down which his friend escaped.

Marruni
Melanesian god of earthquakes.

Marruni had a body ending in a tail. One day, while sunning himself, he was seen by his wives. They saw his tail for the first time and were horrified. He sent them away and cut his tail into bits; from the sections he made the various clans of mankind, and also animals.

Marunogere
Melanesian god who created the female sex; he also taught the Papuans to make longhouses.

Marunogere made a pig out of coconut and sago for a ceremony designed to make men great warriors. The pig escaped and then, as it was being recaptured, was accidentally killed. That meant that men would thereafter be subject to death. It also meant that Marunogere himself had to die. Before he died he created female sexuality by boring holes into the women. That night he waited and watched outside the longhouse. When the humans discovered their sexuality, the house rocked back and forth from their first

362

ecstatic embraces. Marunogere was then happy to die knowing that men would be regenerated.

Matuku Tago Tago

In Polynesian myth the shark who bit off the head of *Wahieroa*. The god hero *Rata* rescued his father's head from Matuku's belly. It was also Matuku Tago Tago who guided *Tahiti Tokerau* to the dwelling of *Puna*. (See *Rata*.)

Maui

The great Polynesian hero-god. The greatest of the tricksters, known as 'Maui of the thousand tricks', 'Maui super-superman'.

It was said that Maui's was a premature birth, that his mother wrapped him in a tuft of hair and cast him adrift. He was covered in a sort of jelly which saved him from becoming a malicious spirit. Tama, the sky, found him and hung him in the rafters to warm up. After a period of time, during which he grew fast and learnt even faster, Maui went in search of his family. He found them at a dance and when it was time to return home, tagged along and included himself in the headcount. Because he was incredibly ugly and because his mother favoured him, Maui's brothers hated him and called him 'the abortion'.

Maui was puzzled by the daily absence of his mother; he changed himself into a pigeon and followed her. She went into a cave and through an underground cavern to a garden, which she tended in company with her divine husband. Maui revealed himself; his father named him but omitted part of the ceremony, thus condemning his son to be mortal.

Maui got up to many a mean trick; he starved his grandmother to death to obtain her jawbone, which had magic powers. In those days the world was as yet unfinished. Maui worked on the side of mankind, trying to get them a better deal. The sky pressed down on the earth and the sun travelled too fast, hardly giving people time to do anything. Maui helped raise the sky and built wedges between it and the earth. He made a flaxen noose and snared the sun; then he beat it mercilessly with the magic jawbone to force it to travel more slowly across the sky. It did so and people were able to tend gardens, cook, and make cloth.

Maui went fishing, using his magic jawbone as a hook. He heaved up a gigantic fish and left it with his brothers while he went to give thanks. His foolish brothers did not wait for instructions but began cutting the fish; it squirmed violently. That is the reason for the unevenness of the New Zealand landscape, for the fish was of course a great island. When Maui returned, the great fish had been cut in two.

Maui arranged the stars and controlled the winds. Then he decided to acquire the gift of fire for mankind. *Mahui-Ike*, the ancient goddess of fire, kept the sacred flame in the Underworld. Maui went to her and requested fire for his oven. She pulled out one of her fingernails which contained fire and gave it to him. He took it away and extinguished it. Then he returned again and again for more, nineteen times in all. Only then did the old goddess realize that she was being tricked. She had only one toenail left. She threw it down furiously and the whole world caught fire. Maui turned himself into an eagle and flew up to escape the flames, but his feathers were singed; so nowadays eagles all have brown feathers. Maui called the rain and it dampened down the fire. As she scampered from the downpour, Mahui-Ike managed to throw a few sparks into some trees. Ever since that time man has got his fire from rubbing wood.

Maui was capable of less creative acts. Just for fun, he changed his brother-in-law into a dog. Maui's wife took a lover, Ri. Maui turned him into a dog as well, not because he was angry or jealous but because his wife paid so much attention to Ri that Maui wasn't getting his meals on time.

Maui's father, despite the fact he knew Maui was mortal, persuaded him to challenge the great goddess of the night, Hine Nui Te Po (*Hina, q.v.*), in order to gain immortality for the whole of mankind. He told Maui what she looked like: hair like seaweed, eyes like red fire, mouth like a barracuda's, sharp teeth, human body. Maui found her asleep. He told his companions, a company of small birds, of the trick he intended to play on her. He would crawl between her legs, enter her body, and climb all the way up inside her and come out of her mouth. He warned them not to laugh until his peculiarly insulting and quixotic journey was over; for if they did, he would die. He took off his clothes and pushed himself between the spread thighs of the sleeping goddess.

Soon only his legs were visible. The birds held their sides in an agony of suppressed mirth at the sight. It was too ridiculous. At last the wagtail could no longer contain himself; he let out a thin giggle. Just one, just a tiny one. But it was enough. Hine awoke and Maui was crushed to death inside her. Ever since then men have been subject to death.

Mesede
Melanesian god of archery.

When Mesede's bow was drawn it would cause fire. He is linked with the terrible goddess *Abere*. He rescued her son from a crocodile and then abducted her daughters. Abere recovered them and, true to character, killed them. She threw the headless body of the youngest and most beautiful girl into the sea. There it hardened, and was later washed ashore where the flies hollowed it out. The spirit Morave took the remains, covered the ends with skin, and made a ceremonial drum called *dibiri*.

Mimi
Alternatively Mini. These charming Australian spirits have such long, brittle bones that they will not go out in the wind for fear their legs or necks will snap. They eat men, and yams.

Morkul Kua Luan
Australian Spirit of the Long Grass. He watched over the wild sorghum which the aborigines use to make meal.

Motikitik
Melanesian hero god. A version of *Maui*.

Motikitik discovered that his mother was getting food from the Underworld; as a result of his discovery death was let loose on earth. He fished up baskets of food from under the sea. Then he fished up the island of Fais. His fishing-hook fell into the hands of the islanders of Yap. This is the origin of the tribute paid by Fais to Yap, for if the hook were ever destroyed or lost then Fais would sink back into the sea.

Munga Munga
Daughters of *Kunapipi* (*q.v.*).

Nakaa

Gilbertese god. Guardian of the tree of life and of the inexhaustible fish-trap.

One day Nakaa discovered that the men and women had touched the tree of life. He took it away, along with the wonderful fish-trap, telling mankind that death had come among them. He then wove a net and sat at the door of the spirit world. As the newly-dead arrived, he netted them. The good people were allowed to join their ancestors, the bad were left to struggle for ever in the meshes of the net.

Nareau

'Spider'; the name for a pair of Micronesian creator-trickster deities. They were father and son, Old Spider and Young Spider.

Young Spider shaped the world with the help of numerous creatures, including the eel and octopus. He set four women at the corners of the sky to hold it up. He crumbled his father's brain and scattered handfuls of it into the sky to make the stars. From his father's flesh he made rocks and soil; from his spine he made the Kai-n-tiku-aba, the 'Tree of the resting-place of lands'. From the branches of this tree came men, called 'The Breed of Matang'. These first men lived in Matang ('paradise'). Nareau, Young Spider, threw flowers down from the tree and they became the islands of the Gilbert chain.

It is said that he was a god without trees or property and so was compelled to wander about the earth, living on his wits. He escaped from an attempted post-hole murder: being used as a blood sacrifice to sanctify a new house was a constant risk of travelling, for people preferred to use strangers as their victims.

Nareau was once challenged to an exchange of food; this custom was a mark of social status. Being without property, he got the ants to pick up crumbs for him. He made up the weight of the food parcel with excrement. At the ceremony he calmly arrived, presented his contribution, sat down and consumed all the food the others had brought. When their turn came to open his package they discovered his foul trick. They were so disgusted that they chased after him angrily. As he ran away Nareau dropped sharp stones, shells, and spiny sea urchins to delay his pursuers. He got clean away.

Ndengei
Fiji serpent god with stone flesh.

Ndengei sent his son Rokomotu to make the land by scraping it up from the sea bed. Then he laid and hatched two eggs; a boy and a girl emerged. Ndengei gave them yams, bananas, and fire.

When Ndengei slept it was night. Then his black dove woke him and it became daylight. The days were far too long for the taste of his nephews. They were boatbuilders and the long days tired them out. They shot the dove in annoyance. Ndengei responded with torrential rain, and the boatbuilders were swept away. They were separated by the floods and distributed among different peoples and tribes. Thus Ndengei punished them while at the same time spreading the craft of boatbuilding to many more communities. When Ndengei turns over his coils there are earthquakes.

Nevinbimbaau
A terrible Melanesian ogress, connected with *Ambat*.

During the initiation ceremonies of Nevinbimbaau's cult her voice could be heard in the bull-roarers. Part of the ritual consisted of a sort of puppet show which included the ceremonial creation and sacrifice of Nevinbimbaau's son-in-law and two wives.

Ngunung Ngunnut
The Bat. Australian totemic deity who created sexuality by turning his companion into a woman.

Ngurunderi, Nurrundere
Aliases for *Daramulun* (*q.v.*).

Nogomain
Australian giver of spirit children, thought to be a vague concept of a supreme being.

Nuga
Melanesian crocodile god.

Nuga made the winding estuaries by lashing his tail in anger at the discovery of his wife's unfaithfulness. He was first made in human form by a god called Ipila, who carved him from a tree. He made the carving live by painting its face with sago milk. Nuga then urged Ipila to create for him three companions. Ipila complied, but the four men began to ignore his teachings. They started killing animals for food instead of preparing sago, and as a result began to look like crocodiles. The half-men tried to create more of their own kind, but Ipila stopped them. He grew so angry with them that he allowed them to become totally crocodile, and condemned Nuga to carry the earth on his shoulders.

Numbakulla
Australian sky gods who came down and made men from the formless *Inapatua*.

Nyungu
Australian totemic ancestor, the pigeon.

Nyungu's daughter was stolen by *Sivri*, the seagull, and taken in the direction of Mabuiag. Before Nyungu left in search of them, he changed his children into ducks and seashells.

Olifat
Micronesian trickster god. Grandson of the sky god *Anulap*.

Born from his mother's head, Olifat was precocious and fast-growing. He was ordered never to drink from the small hole of a coconut, but one day he did. He had to tip back his head and in so doing he saw his father in heaven. Immediately he wanted to visit him. He ascended to heaven on a column of smoke and found there a group of children playing with scorpion fish, sharks and stingrays, who were all harmless creatures at that time. The children refused to allow him to join in their games, so Olifat spitefully gave sharp spines, teeth and stings to the creatures.

The people in heaven were building a house for the spirits of the dead. Olifat helped to dig the post-hole. As he was working down in the hole, he dug out a special sheltering place for himself; for he didn't like the look of the people above him. True to his suspicions, they had decided he would be a suitable sacrifice and rammed the post down on top of him. Olifat crouched in his dugout and spat out a mouthful of red earth. The people thought it was his blood. Then he squirted out a mouthful of chewed leaves, and the people thought the greenish fluid was from his digestive tract. As the people filled in the hole, Olifat enlisted the help of termites; he tunnelled his way up inside the post and reached the rafters. He shouted out, and the men below were terrified to see him grinning down at them from the roof.

Olifat played a constant variety of unpleasant tricks on people. He often soiled food and drink, ruined fishing trips, seduced men's wives, even those of his relatives. He introduced the habit of tattooing, a practice with erotic associations.

Olifat discovered that he had a brother who every night left a gift of fish for their father. Olifat thought up a good trick: he waylaid his brother, killed him, and cut off his head. He left the head in the place of the usual fish. His father brought the lad back to life and shouted angrily at Olifat, who assumed an expression of childish innocence.

Oro
Maori god of war. Son of *Ta'aroa*, he is also known as a peace god, being called 'Oro-of-the-laid-down-spear'.

Palulop
Great sea god and canoe captain of Micronesia; father of *Aluluei* and founder of an important divine family (Aluluei, *Rongerik*, *Rongelap*, *Faravai*).

Pani
A vegetation goddess

Pani, in the form of a mortal woman, figures in the story of the giving of kumara (sweet potato) to the Maoris. *Rongo-Maui* stole the kumara from the star Whahuni. He concealed it in his loincloth, and when he returned to earth he slept with his wife and impregnated her with it. Pani gave birth to kumara in a stream. When she eventually fled to the Underworld, she continued to cultivate kumara there.

Papa
Polynesian earth goddess.

369

Papa was the consort of *Rangi*, the Sky Father. Clasped together in a tight and eager embrace they annoyed the gods, their children, who were compressed into the dark space between the two lovers. The gods became restless; they wanted more elbow room, more light. Some said they should kill Papa and Rangi to separate them. There was a fierce argument, then each god tried to prise the couple apart. *Rongo*, *Tangaroa*, *Haumia*, *Tu* all tried and failed. Then *Tane* placed his shoulders on his mother and, pressing with his legs, gradually pushed his parents apart, deaf to their entreaties. *Tawhiri*, god of winds, was distraught at this treatment of his parents and tried to stop Tane with storms and tempests. Some of the sea creatures fled to the swamps, and this annoyed Tangaroa who lost subjects to his brother Tane. Ever since then they have been enemies. There was battle among the gods, but Rangi and Papa were separated and remained so. Even now he cries for her with rain, and she sighs for him in the mists that rise from the earth.

Pele
Hawaiian goddess of volcanic fire; a personification of the female power of destruction.

A great voyager, Pele arrived from Tahiti, looking for a place to stay. She was washed out of several locations until she burrowed deep into Mount Kilauea, a volcano on Hawaii. Goddess of sorcery and the hula, she constantly maltreated people (see *Ha'iaka* and *Kamapua'a*). Pele's altars were erected beside lava streams, though only those who claimed family descent from her worshipped her.

Porpoise Girl
Micronesian supernatural being

The Porpoise Girl came from the sea at night to watch men dancing, leaving her tail hidden in the rocks. One night a man saw marks on the sand and found it. He took the tail, without which the Porpoise Girl was unable to return home. She married the man, set up house, and had children. One day she discovered her tail hidden in the roof; putting it on, she warned her children never to eat porpoise meat, and then returned to the sea.

Puna
Polynesian god.

He is involved as the guilty party in the revenge story centering about the god *Rata*.

Puntan
Micronesian god who existed before earth and sky. When he died the world was created out of parts of his body.

Qat
Local Melanesian god (Banks Islands) to whom were appended several *Maui*-style trickster tales.

Qat was accompanied in his adventures by a spider. He had eleven brothers and all of them were called Tangaro. Qat fished up the land, made men and women from wood, and charmed them to life by dancing to the beat of a drum. His companion and spider friend *Marawa* (*q.v.*) copied him, but got things wrong, introducing death into the world through his incompetence. Qat was born when his mother, a stone, suddenly burst asunder. Having created all living things, plants, animals, trees and men, he last of all made woman. He made a frame of rods and hoops and covered it with cloth from the sago palm. This very same method of modelling is still used to make ceremonial hats for his festivals.

Qat made a great canoe with sundry interruptions from Marawa. His brothers had grown exhausted by the perpetual daylight which surrounded them, so Qat sailed off to visit I Qong, Night. He bartered with Night and exchanged a pig for nighttime. Night taught him how to sleep and how to make dawn. Qat returned with night-time, birds and roosters. He told his brothers to make beds, then he set night-time going. The sun descended obediently; his brothers were terrified and Qat had to soothe them. He gave them a yawn by yawn commentary on how to fall asleep. The brothers slept. When night-time had run its course the birds began to twitter and the roosters began to crow. Qat took a blade of hard red obsidian, reached up and cut through the mantle of night. Daylight came flooding back again.

Qat finally left his human creations. He entered his canoe which was loaded with all sorts of good things. The canoe, which had been built inshore, tore a passage for itself across the land to the sea. Qat sailed away, but men said that he would return one day with good things for them. When white men first appeared, people believed that Qat had at last come back.

Rangi
Polynesian sky god.

Rangi joined with *Papa* (*q.v.*), Earth Mother, to produce the gods. Their embrace was passionate and long-lasting until the gods, fed up with their cramped quarters between sky and earth, separated them. His aliases are Atea Rangi and *Atea*, meaning 'great expanse of sky'.

Rata
Polynesian hero god. Alias Laka; grandson of *Tawhaki*, son of *Tahiti Tokerau* and *Wahieroa*.

Rata's stories are sometimes confused with those of his grandfather and sometimes with those of *Hina* (*q.v.*). His character was honest, impulsive and brash. While playing with other children, he learnt about his father who had been killed and dismembered by *Puna*. With the enchanted axe of Kui (a bird spirit), the 'Great Axe of Hibiscus Wood', he determined to make a canoe and sail to avenge his father. But every time he cut down a tree it was mysteriously lifted up again. Rata hid nearby to see what was causing this phenomenon, and saw that it was some spirits who were charming the tree back to life. He was so angry that he shouted out from his hiding-place, and the spirits fell over in fright. Rata came forward and spoke to them, explaining what he wanted to do with the tree. The spirits decided that justice was on his side so they built the canoe for him in a single night, transporting it to him on a rainbow. With the spirits crewing for him, Rata sailed to the Land of the Moonlight Border where the gods agreed to support him.

Rata set off to find his father with Kui flying above the canoe as a bird, keeping watch for Puna's sea demons. Rata met and destroyed these demons, who appeared as a shark, a swordfish, and a giant clam. He cut up the monsters, retrieved his father's dissected body, and carefully put the bits into a cloth-lined basket. Now he turned his attention towards Puna.

As Rata approached Puna's island, a reef magically rose from the sea to protect it. Rata smashed a way through the reef with the enchanted axe. Puna was asleep; his lizard guards attacked Rata and the roosters called out a warning. But Rata lassoed his enemy, dragged him to the canoe, and hacked him to bits. On the island he found his mother, who had been blinded and held captive by Puna. He restored her sight and then returned home.

Riiki and Rigi
The first means 'eel', the second 'worm'.

In Micronesia the raising of the sky was performed by one of these two creatures, depending on local tradition, and not by a primal god (*e.g. Tane*). Riiki was set to raise the sky by *Nareau*, who encouraged him by chanting. Riiki lifted and strained, and was successful. But exhausted by the incredible effort, he forthwith expired. He was cast up into the sky and became the Milky Way, while his severed legs fell into the ocean to become eels. In the Rigi version of the story the severed legs become worms.

Rongerik and Rongelap
Divine brothers and eponymous gods of two of the Marshall Islands in Micronesia.

They belonged to the sea-faring family of gods founded by *Palulop*. Rongerik, or 'small cheeks', may be identified with *Longorik* of Ifaluk and Little Rong of the Carolines. His brother, Rongelap, is paralleled by *Longolap* of Ifaluk and Big Rong of the Carolines.

Rongo
Polynesian god of cultivated foods.

Rongo was first of the gods to try and separate *Rangi* ('sky') and *Papa* ('earth') from their blissful embrace (see *Papa*). He and his brother *Haumia* hid themselves inside Papa, while the other gods joined in a furious mêlée of violent dissension over the separation. Rongo was favoured by Papa; she suggested that all red foods should be sacred and should belong to *Tangaroa*. This meant that all the other foods would belong to Rongo, so Tangaroa had to leave and look for new possessions elsewhere.

Rongo's name means 'sound', and he was represented by a great shell, The Resounder. His aliases are Ono and *Lono* (his Hawaiian name). Maoris often represented their gods in godsticks - long carved pieces of wood bound with twine. Rongo's godstick was used by the priests to sanctify planting. The stick, attached to a string, was thrust into the ground. The priest chanted prayers and requests to the god, attracting the latter's attention by tugging on the string. On the Gambier Islands the rainbow was Rongo's symbol, for it heralded the rain needed to nourish the crops.

Ru
Alias 'Ru who explored the earth'; a minor Polynesian god, brother of the goddess *Hina*.

Rua
'The abyss', god of craftsmen

In Tahitian myth Rua tried to separate earth and sky by putting death spells on the great spotted octopus which held them together. He managed to kill the octopus (Tumu-Ra'i-Fuena, 'foundation of earthly heaven') but it still would not release its hold.

Rua invented wood-carving. Once he invited the great god *Tangaroa* to his house. Tangaroa saw two men waiting to greet him; he rubbed noses with the first, then stopped in surprise. Rua appeared, laughing, for the two men were really wood-carvings he had made.

Sido
Melanesian hero-god, alias Hido, Iko.

Sido's beautiful wife Sagaru was abducted by a rival who used a magical stretching tree (a tree that could be made to grow suddenly to an enormous height through the use of a magic spell), to carry her off. Sido fought the abducter, but was killed. He tried to enter the Otherworld but his way was barred by bats, flying foxes, and great thickets of tangled vine. He was forced to wander about the earth as a spirit, and got up to many a low trick, including molesting women and children.

Sido turned himself into a seashell and was swallowed by twins who were joined to each other by their backs. The twins, both women, gave birth to him, and he cut them apart. To avoid death he would change his skin, sloughing off the old one. Whilst doing this he was observed by two children, and the fact that they had seen him meant he would die. He expired, and the now separated twins buried him, keeping his skull as a memento. Sido's spirit travelled west, and each of his resting places became stations on the journey that all souls must make to Adiri, the land of the dead. On his journey, the two women who had given him his second life caught up with him. They gave him a drink from his own skull. This was a spell to ensure he remained dead. In Adiri, Sido planted crops to feed the dead souls. He turned himself into a giant pig, then split open his stomach so that his body became a great house, his spine forming the ridge pole and his flanks the walls. And so his sad wanderings came to an end.

Siho I Salo
A demon from the Solomon Islands.

Siho I Salo had ears like giant pandanus leaves. He would wrap himself in one and lie on the other when he slept. He came from the sky in a rainstorm and approached two fishermen. He ate up whatever they caught. The fishermen got fed up with that and, pretending to fetch more bait, they left. Siho I Salo waited about for quite a while, not realizing he had been duped. He went off after the fishermen and found them in a boathouse, where they were holding an emergency meeting with all the other men. He wandered in, settled himself down, and then ate all the food in sight.

One of the men happened to be a sorcerer, and put a sleeping spell on the demon. Siho I Salo gave a great yawn, unfolded his ears, wrapped himself up, and dozed off. The men fled, barricading the path to the village. Siho I Salo woke up and shambled off; he found himself in the sorcerer's garden, and made himself a nest among the plants before dozing off again. The sorcerer dreamed that the demon was in his garden. He visited Siho I Salo, fed him on raw pork and made a deal with him. The demon agreed to stay in the garden and protect it against ghosts.

375

Sivri
The seagull, Australian totemic deity.

Sivri came from the north and possessed a drum, bow and arrows. As Kwoiam, he was famous for his seagull dances and his spear.

Solang
Micronesian god of carpenters.

He appeared to *Longorik* in the shape of a bird, and organized the building of his canoe with the help of some ants.

Ta'aroa
Creator god of Polynesia; he is linked to the sea god *Tangaroa*.

Ta'aroa existed before creation in an egg which floated on the primal darkness. He may be regarded as darkness personified and from him evolved *Atea* ('light', 'sky'). Some say he created the world and that the effort made him perspire quantities of moisture, thus creating the oceans.

There is a hint of the destructive about Ta'aroa, for as soon as the universe was created, he set fire to it. The fire was put out by three men who hastened to the blaze from earth.

Tahiti Tokerau
Goddess wife of *Wahieroa* and mother of *Rata*.

Both she and her husband fell under the power of *Puna*; Wahieroa was murdered and dismembered and Tahiti Tokerau was blinded and kept captive. She was rescued by her son, the hero god Rata.

Take
Not a god, nor anything created. Take is the 'Root-of-all-existence'; it is the point from which everything in the universe is nourished.

Tane
Maori god of forests and craftsmen.

Tane brought knowledge to earth in three baskets; the priestly schools symbolized this by teaching three strata of learning. He

was also responsible for separating *Rangi* ('sky') and *Papa* ('earth'),
pushing them apart with his feet (see *Papa*). *Ta'aroa'*s craftsmen
fashioned him into a handsome boy, and Ta'aroa exalted him to
his own heavenly dwelling. Tane bored through Atea (the 'great
expanse of sky') to let daylight through to men. As Tane 'the
chirper' and Tane 'the artisan', he was invoked by all who used
wood. In search of a wife, he turned first to Papa, but she rejected
him; as was only right and proper since she was his mother. He
mated with several different beings, but their children were
streams, snakes, grass, and stones; an unsatisfactory state of affairs. So Tane made a woman out of sandstone; he breathed life
into her and she awoke with a sneeze. Their daughter was Hina
Titama, the dawn maiden. Tane took her as his wife; when she
found out that he was her father she ran away to Po, the dark
underworld, and became Hine Nui Te Po, great goddess of death
(see *Hina*).

Tangaloa

Polynesian original god, predating *Rangi* and *Papa*. In other places
he is merely one of the gods, alias *Tangaroa* or *Ta'aroa*.

Tangaroa

Great Polynesian god of the sea; father of fishes and reptiles; god of
carpenters and housebuilders (the first house having been built in
heaven).

Tangaroa was involved in constant warfare with his brother *Tane*,
the forest god. They argued at every chance, destroying each
other's offspring at every meeting. The sea swallowed canoes of
wood, while wooden fish-hooks account for the death of sea
creatures. Tangaroa's children, the fish, are also trapped in nets
provided by flax grown by Tane.

After the separation of *Rangi* ('sky') and *Papa* ('earth') there
were storms and tumults, ending with the sea covering everything.
Tangaroa had the task of recreating the world. In some parts of
Polynesia he is regarded as the sole creator god, emerging alone
from an egg. He made everything, including the other gods. In
other traditions he was the eldest son of Rangi and Papa, or of
Atea and Papa.

Tawhaki
Polynesian god of thunder and lightning.

Tawhaki was noble and handsome, his gleaming red skin a sign of his divine nature. He was so attractive that women grew faint with love when they looked on him. His jealous rivals planned to ruin his beautiful skin. They proposed a diving competition. When it was Tawhaki's turn to dive his rivals turned themselves into fish; they waited under the water and attacked him, tearing off his skin in long shreds. But Tawhaki's grandmother had guessed their plan, and she collected the bits of skin from under the waves. She stuck it all back on to him, but then discovered that there wasn't enough to cover the soles of his feet: the stick insects had stolen some of the skin to put under their arms.

Tawhaki's cousins, the children of *Puna*, hated him because he won all the toy boat races. They beat him up and left him for dead on the beach. Tawhaki recovered and returned home. Seeing he was alive and not too bothered, the cousins began taunting him about his father, Hema. He learnt from them that his father had unwittingly trespassed on the lands of the goblins. The goblins had gouged out his eyes and thrown him into a cesspit. Daylight was fatal to goblins, so they used Hema's eyes as lights at night-time. Tawhaki learnt all this from his tormentors. Pausing only to turn the little beasts into porpoises, he went in search of his father; he rescued him from the cesspit and replaced his eyes. Tawhaki then devised an elegant little plan to trap the goblins. He crept up to their hut and stopped up all the chinks. The goblins woke up, thinking that night had come; but it was really day outside. They were thus trapped in the house, and Tawhaki slew them.

Tawhaki's wife was a goddess. After an argument she went home to mother, and Tawhaki determined to go to heaven and fetch her back. Accompanied by his stupid brother Kariki, he encountered his grandmother, who was blind and guarded the loose vine that led to heaven. She was counting out taro roots to cook. Tawhaki could not resist playing a joke on her. As she counted the roots, he stole them. The bewildered old woman lashed about her with her huge fish-hook and snared Tawhaki. He touched her eyes, restoring her sight. She recognized him and agreed to help him reach heaven. The trick was to climb the vine and swing it in the right direction. Kariki climbed the vine but swung it the wrong way; he was sent home in disgrace. Then Tawhaki got up to heaven and retrieved his wife.

Tawhiri
Polynesian god of storms and winds.

Tawhiri was the only god who was upset at the thought of separating *Rangi* ('sky') and *Papa* ('earth'). He clung to his father, Rangi, and plotted revenge on his brothers, sending squalls, whirlwinds, and hurricanes against them. He wrecked the forests and lashed at the sea, panicking the sea creatures and driving many of them into the marshes, and onto land.

Tilitr
God of song on Ifaluk.

Tilitr enters men and women, causing them to compose songs. In other parts of Oceania men go fishing for new songs. They throw their lines into the sea, and when they feel it moving they are inspired to chant the music.

Tinirau
'Infinite'; god of sea creatures in Polynesia.

Tinirau restocked the oceans from his fish ponds. The whales and sharks were his messengers. Tinirau had two bodies; his divine one was fish-like, his human body handsome and charming. He sometimes had two faces, for he was both benign and sinister. As the good-looking heart-throb, he takes the romantic lead in several stories which involve an adolescent maiden named Hina. Her sexual longings for him were overshadowed by fear, for Tinirau, lord of the ocean, 'The Engulfer', was capable of sudden violence, swallowing people by the boatload. In most of the stories he courts Hina, who rejects him through fear but then relents, going off in search of him.

Tinirau had a pet whale, a marvellous creature who provided delicious steaks without seeming any the worse for it. To honour the priest, Kae, who had officiated at the ceremony of naming his son, Tinirau served meat from this whale. It was so tasty that the priest plotted to get more. He begged to be carried home on the animal. Tinirau generously agreed. The priest repaid this kindness by having the whale killed and cooked. The mouth-watering smell of the cooking meat wafted over the sea to Tinirau, whose suspicions were aroused. He sent a troupe of dancing girls to investigate; they had been told they would recognize Kae by his crooked teeth. The girls arrived at the feast, and danced and sang comic songs so that everyone laughed. Kae held his hand over his mouth when he laughed, but the girls continued their clowning until even he forgot his embarrassment and joined in the abandoned glee. He revealed his teeth, his identity, and his guilt all in one go; for the girls saw between his crooked teeth the telltale shreds of roast whale meat. That night the girls caused an enchanted sleep to fall on the people; then they formed a long line to the shore and passed the sleeping Kae along it to the waiting canoe. He was taken back to Tinirau. Distraught at the loss of his beloved pet whale, Tinirau declared that Kae would suffer the same fate. The deceitful priest was killed and eaten.

Tjilpa
Ancestral totemic cat-men of Australia. They introduced circumcision, genital sub-incision, and ordeal by fire to the aborigines.

Tjinimin
'The Bat'. Australian totemic ancestor.

Tjinimin lusted after the women (called the Green Parrot Girls) who were the sexual companions of the *Great Rainbow Snake* (*q.v.*). He made an excuse to follow them into the bush when they went to search for food. There he forced them to submit to his desires. The next day he followed them again, intending to enjoy them once more. They waited until he approached them across a river, then charmed a flight of bees to attack him. Then the river rose at their command and swept him out to sea. After a while Tjinimin managed to make his way to land, catching sight of the girls who had lit a fire on a clifftop. They agreed to haul him up, but just as he reached the top, they cut the rope. He fell, smashing his bones on the rocks below. Tjinimin believed he could mend his broken bones with magic. But he tested the magic first by cutting off his nose and replacing it. Then he cured himself. Realizing his power, he determined to kill his father, the Great Snake. He made a spear, hid it, and invited everyone to a great ceremony. There was food, drink, music and dancing. At the climax of the dance, he produced the spear and stabbed the Great Snake. All the dancers turned into birds and flew up into the sky. Tjinimin fled.

The Great Snake was badly hurt, and staggered from place to place, trying to staunch his wound. At every stopping place a spring welled up in sympathy with his gushing blood; he left his footprints on the rocks and all his possessions were scattered in his wake. In mortal agony the Great Snake collected all the fire in the world, put it on his headband, and walked into the sea. There was general panic, for all the fire was about to disappear. The last brand was snatched. Too late; it had gone out. There was no more fire! The world would have been without fire forever had it not been for Pilirin, the kestrel. He invented firesticks and passed the knowledge on to men.

To Kabinana, To Karvuvu
Melanesian brother hero-gods.

Of miraculous birth, they set to and began to create women for themselves. They used coconuts, the best raw material they could find. They threw the nuts down from the trees and To Karvuvu, the stupid one of the pair, carelessly let his coconuts hit the ground hairy-end first. The women who emerged from these nuts were ugly creatures with flattened noses. To Kabinana's women, on the other hand, were deliciously beautiful, for he had made sure that his coconuts struck the ground with their 'eye' end. To Karvuvu had the brilliant idea of making something to help him with his fishing. He designed a fast creature with sharp teeth, the shark. He didn't think that the shark would hunt men as well as fish!

The mother of these two gods was a wonderful creature who avoided mortality by the simple expedient of shedding her old skin, appearing once more young and healthy. When To Karvuvu saw her like that for the first time, he was scared and burst into tears, for he didn't recognize her. To pacify him and stop him blubbering, the mother put the old wrinkled skin back on. Ever since then men have been unable to shed their old skins, and so are condemned to die through To Karvuvu's stupidity.

Toru
Polynesian god of the chasms of the deep. He was appointed to paint the fish and the seashells.

Tu
Polynesian god of war. His names include 'Tu of the angry face', 'Tu the lover of war', 'Tu the man-eater', 'Tu of the narrow face'.

Tu suggested killing *Rangi* ('sky') and *Papa* ('earth') to separate them. In the battle which followed the separation he was deserted by his brothers, and took his revenge on them in various ways. He snared the birds of *Tane's* forests, netted the fishes of *Tangaroa's* seas, pulled up the children of *Haumia* and *Rongo* (cultivated and uncultivated plants) by their hair (leaves) and left them to dry out in the sun. He learnt many secret formulae and spells with which to control his brothers. His name means 'to stand' or 'to strike', and he is therefore associated with stability as well as war. He accepted human sacrifices and is the founder of the Ku family of Hawaiian war gods, of whom the most horrific is 'Ku with the maggot dropping mouth'.

Tudava
Trobriand culture-hero.

Like most miraculous children, Tudava grew with astonishing rapidity. His first task was to kill the ogre that had terrorized the land. Then he wandered about, teaching the people the skills of agriculture. Those that received him well were well rewarded, which explains why some crops grow successfully in some areas and fail in others. He created islands by throwing stones into the sea.

Tumbrenjak
Papuan original man.

Tumbrenjak climbed down to earth from heaven in order to hunt and fish. On his return, he found that the rope was cut. He wept and his wife, looking down from the sky, also wept. To help him survive, she threw down fire, fruit and vegetables, including four large cucumbers. Tumbrenjak built a house, and then went off hunting. When he came back he saw that all the housework had been done, and he heard laughter. In his absence the four cucumbers had turned into women.

Tuna

Polynesian eel-lover of *Hina*; from his severed head sprang the coconut palm.

'Tuna-of-the-eternal-waters' was so fearsome a paramour that when Hina tired of him she could not find a replacement; everyone was afraid of Tuna and would have nothing to do with Hina as a result. Then along came *Maui*, more attracted by Hina than deterred by Tuna. He was pursued by Tuna, who came speeding over the breakers. They agreed to fight. Tuna sent three huge waves crashing towards Maui. He resisted the first on his feet, the second knocked him to his knees, and the third nearly overwhelmed him; he had to clutch at his sacred coral slab to save himself. Tuna came in for the kill, riding like a surf champion on a mighty crest. Maui threw his sacred coral up the beach. Tuna grabbed at it, and before he knew it he was stranded high and dry. Before he could recover his wits and wriggle back to the safety of the sea, Maui sauntered over and chopped him up into little bits.

Ungud

The Australian Dreamtime, a previous age in which totemic ancestors shaped the earth and founded the rituals of life. Also called Wongar.

Vari or Vari Ma Te Takere

Polynesian: 'The beginning and the bottom'. Also means 'mud'.

Vari was a primeval self-existent being who dwelt at the bottom of the vast coconut shell which contained the universe. She produced the gods by plucking them from her side. Below her was *Take*, the universal root, and above her were ranged the gods and men.

Wahieroa
Polynesian hero-god. Son of *Tawhaki* and father of the famous *Rata*.

Like his grandfather, Hema, Wahieroa was also destined to be captured, thus providing his own son with the opportunity of saving him and making a great reputation (see *Rata*).

Walutahanga
Melanesian spirit who was born to a mortal woman as a female snake. Her name means 'eight fathoms'.

Walutahanga was hidden from her father, who never saw her. When another child was born to her mother, Walutahanga was set to watch the baby. Her father happened to pass nearby and, hearing her sing a lullaby, peered through the undergrowth. Shocked at what he saw, he leapt forward and chopped her into eight bits. After eight days of rain, Walutahanga was joined together again. She turned nasty and began to eat people; so she was killed and chopped up once more into eight pieces. Then she was cooked, and everyone stopped by to help eat her up. Everyone, that is, except one woman and her child.

But you can't keep a good spirit down, or a bad one either. Walutahanga's bones came together yet again, and she returned to life. She conjured eight huge waves which came crashing over the village, destroying it utterly and drowning everyone. Everyone, that is, except the woman and child who had not partaken of the snake hotpot. Walutahanga looked after these two; she gave them fresh water, yams, taro, and coconut, and ended up being their guardian spirit.

Waramurungundju
Alias *Imberombera*, 'the Mother-who-made-us-all'.

Warohunugamwanehaora
Melanesian hero figure, sometimes called 'Delectable Lizard'.

Warohunugamwanehaora was the youngest of a band of brothers, and was a constant annoyance to them on account of his pert cleverness. They were infuriated beyond endurance and decided to make a new house, using him as the necessary blood-sacrifice. They tried the old post-hole murder routine. (See *Kilibob*.) After ramming the post down on him, they heard his voice – and there he was, grinning at them from the top of the post. Later they tempted him to expose himself to various dangers – a giant clam, a man-eating fish, a huge boar – and left him to his fate. But he was always waiting for them when they arrived home, as cheeky as ever. After several more attempts to get rid of him, he actually reacted. He killed the eldest brother just as a gentle warning to the others.

Wawalug
A pair of fertility goddesses of North Australia.

The Wawalug arrived from the south and were guilty, it was said, of incest. One had a child and the other was pregnant, soon giving birth to a baby girl. In error they set up their camp by a waterhole sacred to Yurlunggur, the *Great Rainbow Snake* (*q.v.*). They made a fire and tried to cook a meal; but everything, be it animal or plant, which they placed on the fire immediately jumped off and plunged into the waterhole. The food had taken on the sacred nature of the place.

One of the Wawalug then unwittingly profaned the waterhole with blood. The pool welled up into flood; rain cascaded down and the great snake of water advanced on them. The Wawalug kept the flood away by singing and dancing, but after many hours of this, and utterly exhausted, they fell asleep. The snake advanced on them, and the sisters and their two children were swallowed up. Yurlunggur then went into the sky where all the other Great Rainbow Snakes were collected. The snakes were talking about what they had recently had to eat. Yurlunggur was ashamed to admit that he had just consumed two women and their children. He threw himself back to earth, splitting the ground as he landed, and spewed out the humans, who were then revived by the bites of ants. The Great Snake then swallowed and regurgitated the Wawalug several times, each time marking out a new sacred spot for future ceremonies.

These ceremonies dramatize the acts of swallowing and re-gurgitation which symbolize the rebirth of children into adults.

The Great Snake is linked to the Great Mother, whose voice is heard in the bull-roarer and whose name is 'Mumuna'. (See *Kunapipi*.)

Wollunqua
The Warramunga name for the *Great Rainbow Snake* of Australia.

Rising from a waterhole, Wollunqua travelled many, many miles; but he was so long that part of him still remained in the hole. It is said that Mumumanugara, a man, emerged from the snake's body and struck him, trying to make him return to the waterhole; so the Great Snake coiled round the man and complied with his wishes. The Warramunga still make ground paintings of this event for use in initiation ceremonies.

Wondjina
The primal beings of the Dreamtime (see *Ungud*) in Australia. Among them are Warana, 'the eaglehawk'; Wodoi, 'the rock pigeon'; Djunggun, 'the owl'; Walangada, 'he who belongs in the sky'.

Wondjina are shown in rock paintings. They are human in shape. They lie on their sides, their heads are haloed, they have no mouths, and their eyes and noses are joined. Like the *Great Rainbow Snake*, they produce both rain and spirit children.

Wuraka
Australian god and companion of the mother creatress *Imberombera*, with whom he came walking out of the sea.

Wuraka had a penis so long and heavy that he was obliged to carry it slung round his neck. A large rock named 'Tor Rock' marks the spot on land where he sat down to rest, no doubt tired out by his burden. Let that be a lesson to us all.

Yalungur
'Eaglehawk'; also called Warana; a totem ancestor of Australia.

Yalungur figures in several stories about the Dreamtime (*Ungud*), that mythical era in which the primal beings shaped the earth and created the rituals that men inherited with it. He created female sexuality and killed the ogress *Kunapipi*.

INDEX OF ENTRIES

(Italics indicate alternative names)

INDEX